Giant tortoises

These naturally occur on Aldabra Atoll but can be seen on many of the Seychelles islands (LM) page 194

D0302089

Snorkelling and scuba diving

The warm tropical waters of the Seychelles are the perfect place to explore the underwater world

(WP/A) pages 69–70

Sir Selwyn Selwyn-Clarke Market

Sample exotic fruits, fresh fish and local spices at Victoria's lively market

(LM) pages 102–3

Seychelles in colour

above left   The clock tower is a good starting point for setting out to explore Victoria on foot (OZ/S) page 97

above right   The intricately painted Hindu Temple on Quincy Street, Victoria (I/D) page 104

below   The beautiful view over Ste Anne Marine National Park, with the islands of Cerf, Long, Round, Moyenne and Ste Anne (RS/STB) pages 119–21

above   There are a number of excellent walking trails in the Morne Seychellois National Park (SS) pages 118–19

right   Pretty St Joseph's Church in Anse Royale nestled between the beach and mountains behind (TA/S) page 111

above left   The Seychellois have a hundred or more uses for coconuts; from thatching roofs to flavouring curries (NP/S) page 31

above right   The early morning catch – a fisherman coming ashore with his bundles of fish (LB) pages 20–1

below   Tea pickers at work on the mountain slopes of central Mahé (SS) page 115

AUTHORS

Lyn Mair is a naturalist and travel guide who specialises in the islands of the western Indian Ocean, West Africa and Antarctica. Passionate about birdwatching, she regularly leads tours to exotic places, and lectures on board ships plying the tropical waters off Africa. When not gadding round the world she is resident in Cape Town, South Africa.

Lynnath Beckley is a professor of marine science at Murdoch University, Perth, Western Australia. She has undertaken scientific research, travelled and sailed extensively in the western Indian Ocean and has been writing for magazines, journals and books for many years.

AUTHORS' STORY

The gangplank of a cruise ship may seem to be an unlikely catalyst for a book. However, that was where we met when, in 1995, as guest lecturers on the MV *Rhapsody*, we were boarding for a cruise to many islands in the western Indian Ocean. Our complementary interests in the terrestrial and marine environments made us well suited to guiding passengers at the many islands we visited. We had loads of fun and thought that it would be appropriate to put together a guidebook to this part of the planet – even getting as far as drafting a contents page while sipping sundowners on the upper deck!

Fortunately, fate intervened after Lyn had spent three months on Aldabra Atoll and Hilary Bradt asked if she would be interested in writing a guide to the Seychelles. Recruiting assistance from Lynnath (fresh from navigating an entry in the round-the-world yacht race), working on the book became an inter-continental exercise in blending the needs of visitors, interests of authors and desires of editors. Several trips to the Seychelles to gather information about the diverse islands, inter-island transport, hotels, restaurants, etc, often tested by Creole laissez-faire, kept us suitably occupied and the book reached fruition.

We still visit the Seychelles as often as our respective careers allow because these multifarious oceanic islands are indeed rather special.

PUBLISHER'S FOREWORD   *Hilary Bradt*

I first met Lyn Mair in the Seychelles when we were fellow lecturers on the *Caledonian Star*, an expedition ship that cruised the Indian Ocean. Although we were both first-timers, Lyn could identify every bird and most of the other animals. Word soon got around among the passengers and they almost fought to get a place in the queue to join her for land excursions (those who were slow off the mark reluctantly came with me). Since then she has made many return visits, and the qualities that make her such a good tour leader spill over into the pages of this book: enthusiasm, knowledge of the natural world, and an instinctive understanding of what tourists want. Her friend and co-author, Lynnath Beckley, brings her extensive experience of marine life to ensure that this continues to be the most comprehensive guide to the Seychelles in print.

Fifth edition published January 2016
First published January 2001

Bradt Travel Guides Ltd, IDC House, The Vale, Chalfont St Peter, Bucks SL9 9RZ, England
www.bradtguides.com
Print edition published in the USA by The Globe Pequot Press Inc, PO Box 480, Guilford, Connecticut 06437-0480

ISBN: 978 1 84162 918 6 (print)
e-ISBN: 978 1 78477 130 0 (e-pub)
e-ISBN: 978 1 78477 230 7 (mobi)

British Library Cataloguing in Publication Data
A catalogue record for this book is available from the British Library

Photographs Alamy: STOCKFOLIO(R) (S/A), Imagebroker (IB/A), Wolfgang Pölzer (WP/A); Dreamstime: 7chriss3 (7/D); Getty Images: F. Lukasseck (F/G); Lyn Mair (LM); Lynnath Beckley (LB); Sandra Fowkes (SF); Seychelles Tourism Board: Gerard Larose (GL/STB), Raymond Sahuquet (RS/STB), Tony Baskeyfield (TB/STB); Shutterstock: Christopher Salerno (CS/S), David5962 (D5962/S), Nick Poling (NP/S), Oleg Znamenskiy (OZ/S), Paladin12 (P/S); SuperStock (SS)
Front cover Anse Source d'Argent, La Digue (F/G)
Back cover Waterfall in Vallée de Mai (GL/STB); Church on La Digue (7/D)
Title page Petite Anse, La Digue (GL/STB); male paradise flycatcher (GL/STB); Ipomea beach creeper (LM)
Illustrations Carole Vincer
Maps David McCutcheon FBCart.S

Typeset by Wakewing, High Wycombe
Production managed by Jellyfish Print Solutions; printed in India
Digital conversion by www.dataworks.co.in

Acknowledgements

Without the assistance of many people this guide would never have been written. My thanks to Hilary Bradt for asking me to write it and my initial visit to the Seychelles would never have happened if it were not for Tony Soper and Mike Mair.

It had always been my dream to stay on Aldabra and when Lindsay Chong Seng of the Seychelles Islands Foundation gave me the opportunity to be the first volunteer working on the atoll as assistant to the warden, I jumped at the chance. My special thanks to Louis Prea, the relief warden, who made my job so easy and who later took me into the warm heart of his family in Mahé. To my other colleagues on the atoll, a huge thank you for your friendship and sharing the secrets of Aldabra – from you I learnt the essence of being Seychellois.

Early on, in the planning stages of the book, I realised I needed someone to contribute to matters marine. My obvious choice was Dr Lynnath Beckley, an author and marine scientist working in the western Indian Ocean. As time progressed, she became more involved with every aspect of the book, beating it into shape with her clear logic and literary skills. She most deservedly became co-author and I am indebted to her for her most valuable contribution.

It is always a pleasure to visit the Seychelles, and doing research for this fifth edition was no exception. As always, the warmth and kindness of everyone we were involved with was remarkable. The Seychelles Tourism Board was exceptionally helpful; special thanks to Myra Fanchette who arranged much of our itinerary and David Germain, at the Cape Town office, for his continued support. Creole Travel Services provided much-appreciated assistance, Marie Reix introduced us to the Hilton properties and Li Boatwright facilitated our visit to Desroches. Once again, it was lovely to stay at the Coco de Mer on Praslin where Bart and Matt Labuschagne were delightful and generous hosts.

Now we would just like to go to the Seychelles on holiday!

Lyn Mair

UPDATES WEBSITE AND FEEDBACK REQUEST

At Bradt Travel Guides we are aware that guidebooks get out of date very quickly. So, why not write and tell us about your discoveries? We will be pleased to include you in the acknowledgements of the next edition of the guide if we use your feedback. Email e info@bradtguides.com, or write to Bradt Travel Guides, IDC House, The Vale, Chalfont St Peter, Bucks SL9 9RZ, England. Alternatively you can add a review of the book to www.bradtguides.com or Amazon. Your comment may be used as a 'one-off update' on the Bradt website at www.bradtupdates.com/seychelles. You can also visit this website for updates to information in this guide.

Contents

LIST OF MAPS

Introduction

In the deep blue of the western Indian Ocean, 115 unique and exquisite islands lie randomly scattered like emeralds and sapphires from a jeweller's purse. The Seychelles are famous for their palm-fringed silvery sands, secluded coves bounded by granite boulders, misty mountain peaks cloaked in forest and coral reefs extending into the warm ocean. Coupled with idyllic days in the tropical sun, velvet nights under starry southern skies, delightful people and charming Creole culture, they beckon discerning travellers to their shores.

The main, populated islands of the Seychelles lie a few degrees south of the Equator and rise from shallow banks as huge granite rocks, reflecting their ancient continental origin. Other remote, coralline islands, inhabited by millions of seabirds, arc out towards the shores of Africa and Madagascar. One of these is Aldabra – a wilderness atoll where time flows with the tides and nature rules supreme.

Aldabra was the first Seychelles island I set foot on, but before going ashore a quick dive into the clear water assaulted my senses with an array of corals teeming with colourful reef fish. When I took a break from the underwater scenery, I found that I was being scrutinised by a couple of inquisitive fairy terns while other seabirds – frigates, boobies and noddies – circled overhead. Traversing the mangrove-fringed lagoon, I watched turtles and rays lazing in the clear turquoise water. I was able to explore a small part of the rugged, limestone interior where giant tortoises slept in the shade of salt-resistant bushes shaped by the persistent trade winds. I was completely captivated by the wild, remote and near-pristine atoll. My love affair with the Seychelles began right there and then. After visiting the Seychelles on numerous subsequent occasions and getting to know many of the other islands, I had the good fortune actually to stay on Aldabra as the assistant to the warden.

The Seychelles has a short, but fascinating, history of explorers, pirates and settlers. The Creole people, a harmonious mélange of African, European and Asian descent, have a happy-go-lucky lifestyle and, although global travel has come to them, they maintain their traditions of language, music, dance and food.

The Seychelles has an ambience of remoteness. It is a modern country with accommodation ranging from exclusive lodges to family-run guesthouses. Island-hopping can be accomplished with ease using fast ferries, aeroplanes and helicopters, and what better way to explore than in your very own (or chartered) yacht? However, there is more to the Seychelles than basking in the sun. The Seychelles has many secrets, discovered as you explore the islands – coco de mer palm forests, the busy little capital of Victoria, picturesque La Digue, island bird sanctuaries, weather-beaten *glacis*, the local market, Creole cuisine… After a day's exploring, savour the evening. Sip a Seybrew on a beach coloured by a fiery sunset, wait for the southern constellations to grace the enveloping night, and plan another perfect day in paradise.

Lyn Mair

Part One

GENERAL INFORMATION

Location Indian Ocean

Islands 115 islands

Size 455km^2 across 1.3 million km^2 of ocean

Climate Equatorial; temperatures 24–30°C

Status Republic

Population 91,000 (2014)

Main islands Mahé (78,600), Praslin (8,600), La Digue (2,700) and outer islands (1,042)

Capital Victoria (on Mahé) (population 26,500 including surrounding districts)

Life expectancy 73 years (2013)

Economy Fishing, tourism

GDP SR11,621 million (2010)

Languages Creole, English, French

Religion Predominantly Roman Catholic

Currency Seychelles rupee (SR)

Exchange rate £1 = SR20.16, US$1 = SR13.14, €1 = SR14.83 (October 2015)

International telephone code +248

Time GMT+4. Sunrise 06.15 approx, sunset 18.30 approx

Electrical voltage 240 volts; three-point, square-pin plugs

Weights and measures Metric

Flag Five colours (green, white, red, yellow and blue) radiating out from bottom left

National anthem *Koste Seselwa* ('Come together Seychellois')

National flower Tropicbird orchid

National bird Black parrot

Public holidays 1–2 January, Easter, 1 May, 5 June, 18 June, 29 June, 15 August, 1 November, 8 December, 25 December

1

Background Information

The magnificent Seychelles islands are spread out over a vast swathe of tropical Indian Ocean between Madagascar and India. They extend over a straight-line distance of some 1,500km from Aldabra (located at 9°S 46°E) in the southwest to Denis and Bird (both near 3°S 55°E) to the northeast. The ecology of the islands and surrounding waters reflects the complex geology, oceanography and climate of the region.

GEOGRAPHY

LOCATION The 115 islands of the Seychelles, with a collective land mass of only 455km², are surrounded by a vast oceanic Exclusive Economic Zone (EEZ) of 1.3 million km². The islands are located in the western Indian Ocean, between latitudes 3°S and 10°S and longitudes 46°E and 56°E. The nearest neighbours are Madagascar and the great continent of Africa.

Geologically, the islands of the Seychelles have two distinct origins. The inner islands are continental, granitic remnants and the outer islands are coralline in nature. About 30 of the islands are inhabited while the others exist as sandy cays, atolls, coral reefs and great clumps of rock, uninhabited except for noisy seabird colonies.

LARGE GRANITIC ISLANDS
Mahé This is the largest granitic island (152km²). It is spectacular with grey, granite boulders dotting the verdant slopes that rise steeply out of the blue ocean to form a range of mist-enshrouded peaks, the highest being 905m above sea level. The town of Victoria, the busy commercial and administrative capital of the Seychelles, nestles below the mountains on the east coast.

Praslin The second-largest island (37km²) lies 45km northeast of Mahé. The central hills, which reach a height of 367m, rise up from the soft, white, sandy beaches and are covered in palm forests. The voluptuous coco de mer palm is protected in the Vallée de Mai, a World Heritage Site.

Silhouette This is the third-largest island, covering 20km² and reaching a height of 740m. It lies 19km to the northwest of Mahé but it has only a small population and very little development.

La Digue With its majestic, sculptured boulders creating sheltered and secluded beaches, La Digue is 5km from Praslin and 50km from Mahé. It covers an area of 10km² and rises to a height of 333m.

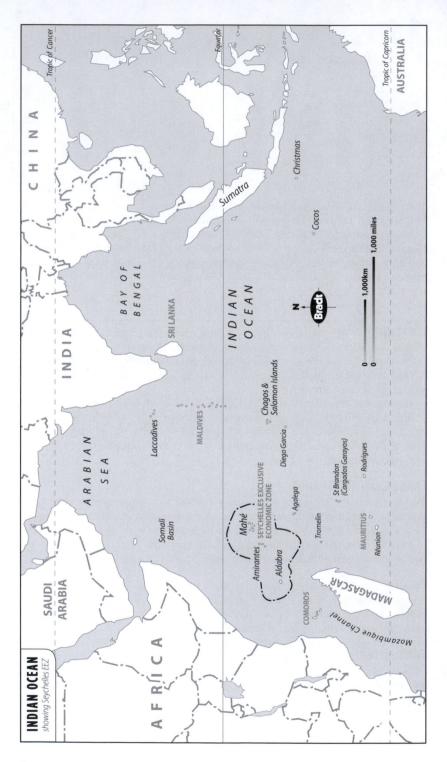

INDIAN OCEAN
showing Seychelles EEZ

ISLANDS OF THE SEYCHELLES

Names in italics indicate major islands

GRANITIC ISLANDS

Mahé	Ile aux Vaches	Chauve Souris	Grande Soeur
Anonyme	Long	Ile St Pierre	Ile Cocos
Beacon	Mamelles	Round	Ile la Fouche
Cerf	Moyenne	*Curieuse*	Ile aux Récifs
Conception	Rat	*Aride*	Marianne
Hodoul	Round	Booby	Petite Soeur
Ile Cachée	Ste Anne	*Cousin*	*Frégate*
Ile Chauve Souris	Thérèse	*Cousine*	L'Ilot Frégate
L'Ilot	*Silhouette*	*La Digue*	
L'Islette	*North*	Zave	
Ile Souris	*Praslin*	*Félicité*	

CORALLINE ISLANDS

Bird	*Coëtivy*	*Denis*	*Plat*

AMIRANTES GROUP

African Banks	*Desnoeufs*	Fouquet	Vars
Rémire	*St Joseph's Atoll*	Grand Carcassaye	*Poivre Atoll*
D'Arros	Banc Cocos	Ile Paul	Florentin
Desroches	Banc Ferrari	Pélican	Ile du Sud
Etoile	Banc de Sable	Petit Carcassaye	Poivre
Boudeuse	Benjamin	Ressource	
Marie-Louise	Chien	St Joseph	

ALPHONSE GROUP

Alphonse	Bijoutier	St François	

FARQUHAR GROUP

Providence Atoll	Providence	Ile Déposé	Lapin
Banc Providence	St Pierre	Ile du Milieu	Manaha Milieu
Banc de Sable	*Farquhar Atoll*	Ile du Nord	Manaha Nord
Ile Cerf	Goëlette	Ile du Sud	Manaha Sud

ALDABRA GROUP

Astove	Ile Moustiques	*Aldabra Atoll*	Ilot Lanier
Assumption	Ile du Nord	Grande Terre	Ilot Magnan
Cosmoledo Atoll	Ile Nord Est	Ile aux Cèdres	Ilot Parc
Goëlette	Ile Sud Ouest	Ile Esprit	Ilot Yangue
Grand Ile (Wizard)	Ile du Trou	Ile Michel	Malabar
Grand Polyte	Menai	Ile Moustiques	Picard
Ile Baleine	Pagode	Ilot Dubois	Polymnie
Ile Chauve Souris	Petit Polyte	Ilot Emile	

MANMADE ISLANDS

Off *Mahé*	Ile Persévèrence	Off *Praslin*
Eden Island	Ile de Romainville	Eve Island
Ile Aurore	Ile Soleil	

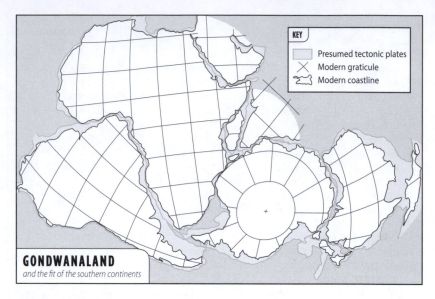

GONDWANALAND
and the fit of the southern continents

KEY
◻ Presumed tectonic plates
✕ Modern graticule
⌇ Modern coastline

Other islands There are about three-dozen smaller, satellite, granitic islands in close proximity to the main islands. **Bird** and **Denis** are different in that they are volcanic in origin and lie to the far north, on the edge of the Seychelles Bank.

OUTER CORALLINE ISLANDS The outlying coralline islands trickle away to the south and west of the granitic islands.

The Amirantes These straddle 6°S, and stretch from the African Banks to Desnoeufs. Other islands in this group are Rémire, Desroches, St Joseph's Atoll, D'Arros, Poivre and Marie-Louise.

The Alphonse group At 7°S, this comprises Alphonse with its own satellite islands of Bijoutier and St François.

The Farquhar group At 10°S, this consists of the atolls of Providence and Farquhar, each composed of small islands.

The Aldabra group With the island of Assumption and the atolls of Aldabra, Astove and Cosmoledo, this is the most southwesterly part of the Seychelles land territory. Aldabra, a World Heritage Site, is the largest raised coral atoll in the world and is situated near 9°S.

GEOLOGY The geological origins of the Seychelles can be traced to the disintegration of the Gondwanaland super-continent over 100 million years ago. The drifting apart of the tectonic plates in various directions gave rise to the continents of South America, Africa, Australia and Antarctica. At the end of the Cretaceous period, Madagascar and India, to which the Seychelles Bank was attached, drifted northeastwards. Before India crashed into Asia (producing the Himalayas) the Seychelles Bank separated off and lodged in its current position. The Seychelles Bank and its islands thus constitute a 'micro-continent' isolated by the slow process of sea-floor spreading in the Indian Ocean. The Seychelles Bank, surrounded by deep ocean, is a shoal area of some 31,000km² with water depths less than 60m. Rising from the Seychelles Bank are about 40 granitic islands and islets, located from 4° to 5°S, 55° to 56°E. The largest island, Mahé, with an area of 152km², rises to 905m in Morne Seychellois, the highest point in the group. Praslin, which has an area of 37km², rises to 367m and Silhouette, with an area of 20km², rises to 740m. These islands consist of rugged granitic mountains – often with smooth, bare rock slopes known as *glacis*, surrounded by narrow coastal plains and marsh. The granitic rocks of Mahé are reputed to be over 500 million years old. The other islands in the Seychelles comprise low sand cays on sea-level platform reefs, atolls or raised atolls. The sand cays are usually less than 5m above sea level, while the raised reef islands are about 8m above sea level, though some may have sand dunes up to 32m high. Low sand cays include Bird and Denis on the Seychelles Bank, Plat and Coëtivy, some of the Amirantes islands and Providence. Farquhar is the largest true atoll. Raised coral atolls include Aldabra, Cosmoledo and Astove, which all enclose central lagoons. On Aldabra there are two distinct terraces at 8m and 4m above sea level which formed as the sea level fell. Most of the atolls also reflect a history of recent erosion by sea water with characteristic mushroom-shaped undercut limestone platforms known as *champignon*.

RESHAPING THE SEYCHELLES

Seventy million years ago, after the break-up of the super-continent of Gondwanaland, the granitic Seychelles islands separated from Madagascar and India and lodged near their current position just south of the Equator in the western Indian Ocean. Rising from the shallow Seychelles Bank, the granitic islands have, over eons of time, developed substantial fringing coral reefs. These reefs protect the islands from coastal erosion, support valuable fisheries and attract thousands of tourists, the mainstay of the Seychelles economy.

In the 1960s, a considerable amount of reef was reclaimed on the east coast of Mahé to provide sufficient land for the construction of the Seychelles International Airport. Recently, in an ambitious, even larger scheme, the Seychelles government has gone ahead with the reclamation of enormous amounts of fringing reef around the capital, Victoria, to provide land for industrial development and housing.

Large tracts of fringing reef extending over about 10km, from the southeast near Ile Anonyme, along the Mahé side of Cerf Passage, past the port of Victoria, and up to North East Point, were encircled by vast enclosures of granite boulders quarried from the island. Simultaneously, a huge dredging operation to deepen access to the port took place, with the dredging spoil pumped into the enclosures, thereby filling them with sand and reef rubble and destroying the reefs. In total, six manmade islands have been created off the northeast coast of Mahé and these include the tourist node of Eden Island. On nearby Praslin, the horseshoe-shaped embayment of Baie Ste Anne has also succumbed to the reclamation process. The dredger deepened the approaches to the jetty and the spoil was dumped into yet another enclosure over the reefs along the western side of the bay to create Eve Island.

It is well nigh impossible to mitigate against such an environmental onslaught and rather difficult to believe that such enormous amounts of reclaimed land are necessary for a country with such a small total population.

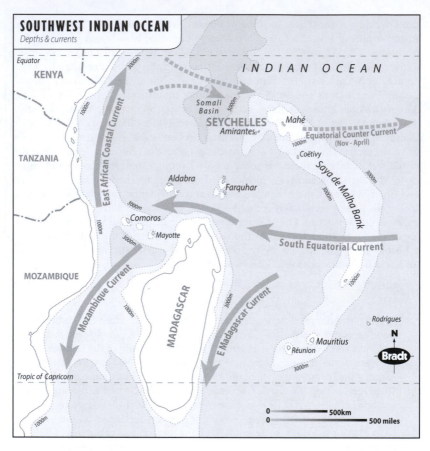

SOUTHWEST INDIAN OCEAN
Depths & currents

Equator

KENYA

INDIAN OCEAN

Somali Basin

SEYCHELLES

Amirantes

Mahé

Equatorial Counter Current
(Nov - April)

Coëtivy

TANZANIA

Aldabra

Farquhar

Saya de Malha Bank

East African Coastal Current

Comoros

Mayotte

South Equatorial Current

MOZAMBIQUE

Mozambique Current

MADAGASCAR

E Madagascar Current

Rodrigues

N

Bradt

Mauritius

Réunion

Tropic of Capricorn

| 0 | 500km |
| 0 | 500 miles |

OCEANOGRAPHY Ocean depths around the Seychelles are generally about 3,000–4,000m but in the Somali Basin, located between the Seychelles and Africa, the inky depths exceed 5,000m. In addition to the Seychelles Bank, there are several other shallow banks in the Seychelles EEZ, and the large granitic Saya de Malha Bank extends southeastwards in a gentle arc towards Mauritius.

Ocean currents are an important feature of the Indian Ocean and they vary seasonally with the monsoons. The main stream of the South Equatorial Current flows westwards across the Indian Ocean at about 10°S. When it reaches the western Indian Ocean it splits into the southward-flowing East Madagascar and Mozambique currents and the northward-flowing East African Coastal Current. However, during the northwest monsoon (November to March), the northerly flow of this current is reduced and its course changes, becoming the Equatorial Counter Current which flows eastwards through the Seychelles.

Tides in the Seychelles are semidiurnal, with two high tides and two low tides daily. Tidal amplitude is generally small but, at those islands located in the southwest nearer the Mozambique Channel, amplitude increases. So, for example, at Mahé spring tidal range is only about 1.2m, while at Aldabra it is about 2.6m. Mean local time of low spring tide is 11.00, so during full- and new-moon periods one can expect beaches and the tops of fringing reefs to be exposed around this time. In islands with lagoons, tidal currents can be quite considerable, particularly

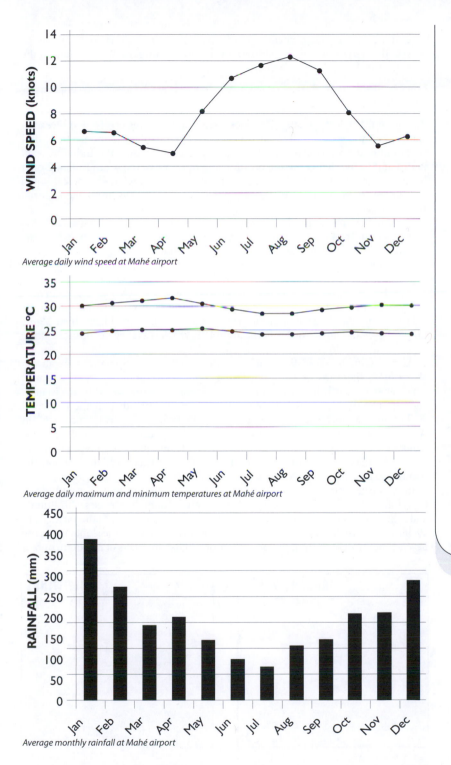

Average daily wind speed at Mahé airport

Average daily maximum and minimum temperatures at Mahé airport

Average monthly rainfall at Mahé airport

around mid tide as water enters or leaves the lagoon through narrow channels or passes. The water is warm all year round with temperatures of 27–28°C during the summer and 23–24°C in the winter.

CLIMATE

The humid, tropical climate of the Seychelles and the western Indian Ocean is controlled by a host of interrelated factors. These include the monsoonal wind shifts induced by seasonal barometric pressure changes over the Indian Ocean, Africa and India; changes in the position and intensity of the south Indian Ocean high-pressure zone; seasonal migration of the complex inter-tropical lows; and ocean currents and sea surface temperature patterns in the equatorial Indian Ocean.

Wind direction and speed in the Seychelles display clear seasonal patterns. In the southern hemisphere winter (May to October), southeast trade winds (*vent swet*) extend over the western Indian Ocean south of the Equator and, in the Seychelles, there is dry weather with low rainfall. In the southern hemisphere summer (December to March), on the other hand, the south Indian Ocean high-pressure system shifts southwards, and the rainy northwest monsoon (*vent nord*) sets in over the islands. In the transitional months of April and November winds tend to be light and variable. In general, mean wind speed is higher in Aldabra than Mahé. Tropical cyclones do not occur in the granitic Seychelles as they lie too close to the Equator but they do occur infrequently on Aldabra and Assumption.

Annual rainfall exceeds 800mm on all the islands and temperatures are always above 20°C. There are, however, important climatic variations between the islands which arise primarily because of the wide expanse of ocean covered by the islands, and altitudinal differences between the high granitic islands and the low coral atolls. Mean annual temperatures in Mahé (Victoria) are 26.6°C and 27°C on Aldabra, with only a 3°C seasonal variation. In the mountainous granitic islands, temperature decreases with increasing altitude. Humidity is usually around 75–80% and varies little with the season. Humidity does vary with altitude and the mountains are often shrouded with mist for long periods.

In all the granitic islands, rainfall reaches a maximum in summer. Altitude and aspect strongly influence the amount of rain received (rainfall increases with altitude and is higher on north-facing slopes). Average annual rainfall on Mahé varies from 1,846mm at Anse Royale on the coast to 3,250mm at Salazie on the slopes of Morne Seychellois. Most of the mountainous interior receives in excess of 2,500mm of rain

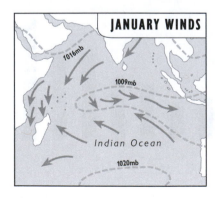

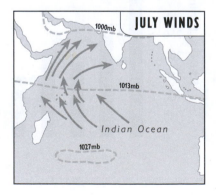

per year. Similarly, on Praslin, the rainfall at Côte d'Or (2,306mm) on the east coast is higher than Baie Ste Anne (2,130mm) on the south coast. Average annual rainfall on the northeastern islands of Bird (1,973mm) and Denis (1,730mm) is twice as high as the southwestern atolls of Aldabra (966mm) and Assumption (867mm). The duration of the dry season (less than 100mm rain) increases southwestwards from only one month at Denis to eight months at Aldabra. The contrast in length of the wet season between the northeast and southwest islands is of fundamental importance in accounting for the striking ecological contrasts that exist amongst the Seychelles islands.

HISTORY

For centuries, the islands of the Seychelles lay hidden in the glossy, blue-black waters of Bahr el Zanj, the ancient Arab name for the tropical ocean extending eastwards from the shores of Africa. Terrifying legends of deep, dark waters, treacherous currents and monstrous waves were born in this mysterious sea. There were stories of strange lands and many islands filled with wondrous plants and peculiar animals, but the exact whereabouts of these mythical places will forever remain a mystery, lost in the cobwebs of time.

From as early as the 7th century, Arabs in their stately dhows plied the trade routes between Arabia, India and Africa. Forts and settlements were created on the east coast of Africa from Mogadishu (Somalia) southwards to Sofala in Mozambique for trading in slaves, ivory, gold and other precious metals. With the seasonal southeasterly trades and northwesterly monsoons, the Arab sailors visited the Comoros and Madagascar, so it is quite conceivable that the Seychelles islands were encountered by Arab dhows. In fact, a series of islands in roughly the same position as the Seychelles appeared on Arab documents dated AD851. A cluster of mouldering graves, believed to be those of Arab sailors, has also been found on the island of Silhouette. However, hundreds of years slipped by before the uninhabited, wooded island gems of the Seychelles were revealed to the Western world.

CHRONOLOGY

851	Islands in the vicinity of the Seychelles appear on Arab documents.
1501	First recorded discovery of the Seychelles by João de Nova.
1502	Amirantes group discovered by Vasco da Gama.
1506	The granitic islands of the Seychelles appear on Portuguese charts as *Sete Irmanas*.
1609	The first British expedition in the ship *Ascension* lands on Mahé.
17th and 18th centuries	Plundering pirates roam the western Indian Ocean.
1730	Olivier Le Vasseur, La Buse, the well-known Seychelles pirate, publicly hanged in Réunion.
1742	*Elisabeth* and *Le Charles*, under the captaincy of Lazare Picault, anchored off Mahé.
1744	Lazare Picault's second exploring trip to Mahé and Praslin.
1756	Captain Corneille Nicholas Morphey led an expedition to the Seychelles and the islands were given their present name. A Stone of Possession was laid to symbolise ownership by France.
1768	Expedition by Marion Dufresne which explored Praslin and discovered the source of coco de mer nuts.

1770	First settlers arrived to set up spice gardens on Ste Anne and Mahé.
1788	Jean Baptiste Philogene de Malavois became commandant of the Seychelles.
1792	Chevalier Queau de Quinssy took over as commandant.
1814	The Seychelles officially declared a British colony, administered as a dependency of Mauritius. Queau de Quincy (formerly Quinssy) stayed on as administrator for the British.
1832	Whaling station opened at Ste Anne.
1835	Abolition of slavery.
1841	Main town on Mahé given the name of Victoria.
1862	St Louis avalanche killed 75 people in Victoria.
1890	First Seychelles stamps issued.
1903	The Seychelles became a Crown Colony with Ernest Bickham Sweet-Escott as first governor.
1914–18	World War I caused severe economic hardship in the Seychelles. German warship *Koenigsberg* reputedly hid in Aldabra lagoon.
1939–45	World War II. The Seychelles became an important refuelling base for British ships and flying boats.
1940	Seychelles currency replaced coins and notes from Mauritius.
1948	First elected representatives in the Seychelles government.
1964	Seychelles Democratic Party and Seychelles People's United Party formed.
1965	Annexation of Farquhar, Desroches and Aldabra as part of the British Indian Ocean Territory.
1967	Universal suffrage introduced in the Seychelles.
1970	Seychelles Constitutional Conference and creation of Legislative Assembly.
1971	International airport opened on Mahé.
1976	The Seychelles became an independent republic. Aldabra, Farquhar and Desroches returned to Seychelles administration.
1977	Armed coup resulting in the Seychelles becoming a single-party state with France Albert Rene as president.
1978	The Seychelles declared its Exclusive Economic Zone.
1982	Aldabra proclaimed a UNESCO World Heritage Site.
1983	Vallée de Mai on Praslin proclaimed a UNESCO World Heritage Site.
1991	Return to multi-party democracy in the Seychelles.
1993	Multi-party elections held – France Albert Rene took office as president.
2004	Rene retired and handed over to James Alix Michel as the new president.
2006	Presidential elections – James Michel retained his position as president.
2007	General elections with the ruling party, Seychelles People's Progressive Front (SPPF), being returned to power.
2009	Somali pirate activity impacts on the Seychelles. The Seychelles and the European Union sign an agreement allowing EU troops to be deployed in the islands.
2011	Presidential elections – James Michel retained his position as president.
2016	Presidential elections due.

EXPLORERS The great Portuguese admiral, Vasco da Gama, opened up the sea route from Europe to India when he rounded the Cape of Good Hope in 1498. João de Nova, another pioneering Portuguese navigator, followed in his wake and made the first recorded discovery of the Seychelles in 1501 when he came upon a group of low coral islands, which were named in his honour. However, in 1824 they were renamed the Farquhar group after Sir Robert Townsend Farquhar, the

WRECKS OF THE SEYCHELLES

Modern navigation is a far cry from that of the early explorers who found their way around the Indian Ocean with sun, stars, sextants and leadlines. Over the years, the variable currents and the countless reefs and shoals around the Seychelles have resulted in many craft coming to grief.

One of the earliest was a wooden Portuguese vessel which foundered on Boudeuse cay in the Amirantes in 1550. Various artefacts have been recovered, including bronze cannons, copper nails, and a coin bearing the royal crest of Portugal. The *Dom Royal*, another Portuguese ship laden with treasures and slaves, ran aground on Astove in 1760. The slaves survived on the island for 26 years before they were eventually recaptured. Some gold coins and silver cutlery, reputedly from the *Dom Royal*, have been salvaged by divers.

In 1763, the French frigate *Heureuse* was wrecked off Providence in the Farquhar group, the start of a long list of ill-fated vessels that have succumbed on this atoll. Others include the British brigantine *Aure* (1836), the French barque *Fédération* (1894), the British schooner *Maggie Low* (1901), the British *Endeavour* (1906), the Norwegian *Jorgen Bank* (1906) and the *Dagmar* (1907). Other Farquhar islands have also claimed craft, including SV *St Abbs* which in 1854, *en route* from London to Bombay, hit a reef. There were only six survivors and an account by one of them, Edward Ross, is held in the Seychelles archives. In 1897, the British ship *Aymestry* went down off Ile Déposé; five years later, SS *Hardwick Castle* was wrecked on Farquhar, and *Norden* hit St Pierre in 1906.

The Amirantes claimed the British sloop *Spitfire* at Rémire (1801), the slave trader *La Louise* at Desroches (1809) and SS *Sir Celicourt Antelme* at Marie-Louise (1905). The French coal burner SS *Dot* was wrecked on Alphonse (1873), as was *Tamatave* (1903). Coëtivy claimed the corvette *Eclair* (1787) and the lugger *Alice Adeline* (1906). The whaler *Greenwich* was wrecked off Bird (1833) and *La Perle* succumbed on Plat (1863). The southern islands of the Aldabra group also have their share of wrecks with Cosmoledo claiming *Merry Monarch* (1874), the Norwegian barque *Hamengia* (1913) and, a decade later, the auxiliary schooner *Meredith A White*. In 1915, SS *Glen Lyon* was wrecked on Aldabra, and the lugger *Reve* hit the reefs of Assumption.

Over the years various vessels have disappeared without trace in Seychelles waters, amongst them *Briton*, *Cupido*, *Sea Queen* and *Lord of the Isles*. Others such as *Parachi Pachia* and *Voyageur* have sunk in the precincts of the port of Victoria. The Royal Fleet Auxiliary tanker *Ennerdale* hit a rock about 15km northeast of Victoria in June 1970 and sank. In order to disperse the oil remaining in its tanks, Royal Navy divers placed charges on the vessel and attached the fuses to a helicopter overhead for ignition while the divers raced clear in an inflatable boat! The wreck, which is now a favoured diving site, lies about 2km southwest of Mamelles islet between Mahé and Praslin.

first British governor of Mauritius. (A tiny island in the Mozambique Channel is now called Juan de Nova.) On his second voyage to India in 1502, Vasco da Gama encountered another group of coral islands, which were named Ilhas do Almirante in honour of the admiral, and the name Amirantes is still in current use. The granitic islands of the Seychelles appeared on Portuguese charts in 1506 as *Sete Irmanas*, 'Seven Sisters', but there are no records of what those intrepid mariners found on the islands.

During the 16th and 17th centuries, the race was on between the great seafaring nations to locate and claim all the land they could for their respective countries, and to establish replenishing stations for their ships plying the trade route to India. As a result, Madagascar and the Mascarene Islands of Mauritius, Réunion and Rodrigues became known to the explorers. The Seychelles was left in undisturbed tranquillity until 1609 when the British ship, *Ascension*, under Captain Alexander Sharpeigh, anchored off Mahé. John Jourdain, who was on board the *Ascension*, described in his journal the uninhabited islands, the fresh water, the excellence of the timber and coconuts and the plentiful birds, tortoises and fish. He commented that the tortoises tasted like beef but looked so ugly before they were cooked that the men refused to eat them. After a ten-day sojourn, the *Ascension* left the islands, which were described as places with nothing to fear except the crocodiles. We can only imagine the exquisite beauty of the pristine islands and, although the secret was out, there was no stampede to visit them, and the earthly paradise was to remain uninhabited for a further 160 years.

PIRATES By the early 17th century, trade between Europe and the East was in full swing, and the islands of the Seychelles were stepping stones in the Indian Ocean. Caravels and Indiamen, laden with silks, rare jewels and exotic spices sailed for the demanding markets of Europe. The East India Company, with headquarters in England and Holland, flourished, and trade with the East reached new heights. The heavy, cumbersome vessels transporting these fabulous cargoes were sitting ducks for pirates and brigands in the Sea of Zanj. The tiny, secluded bays, coves and gentle beaches of the Seychelles were ideal hiding places for these robbers of the high seas. Fine hardwood to repair their boats was plentiful, and an abundance of fresh water, fish and meat from turtles and tortoises provided sustenance for the motley crews.

Pirate 'head office' was set up on the tiny island of Ile Ste Marie off the east coast of Madagascar. This was the meeting place of the rogues, where they would divide up their spoils and indulge in drunken debauchery with the local women. In the Caribbean, the Philip Bros of Amerika Company dealt in plundered goods and, as there was so much pirate activity going on in the Indian Ocean, they sent a representative, Adam Baldridge, to expand their business there. Baldridge set up a small shop on a tiny islet at the entrance to the lagoon of Ile Ste Marie, and from there he bought and sold the loot. Very often, the plundered treasures would end up exactly where they had originally been destined, only at a greater cost, having passed through many middlemen on the way.

These oceanic hijackers were a rough and brutal lot. Many had turned to piracy to escape the degrading life experienced in the merchant navies of the time. To survive and outwit each other they had to be strong, wily, fearless and bold. A well-known rascal operating out of the Seychelles was a Frenchman, Olivier Le Vasseur, known as La Buse. With his cronies he made a daring raid on a crippled ship lying in the port of Réunion. The ship was loaded with rich treasures: chests of gold and silver, sparkling diamonds, precious pearls and fabulous silks. The Portuguese viceroy and Archbishop of Goa were both travelling on board, adding their own ceremonial and religious regalia to the priceless treasure trove. La Buse made off with the treasure but was eventually captured and publicly hanged on Réunion on 17 July 1730. Just before he died, he flung a scrap of paper into the air. This contained cryptic clues as to the whereabouts of his hidden treasure, and there is great speculation that it is stashed on Mahé, somewhere in the region of Bel Ombre. To this day, the treasure trove has never been found.

Further clues to pirate activity in the Seychelles linger on in names such as Ile Cachée, Anse Forbans on Mahé, Côte d'Or on Praslin, and Source d'Argent on La Digue. Not all pirates were rogues, however, and Jean-François Hodoul, a corsair operating out of Mahé, gave up his swashbuckling ways and became a most respectable justice of the peace. His name has been given to a tiny island – no more than a clump of casuarinas in the yacht harbour at Victoria – and to the most easterly point of Aldabra.

In recent years, the romantic notion of corsairs has been dispelled with the dramatic increase in Somali pirate activity in the western Indian Ocean. This is cause for great concern amongst the global shipping industry and, in particular, has impacted on the Seychelles itineraries of cruise ships and yachts. The Seychelles Coast Guard, in collaboration with navies from the European Union, China and India, has captured some Somali pirates who are now languishing in a Seychelles jail. By 2015, the piracy threat had diminished considerably, but caution in the Outer Islands is still necessary.

SETTLERS During the 18th century, Mauritius developed into a thriving island community under the very able direction of an exceptional man, Bertrand François Mahé de Labourdonnais. He was appointed governor in 1735 by the French East India Company, which was running the island with approval from the French courts. He successfully served the French in their India campaign, and his leadership was instrumental in the capture of the town of Mahé on the Malabar coast of India, giving him the right to add Mahé to his name. He transformed the straggling little community on Mauritius into a prosperous settlement. In order to secure more food resources, he fitted out two ships, *Elisabeth* and *Le Charles* and, under the captaincy of Lazare Picault, sent them on a voyage of exploration. On 22 November 1742, almost 150 years after the visit by the *Ascension*, Picault anchored in a superbly beautiful bay off an unknown island. It is presumed to have been Anse à la Mouche on Mahé. There, they found mountains densely covered in tall, straight trees, clear rivers, tumbling waterfalls, a profusion of tortoises, birds and turtles and no sign of human habitation. So overwhelmed were they with this multifarious wildlife that they simply called the island Ile d'Abondance. Loading up a supply of tortoises and coconuts, they returned to Mauritius. De Labourdonnais was impressed with all he heard, and two years later sent Picault back to the islands, this time with a competent mapmaker on board, and instructions to find out all he could about the surrounding islands. On this expedition, Picault named the large island Mahé in honour of the governor, and the entire group of islands he called Iles de Labourdonnais. An island covered in palm trees, a little to the northeast of Mahé (the present-day Praslin), was given the name of Ile de Palme although he made no specific reference to the mysterious coco de mer.

The French influence The islands were left in peace for another few years until it was rumoured that the English were about to occupy them. Governor Magon of Mauritius quickly stepped in and, in 1756, sent Captain Corneille Nicolas Morphey in command of two vessels, *Le Cerf* and *Le Benoit*. Mahé was thoroughly explored, and the Iles de Labourdonnais were renamed Sechelles, honouring Vicomte

Moreau des Sechelles, the French Comptroller General of Finances ('Sechelles' later became 'Seychelles'). Amid patriotic cries of '*Vive le roi!*', gun salutes and a flag-raising ceremony, the islands were formally possessed by France and the French East India Company. A Stone of Possession designed with a fleur-de-lis and the crown of Louis XV was set in front of the harbour, near present-day Victoria. Captain Morphey and his two ships sailed away, and the Seychelles continued to exist as peaceful, uninhabited islands.

Exactly 12 years later, another expedition under the patronage of Mauritius reached the verdant islands. Marion Dufresne, in command of two ships, *La Digue* and *La Curieuse*, had been sent on a specific undertaking to exploit the fine timber. There was a more thorough exploration of Ile de Palme which was renamed Praslin after Gabriel de Choiseul, Duc de Praslin, French minister of marine affairs. During the exploration of Praslin, the surveyor, Barre, collected some coco de mer nuts, which he took back to Mauritius. The secret source of the fabled nuts had been revealed!

It was not until 1770 that the first wave of settlers arrived in the Seychelles. Brayer du Barré, an entrepreneur, raised enough money to set up a spice-growing industry on the island of Ste Anne. The first group of settlers consisted of 14 Frenchmen, seven slaves, five labourers from Malabar and a lady named Maria. Du Barré remained in Mauritius in relative comfort! At the same time, spice gardens were also being created on Mahé itself at Anse Royale, with seeds procured by Pierre Poivre of Mauritius. Nutmeg, cloves and pepper came from India and cinnamon from Ceylon. Neither venture was particularly successful.

Around this time, the English showed a renewed interest in the islands. In 1778, France decided it was imperative to protect its Indian Ocean assets, and Lieutenant de Romainville was sent to set up a military base on Mahé. By 1786, there were 24 military personnel, four civilians and 122 slaves. Agriculture had almost been abandoned in favour of the indiscriminate felling of timber and purveyance of tortoise and turtle meat to passing ships.

Things started looking up in 1788 when Jean Baptiste Philogene de Malavois took over as commandant. He created law and order on Mahé, and the land was apportioned to married men only. He was the first person to take active steps to control the exploitation of the natural resources. He prohibited the cutting down of trees for firewood and the capture of hawksbill turtles and tortoises, but allowed the harvest of green turtles for personal use only.

Chevalier Jean Baptiste Queau de Quinssy arrived in the Seychelles in 1792 as the French commandant. He guided the Seychelles through the last years of French administration, which included the upheavals caused by the Napoleonic Wars. Probably the most difficult time he encountered was during the period when the French and English were alternately laying claim to possession of the Seychelles. Diplomatic de Quinssy reputedly capitulated seven times to the British but reverted to his French allegiance each time the British sailed away. Simultaneously, corsairs with letters of marque from their respective governments entitling them to plunder enemy ships caused havoc on the seas around the Seychelles.

The British influence Mauritius eventually fell to the British in 1810 and, in 1814, consequent upon the Treaty of Paris, the Seychelles was officially declared a British colony administered as a dependency of Mauritius. De Quincy (the spelling of his name changed) continued as the Seychelles administrator for the British. Most of the French laws remained and the planters continued growing their crops with slave labour. By 1816, the Seychelles had a thriving community with a population of 7,500 of whom 6,600 were slaves. A whaling station was opened on Ste Anne in 1832 introducing a rough element to the population. Grand-scale cotton production in America caused the crash of the industry in the Seychelles and subsequently, in 1840, the era of copra (dried kernels of coconut) production commenced. The British influence started creeping in, and the main town was given the name of Victoria in 1841.

The abolition of slavery in 1835 brought an influx of freed slaves, mainly of African descent, from ships captured by the British. The slaves were liberated in the Seychelles and provided a labour force for the emergent coconut plantations.

EXILES IN PARADISE

The Seychelles, because of its remoteness, has long been a dumping ground for various undesirable or politically embarrassing characters. Napoleon deported several Jacobin thugs who tried to assassinate him in Paris in 1800. They spent some time in the Seychelles before being sent on to the Comoros. During the 19th century, after the abolition of slavery, British vessels patrolling the waters of the western Indian Ocean captured many Arab dhows still engaged in the illegal practice. Though not strictly exiles, over 2,500 slaves of mainly African origin were released on the Seychelles and formed the basis of the Creole nation.

In 1877, ex-sultan Abdullah of Perak, who was allegedly involved in the murder of a British person, arrived in the Seychelles with his 37-strong entourage. Several African kings were also exiled on Mahé. King Prempeh of Ashanti and his entourage spent their time at Les Mamelles from 1900. The king discarded his African tribal robes, adopted a Western style of dress, and eventually became a Christian. Members of his party received a Western education and one of his sons even became a priest. When he returned to Africa in 1924, he was clothed in a full morning suit complete with a top hat. He was re-elected Head Chief of the Kumasi tribe on the Gold Coast, now Ghana. Two Ugandan kings, Mwanga, King of Buganda, and Kabalega, King of the Bunyoro, were exiled to the Seychelles in 1901. Mwanga died in 1903 but Kabalega spent 20 years in exile. Mahmood Ali Shirreh, Sultan of the Warsangli tribe of Somaliland, was deported to the islands in 1920 and was held until 1928.

More political outcasts arrived in 1921, in the form of Said Khalil bin Bargash, an Arab who was claiming the throne of Zanzibar. He too had a large entourage, which included his two sons and 19 other hangers-on. A year later, the Egyptian premier, Saad Zaghloul Pasha, and five of his cabinet ministers arrived. They did not stay long as the premier was dispatched to Gibraltar for medical treatment. Six Muslim detainees were sent from Aden in 1933, and in 1937 a group of Palestinian freedom fighters were sent to the Seychelles by the British for creating disturbances leading to the death of the district commissioner of Galilea. Their exile was short, and they were repatriated two years later.

Archbishop Makarios of Cyprus spent a year in exile in the Seychelles living in a large house on the Sans Souci Road which is now the home of the American ambassador. The archbishop used to climb to the summit of Morne Seychellois clad in his flowing black robes. He was also reputedly known for his fine singing in the garden, especially after consuming generous amounts of his favourite wine!

During the second half of the 19th century, the production of copra dominated the scene with hundreds of thousands of litres of coconut oil being produced annually. Vanilla became an important cash crop, outstripping copra in 1899. Cinnamon oil was produced in quantity, and cloves were grown on the hill slopes. On the outer coralline islands, which had the most important coconut plantations, guano mining gained momentum, and turtles were heavily exploited for their meat and shells.

THE 20TH CENTURY The Seychelles ceased to be a dependency of Mauritius in 1903, and Ernest Bickham Sweet-Escott was installed as the first governor and commander-in-chief. Although the islands were under British jurisdiction, and the English language was used in law and business matters, the French way of life persisted, and French remained the dominant language. But the Seychelles was in for a rough time as the discovery of synthetic essence caused the world price for natural vanilla to fall dramatically. Then, with the outbreak of World War I, ships no longer called for cargoes of coconut oil. Poverty became widespread and crime was rife. Political detainees arrived to spend years in exile. They were a diverse lot – kings from various tribes in Africa, sultans from the Middle East and Zanzibar, the Egyptian premier plus cabinet members, and Arab freedom fighters.

World War II saw the Seychelles playing an important role as a refuelling station for British ships. Seychelles troops were sent to Africa and saw action at El Alamein and Tobruk. Ultimately, though, the war caused continued financial woe in the Seychelles, as did a fall in world demand for coconut oil. After the war the exploitation of the natural resources of the Seychelles continued unabated with millions of seabird eggs taken annually and, as the demand for turtle soup and tortoiseshell ornaments grew, turtles were harvested in large numbers. Patchouli oil for the perfume industry also became an important, but short-lived, product.

The modernisation of the Seychelles began with the first commercial bank opening in 1959. When space exploration became an exciting new phenomenon, even the isolated Seychelles was drawn in. The Americans set up a satellite-tracking station on the mountain above Victoria with two enormous 'golf ball' receivers as part of the station. Although the Americans withdrew at the end of the programme, the 'golf balls' remained for several years before being removed. A large Arabian-owned mansion has now been built on the site.

The Seychelles did manage to escape a potential disaster during the Cold War. In 1965, Britain, with Anglo-American defence strategy in mind, annexed Farquhar, Desroches and Aldabra as part of the British Indian Ocean Territory. A large air-force base was planned for Aldabra but environmental lobbyists, spearheaded by Julian Huxley, succeeded in overturning the venture, and Aldabra eventually became the world's first coral atoll World Heritage Site in 1982. Since the international airport opened in 1971 linking Mahé with major cities in Europe, tourism has become an increasingly important part of the Seychelles economy.

In common with much of the world, the era of party politics dawned in the Seychelles, and the government included its first elected representatives in 1948. At that time the franchise was extended to property owners only, and it was not until 1967 that universal suffrage was introduced. Two political parties were formed in 1964. The Seychelles People's United Party (SPUP), led by France Albert Rene, was strongly committed to achieving Seychelles independence, while the Seychelles Democratic Party (SDP), led by James Mancham, was keen to maintain ties with Britain. A constitutional conference in 1970 discussed the future of the Seychelles and set up a 15-member Legislative Assembly. After the election, James Mancham became chief minister, his SDP winning six seats to the five seats of the SPUP. In the

1974 elections, the SDP maintained their slender lead. In June 1976, the Seychelles became an independent republic with colourful Mancham as president and Rene as prime minister of the coalition government. A year later, on 5 June 1977, while Mancham was out of the country attending a Commonwealth conference in London, the SPUP staged an armed coup, and the Seychelles became a single-party socialist state with Rene as president. The SPUP was renamed the Seychelles People's Progressive Front (SPPF).

Rene survived several attempted coups of which the most publicised was in November 1981. The responsible mercenaries were arrested, tried and imprisoned in the Seychelles and South Africa. In 1991, there was a return to a multi-party democracy, James Mancham was welcomed back, and eventually a new constitution was produced in June 1993. Multi-party elections were held a month later and Rene defeated Mancham with 59% of the votes. Rene was returned to office in the 1998 elections and again in 2001 with James Alix Michel as his vice-president.

INTO THE 21ST CENTURY On 14 April 2004, France Albert Rene retired and handed over to his vice-president, James Alix Michel, with no major changes taking place. In the 2006 general election Michel was returned to office with a marginal lead. The opposition Seychelles National Party led by Wavel Ramkalawan obtained 46% of the vote.

In addition to the portfolios of defence, police, internal affairs, finance and economic planning, there are a further ten government departments including education and youth, local government, sports and culture, environment and natural resources, agriculture and marine resources, industry and international business, social affairs and employment. Local residents and their employers pay a social security tax for services such as healthcare, education and old-age benefits. In May 2011, Michel once again was returned to office with 55% of the votes ahead of the 43% of Wavel Ramkalawan. The Legislative Assembly is in Victoria and the next presidential election is due in 2016.

ECONOMY

The Seychelles economy depends largely on fishing (chiefly based on tuna processing) and tourism as earners of foreign exchange. Over 230,000 tourists visited the islands in 2014 with 75% of the visitors from Europe. On the home front, agriculture provides a limited amount of food for local consumption, restricted arable land being the controlling factor. Local industries are developing, and the Seychelles government is expanding foreign earnings by entering the global business and financial markets and encouraging offshore investment in the country.

TOURISM Since 1971 and the opening of the international airport, tourism has been a major earner of foreign exchange, with the industry employing a large percentage of the population. In addition to the obvious jobs in aviation, hotels and restaurants, the spin-off work in the supply of services by tour operators, taxis, car hire, inter-island ferries, dive operators, guides, souvenir sellers and so on, is considerable. The Seychelles, through government policy, has tried to maintain the charm of the islands, and buildings higher than the coconut palms are rarely permitted. Instead of catering for mass tourism, the Seychelles strives to provide small, exclusive resorts and there are only 6,550 hotel beds available amongst all the islands. An international convention centre, able to handle meetings for up to 600 delegates, is located in Victoria near Le Chantier traffic circle.

Tourism is increasing, with the majority of visitors coming from Europe, the UK, Russia and the Middle East, with growing numbers from China and the southern African region. Package tours are often the most cost-effective way to travel to this safe destination. Since 2009, several large resorts have been constructed in the Seychelles. The two most noteworthy are the 67-villa resort of Four Seasons, set in the once-pristine hillside of Baie Lazare, Mahé, and the even bigger 86-villa Raffles on Praslin. More recently, the 163-room Russian-owned Savoy Resort & Spa has been constructed at Beau Vallon and the old Plantation Club has become the 150-room Kempinski Resort at Baie Lazare. All are high-end developments, and the villas have their own pool and the hotels have every opulent facility. Eden Bleu, an 87-room hotel, opened in November 2014 on Eden Island, has conference space for up to 340 delegates. There are several more hotels in the planning stages and many of the developments are owned by Middle East companies. Eden Island, the manmade island off Mahé, offers residential properties for sale, giving the owners rights to Seychelles residency. This large development has all the accompanying facilities of a yacht marina, fancy restaurants, bars and shops.

A number of international cruise ships also visit the islands. Passengers generally spend their days ashore exploring the islands but return to the ship at night. Although most visitors come for the sun, sea and sand aspects of a Seychelles trip, scuba diving, snorkelling, birdwatching, walking in the mountains, cruising and deep-sea angling are particularly alluring.

FISHING Fishing and related activities are a major component of the Seychelles economy, contributing about half of the country's foreign exchange inflow. The main fisheries sectors are the local artisanal fishery, which targets reef fish, and the multi-national tuna fishery which targets tuna in the widespread waters of the Seychelles Exclusive Economic Zone (EEZ).

The artisanal fishery uses both hook and line, and traps, and operates a fleet of some 400 small vessels which, by and large, ply the shallow waters around Mahé, Praslin and La Digue. These vessels include pirogues, whalers, schooners and sport-fishing boats. The major species in the catch are *karang* (trevally), *bourzwa* and *bordmar* (red snappers), *zob* (jobfish), *kaptenn* (emperors), *bonit* (bonito), *vyey* (groupers), *kordonnyen* (rabbitfish) and *makro dou* (mackerel). The annual catch has declined during the past decade, and in 2012 it was around 2,500 tonnes. Semi-industrial longline fishing for sharks, tuna and swordfish was introduced after the Seychelles government banned the use of gill nets because of the by-catch of turtles and dolphins. There has been a rapid development of a sea-cucumber fishery in recent years with most of the dried product exported to Asian markets.

A fleet of 40 purse-seine vessels fish for tuna in the Seychelles EEZ. The majority of these are registered in Spain and France with only nine registered in the Seychelles. The total annual catch is about 231,500 tonnes and comprises mainly skipjack and yellowfin tuna, most of which is trans-shipped in Mahé. There is also a foreign longline fishery for tuna in the Seychelles EEZ with the majority of the 140 licensed vessels using this technique from Taiwan or Japan.

Port Victoria, with its four berths and one bunker pier, is extremely busy and is the main tuna trans-shipment port in the Indian Ocean. Landed catches go to the Indian Ocean Tuna canning factory which, after expansion, produces about 30,000 tonnes of canned tuna per year. This factory employs almost half of the estimated 6,000 persons involved in the fishing industry.

Prawn farming started over a decade ago with the first aquaculture ponds built at Coëtivy. There were around 200 ponds, a hatchery and a processing plant, but the entire project collapsed and the island is, at present, a penal settlement with some agriculture. Giant clam and pearl oyster farming are other aquaculture ventures in the Seychelles and can be seen at Amitié near the airport on Praslin as well as in the channel between Praslin and Curieuse. The pearls are proving popular in jewellery sold to foreign visitors.

AGRICULTURE The early economy of the Seychelles was based on the production of copra and coconut oil, and remains of the plantations are seen all over the islands. Vanilla, also once important, is still grown in a small way on Mahé and La Digue. Other spices, like cinnamon, continue to be cultivated commercially, and can be purchased at the market in Victoria. Vegetables are grown around Anse Royale and Anse Boileau on Mahé, lettuce and tomatoes being important crops. The government is actively encouraging further vegetable farming in this area. There are several plant nurseries, and orchids and heliconiums are grown for export and local use in hotel decoration. On the misty mountain slopes of Mahé, tea is a successful crop, and the neatly trimmed bushes can be seen from the Sans Souci Road. Tea is marketed as SeyTé for the domestic market.

TRADE, INDUSTRY AND INVESTMENT Local industry is poorly developed and, with the exception of the tuna processing plant, a paint factory and Seybrew, manufacturing beer and soft drinks, there is little manufacturing in the Seychelles. Most processed foods and manufactured items are imported and distributed through the Seychelles Trading Company. All petroleum products are imported.

The **Islands Development Company** (*IDC; PO Box 638, New Port, Latanier Rd, Victoria;* 4384640; www.idc.sc) is a para-statal organisation that maintains coconut plantations and tourist facilities on some of the outlying islands. The Seychelles has, however, entered the global economy with tax incentives and many other benefits available to foreign investors. The **Seychelles Investment Board** (*SIB;* 4295500; e info@sib.gov.sc; www.sib.gov.sc) has been set up to promote, attract and retain investment in the various sectors – agriculture, fisheries, tourism, general and financial investment. The **Development Bank of Seychelles** (4294400; www.dbs.sc) is geared up to handle the financing of projects in agriculture, fishing, tourism, light industry and the service sectors. In recent years there has been a significant increase in foreign investment by China and some of the Arab countries, while Russians have invested in hotels.

PEOPLE

When the earliest explorers discovered the Seychelles, there were no people living on the islands. The first group of 18th-century pioneers comprised French settlers, African slaves and Indian workers. More people from France and Mauritius, as well as many slaves from Africa and Madagascar, came to the islands, and before the abolition of slavery, 90% of the population was slaves. After the abolition of slavery in 1835, shiploads of slaves, previously destined for the world markets, were set free in the Seychelles. Political prisoners from France were dumped on the oceanic islands during, and after, the French Revolution. Although the Seychelles was a British colony from 1815, there was never a great influx of English settlers, and the dominant French influence remained. Indian and Chinese traders arrived at the beginning of the 20th century to take advantage of the developing economy. There was, and still is, an easy-going attitude to love and romance, and relationships between the races are commonplace, giving rise to the cosmopolitan, dusky-skinned Seychellois people. Today's inhabitants are a cheerful mix of every race imaginable, and they are proud to count how many nationalities can belong to one family.

POPULATION The total population of the Seychelles is approximately 91,000, with 90% living on Mahé. About 26,000 people live in and around Victoria, and the most populated areas are at St Louis, Bel Air and Mont Fleuri. Other well-populated areas are Bel Ombre, Glacis, Anse Royale and Anse Boileau. Praslin, with 8,600 inhabitants, has no really densely populated areas, although most of the people live around Baie Ste Anne, Grande Anse and Anse Volbert. On La Digue, most of the 2,700 residents live on the west coast between La Passe and Anse la Réunion. The average size of families is five, and 29% of the population is under the age of 15.

The people of the granitic islands are, by and large, employed in government service, tourism, fishing, construction or agriculture. The outer islands are sparsely populated by a special breed of people who are happy with the quiet and isolated lifestyle. The remote islands that are run as coconut plantations have basic communications with Mahé but there are virtually no community activities apart from fishing.

LANGUAGE

In the Seychelles there are three languages. Creole is the most commonly spoken language though French and English are widely used and understood, with English the language of commerce and law. Creole, a French patois, was developed during the slave era with the French plantation owners needing to communicate with African and Malagasy slaves. Much of the Creole vocabulary is similar to French although the grammar is simplified, and words and phrases from other tongues such as Swahili or Arabic have been incorporated.

It is only in recent years that the language has been put into a written form by the Creole Institute, Lenstiti Kreol, located at Anse aux Pins on Mahé. It is a phonetic language so, for example, the French *petit* becomes *pti* in the new written language. School books and reading books for children are now being produced in Creole. The local newspaper, *The Nation*, carries articles in both English and Creole. See page 199 for useful Creole words and phrases.

RELIGION

The French and English brought their religions to the islands and there are two cathedrals on Mahé: the Catholic Cathedral of the Immaculate Conception and St Paul's Anglican Cathedral. About 90% of the people are Catholic, and the cathedral in Victoria is usually packed to capacity every Sunday. Mahé must be the origin of the saying 'dressing up in your Sunday best' – the ladies wear their best straw hats with flowers, the little girls are in their frilly dresses, white socks and shiny shoes, while the men are resplendent in clean, ironed shirts and long trousers. Besides the religious aspect, church is an important social event as it is a gathering place to catch up on the gossip of the week, and is also a respectable place for young people to meet and get together. Anglicans account for 8% of the population and their small cathedral was built on the water's edge in Victoria but, with land reclamation, it is now some distance from the ocean. There are churches on most of the inhabited islands, and even on the smallest islands there will be a tiny church. There is also a smattering of Seventh-Day Adventists.

Some of the Indian community use the beautifully decorated Hindu temple in Quincy Street, Victoria, while the Sheikh Mohamed bin Khalifa Mosque in Francis Rachel Street is in daily use for the prayers of the small Muslim community. A Baha'i centre in Praslin, with a commanding view over the harbour, has a following on the island.

EDUCATION

The Seychelles government considers education to be one of its priorities and 20% of the budget is spent on schooling, which is compulsory and free up to the age of 17 years. After this, students may continue working towards A levels for a further two years. Schools are located in most of the larger centres on the three main islands and a regular bus service enables the children to get to school easily. Lessons are conducted in the mother tongue, Creole, but in secondary school, many of the lessons are in English or French because of the lack of more advanced textbooks in Creole. The literacy rate is 96%. A privately run International School is located in Mont Fleuri and a second International School is operating on Praslin.

Tertiary education is continued at the various polytechnics, and practical subjects that can lead to employment are offered. Diploma courses include healthcare, design, computers, marine studies, agriculture, mechanics and building techniques. The Seychelles Hotel and Tourism Training School is accommodated in the hills of La Misère, and courses cover the many facets of the hospitality industry.

In 2009, the first university opened its doors in the Seychelles, offering degree programmes through the University of London. The Anse Royale campus was officially opened by HRH Princess Anne and hosts the faculties of Business, Law, Humanities and Science. The School of Education campus is in Mont Fleuri, which is also home to the India–Seychelles Centre for Information and Communication Technology, and the Guy Morel Institute in Ma Joie offers a training centre for private and public organisations.

CULTURE

The cosmopolitan Seychellois have a charming Creole culture which stems from the African, European and Asian roots of the people. From the slave background, a camaraderie developed and there was a great sense of sharing which is still noticeable today. In fact, sharing is the essence of the Creole culture – sharing of mixed

NATIONAL EMBLEMS

The **Seychelles coat of arms** has been adapted from the original drawn by General Gordon in 1881. The circular, central shield has a tortoise, a coco de mer, and a two-masted sailing vessel approaching a granite hill. The shield is flanked by two sailfish above which are heraldic feathers and a silver helmet. Flying over the grand design is a white-tailed tropicbird. A folded ribbon at the base carries the motto *finis coronat opus* ('the end crowns the work'). The **national flower** is the tropicbird orchid. The Creole name is *fleur payanke* and the French call it *fleur paille en queue*. The **national bird** is the black parrot, found on Praslin and Curieuse. The Seychelles **flag** has five bright colours (green, white, red, yellow and blue) radiating out from the bottom left of the flag.

traditions and languages to build up one culture that is unique to the Seychelles. The slaves brought traditional African and Malagasy cultures encompassing witchcraft and superstition. Some islanders still believe in the power of magic (*gris-gris*) and will spend a lot of money consulting the *bonnomm dibwa* (medicine man) when needing to resolve issues such as a lovers' dispute. The *bonnomm* is also believed to have healing powers and will sometimes be consulted in cases of illness.

Families are generally large and everyone seems to be related to, or at least know, everyone else. Children grow up in a most uncomplicated way playing in the gentle waves, going fishing and messing about in little boats. Grandmothers and aunts are always around to take care of the children when parents are at work. There is a free and easy approach to marriage: many couples never marry and partner changes are quite acceptable. Children tend to stay with their mothers, regardless of her partner, and the woman is generally the head of the household as fathers sometimes shirk the responsibilities of child rearing.

Life in the Seychelles is interwoven with the sea. The deep-blue ocean with its variable winds and currents is always in sight, and one is never far from the sound of the surf. In the early days, fishing from small boats provided the daily food, and news of the outside world arrived intermittently by ship. Today, more sophisticated communication networks prevail but the old days set the scene for the present laid-back lifestyle. The relaxed islanders do not know the word 'hurry'. Tomorrow, very often, does just as well as today. The Seychellois believe that life is to be enjoyed, and they will find any excuse for a celebration with music, dance and plenty to eat and drink.

MUSIC AND DANCING The rhythm of the ocean is mirrored in the lively Creole music which can be sweet and gentle or wild and lively, incorporating the deep-seated pulses of Africa and Madagascar. The drums or *tamtam*, made from a hollowed tree trunk, and the *tambour* with its skin cover are deeply reminiscent of Africa. String instruments, the *zez* and the *mouloumpa*, are made from calabashes or bamboo, and create sounds hauntingly suggestive of Madagascar. Nowadays, though the sounds are often made on modern guitars and keyboards, and the music of the younger generation is influenced by country and western and reggae, it still has that evocative Seychelles quality, and the rhythmic beats are a clear invitation to dance.

The *sega*, danced to the rhythm beaten out on a drum, is pure African in origin. Couples dance sensuously facing each other, without touching. Adapted versions of the *sega* are performed for tourists. The traditional *moutya*, derived from the slave days, is a gathering which takes place on the beach by the light of the moon and the stars. A great fire blazes and everyone sits around drinking *kalou*, a potent brew made from the sap of the coconut palm, fermented with sugar. Heat from the fire is used to tighten the goatskin drums. The music gets off to a slow start and the dancing is slow and erotic. As the beating of the drums increases, so does the rhythm of the chanting and, as the men and women reply to each other, so the dancing becomes more provocative and sensual. The best place to enjoy the drumming and dancing is on Beau Vallon Bay each Wednesday evening in conjunction with the Beau Vallon Bay Bazaar.

THE KREOL FESTIVAL At the end of October each year, the Kreol identity is celebrated with a week-long festival. A wide range of events takes place based on music, singing, dancing and the visual arts. Vibrant street performances liven up Victoria, fashion shows are held, schoolchildren put on variety shows and the elderly are treated to special teas and lunch outings. Other traditional aspects of Creole life are given a forum, with subjects like Creole cuisine and herbalism coming under discussion. Lenstiti Kreol plays an important role in the festivities with plays, poetry readings and literary workshops. The festival week ends with a ball and award ceremonies for the winners of the competitions. Visitors from many other Creole countries descend on the Seychelles and participants from Mauritius, Réunion and Rodrigues join with revellers from some of the Caribbean islands. Madagascar, though not a Creole country, also comes to the party.

ART Sensual scenery, lush tropical vegetation, glorious beaches and a relaxed harmony between all the people of the islands inspires creative expression in the arts. Many foreigners have also settled in the islands, bringing with them their artistic talents in different forms such as painting, sculpture and batik. Many artistic Seychellois have trained and worked abroad and there are artists scattered throughout the islands. Art is strongly encouraged in the schools and exhibitions of children's art can often be seen in unexpected places.

The National Cultural Centre building houses a gallery, which is always worth a visit. Across the road is Kenwyn House, a beautifully restored and renovated Creole house; the lower floor is a gallery showcasing the works of local Seychellois artists. Studios, galleries and boutiques are dotted all over the islands, and artistic treasures from simple sketches to marvellous collector's items are available. Paintings are often vividly coloured interpretations of the surroundings, and there are drawings of people and local scenes as well as magnificent sculptures in bronze or wood. Creative jewellery made from gold, pearls, shells and other items can be found in boutiques on Mahé and Praslin.

the seychelles islands
another world
www.seychelles.travel

The Seychelles Islands...
land of perpetual summer

2

Biodiversity

The islands of the Seychelles, as a result of their fascinating, continental past and equatorial, oceanic location, support a wide diversity of terrestrial and marine fauna and flora. In general, the terrestrial plants and animals have links with Africa, Madagascar and Asia while the marine life is largely characterised by species that are widespread in the tropical Indo-Pacific region. There are two UNESCO World Heritage Sites: Vallée de Mai on Praslin, and Aldabra Atoll (see pages 132–6 and 190–8 respectively).

PLANTS

When Nicholas Morphey made the first detailed account of the vegetation around Mahé in 1756, almost impenetrable mangrove forests lined the shores, coconut palms fringed the beaches and the narrow coastal plains and mountain slopes were covered with dense hardwood forests. Subsequently, there have been several botanical surveys of both the granitic and coralline islands. These have revealed that, at present, there are 766 species of flowering plants and 85 ferns known from the granitic islands, of which 69 are endemic (occur only in the Seychelles). The flora of the drier coralline islands is less prolific, supporting 257 species with 34 endemics.

The impact of man has significantly altered the vegetation on every island although, in some places, patches of natural vegetation still exist. The tall, lowland forests of the coastal plains have been the most denuded of all, but small enclaves still exist on Félicité and Silhouette, and some tiny patches can be found on Mahé. The timber was used for houses, boats and furniture, and the land was cleared to make way for agricultural purposes, mainly coconut and vanilla plantations. Shorelines of the granitic islands have been robbed of their mangroves in many places but magnificent, intact mangrove forests still fringe the inner lagoon of Aldabra Atoll.

SEAWEEDS AND SHORE PLANTS The seaweeds of the Seychelles have only recently received scientific attention and there are some 350 species of red, brown and green seaweeds known from the islands. There are nine species of **seagrasses** occurring in lagoons, namely *Cymodocea serrulata*, *C. rotundata*, *Halodule universis*, *Halophila decipiens*, *H. ovalis*, *H. stipulacea*, *Syringodium isoetifolium*, *Thalassia hemprichii* and *Thalassodendron ciliatum*. The leafy seagrasses form the major part of the diet of green turtles, and the juveniles of many fish spend the early part of their lives sheltering and feeding in seagrass beds – veritable nursery areas.

Shore plants, which are generally adapted to survive wind and salt spray, characterise the shores of the islands, and 54 species, mainly of Indo-Malay origin, are found in the Seychelles. The creeping beach convolvulus (*Ipomoea pes-caprae*), with purplish-pink flowers and large, tough leaves, is the first of the beach pioneers and is common on all the islands. The two most commonly distributed plants on the beach crest are the scrambling, shrubby salt bush (*Scaevola sericea*), known locally as *veloutier*, which has clusters of white flowers frequented by sunbirds, and *Tournefortia argentea*, with the Creole name of *bwa tabac*, which has thick, fleshy leaves covered in fine hairs. The ubiquitous **coconuts** (*Cocos nucifera*) and **casuarinas** (*Casuarina equistifolia*) are to be found fringing the shores of all the islands. The origins of both are unclear but mention of the presence of coconuts appears in the earliest records about the Seychelles. Casuarinas were recorded from Aldabra in 1815 but, as these widespread coastal trees were present in Madagascar in pre-European times, and as the seeds are easily dispersed, they could have spread naturally to the neighbouring Seychelles. Noteworthy trees of the shoreline include the Indian almond (*Terminalia catappa*), and the Alexandrian laurel (*Calophyllum inophyllum*), commonly known as the *badamier* and *takamaka*, respectively.

MANGROVE FORESTS Mangroves, *mangliye* in Creole, are evergreen trees which have adapted to growing in muddy, intertidal areas. Special root systems have evolved to withstand periods of inundation and exposure as the tides ebb and flow. Their strangely shaped roots or pneumatophores are, in fact, breathing roots adapted to cope with the lack of oxygen in the waterlogged mud. They can be seen poking straight up through the mud like long pencils or they can be angled with knobbly knee-roots. Many mangroves have sturdy prop- or stilt roots for support. The seeds of some mangrove species are torpedo-shaped and actually germinate on the parent tree. When they drop, they get vertically impaled into the soft mud, and roots can start to develop within hours.

Mangrove forests are a unique and important ecosystem that functions to protect the coast from erosion as well as providing a habitat for all sorts of animals including specialist crabs and snails. Mangroves provide nursery areas for juvenile fish, shelter for young hawksbill turtles and secluded feeding and breeding grounds for shorebirds and seabirds. On Aldabra, frigatebirds and red-footed boobies nest, side by side, in vast numbers in the mangrove canopy.

Most of the mangroves have all but disappeared from the granitic islands with only tiny patches left on Mahé, La Digue and Praslin. There are still small mangrove-forested areas on Silhouette and Curieuse. Amongst the coralline islands, St Joseph's Atoll, Farquhar, Cosmoledo, Astove and Aldabra still support healthy mangrove communities. Aldabra has an estimated 800ha of these forests, with the largest

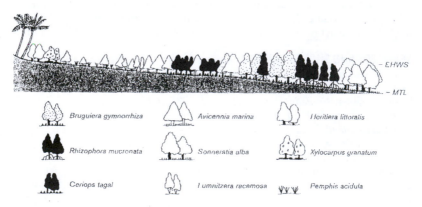

Mangrove tree species and zonation (EHWS: Extreme high water springs; MTL: Mean tide level). Reprinted with permission from Richmond (1997).

areas located at Bras Takamaka and Bras Cinq Cases. The most commonly found species are: the white mangrove (*Avicennia marina*), the black mangrove (*Bruguiera gymnorrhiza*), the red mangrove (*Rhizophora mucronata*) and the Indian mangrove (*Ceriops tagal*). In certain restricted areas, *Lumnitzera racemosa*, *Sonneratia alba*, *Heritiera littoralis* and *Xylocarpus granatum* can be found. Mangroves generally have specific zonation patterns on the shore relative to tidal height (page 196).

Besides mangroves, there are many other plants and trees associated with brackish and freshwater swamps. Reeds, sedges, grasses and water ferns inhabit these areas, which are often shaded by water-loving trees. The beach hibiscus (*Hibiscus tiliaceus*), with golden flowers that turn burnt orange and drop to the ground, are widespread. They are particularly common on the landward side of the mangrove forest at Curieuse. Other conspicuous trees of this area are *Barringtonia racemosa* with long sprays of pale pink flowers, and *Barringtonia asiatica* (Creole *bonnet kare*) with pink, powder-puff flowers and large, quadrangular seeds which are dispersed by the sea.

GRANITIC ISLAND VEGETATION

Coastal plains The narrow, confined coastal plains of the granitic islands were originally covered in fine, Seychelles hardwood trees like *takamaka* and *badamier*. However, most of the flat land was cleared to make way for plantation agriculture in the late 1800s and the original vegetation survives only in small, isolated pockets. Coconuts, vanilla (*Vanilla planifolia*) and cinnamon (*Cinnamonum zeylanicum*) were extensively planted and they can all be found growing wild, and in profusion. On some of the smaller granitic islands, which are now being conserved, woodland plants like *Pisonia grandis* and tortoise tree (*Morinda citrifolia*) are regenerating well. The human settlements on the islands have generally developed on the restricted flat land near the coast; here, introduced ornamental plants like frangipani, bougainvillea and hibiscus are common.

Mountains Away from the coastal habitat to the mountain slopes and valleys, the vegetation is defined by the amount of rainfall received, and this can vary significantly from area to area. Originally covered in hardwood forests, the lower slopes have been extensively cleared for agricultural purposes. Cinnamon, vanilla and other spices were planted on the hillsides and they have invaded the terrain, along with many other introduced plants. Productive tea plantations cover the slopes of central Mahé. The higher slopes retain more of the endemic species and have less introduced vegetation. Some of the endemic trees in the higher rainfall areas are *Dillenia ferruginea*, known locally as *bwa rouz*, and *Northea hornei*, a tall hardwood tree with a distinctive seed shaped like a monk's cowl, hence the Creole name *kapesin*.

Interspersed amongst the hardwood trees in the moist forests are a variety of endemic palms. *Verschafeltia splendida*, known by its Creole name of *latanyenn lat*, has a cone of stilt roots at the base. *Roscheria melanochaetes*, or *latanyenn oban* is the smallest and rarest of the endemic palms. Examples of the interesting pandanus or screw pine family can also be seen in the moist forest. Horne's pandanus (*Pandanus hornei*) or *vakwa parasol* in Creole, has a tall, thin, straight stem and an umbrella of prickly leaves at the top. *P. seychellarum*, or *vakwa maron*, has an even more accentuated wigwam of stilt roots.

Mosses and ferns are associated with the moist forests. An endemic fern, *Angiopterus evecta*, with the Creole name *baton monsennyer*, as the unopened fronds resemble a bishop's crook, and the bird's nest fern (*Asplenium nidus*) adorn many trees in the forest. The tree fern (*Cyathea sechellarum*) and the giant fern (*Angiopteris evecta*) favour the darker slopes of ravines traversed by streams.

There are spectacular, drier forests on Praslin, Curieuse and Silhouette. Though much of the original forest was altered by the removal of large *bwa rouz* and *kapesin* trees in days gone by, there are parts that are fairly intact and the prime example of this type of forest is the Vallée de Mai on Praslin. All six endemic palms can be seen in the Praslin National Park, the most spectacular of which is the **coco de mer** (*Lodoicea maldivica*), with its famous, suggestive, double nut. The other five palms, which each have a scientific name and a Creole name, are *Deckenia nobilis* or *palmiste*, *Nephrosperma vanhoutteanum* or *latanyenn milpat*, *Phoenicophorium borsigianum* or *latannyen fey*, *Roscheria melanochaetes* or *latannyen oban*, and *Verschafeltia splendida* or *latanyenn lat*. Four species of pandanus thrive in this relatively dry forest: *Pandanus hornei*, *P. sechellarum*, *P. balfourii* and *P. multispicatus*. See pages 134–6 for more information.

Glacis Glacis is weathered granite and these exposed areas on mountainsides have small pockets of peaty, shallow soil which support a number of interesting plants. The **pitcher plant** (*Nepenthes pervillei*), with its nearest relatives in Madagascar and Asia, is a low-growing, scrambling plant with pitcher-like receptacles that extend from the leaf midrib. The pitcher contains a liquid capable of digesting unsuspecting insects that fall into it. An interesting exception is the small endemic mosquito, *Uranotaenia nepenthes*, which actually breeds in the pitcher. *Pandanus multispicatus* also occurs on the wind-blown, misty *glacis* slopes. Several **orchids** are able to thrive on the *glacis*, and include the endemic Seychelles vanilla orchid (*Vanilla phaleanopsis*), which produces beautiful, waxy-looking, white flowers flushed with pink, on a thick, fleshy, leafless vine. The Seychelles national flower, the tropicbird orchid (*Angraecum eburneum*), is also able to survive on these inhospitable rocky slopes, and can even be found on the dry, craggy limestone *champignon* of Aldabra. *Malaxis seychellarum*, another small orchid which has greeny-yellow or purple flowers, can be found on the rocks or trees. There are another 22 species of orchids, both terrestrial and epiphytic (growing on other plants), but none is particularly spectacular.

Glacis in the drier parts does not have the thick, peaty mats of the moist locations and, though the plant life is similar, there are also some interesting differences. Occurring on the drier *glacis* slopes of Mahé are a few specimens of a most unusual tree, the **jellyfish tree** (*Medusagnye oppositaefolia*). This species is in a plant family all its own, and was thought to be extinct until rediscovered on Mahé in 1970. The flower is small, white and insignificant, and the dry, open fruit resembles a dark jellyfish.

CORALLINE ISLAND VEGETATION A beach-crest hedge of mostly *Scaevola* and *Tournefortia* characterises the shoreline of the coralline islands, and coconuts and casuarinas fringe many of the beaches. *Suriana maritime*, a low, scrambling coastal shrub with little yellow flowers, is common on the coralline islands and is known as *bois d'amande* in Creole. Two other trees found around the coasts are *Cordia subcordata*, known locally as *bwa porcher*, which has bright orange, bell-shaped flowers, and *Guettarda speciosa* or *bwa cassan*, which has bunches of creamy-white flowers producing a heady fragrance at night.

Pemphis acidula forms dense, impenetrable thickets up to 6m high on Aldabra. It grows in the rocky limestone and is able to withstand the brackish nature of the water. It has small, white flowers frequented by sunbirds. *Pemphis* is also found on Cosmoledo, Astove, Farquhar, Poivre and St Joseph's but does not occur on the granitic Seychelles islands.

Much of the natural forest of the coralline islands was removed for phosphate and guano mining, and later for coconut plantations. However, small patches of these trees surrounded by coconuts can still be found. The most widespread is *Cordia*, while *takamaka* occurs in groves on Aldabra and D'Arros, and is fairly common on many of the other coralline islands. There is also an evergreen mixed scrub cover on the raised limestone atolls with a wide variety of understorey species. Aldabra supports a surprising number of endemic plants including *Pandanus aldabrensis*, the Aldabra lily (*Lomatophyllum aldabrense*), and a subspecies of the tropicbird orchid, *Angraecum eburneum* (more details on page 195).

INTRODUCED PLANTS There are trees and shrubs that have been purposely introduced to the Seychelles for erosion control. They include mahogany (*Swietenia macrophylla*), the cocoplum (*Chrysobalanus icaco*), with its edible fruits, and the tall, flat-crowned albizia (*Paraserianthes falcataria*), which has become an invading nuisance. A wilt disease has spread among many of the large trees in the Seychelles with most of the sandragons and albizias being affected, as well as many of the *takamakas*. The brown, dead trees make a stark statement against the remaining green of the forest.

Many of the plants introduced for agricultural purposes have become naturalised and are widespread throughout the Seychelles. Coconuts dominated the Seychelles agriculture from the mid 1800s to around 1960 and, though no longer always grown in managed plantations, it is still the dominant species on many of the low coralline islands. Seedlings are grown from the germinating nut and the tree becomes productive after 15–18 years. They bear fruit for about 50 years and each coconut weighs about 1.5–2kg. The Seychellois have 100 or more uses for coconuts. Fronds provide thatching for walls, roofs and fences while trunks make sturdy timber for furniture. Leaves are used to make hats, bags, baskets, brooms, brushes and mats. Fermenting sap makes a potent toddy, *kalou*, and the growing shoot is a delicious substitute for the *palmiste* in a millionaire's salad. Green coconuts provide a cool, hygienic and refreshing juice that can be drunk straight from the nut. The thick, white flesh of mature coconuts is delicious as a filling snack, and coconut milk squeezed from the grated flesh is an important component of Creole cuisine. Copra is the dried flesh from which coconut oil is extracted, and that too has umpteen uses. Even the dry, brown coconut husks have uses – they make excellent charcoal as well as providing fuel for copra driers or calorifiers.

Cinnamon was once an important crop, with the bark providing cinnamon quills and powder, and the oil, distilled from the leaves, used in the perfume industry. Cinnamon trees are now widespread throughout the mountain slopes of the granitic Seychelles. Vanilla used to account for a significant amount of foreign earnings, but since the manufacture of synthetic essence it has become unprofitable. The vines have become naturalised and can be seen creeping on many of the mountainsides.

Fruits of a great variety are widely grown on the islands. Jackfruit, locally called *zak*, has large, oval, edible fruits growing directly from the trunk. Breadfruit has the wonderful Creole name of *fraipen*, probably because it is so commonly fried in a pan and eaten. It has distinctive, palmate leaves and large, round fruits growing from the branches. The story goes that any foreigners eating the fruit will surely return to the Seychelles! Other common fruits include banana, mango, papaya, crispy white jamalac, smelly durian, guava and spicy nutmeg. The market in Victoria is probably the best place to see and sample many of these exotic fruits.

Many of the brightly coloured flowering trees and shrubs that you see growing in profusion on many of the islands have been introduced to the Seychelles where they thrive in a riot of colour. Heady perfume from the frangipani *Plumeria obtuse* fills the sultry evening air and the creamy flowers are often put on the hotel beds in the evening or woven into a garland to greet new arrivals at the airport. Frilly crimson, orange or yellow hibiscus are to be found all over the islands and originated in south China. The flamboyant or flame tree, *Delonix regia*, is a native of Madagascar and is an umbrella of fiery, flame-coloured flowers in December and January. The tall **cannonball trees** have red, waxy flowers growing straight from the tree trunk and the round fruits give it its name. There is a beautiful specimen growing along the driveway into the Northolme Hilton in Mahé. It can also be found in the Botanical Gardens in Victoria. A common street tree in Victoria is the geiger tree *Cordia* which has clusters of bright orange flowers. There are a host of gorgeous lily species that grow in unlikely places. The spider lily (*Hymenocallis littoralis*) has long perianth segments drooping from the white trumpet-shaped flower and is often found in the

SCIENTIFIC NAMES

The system of scientific names given to animals and plants is best understood if it is regarded as a hierarchical address system in which each species is positioned according to its relationship with other species. At the broadest level, the animal kingdom is divided into phyla which are groups of animals which share a similar overall body plan. Each phylum is then subdivided into more closely related classes, which in turn contain orders, families, and finally genera and species. Each species is allocated a pair of names; in text, these are printed in italics. The first word of the pair is the genus name, while the second, always written in the lower case, identifies the individual species. Closely related species thus share the same generic names. The specific epithet is meaningless when written alone because many different species in different phyla may have the same specific epithet. For example, the Seychelles warbler, *Acrocephalus seychellensis*, has the same specific epithet as the Seychelles tree frog, *Tachycnemis seychellensis*. So do many other animals and plants of the Seychelles – possibly indicative of poor imagination on the part of museum-bound taxonomists!

This binomial nomenclature was invented by the Swedish scientist Linnaeus in the 18th century, and has been slavishly adhered to by biologists ever since. Unique scientific names (in Latin) are established for every known species, and these are universally recognised, unlike common names, which for the same species may differ from location to location. In this book we sometimes only give the generic name if several species of the same genus are involved. If referring to several species within the same genus, the genus name is abbreviated to the first letter. As an example, the classification of the emperor angelfish would be as follows:

Phylum	Vertebrata
Class	Osteichthyes
Order	Perciformes
Family	Pomacanthidae
Genus	*Pomacanthus*
Species	*imperator*

dry areas above the beach crest. Crinum lilies can be found in gardens and along roadsides. There are several species as well as hybrid varieties and most have long, strap-like leaves and showy clusters of bright pink and white trumpet-shaped flowers.

INVERTEBRATES

The various habitats of the Seychelles are home to an amazing variety of creepy-crawlies. Over 3,500 species of insects have been documented, and there is a close association between endemic insects and endemic plants. Beetles are the best group with about 700 species, followed by some 400 species of flies. One endemic insect of note is the **giant tenebrionid beetle** (*Pulposipes herculaenus*), which is found only on Frégate. The spherical, mud nests of potter **wasps** are frequently seen but the yellow wasps, with their paper-like hanging nests, should be avoided as they can inflict a nasty sting. The insect faunas of the high granitic islands and low coralline islands are remarkably distinct with less than 10% shared between the two types of islands. **Butterflies** provide a good example of this, with surprisingly few found in the granitic Seychelles but numerous, brightly coloured species flutter around the islands of the Aldabra group. There are some introduced insect species, most of which have become pests. One of these is the **crazy-ant** (*Anopolepsis longipes*), which reportedly arrived in Mahé from southeast Asia in 1962, and is now infesting various seabird colonies.

Large, harmless, orange-legged **millipedes** are frequently seen on the granitic islands, but be careful of the **centipedes** as they have a nasty bite. The golden orb **spider** (*Nephila madagascariensis*) is abundant in the granitic Seychelles and their conspicuous webs are often seen glistening between trees. On Frégate, there is the extremely large, flattened **whip spider** (*Amblypige*), which reaches up to 25cm across, as well as the **Seychelles giant scorpion** (*Chiromachus ochropus*), which is found under rocks or piles of coconut husks. Two species of **ticks** have been found to parasitise nesting seabirds in the Seychelles and ticks are also found on domesticated animals such as dogs and cattle.

Land and freshwater **molluscs** in the granitic Seychelles are generally endemic, small and dull in colour, and most survive in the relic forests on the summits of the islands. In the Vallée de Mai on Praslin the large snail (*Stylodonta studeriana*) and the Praslin snail (*Pachnodus praslinus*) can be seen on coco de mer palm leaves and stems while the white slug (*Vaginula seychellensis*) frequents the male flowers.

There are 32 species of land and freshwater **crabs** known from the Seychelles, and these include one endemic freshwater species, *Deckenia alluaudi*, which is found in streams on Mahé and Praslin. The land crab (*Cardisoma carnifex*) is the most common terrestrial crab, and is widespread throughout the Seychelles. They are large, nocturnal scavengers that, though they spend most of their lives ashore, must return to the sea to spawn. Similarly, the large robber or coconut crabs (*Birgus latro*) also have to return to the sea to spawn. They are the largest terrestrial crabs and can attain 4kg in weight. They have big, strong claws and, when not foraging, shelter between tree roots and in burrows. They feed on a wide variety of plant material as well as scavenging on turtle eggs and hatchlings. They even climb *Pandanus* to feed on the fruits and are able to tear open fallen coconuts.

AMPHIBIANS

Despite the oceanic location of the Seychelles, the continental origin of the granitic islands accounts for the occurrence of 12 species of amphibians (11 endemic). Five of these are true frogs, and include three species of minute, secretive **sooglossids**

2

which live at altitudes exceeding 200m on Mahé and Silhouette. They deposit their eggs in terrestrial nests in moist places, and, upon hatching, the tadpoles of *Sooglossus sechellensis* clamber onto the back of the parent male and remain there until metamorphosing into small frogs. In contrast, in *S. gardineri*, no tadpole-carrying occurs, and fully developed froglets hatch from the egg capsules. **Caecilians**, which are specialised, burrowing, legless amphibians, are represented by seven species and they spend their lives hidden in rotten logs and in moist leaf litter. *Hypogeophis rostratus* is ubiquitous through the granitic islands but *Grandisonia brevis* and *G. diminutiva* are endemic to Mahé and Praslin, respectively. The tree frog (*Tachycnemis seychellensis*) is found on Mahé, Praslin and La Digue. Interestingly, the green-coloured females deposit their eggs in vegetation over streams and, after hatching, the long-tailed tadpoles drop into the water below. The most wide-ranging frog in the granitic Seychelles is the African species, *Rana mascareniensis*, which occurs from marshy ground near the coast up into mountain forest. There are no frogs on the outer coralline islands of the Seychelles.

REPTILES

The islands of the Seychelles are surprisingly well endowed with reptiles, ranging from tiny lizards to giant tortoises. Early explorers documented the occurrence of large crocodiles along the coast of Mahé, but they were hunted to extinction, the only remaining evidence now residing at the Natural History Museum in Victoria. Smaller, less dangerous relatives proliferate today, and scuttling skinks and gaudy geckos are characteristic of both the granitic and coralline islands.

LIZARDS The brightly coloured, endemic *Phelsuma* **geckos**, which are of Malagasy origin, have radiated throughout the Seychelles and various species and subspecies are found in the granitic islands and the Amirantes and Aldabra groups. A visit to the Vallée de Mai on Praslin will guarantee sightings of green *Phelsuma* geckos, *P. astriata* and *P. sundbergi*, as they scuttle up and down coco de mer trunks feeding on insects. These geckos are known as *leza ver* in Creole. The bronze-eyed gecko (*Ailuronyx seychellensis; maguya* in Creole), which is active at night, generally hides in crevices and leaf bases of palms during the day. The larger giant bronze gecko (*A. trachygaster*) has a much broader and bigger head than *A. seychellensis*, and has recently been studied in the Vallée de Mai. *Cryptoblepharus boutonii* is a widely distributed gecko inhabiting the shore and tideline of many islands but on Aldabra it extends all over the atoll. *Gehyra mutilata*, the introduced house gecko (*leza disik*), is common on the inhabited islands and can often be seen feeding on insects attracted to lights.

Other lizards widely distributed in the granitic islands are *Phyllodactylus inexpectatus*, chameleons (*Chamaleo tigris*) and *Scelotes* and *Mabuya* **skinks**. The endemic *Mabuya* skinks (*leza sek*) are predators feeding chiefly on seabird eggs and chicks, and the two species *M. sechellensis* and *M. wrightii* are remarkably abundant on islands like Cousin, Aride and Frégate. The *Scelotes* skinks (*S. braueri* and *S. gardineri*), which live in and under leaf litter, are also widespread, extending up into the mountains.

SNAKES Three harmless species of snakes occur on the central granitic islands. The endemic Seychelles **house snake** (*Boaedon geometricus*) is found in forests, coconut plantations, rocky slopes and villages. It is a thick-bodied, short, greyish snake with a white snout and two white stripes behind the eye. It is nocturnal and preys on rats, mice, birds, lizards and frogs. The endemic **Seychelles wolf snake** (*Lycognathopsis* *seychellensis*) attains 1.2m in length. It is an active, diurnal species found at all elevations and preys on lizards. It has two colour phases, namely 'yellow' when the animal is bright yellow on the underside and brown on top, and 'dark' when it is dark grey with black spots dorsally and a white underside. The **burrowing snake** (*Rampotyphlops braminus*) is a small, dark grey, blind creature that resembles an earthworm. It burrows in damp soil and leaf litter but has also been recorded living in beach sand. This species is broadly distributed outside the Seychelles and was probably inadvertently introduced by man.

TORTOISES AND TERRAPINS Giant tortoise populations in the Indian Ocean were first discovered in the 16th century. Subsequently, natural populations were exterminated from all the Seychelles islands except Aldabra by seafarers who ruthlessly exploited the lumbering creatures as a source of fresh meat. The only surviving population was saved by the first lessee of Aldabra, James Spurs, who in 1891 prohibited the killing of the giant tortoises on the atoll. *Geochelone (Dipsochelys) gigantea* is now thriving on Aldabra, and the most recent population estimates are in the region of 100,000 animals, living principally on Grande Terre.

The very existence of these ancient chelonians is limited by food, water, nesting sites and shade from the tropical sun. In order to survive – and avoid literally being cooked in their dome-shaped shells – the tortoises have to seek shade during the day, where they rest in groups under trees and shrubs. When they are out feeding in the early morning and late afternoon they generally orientate themselves so their backs face the sun, thus ensuring that their head, neck and front legs are in shade. The tortoises feed chiefly on grass turf, tree leaves, flowers and fruits.

Most mating takes place from February to May and this is a noisy affair. The heavy male, encumbered by both his and her carapace, climbs onto the female and attempts to curve his tail under her carapace to reach her cloaca. Apparently, the success rate of matings is low! Females nest between June and September, digging holes in the ground at night into which they lay clutches of golf-ball-sized eggs enveloped in thick mucus. They then cover the nest with soil, the whole nesting process taking about 11 hours. The period of incubation varies from 73 to 160 days, and the hatchlings emerge from the nest just before the rainy season. They then have to survive the ravages of predators such as coconut crabs, land crabs, rats and birds. The average weight of tortoises on Grande Terre is about 21kg but on Malabar and Picard, where there is more food, they are more than double this weight and reach reproductive condition earlier than those on Grande Terre.

Aldabra tortoises have been translocated to many of the granitic islands, and visitors to Mahé can see captive ones at the Botanical Gardens in Victoria and in the grounds of several of the hotels. On Curieuse, there is now a thriving tortoise population, and these can easily be viewed on a day trip over from Praslin. There are also free-ranging tortoise populations on Frégate, Moyenne and Cousin.

Three species of freshwater **terrapins** from the genus *Pelusios* have been found in the Seychelles. Although La Digue is regarded as the home of the *tortues-soupapes* as they are known in Creole, *Pelusios seychellensis*, *P. subniger* (star-bellied terrapin) and *P. castanoides* (the yellow-bellied terrapin) are also found on Mahé, Praslin and satellite granitic islands. They are carnivorous but sometimes feed on plants. Extensive draining of coastal swamps is, however, threatening some populations.

MARINE TURTLES Four species of marine turtles are known from the Seychelles. Two of them, the **leatherback** (*Dermochelys coriacea*) and the **loggerhead** (*Caretta caretta*), although found in other parts of the western Indian Ocean, are rarely seen in Seychelles waters. The **hawksbill turtle** (*Eretmochelys imbricata*) and the **green turtle** (*Chelonia mydas*) are widespread throughout the Seychelles, although their populations have been decimated by harvesting for 'tortoiseshell' and meat.

Turtles have a complicated life history that includes both terrestrial and marine phases, and visitors to the Seychelles have the possibility of seeing them in both environments. Mating of turtles occurs at sea, and the females come ashore on sandy beaches to lay their eggs in holes they dig above the high-tide mark. The eggs hatch after about two months, and the little hatchlings emerge from the sand to make their way down to the water's edge. On entering the water, the hatchlings are widely dispersed by ocean currents. They then enter the feeding phase, which is largely in coastal waters, and attaining reproductive maturity, start the breeding phase. There are often clear migrations between feeding and breeding grounds. Hawksbill turtles are usually seen in association with coral reefs where they feed on coral polyps and sponges. Green turtles, by contrast, are largely vegetarian and feed on seagrasses and seaweeds.

Both species nest on sandy beaches although the hawksbill appears to prefer more protected beaches. Although the green turtle has been reported to nest year-round, nesting peaks during the southeast trade wind period from June to September, whereas nesting by the hawksbill occurs mainly during the northwest monsoon from October to January. Hawksbill turtles usually attempt to nest under vegetation above the high-tide mark and, surprisingly, in the Seychelles have a tendency to nest in daylight hours. Although hawksbill turtles may nest up to five times per season, the average seasonal complement is two, and there is 'site tenacity', with females known to return to the same beach. Hawksbill turtles do not appear to nest annually, and studies of tagged animals on Cousin show inter-season intervals of

INTERNATIONAL TRADE IN ENDANGERED SPECIES

In 1963, the International Union for the Conservation of Nature (IUCN) called for an international agreement on trade in animal species and their products in response to the impact that increased trade was having on wild populations of many species. Ten years later, the Convention on International Trade in Endangered Species of Wild Fauna and Flora (CITES) was negotiated in Washington, DC, and it came into force in July 1975 after ten nations had ratified it. To date, some 175 countries have signed the convention and the Seychelles was one of the early signatories in February 1977.

CITES regulates international trade in animals and plants whose survival may be threatened by trade. CITES operates on a permit system corresponding to species listed on three appendices. Generally, import and export permits are required.

The convention is administered via a secretariat based in Geneva and, within party countries, management authorities issue permits based on advice from their scientific agencies. A conference of signatory parties is held every two years to evaluate implementation of the treaty and consider ways to improve efforts. The most recent meeting was held in Bangkok, Thailand in March 2013.

In the Seychelles, attempts to stop the sale of turtle products (all turtles are CITES species) were only effective when the World Bank and the Seychelles government funded a programme to curb the tourist-based demand for turtle-shell products and provide artisans with alternative occupations and compensation.

two to four years. Clutch size averages about 170 eggs. Green turtle nesting has been reported at more than 20 islands in the Seychelles, but they have been most studied in the Aldabra group where they nest just above the beach crest in unvegetated sand. Green turtles nest at night, about three times in a season, and show nest-site tenacity with a two- to three-year period between nesting. Clutch size is about 125 eggs. Ghost crabs are voracious predators on turtle eggs and hatchlings, while birds frequently attack hatchlings as they make their way to the sea. Feral rats and dogs can also impact turtle populations by digging up nests.

MAMMALS

TERRESTRIAL MAMMALS Bats are widespread throughout the Seychelles, and two species of endemic bats are found on the granitic islands. The **Seychelles fruit bat** (*Pteropus seychellensis*) spends much of the day roosting in casuarina and albizia trees. Also known as flying foxes, they usually emerge at dusk to feed on soft, sweet fruits. These bats can be quite large, and adult males reach up to 600g. The **sheath-tailed bat** (*Coleura seychellensis*) is much smaller (only weighing about 10g) and much rarer. They are insectivorous, and roost in caves on the granitic islands. The fruit bat also occurs on the atolls of the Aldabra group, together with three other species of small bats, namely *Taphozous mauritianus*, *Triaenops furculu* and *Tadarida pusilla*.

There have been several species of mammals introduced to the Seychelles over the years. The **tenrec** (*Tenrec ecaudatus*), which is rat-like, light brown in colour with quills on the neck and back, has spread through much of the hill forest where they forage on leaf-litter invertebrates and fallen fruit. Rats and mice were introduced during the late 18th century and now occur on most of the islands. Rats cause damage to crops, and also prey on eggs and chicks. Rabbits, cats and dogs have also been introduced and feral cats have been blamed for the decline in several bird species. Domestic pigs, goats, cattle and horses are found on the farms. Feral goats prevent regeneration of natural vegetation and have been a problem on Aldabra.

MARINE MAMMALS The distribution ranges of many species of **whales** and **dolphins** include the waters of the Seychelles EEZ. Prior to 1915, sperm whales (*Physeter catodon*) were harvested around Bird and Denis islands on the edge of the Seychelles Bank, and the carcasses were towed to the whaling station on Ste Anne for processing. Recent boat-based and aerial surveys have confirmed that sperm whales and their calves still frequent this area. Humpback whales (*Megaptera novaeangliae*) are sighted from Aldabra during the winter and spring months when these large baleen whales migrate from Antarctica to the tropical waters of the western Indian Ocean for breeding purposes. Bottle-nosed dolphins (*Tursiops truncatus*), Risso's dolphins (*Grampus grisius*), spotted dolphins (*Stenella attentuata*) and the acrobatic spinner dolphins (*Stenella longirostris*) are regularly sighted from vessels traversing Seychelles waters. The strange-looking vegetarian **dugongs** (*Dugong dugon*), which frequent shallow, tropical lagoons where they feed on seagrasses, used to occur throughout the Seychelles but are now only seen on very rare occasions in the Aldabra lagoon.

BIRDS

The Seychelles, uniquely positioned in the western Indian Ocean, is home, breeding site and migratory stopover for a wide variety of birds. The Seychelles land birds, with affinities to Madagascar, Asia and Africa, have evolved into new species and subspecies over the millennia, and there are 17 endemic species. Many of the Seychelles islands are globally important seabird breeding colonies, and the majority of the birds nest during the southeast trade wind season, from April to October. Although the actual number of species is relatively low, a staggering number of seabirds breed on the coralline islands. Many can also be seen around the inner granitic islands of Aride, Cousin and Bird. Palaearctic migrants from Europe and Asia stop over in the Seychelles and some stay the entire season, while others are mere passing travellers.

One bird species has become extinct in the Seychelles since man intervened on these fragile islands. Habitat destruction was the main cause of the demise of the green parakeet (*Psittacula eupatria*), but it was also indiscriminately shot as it was believed to devour the crops.

LAND BIRDS It is quite remarkable that, on such a tiny land mass as the Seychelles, there are 17 endemic land-bird species, 12 of which are found on the granitic islands and five in the Aldabra group. The other two-dozen species of land birds occurring in the Seychelles are also found in Madagascar and the Comoros, making them endemic to the western Indian Ocean. However, some of the most commonly seen birds are introduced species that have developed successful breeding populations in the Seychelles.

The most commonly seen bird is the **Madagascar fody** (*Foudia madagascariensis*). In the breeding season, the male assumes a glowing orange-red plumage while the female is always a dull streaky brown. The noisy, gregarious **Indian mynah** (*Acridotheres tristis*) is widespread, and the white window patches on the wings are conspicuous when in flight. One of the characteristic bird sounds of the Seychelles is the gentle cooing of the **barred ground dove** (*Geopelia striata*).

The most amazing assortment of birds arrives on the Seychelles islands during seasonal migrations as it is the only landfall in a huge expanse of ocean. They range from Eleanor's falcon to European rollers, tree pipits, hoopoes and barn swallows, as well as a selection of waders such as terek sandpipers, greenshanks and godwits.

ENDEMIC BIRDS OF THE GRANITIC ISLANDS The national bird, the **Seychelles black parrot** (*Coracopsis barklyi*), is closely related to the Vasa parrots of Madagascar. It is not really black, more of a dark chocolate colour, and can be found on Praslin and Curieuse foraging in the forests for fruits. The **Seychelles blue pigeon** (*Alectroenas pulcherrima*) is a handsome bird, deep blue with scarlet wattles, and it occurs around fruiting trees on the main islands.

One of the most beautiful birds is the **Seychelles black paradise flycatcher** (*Tersiphone corvine*). There are only about 300 left, with a stronghold on La Digue where they can be seen in the flycatcher reserve and elsewhere on the island. The striking long-tailed male, black all over with a dark blue bill, differs from the female which has a shorter tail, white underparts, a black head and ginger upperparts. A population of 23 flycatchers was relocated to the far northern island of Denis in 2009, where the birds are now breeding and the small population appears to be doing well. This translocation programme took many years of planning to implement. Dense coconut plantations were cleared and planted with indigenous plants and a rat eradication programme was carried out to make Denis one of the few rat-free islands in the Seychelles. The relocation was achieved with funding from the Darwin Initiative and the Durrell Institute of Conservation, expertise from Nature Seychelles and wonderful co-operation from the management of Denis and the Department of Environment.

The **Seychelles magpie robin** (*Copsychus sechellarum*) is teetering on the edge of extinction as habitat destruction and introduced cats and rats caused a rapid decline in their numbers. These black-and-white birds spend most of their time grubbing in the leaf litter feeding on insects. The last remaining foothold of the magpie robin was on the island of Frégate but the population reached an alarming low of only 24 birds. Several were relocated to Cousin where they started breeding to the point where the island has almost reached carrying capacity. More recently, they have been relocated to Cousine, Denis and Aride, where they have settled and are breeding successfully. There are now over 260 magpie robins on five islands. The survival success story, however, belongs to the **Seychelles warbler** (*Acrocephalus seychellensis*). From a mere 29 birds, endangered and on the Red Data List, there are now several hundred, breeding well and thriving on Cousin, Cousine, Aride, and now also on Denis. The warbler, a dull olive-brown, is easy to see on these islands as it flits through the undergrowth calling and chattering.

One of the rarest birds is the **Seychelles scops owl** (*Otus insularis*). It is confined to Mahé where it resides in the deep forests of the Morne Seychellois National Park and can be heard making its deep croaking call in the evenings. Little is known about this enigmatic little brown owl, and the first nest was only discovered in 1999.

The **Seychelles white-eye** (*Zosterops modestus*) is a tiny, grey bird with a white eye-ring. They are difficult to find but they frequent degraded woodland. Small groups can be observed at La Misère near the hotel school, and a large population (around 200) exists on Conception off the west coast of Mahé, but getting there to see them is extremely difficult. A small group was transported to Frégate, where they are thriving. In July 2007, 20 birds were relocated to North Island and a further 20 to Cousine in specially constructed, soundproof, ventilated Helibird boxes with the kind assistance of Helicopter Seychelles. All appear to be doing well and there are now 400 altogether.

Another little bird found on the granitic islands is the **Seychelles sunbird** (*Nectarinia dussumieri*). It has a typical, long, curved bill for sipping nectar and the male shows a deep blue iridescence on the throat and breast. In 2006, 33 sunbirds were relocated to Bird Island where they have been breeding successfully. The **Seychelles fody** (*Foudia seychellarum*) is dull brown with a large, wedge-shaped bill, but in breeding plumage the male has a bright yellow face. These birds, known locally as the *tok-tok*, scavenge untended seabird eggs, and are confined to Cousin, Cousine, Denis and Frégate.

The **Seychelles kestrel** (*Falco araea*) preys on lizards, including geckos, and is most commonly seen on Mahé on top of buildings or around rock faces. Its call, described as 'ti-ti-ti', gives rise to the Creole name of *katiti*. The widespread **Seychelles turtle dove** (*Streptopelia picturata*) has interbred to a large extent with the Madagascar turtle dove and it is not clear whether any pure forms still exist. The **Seychelles swiftlet** (*Collocalia elaphra*) is the only small swift. They are often seen flying in groups near the mountains of Mahé, Praslin and La Digue where they nest in rocky areas. One of the most commonly heard birds in the forests is the noisy **Seychelles bulbul** (*Hypsipetes crassirostris*), which has an untidy black crest and an orange bill.

BIRDS OF THE ALDABRA GROUP Five endemic species are known from the Aldabra archipelago. The last remaining flightless bird of the Indian Ocean is the **Aldabra rail** (*Dryolimnas aldabranus*). Confined to Aldabra, the rails are surviving well on the islands of Picard, Polymnie and Malabar, which are the best places to see these fearless and curious birds. The **Aldabra drongo** (*Dicrurus aldabranus*), black with a forked tail, is a very territorial bird and will even chase the kestrels and crows. The **Aldabra fody** (*Foudia aldabrana*), a nondescript bird (LBJ, or little brown job) can be seen around the settlement on Picard. In breeding plumage, however, the male develops a yellow belly and bright red head, chest and rump. **Abbot's sunbird** (*Nectarinia abbotii*) is found on Cosmoledo, Astove and Assumption but not on Aldabra where the Souimanga sunbird rules the roost. In breeding plumage the male has a green iridescence over the head and chest and a black belly. Despite extensive searches, the **Aldabra brush warbler** (*Nesillas aldabrana*) has not been seen since 1983.

Other land birds common in the Aldabra archipelago share an ancestry with those from Madagascar or the Comoros. The **Madagascar sacred ibis** (*Threskiornis bernieri*), with sky-blue eyes, can be seen around the settlement on Picard. Others include: the **Madagascar coucal** (*Centropus toulou*); **Madagascar nightjar** (*Caprimulgus madagascariensis*); **Madagacar bulbul** (*Hypsipetes madagascariensis*) and the **Souimanga sunbird** (*Nectarina souimanga*). Found only on Cosmoledo and Astove, the **Madagascar cisticola** (*Cisticola cherina*) is easily seen flitting between the rocky islets.

SHORE BIRDS Also known as wading birds, most of the birds along the shores of the Seychelles are migratory and breed in Europe. These Palaearctic species winter in the southern hemisphere spending the entire non-breeding period in the Seychelles where they frequent both granitic and coralline islands. **Whimbrels** (*Numenius phaeopus*), **plovers** (*Pluvialis*) and **sandplovers** (*Charadrius*) are common, and **ruddy turnstones** (*Arenaria interpres*) can be seen throughout the year. Flocks of several hundred **crab plovers** (*Dromas ardeola*) occur on Aldabra and Cosmoledo and there are sometimes over 1,000 on St François in the Alphonse group. There are usually a couple of these enigmatic birds that breed in the Gulf of Oman, to be found on Mahé and Silhouette.

SEABIRDS Eighteen species of seabirds breed in the Seychelles and it is possible to see most of them on the granitic islands of Aride, Cousin and Bird.

Nine tern species breed in the Seychelles and the most spectacular are the hundreds of thousands of **sooty terns** (*Sterna fuscata*) that nest, during the southeast trades, on the low coralline islands and Aride (the only hilltop granitic breeding site). Sooty terns are the most aerial of all birds, spending many years on the wing before reaching breeding maturity. Their mottled eggs are laid on the sand. The most extensive breeding colony is on Cosmoledo with an estimated 1.2 million pairs. Sooty tern eggs are considered a great national delicacy: from 1944 to 1965, one million eggs were collected annually. There were sufficient for the local market and the yolks were also exported. At present, in June each year, some eggs are still collected from Bird and Desnoeufs under the control of the Islands Development Company.

Brown noddies (*Anous stolidus*) and **lesser noddies** (*A. tenuirostris*) are brown-coloured terns and difficult to tell apart at a distance. Both species breed throughout the Seychelles. Up to 170,000 pairs of lesser noddies can breed on Aride in a season. Numbers do fluctuate enormously and are dependent on food supplies. The pure **white fairy tern** (*Gygis alba*) is common on most of the islands. The single, mottled egg is laid in a slight groove on a bare branch, and, as the chick hatches, the feet emerge first and cling on to the branch for dear life. Fairy terns breed throughout the year and can be found on nearly all of the Seychelles islands. The largest tern is the **Caspian tern** (*Hydroprogne caspia*), which has a massive red bill. A few pairs nest on Aldabra, the only known oceanic breeding site in the world. The **swift** or **crested tern** (*Sterna bergii*) is smaller than the Caspian tern, has a yellow bill and also breeds on Aldabra on rocky îlots in the middle of the lagoon. Also breeding on Aldabra is the elegant **black-naped tern** (*S. sumatrana*), which lays its eggs on the bare *champignon*. One of the most beautiful terns is the **roseate tern** (*S. dougalii*), which has accentuated tail streamers and a rosy flush to the breast in the breeding season. These birds breed on Aride, but numbers appear to be declining for no apparent reason. **Bridled terns** (*S. anthetus*) are never seen in large numbers. They can be confused with sooty terns but are seldom seen far out to sea as they generally return to roost at night.

White-tailed tropicbirds (*Phaethon lepturus*), which have long, white tail streamers, fly gracefully around most of the granitic islands. They nest on the ground close to a protective rock or tree trunk. The larger **red-tailed tropicbird** (*P. rubricauda*) is not as easily observed as only a few nest on Aride and most are on Aldabra and Cosmoledo.

Greater frigatebirds (*Fregata ariel*) and **lesser frigatebirds** (*F. minor*), with their long, angled wings and deeply forked tails, are the most spectacular aerial birds. The males are generally black but the females have more white on the chest. As they take about five to six years to mature, the varying juvenile plumage can cause identification problems. They nest in profusion in the mangroves of Aldabra, cheek by jowl with the unsuspecting red-footed boobies, which they harass until the boobies regurgitate their last meals. As the frigatebirds do not have a good waterproofing system on their feathers, they do not dive into the water. During the non-breeding season, frigatebirds roost on Aride and Bird and can be seen soaring over the islands.

Boobies belong to the same family as gannets, and three species breed on the outer coralline islands. The most commonly seen is the **red-footed booby** (*Sula sula*), with thousands nesting in the mangroves in the Aldabra archipelago. They are characterised by their distinctive red feet. These birds will spend hours circling a ship at sea, and will often perch on the rigging. The large, ground-nesting **masked booby** (*S. dactylatra*) is not a widespread bird but can be seen in the vicinity of Cosmoledo where it breeds. Also breeding on Cosmoledo is the **brown booby** (*S. leucogaster*), which has a brown chest, and can be confused with young masked boobies.

Wedge-tailed shearwaters (*Puffinus pacificus*) and **tropical shearwaters** (*P. bailloni*), which nest in burrows are seldom seen on land during the day as they spend most of the daylight hours fishing far out to sea.

CORAL REEFS

Coral reefs are the most characteristic feature of the turquoise-blue waters surrounding the Seychelles islands. They are extremely important in ensuring coastal protection, supporting artisanal fisheries and providing the focus for diving tourism. There are three main types: fringing reefs, platform reefs and atolls. Barrier reefs are absent from the Seychelles, although they occur in other parts of the western Indian Ocean.

REEF TYPES **Fringing reefs** are associated with the granitic islands of the Seychelles Bank and are most extensive on Mahé and Praslin. There are considerable differences between reefs exposed to the southeast trade winds and those in more sheltered localities. The reefs along the southeast coast of Mahé are continuous and vary in width from 500m to 750m. The reefs along the west coast of Mahé are small and discontinuous, and are mainly found in bays like Baie Ternay and Port Launay. Between the bays, the high granite cliffs drop steeply into the sea and may lack reefs altogether, though some corals grow directly on the granite. On Praslin, the fringing reefs are much more extensive relative to the size of the island. They are widest on the southwest coast where they extend nearly 3km seawards, though elsewhere they may be as narrow as 400m. On La Digue, the reefs are widest on the west coast.

Platform reefs occur at several islands and at Coëtivy and D'Arros large parts of their upper surfaces are covered with land. At Plat and Providence, however, the

2

platform reefs have large shallow lagoons and very little land area. Assumption and St Pierre consist of raised platform reefs which do not exceed 8m above sea level.

There are several true **atolls** in the Seychelles. Farquhar (172km²) is the largest with the main peripheral reef about 1km wide surrounding a lagoon of about 14m in depth. St Joseph's in the Amirantes is much smaller with the peripheral reef ranging from 0.6km to 1.2km in width, and surrounding a shallow lagoon of about 6m in depth. The vertical thickness of the coral in the Amirantes has been determined to be about 1km.

The main **raised atolls** of the southern Seychelles are Aldabra, Cosmoledo and Astove. Aldabra is 34km long and up to 14km across with a rim of raised reef limestone which averages 2km in width. There are four coral-encrusted entrance channels into the lagoon – Grande Passe is 20m deep. The lagoon itself is shallow, and the lagoon floor consists of scoured bedrock with a thin veneer of sediment. The coastal cliffs on the seaward side of these atolls rise about 4m above the level of the reef flat. On Aldabra, there is a conspicuous terrace at about 4m and a higher surface level at about 8m. These features indicate a complex history of submergence and emergence. Geophysical evidence from Aldabra indicates that the coral cap varies between 0.6km and 1.6km in thickness.

CORALS AND REEF ZONATION

The western Indian Ocean is a centre for diversity of corals, and some 51 genera of scleractinian or **hard corals** are known from the granitic Seychelles islands and 47 genera from Aldabra. Recent scientific expeditions have recorded a further 40 hard coral species to bring the Seychelles species list to some 161 (excluding *Acropora* species). Hard corals are essentially colonies of polyps living within a communal calcium carbonate skeleton. The colonies can take on many shapes and forms which, amongst others, may be branching, columnar, tabular, encrusting or massive domes. Identification of many of the species requires examination of microscopic features of the skeleton but some of the more well-known species include: staghorn coral (*Acropora formosa*); table coral (*Acropora clathrata*); knob-horned coral (*Pocillopora verrucosa*); massive domes of *Porites lutea* and *P. solida*; brain coral (*Platygyra daedalea*); honeycomb corals (*Favites*); and turbinate

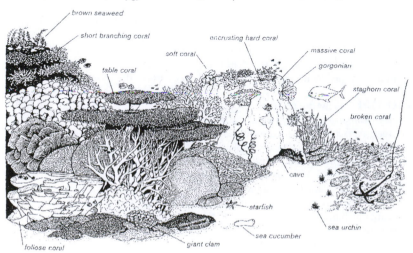

Typical shallow-water coral reef of the western Indian Ocean.
Reprinted with permission from Richmond (1997)

coral (*Turbinaria mesenterina*). Also easily recognised are mushroom corals, *Fungia scutaria*, which are actually solitary flat polyps, and colourful cup or turret corals (*Dendrophyllia*), which are solitary but grow in clumps on rock surfaces.

Soft corals are important components of coral reefs and, again, identification to species level often requires microscopic examination of various anatomical features. Some of the most well known are: organ-pipe coral (*Tubipora musica*); dead man's fingers (*Alcyonium flaccidum*); leather corals (*Lobophyton*); soft-lobed corals (*Sinularia*); fleshy mushroom corals (*Sarcophyton glaucum*); thistle corals (*Dendronephthya*); branching soft corals (*Nephthea*) and stalked soft corals like *Xenia crassa* and *Anthelia glauca*.

Spiral black coral (*Cirrhipathes*) and bushy black coral (*Antipathes*) are other easily recognised corals usually found on deeper reefs together with seafans or gorgonians like *Supergorgia* and *Rumphella*. **Fire coral** (*Millepora*), although not actually a true coral, appears in various forms and subjects the unwary diver who touches it to an extremely painful sting.

The zonation of the shallow fringing reefs of the granitic islands differs considerably from that on the exposed oceanic atolls. At Mahé or Praslin, if one swims out to the fringing reef from the beach at high tide, one will pass over a rippled sand zone followed by beds of seagrasses. The sand will then become interspersed with cobble ridges, seaweeds like *Sargassum*, *Turbinaria* and *Halimeda*, and large coral colonies of *Acropora*, *Pocillopora*, *Porites*, *Goniastrea* and *Favia*. Before reaching the reef edge one will encounter a narrow seaweed ridge with small coral colonies which dries at low tide. The reef edge has a gentle seaward slope and much of the surface is covered with encrusting calcareous algae. The common encrusting corals in this rough water habitat are *Pocillopora*, *Acropora*, *Goniastrea* and *Millepora* (fire coral). On the outer slopes of the reef various species of *Acropora* are dominant, and massive corals like *Porites*, *Favia* and *Leptoria* are more common on the lower slope. Corals decrease rapidly in abundance below 10m depth.

At Aldabra, the zonation of the reef is more vertical. In shallow water from 0m to 6m there are branching and columnar corals like *Acropora*, followed by a highly diverse zone of soft and honeycomb faviid corals which extends to about 14m depth. Below this, down to about 28m, the reef is dominated by honeycomb faviid corals.

CORAL BLEACHING During the summer of 1997–98, raised coastal water temperatures throughout the western Indian Ocean (attaining 34°C) led to wide-scale bleaching of corals in the shallow waters surrounding most of the Seychelles islands. This resulted in the death of the coral polyps, followed by colonisation and growth of algae on the remaining coral skeletons. As the corals are dead, boring organisms undermine the colonies, and they slowly break up and become reduced to rubble. Scientific investigations have revealed that corals on the deeper reef walls of many of the southern islands were not as badly affected. Recent reports indicate that regeneration is occurring in some places with settlement of young corals particularly evident around the granitic islands where the corals often grow directly on the granite. However, regeneration around Victoria and Ste Anne appears to have been slow. The Island Conservation Society has been involved in coral transplantation with 27,000 fragments transplanted at Cousin Island and 2,000 fragments transplanted at Praslin near Lemuria.

MARINE INVERTEBRATES

A huge variety of marine invertebrates including encrusting sponges and tunicates (sea squirts), tubeworms, crustaceans, molluscs and echinoderms are associated with coral reefs and other coastal habitats of the Seychelles. Sponges are extremely

SEYCHELLES CORAL REEF RECOVERY

Dr Karen Chong-Seng

Seychelles coral reefs, similar to many worldwide, are facing increasingly frequent and intense disturbances such as overfishing, thermal anomalies and storms. In particular, the reefs around the inner granitic Seychelles islands were affected by an El Niño coral bleaching event in 1998, the effects of which were probably worse as a result of chronic overfishing and sedimentation. Up to 90% of coral cover was lost in 1998, and today, recovery is occurring, but at very different levels between reefs. Recovery requires not only that overall coral cover approximates pre-disturbance levels, but also that the communities within the ecosystem such as corals, fish and algae remain fairly consistent. As a result of low coral cover, other organisms such as macro-algae or soft corals can dominate. These organisms are less desirable because they do not create the highly complex structures of hard corals, reducing the habitat availability provided by a reef. This has knock-on effects, affecting the populations of reef organisms that depend on corals, both directly (eg: for food and/or shelter) and indirectly (eg: their prey lives in corals).

Some key ecological processes have been identified as influential to a reef's recovery potential: coral recruitment (inflow of new coral juveniles), bio-erosion (stability of the reef matrix – loose rubble pieces are detrimental), herbivory (the consumption of algae on reefs) and the recovered fitness of remaining coral colonies to ensure continuity of the population. After 1998, the isolated nature of the inner Seychelles islands and the low numbers of fecund adult colonies were thought to make the reefs particularly vulnerable to recruitment failure. Happily, studies have shown that there is a supply of coral larvae to the reefs. However, on reefs where recovery is taking longer to initiate, and reef condition has degraded, mortality of coral recruits is high. The altered conditions, either overgrowth of macro-algae, or rubble fields, are further delaying recovery by preventing re-establishment of a dwindling coral population. Fishing of herbivorous fish is an important livelihood and protein source for the general population, yet these targeted species may be vital for the continuation of the ecosystem. Indeed, reefs were found to have very different types of herbivorous fish operating depending on whether they were recovering, or appeared degraded. The fishery is being strictly managed, and research is ongoing to determine the best catch levels and practices. Other stressors such as coral diseases, which have impacted many regions around the world, are present on some reefs although, currently, their effects are minimal as their prevalence is still low. There remains uncertainty as to the causes of the variability in recovery levels between reefs in the Seychelles and considerable research is being undertaken.

common and diverse, and range from encrusting species growing on granite boulders to huge barrel sponges. Tunicates, particularly the colonial species, are often confused with sponges, and both groups have been poorly studied in the western Indian Ocean. Many species of tubeworm are found on the reefs but the most spectacular is *Sabellastarte sanctijosephi* which has a brightly coloured featherduster-like crown which is quickly retracted into the tube when disturbed by divers.

The **crustaceans** include various types of colourful snapper shrimps (Caridea), coral crabs (Trapeziidae) and anemone crabs (Porcellanidae). Spiny lobsters,

Panulirus versicolor and *P. longipes*, respectively known as *omar ver* and *omar rouz*, generally hide in caves and crevices in the reef. Ghost crabs (*Ocypode*) frequent sandy beaches, and sunbathing visitors will probably notice numerous holes with little mounds of sand adjacent to them. These are the burrows of ghost crabs, and these swift decapods are most active at night when they can be seen scuttling along the water's edge scavenging for food. Coconut or robber crabs (*Birgus latro*) are sometimes found on the upper shore but generally inhabit beach vegetation, coconut groves and pandanus thickets. Three species of rock crabs (Grapsidae) can be seen scampering over rocky intertidal areas, while on mudflats and amongst mangroves, several species of burrowing fiddler crabs, *Uca*, and marsh crabs (Sesarminae) are found. Male fiddler crabs have a characteristically enlarged claw which they use in waving displays to establish territories and attract females. The marsh crabs typically have equal-sized, bright red or orange claws.

Echinoderms are a noticeable part of the marine fauna in the Seychelles, and most of the 150 species are widespread tropical Indo-Pacific forms. The long-spined black sea urchin (*Diadema savignyi*) is common, particularly where the reefs have been damaged. When diving or wading, care should be taken not to get spiked by their sharp spines as such an injury can be very painful. Slate pencil urchins (*Heterocentrus*) are also found on exposed reefs whilst, in sandy areas, fragile sand dollars (*Echinodiscus*) and heart urchins occur. Sea cucumbers are abundant on reef flats and seagrass beds, and range from the stocky species like *Holothuria nobilis* to the long, snake-like species *Synapta maculata* that can attain over 2m in length. Starfish include large cushion stars, *Culcita*, the long-armed, colourful *Linkia*, and the undesirable and extremely prickly crown-of-thorns starfish (*Acanthaster planci*), which is notorious for its reef-devouring habits. Brittle stars with their snake-like legs are generally difficult to spot and their close relatives, the basket stars, are also usually well hidden during the day, but at night they creep out and extend their arms into the water column to trap food particles. Similarly, the feather stars are also active at night and also hang onto corals, extending their arms to sieve food from the water.

Marine **molluscs** in the Seychelles are well represented by about 450 species of bivalves, gastropods (snails) and nudibranchs. Giant clams (*Tridacna*) are some of the most conspicuous bivalves but there are many smaller species in tropical waters. These include *Donax* which are small, wedge-shaped mussels that actively burrow on sandy shores. They are favoured by the Seychellois for *tec-tec* soup. Large conchs (Strombidae), a variety of cowries (*Cypraea*), snow-white egg shells (*Ovula ovum*), green turbans (*Turbo marmoratus*), helmet shells (Cassidae), tritons (Ranellidae), murex shells (Muricidae), olive shells (Olividae), and the poisonous cone shells (*Conus*), are some of the more well-known gastropods occurring on coral reefs. Nudibranchs, which are marine snails without shells, display some of the most striking colours found on reefs, and numerous species including the large (up to 30cm) Spanish dancer (*Hexabranchus marginatus*) are found on the Seychelles reefs. Frequently, while diving you can spot shoals of small squid (Loliginidae) swimming in the water column. Their jet-like propulsion and chameleon-like ability to change colour rapidly make them fascinating subjects to observe. Well-camouflaged octopuses are also sometimes seen hiding in crevices of the reefs.

FISH

A huge variety of marine fish are found in the Seychelles waters, and latest lists indicate that nearly 1,000 species have been recorded in the area. However, there is only one species of freshwater fish, the endemic Seychelles killifish (*Pachypanchax playfairii*), which is found in streams on some of the granitic islands. Most of the fish are widely distributed Indo-Pacific species associated with coral reefs, but wide-ranging open-water fish like tuna and billfish are also common in the oceanic waters of the EEZ. Endemism among fish in the Seychelles is very low. There are some specific variations in distribution and abundance of fish amongst the islands which can be related to the availability of suitable habitats, the ability of the species to disperse and the role of human fishing pressure.

Coral reef fish communities are a kaleidoscope of colour, and are characterised by numerous small species from many fish families. They include the butterflyfish (Chaetodontidae), angelfish (Pomacanthidae), surgeonfish (Acanthuridae), damselfish (Pomacentridae), wrass (Labridae), cardinalfish (Apogonidae), goldies

MARINE PROTECTED AREAS

The Seychelles has designated some 140km² of its territory for conservation of marine ecosystems, and the country has the distinction of having established the first marine park in the western Indian Ocean. The Ste Anne Marine National Park, which was proclaimed in March 1973, is probably the best known and, because of its proximity to Mahé, is visited by boatloads of tourists. The park encompasses the islands of Ste Anne, Moyenne, Round, Long and Cerf, together with the adjacent reefs and sea, an area of 15km². The park offers a diversity of marine habitats including fringing coral reefs, patch reefs, coral-encrusted granite boulders, seagrass beds, sand flats, intertidal rocks and sandy beaches. Snorkelling is permitted and, if you don't wish to get wet, tours by glass-bottom boat set out from the Marine Charter Association jetty in Victoria. Fishing by visitors is prohibited, as is collecting shells and coral.

The Seychelles Marine Parks Authority was created in September 1996 and in 2003, it merged with the Seychelles Centre for Marine Research and Technology (SCMRT-MPA). In 2010, major consolidation took place with the Seychelles National Parks Authority now being responsible for management of all marine and terrestrial protected areas, encouraging private investment within the parks (ecotourism), and collecting fees from tourist visitors (*PO Box 1240, Victoria, Mahé;* 4225114; *www.snpa.sc*).

The other marine protected areas managed by the Seychelles National Parks Authority include Curieuse, Baie Ternay, Port Launay, Silhouette Marine National Park and the area surrounding Ile Cocos. The Curieuse Marine National Park was established in 1979, and extends from the northeastern shores of Praslin across to, and around, Curieuse and Ile St Pierre. Baie Ternay and Port Launay, adjacent areas at the western extremity of Mahé, were also established as marine parks in 1979; these bays are characterised by fringing reefs which can be viewed by snorkelling or glass-bottom boat trips. Silhouette Marine National Park was designated in 1987 and comprises an area 1km wide around the perimeter of the island famous for its *glacis* that slope steeply into deep water.

Aldabra, a World Heritage Site, serves as a flagship marine protected area and is administered by the Seychelles Islands Foundation. Similarly, the marine areas around Cousin and Aride are protected through the respective efforts of Nature Seychelles and the Island Conservation Society. African Banks, through its allocation to the Ministry of Defence, also offers some protection to the marine life in the area.

(*Anthias*), triggerfish (Balistidae), filefish (Monacanthidae) and the majestic Moorish idols (*Zanclus cornutus*). These fish generally swim around the coral heads, often ducking for cover as a snorkeller or scuba diver approaches. Larger species found on the reefs include snappers (Lutjanidae), parrotfish (Scaridae), batfish (Ephippidae), groupers (Serranidae), emperors (Lethrinidae) and sweetlips (Haemulidae). By day, the red soldierfish and squirrelfish (Holocentridae) are rarely seen as they hide in caves and crevices but, at night, they emerge to feed on the reef. Shoals of sweepers (*Pempheris*) often form a silvery-brown curtain at the entrance to caves and overhangs. Well-camouflaged species include lizardfish (Synodontidae), hawkfish (Cirrhitidae), small gobies (Gobiidae) and blennies (Blenniidae), and other larger poisonous species like stonefish (*Synaceia verrucos*) and scorpionfish (Scorpaenidae). The magnificent lionfish (*Pterois*), with their elongate fins, are usually seen hovering nearly motionless over the reef but, beware; they can inflict nasty injuries to unwary divers. Several species of moray eels (Muraenidae) frequent crevices, holes and caves in the reefs, and care should be taken not to stick your hands into such places.

Coral reefs are also home to some of the strangest fish. Divers are often surprised when they see the elongate, tubular-snouted trumpetfish (*Aulostomus chinensis*) and cornetfish (*Fistularia petimba*) hovering over the reef. Some of the oddities of the reefs include boxfish and cowfish (Ostraciidae) with their bodies encased in bony plates; pufferfish (Tetraodontidae) which, as a defence against predators, can inflate their bodies into spherical balls by swallowing water or air; and porcupine fish (Diodontidae) which, in addition to being covered with prominent spines, can also inflate their rotund bodies. Whilst on the subject of peculiar fish, flying fish (Exocoetidae) cannot be omitted. These fish, spotted when voyaging between the islands, are characterised by elongate pectoral fins and a forked tail with an enlarged lower lobe. When chased by predators, they erupt from the surface of the water and glide in the air for considerable distances, frequently dipping their beating tails into the water for extra propulsion.

Coral reef fish also exhibit peculiar lifestyles and associations. For example, the little cleaner wrasse (*Labroides dimidiatus*) removes parasites from other fish. When diving, stopping to observe the agility and apparent foolhardiness of the wrasse as it nimbly nips parasites from inside the mouths and gill covers of large predators like groupers, is a worthwhile diversion. In fact, the wrasses have 'cleaning stations', and one can often see fish queuing up for the service! Cleaner shrimps provide a similar service. Another interesting association is that of the clownfish and anemone. Clownfish pairs (*Amphiprion*), immune to the stings of the anemones, shelter from predators among the tentacles of their hosts. These fish attach their eggs to the reef near the anemone, and guard them aggressively until the little larvae hatch out. Look carefully at the shoals of goldies (*Anthias*) over the reef and you will see that the larger ones are more reddish in colour with elongate dorsal and tail-fin filaments. These are the males; the gaggle of other bright-orange goldies are the females in the harems. Interestingly, these fish are hermaphrodite and capable of changing their sex. If the male is removed, one of the females will change into a male. Similarly, the parrotfish can also change sex and, as they exhibit colour changes with age and sex, there have been several instances where ichthyologists have actually described juveniles, males and females as separate species!

While scuba diving, take time out from peering at the reef to stop and look up into the water column. You will be richly rewarded as, above the reef, shoals of iridescent blue and gold fusiliers (Caesionidae) provide a breathtaking mobile canopy. Roving predators like jacks and trevallies (Carangidae) could be passing by, and you could even spot a lurking barracuda (*Sphyraena*) waiting for a meal. The pelagic domain is also home to shoals of mackerel (*Rastrelliger kanagurta*), as well as the fast-swimming tunas and billfish, and underwater sightings of these are always exciting.

The seagrass beds inshore of the reefs provide an important nursery area for juveniles of numerous fish species, and snorkelling in these areas can reveal all sorts of strange and unusual species. Shoals of herbivorous rabbitfish (Siganidae) and juvenile parrotfish (Scaridae) are common, and goatfish (Mullidae) with their chin barbels, flattened soles (Soleidae and Cynoglossidae) and flounders (Bothidae) can be spotted in sandy areas around seagrass beds. Some unusual species like elongate pipefish (Sygnathidae), seahorses (*Hippocampus*) and the strange razorfish (*Aeoliscus strigatus*), which swim with their heads pointing downwards, find shelter amongst the seagrass. Silvery half-beaks (Hemirhamphidae) also shoal near the surface in sheltered lagoons.

Sharks are plentiful in tropical waters, and around reefs the most likely ones to be seen are the nurse shark (*Nebrius ferrugineus*), the whitetip reef shark (*Triaenodon obesus*) and the blacktip reef shark (*Carcharinus melanopterus*), which has been known to attack man, so do exercise caution. Whale sharks (*Rhincodon typus*), which can exceed 15m in length, occur in the waters around the Seychelles, particularly during the months of August to November. Despite being the largest fish in the sea, their diet consists mainly of plankton which they filter from the water passing over their specialised gills. A dive with these harmless circum-tropical monsters of the deep is an awesome experience.

Various species of **rays** frequent reefs, and some of those most likely to be seen are eagle rays (*Aetobatus narinari*), which seem to glide effortlessly over the reef, and stingrays (Dasyatidae), which usually hide in caves. It is always spectacular to see a manta ray (*Manta birostris*) underwater especially as wing-to-wing they can exceed 6m. When voyaging between the islands one sometimes sees them leaping out of the water and landing with a big splash, a behaviour believed to dislodge persistent parasites.

3

Practical Information

The Seychelles, isolated in the crystal-clear, equatorial waters of the Indian Ocean, provides a superb destination for those seeking sun, sea and sand. However, the islands with their Creole culture, as well as unique biodiversity, afford discerning visitors a whole lot more.

WHEN TO VISIT

The equatorial climate is hot all year round, and is governed by the two wind regimes. The southeast trade winds blow steadily from May to October and, during these months, very little rain falls and the days are hot, humid and sunny. The seas are not as calm as during the northwest monsoon period from November to March. The highest rainfall occurs in December and January but don't let that put you off as, even when it pours, it is not cold. The tropical downpours tend to occur in the afternoons and are short and sharp. Getting drenched in a tropical downpour could be a whole new experience!

Seychelles meteorological office ✎4384070

HIGHLIGHTS

The Seychelles is the ultimate sun, sea and sand destination, and the many beachfront hotels are geared up to cater for idyllic and relaxing holidays. A full spectrum of watersports is on offer at the larger resorts, and the smaller hotels and guesthouses can easily arrange such activities. Good local infrastructure is in place for scuba diving, snorkelling, fishing, sailing, birdwatching and hiking, and there are dive centres, watersports operators, charter boats, tour operators and well-trained local guides on hand. Beau Vallon offers the lot!

But there is much more to the Seychelles, and the islands are just asking to be explored.

MAHE Make the effort to take a walk in the **Morne Seychelles National Park**. Go early in the morning with a guide and experience the mosses and mists of a high-altitude tropical forest with fabulous views over the granitic inner islands; you can look for bizarre pitcher plants, jellyfish trees and the tiny *Sooglossus* frogs. Visit the **Jardin du Roi** to find out about exotic spices and then drop in at **Kot-Man-Ya** to see a profusion of striking and colourful ornamental flowers. Make a stop at a studio of one of the many local artists and revel in the vibrant styles depicting the beauty of the islands. Pay a visit to the **Selwyn-Clarke Market** in Victoria for a glimpse of local life. Amid the hustle and bustle, take in the noisy fish market and the colourful stalls of tropical fruits, vegetables, flowers and fragrant spices. Explore the **Beau Vallon** area with its gorgeous beach and glorious view over to Silhouette. Join the locals at **Bazar Labrin** on a Wednesday evening or the last Saturday of the month to taste the freshest barbecued fish and other local delicacies and purchase your souvenirs from the cheerful stalls under the trees. Enjoy a **sunset cruise** on a lovely old sailing boat and, for a taste of the nightlife, watch a *sega* dance show. For some adventure, go **zip lining** at Ephelia Hotel.

PRASLIN Experience the magnificent **Vallée de Mai**, the World Heritage Site that protects the remarkable coco de mer palms. Laze on **Anse Lazio**, one of the finest beaches in the world.

LA DIGUE Hire a bicycle and explore this leisurely island making a recommended stop at **Anse Source d'Argent** where the famous beaches are surrounded by naturally sculpted, granite rocks. A little more energy is required to cycle over the low hill to the magnificent stretch of beach at **Grand Anse**.

OTHER ISLANDS The fantastic scenery and interesting biodiversity are increasingly attracting ecotourists to the Seychelles. Entire islands have been set aside as nature reserves and there are marine parks as well as mountain and forest reserves for the nature lover to explore. Make an expedition to one or more of the tiny **satellite islands** surrounding Mahé, Praslin and La Digue – some require a whole day while others can be enjoyed in a morning or afternoon.

Curieuse Spend the morning walking the coastal trail amongst the imposing black granite rocks and mangroves and see the wild, giant Aldabra tortoises up close.

Cousin A guided trip to this island reserve set aside for breeding seabirds allows close-up viewing of white fairy terns, noddies and tropic birds without disturbing them.

Ile Cocos and Les Soeurs A snorkelling trip followed by a beach barbecue to these granitic outcrops is a great experience.

SUGGESTED ITINERARIES

The Seychelles has a charming, relaxed lifestyle and we suggest that you spend at least a week there to really enjoy what these marvellous islands can offer. We also recommend that you make the necessary arrangements beforehand to ensure that your transport is ready and waiting. If you have a short sojourn in the Seychelles, it may be worthwhile to use one of the local tour operators to ensure that your time is well spent (page 84).

ONE DAY If you really only have one day in the Seychelles, take the earliest ferry or short flight from Mahé to Praslin and spend the morning walking in the Vallée de Mai World Heritage Site to see the endemic coco de mer palms with their remarkable nuts and, if you are lucky, the black parrots. After lunch return to Mahé and enjoy the late afternoon at Beau Vallon, walk along the beach and, to cool down, take a dip in the gentle sea.

If you do not want to venture away from Mahé, hire a car and drive around part of the island, making sure to stop somewhere around midday for a tasty Creole buffet lunch. One option is to go to Beau Vallon, spend time at the beach and then, via the north of the island, return to Victoria and do some exploring in the capital. Another option is to head across the island by taking one of the mountain passes; the Sans Souci Road is a good one as it has spectacular views, passes through the Morne Seychellois National Park and you can stop at the old Capucin Mission Ruins and the Tea Factory on the way. Once on the west coast, Port Launay Marine National Park is a good place to go snorkelling. Return to Victoria via Chemin La Misère, allowing some time to wander in the town. If you are at the airport, another option is to head south to Anse Royale and take Chemin Les Canelles across the island which will provide an opportunity to visit the Jardin du Roi spice garden as well as the Tom Bowers sculpture studio. Return to Victoria via Chemin La Misère for spectacular views of the inner islands. See also page 117.

TWO DAYS On the first day, drive around Mahé on any of the routes described above but give yourself a little time early in the day to experience the hustle and bustle of the colourful Selwyn-Clarke Market in Victoria. In the late afternoon, take the ferry or fly to Praslin, stay overnight and, early the next day, nip over to Cousin to have very close encounters with thousands of seabirds. A late morning return to Praslin will give you time for an afternoon visit to the Vallée de Mai before catching the ferry or flight back to Mahé.

THREE DAYS You can do the same as described above for a two-day trip but, in the late afternoon of the second day, take the *Cat Rose*'s ferry from Praslin to La Digue, overnight there and explore the island and its marvellous beaches. Depending on your budget you could return to Mahé by helicopter or use the ferry.

FOUR DAYS If you are really keen to explore a little more, you should spend an extra night on one of the tiny islands. Silhouette is an hour away by boat and the islands in the Ste Anne Marine Park are only a 15-minute boat ride away.

ONE WEEK This would allow you many variations on the three-day inner-island itinerary with a couple of nights on Mahé (include a walk in the Morne Seychellois National Park) before going over to Praslin and/or La Digue for a few nights. This would enable you to visit Curieuse and see the giant Aldabra tortoises and enjoy the fine beaches and restaurants of Praslin. A couple of nights on La Digue would allow for leisurely exploration of the island, looking for the black paradise flycatcher, discovering Grande Anse and Anse Source d'Argent, and even having a morning snorkelling trip to Ile Cocos.

TWO WEEKS Now you will have time to do things in a more relaxed fashion and add to the one-week itinerary with a stay of a few days on one or two of the other islands. **Denis** and **Desroches** are renowned for deep-sea fishing and diving. **Bird Island** has a relaxed informal family-run hotel with masses of sooty terns nesting on the island around June. **North, Frégate, Silhouette, Ste Anne, Cerf and Cousine** are all other nearby islands where you could enjoy the peace and quiet of the Seychelles in the comfort of luxurious villas. For something different, you could spend some time at the Station on Mahé and enjoy yoga, massages and homeopathic treatments.

TOUR OPERATORS

The main tour operators in the Seychelles are represented on Mahé, Praslin and La Digue. Several smaller tour companies can also be found in Victoria. The larger operators will efficiently deal with package tours or cruise ships as well as small or even individual tours. All the operators will be able to arrange a variety of day or half-day tours, with or without guides, on all the main islands. They can also organise visits to the different islands with relevant flights or boat transfers. Some of the privately owned islands have their own offices in Victoria and will make all the relevant arrangements necessary for a visit. Specialist tours often focus on natural history of the islands and can be selected according to one's interests, for example, birdwatching, scuba diving or fly-fishing. Honeymoon arrangements, luxury getaways and tailor-made itineraries are possible through most of the companies.

UK

Abercrombie and Kent Travel ✆+44 (0)1242 547700; e rpakes@abercrombiekent.co.uk; www.abercrombiekent.co.uk

Cox & Kings Travel ✆+44 (0)20 7873 5000; e cox.kings@coxandkings.co.uk; www.coxandkings.co.uk

Naturetrek ✆+44 (0)1962 733051; e info@naturetrek.co.uk; www.naturetrek.co.uk

Rainbow Tours ✆+44 (0)20 7226 1250; e info@rainbowtours.co.uk; www.rainbowtours.co.uk

Reef and Rainforest Tours ✆+44 (0)1803 866965; e alan@reefandrainforest.co.uk; www.reefandrainforest.co.uk

W&O Travel ✆+44 (0)20 7666 1306; www.westernoriental.com; see ad, 2nd colour section

SOUTH AFRICA

Seyunique ✆+27 (0)11 453 2933; e reservations@seyunique.co.za; www.seyunique.co.za

Thompsons Holidays ✆+27 (0)11 770 7511 or +27 21 408 9500; e info@thompsons.co.za; www.thompsons.co.za

USA

Frontiers International Travel ✆+1 724 935 1577; e jkoziara@frontierstravel.com; www.frontierstravel.com

New Adventures ✆+1 888 437 8456; e jeffl@newadventures.com; www.newadventures.com

Zegrahm Expeditions ✆+1 206 453 2217; e zoe@zeco.com; www.zeco.com. This company specialises in high-end expedition-type cruises.

AUSTRALIA

Above & Beyond ✆+61 1300 362 166; e sales@aboveandbeyondholidays.com.au; www.aboveandbeyondholidays.com.au

SEYCHELLES TOURIST OFFICES

Seychelles Tourism Board PO Box 1262, Victoria, Mahé; ✆+248 4671300; e info@seychelles.travel; www.seychelles.travel; see ad, page 26

China Seychelles Tourism Board, #8 Dongdaqiao Rd, The Spaces, Chaoyang District, Room 1105, Beijing 100020; ✆+86 105 870 1192; elrjll.sey@gmail.com

France, Belgium, Netherlands & Luxembourg Office du Tourisme des Seychelles, 18 Rue Mogador, 75009 Paris; ✆+33 1 44 53 93 20; e info-tourisme.fr@seychelles.travel; www.seychelles.travel

Germany Seychelles Tourist Office, Hochstrasse 17, 60313 Frankfurt am Main; ✆+49 69 2972 0789; e info@seychelles-service-center.de; www.seychelles.travel

Italy Seychelles Tourism Board, Via Pindaro 28N, Axa 00125, Rome; ✆+39 6 50 90 135; e info-tourismo.it@seychelles.travel; www.seychelles.travel

Middle East Mohamed Al Geziry Consultancy, 100 Al Fattan Plaza, PO Box 36345, Dubai, UAE; ✆+971 4 2865586; e info-tourism.me@seychelles.travel; www.seychelles.travel

Russia Access Russia, Vorotnikovskly Lane 8, Bld 1 of 12, 1270006 Moscow; ✆+7 495 699 9351; e erussiayanova@accessrussia.ru

Singapore 360 Orchard Rd,12-02 International Bldg, 238869, Singapore; ✆+65 67362202; e admin@sbacasia.com.sg; www.seychelles.travel

South Africa Cape Holiday Services, 402 Bree Castle Hse, 68 Bree St, Cape Town; ✆+27 21 426 0104, +27 826945329; e seychelles@stoza.com; www.seychelles.travel

South Korea #411, Doosan We've Pavillion, 58 Susong-dong, Jongno-gu, Seoul; ✆+82 2 7373235; e sey@seychellestour.co.kr; www.seychellestour.co.kr

Spain Calle Princesa 40, 28008 Madrid; ✆+34 91 702 0804; e info@turismoseychelles.com; www.seychelles.travel

UK Seychelles Tourist Office, 4th Floor, 11 Grosvenor Crescent, London SW1X 7EE; ✆+44 (0)20 724 56106; e info-tourism.uk@seychelles.travel; www.seychelles.travel

RED TAPE

On arrival, it is necessary to have a current passport that is valid for six months after the scheduled date of departure from the Seychelles and a return ticket. Proof of accommodation is also necessary and, if you have not made a booking, an official at the airport will take you aside and organise your accommodation there and then, even if it is late at night. A one-month entry permit will be issued on arrival, and this may be extended for a further two months provided you have proof of funds to cover your stay. Extensions may be obtained from the Department of Immigration (*Independence Hse, Victoria;* ✆ *4293636;* e *info@immigration.sc*). No vaccinations are necessary unless you have been in a yellow fever country within the last six days, in which case a yellow fever vaccination certificate is needed.

CUSTOMS REGULATIONS Visitors over 18 years of age have a duty-free allowance of 200 cigarettes or 250g of tobacco, two litres of wine, two litres of spirits, and 200ml perfume or eau de toilette. Tea, seeds, plants, flowers, raw meat and meat products are prohibited. Drugs such as cannabis, cocaine, LSD and other narcotics are not allowed into the Seychelles and severe penalties are enforced. It is strictly prohibited to take firearms and ammunition, stun-guns, mace, knuckle-dusters, daggers, swords, tear gas, harpoons and spearguns into the Seychelles. A special permit is required for the exportation of coco de mer, and a certificate must be obtained from the seller. It is prohibited to export live shells, tortoises and birds, and the possession or exportation of turtles or turtle products is illegal. There is a customs office at the airport.

EMBASSIES AND CONSULATES

The following countries have diplomatic representation on Mahé:

E **Belgium** Consulate, Eden Marina Hse, Eden Island, Roche Caiman; ✆4346161; e xavier.heinen@gmail.com

E **China** Embassy, St Louis, PO Box 680, Victoria; ✆4671700; e chinaemb_sc@mfa.gov.cn

E **Cuba** Embassy, Bel Eau; ✆4224094; e cubasey@seychelles.net

E **Cyprus** Honorary Consul, PO Box 450, Victoria; ✆4381750; e panosco@cytanet.com.cy

E **Denmark** Consulate, PO Box 231, Victoria; ✆4285700; e bodco@seychelles.net

E **Finland** Honorary Consulate, Bodco Ltd; PO Box 1191, Victoria; ✆4224710; e mkarjalainen@gmail.com

E **France** Ambassador, La Ciotat Bldg, Mont Fleuri, Victoria; Chancellerie: ✆4382500; e ambafrance@intelvision.net; Alliance Française: ✆4282424

E **Germany** Honorary Consul, PO Box 1310, Victoria; ✆4601160; e germanconsul@natureseychelles.org

E **Hungary** Consulate, PO Box 475, Victoria; ✆4292800; e anna@7south.net

E **India** High Commission, PO Box 488, Victoria; ✆4610301; e hc.mahe@mea.gov.in

E **Indonesia** Consulate, 2 Oceangate Hse, PO Box 31, Victoria; ✆4224835; e tass@seychelles.net

E **Italy** Consulate, PO Box 499, Victoria; ✆ 4344551; e consulitaly@seychelles.net

E **Mauritius** Consulate, Conservation Centre, Roche Caiman, PO Box 1310, Victoria; ✆4601100; e nirmalshah@natureseychelles.org

E **Morocco** Consulate, PO Box 215, Victoria; ✆4380700; e hon.consulofmorocco@seychelles.net

E **Netherlands** Consulate, PO Box 372, Glacis; ✆4261111; e consulgeers@hotmail.com

❺ **Norway** Consulate, PO Box 732, Victoria; m 2512220; e chrystold@gmail.com
❺ **Oman** Consulate, PO Box 672, Victoria; ☎4385600; e Frank.horeau@bmibank.com
❺ **Russia** Embassy, PO Box 632, Le Niol; ☎4266590
❺ **Serbia** Consulate, PO Box 1001, Glacis; ☎4261175; e drtodo@gmail.com
❺ **Slovakia** Consulate, PO Box 611, c/o Creole Travel Services; ☎4297000; e joseph.albert@creoletravelservices.com
❺ **Sri Lanka** Embassy, Suite 3-01, Capital City Bldg, Independence Av, Victoria; e slhcseychelles@yahoo.com

❺ **Sweden** Consulate, PO Box 231, Victoria; ☎4285700; e soundy@seychelles.net
❺ **Spain** PO Box 14, Victoria, ☎4380300; e hundel@seychelles.net
❺ **Switzerland** Consulate, PO Box 935, Victoria; ☎4374278; e swissconsul@seychelles.sc
❺ **Thailand** PO Box 933, Victoria; ☎4224547; e jmsa@seychelles.net
❺ **UK** High Commission, Oliaji Trade Centre, PO Box 161, Victoria; ☎4283666; e bhcvictoria@fco.gov.uk
❺ **USA** Consulate, Oliaji Trade Centre, Francis Rachel St, Victoria; ☎4225256; e consularagencyseychelles@gmail.com

SEYCHELLES CONSULATES Seychelles representation overseas is fairly limited:

❺ **Belgium** 1st Floor, 28 Bd St Michel, 1040 Brussels; ☎+32 2 733 6055; e brussels@seychellesgov.com
❺ **China** Room 1105, The Spaces, No 8 Dongdaqiao Rd, Chaoyang District, 100020 Beijing; ☎+86 10 5870 1192; e amb.legall@yahoo.com
❺ **Ethiopia** Bole, Woreda13, Addis Ababa; ☎251 11 6297 721; e jnourrice@gmail.com
❺ **France** 51 Av Mozart, 75016 Paris; ☎+33 1 42 30 57 47; e ambsey@aol.com
❺ **India** F-4 Anand Niketan, New Delhi 110021; ☎+91 11 241 14102; e seychelleshighcommission@gmail.com

❺ **South Africa** Unit D02/01 The Village, cnr Glenwood & Oberon Av, Faerie Glen, Pretoria 0043; ☎+27 12 348 0270; e sez@seychelles.net
❺ **Switzerland** Chemin Louis-Dunant 15b, 1202, Geneva; ☎+41 22 730 1729; e geneva@seymission.ch
❺ **UAE** Villa no 15 Muroor Area, 23rd St, Abu Dhabi; ☎971 2 491 7755; e seychellesembuae@gmail.com
❺ **UK** 4th Floor, 130/132 Buckingham Palace Rd, London SW1W 9SA; ☎+44 20 7730 2046; e seyhc.london@btconnect.com
❺ **USA** Suite 400C, 4th Floor, 800 2nd Av, New York, NY 10017; ☎+1 212 9721 785; e seychelles@un.int

GETTING THERE AND AWAY

As the Seychelles islands are in the middle of the ocean, almost 1,000 miles from anywhere, there are only two ways to get there – by air or by sea.

BY AIR Regular flights link the Seychelles with Europe, Africa and the Middle East. **Air Seychelles** (*www.airseychelles.com*), with its bright red, green, blue and white livery and the white fairy tern logo, is the national carrier. It originally only provided a service from Mahé to Praslin and Frégate with foreign airlines bringing in the tourists. However, in 1983, Air Seychelles launched its first international flight from Gatwick, London, using a DC10 aircraft.

Recently, Air Seychelles has been restructured, is code sharing with Etihad Airways, and is presently flying only between Mahé, Johannesburg, Mauritius, Antananarivo, Dar es Salaam and Mumbai.

Several other airlines fly to the Seychelles: these are **Kenya Airways** (*www.kenya-airways.com*); **Emirates Airlines** (*www.emirates.com*); **Etihad Airways** (*www.etihadairways.com*); **Ethiopian Airlines** (*www.ethiopianairlines.com*) and **Mihin Lanka** (*www.mihinlanka.com*). There are also frequent unscheduled seasonal flights linking up with package tours and cruise ships. They include Air Austral (*www. air-austral.com*), linking Réunion and Mahé, Condor (*www.condor.com*), taking passengers from Munich, Blue Panorama (*www.blue-panorama.it*) and Transaero Airlines (*www.transaero.com*) from Moscow, as well as other flights from eastern Europe and China. Flight schedules vary so check websites for details.

The busy **Seychelles International Airport** (*domestic flight enquiries,* 4391230; *international flight enquiries,* 4384000; *customer care services,* 4391000; e *customer@airseychelles.com*) is located on Mahé, right on the edge of the ocean, just 9km south of Victoria. Constructed in 1971, on land reclaimed from the sea, the international airport terminal buildings have undergone major renovations and there is now a proper baggage carousel instead of having luggage all piled up on a shelf. There is a tourist information office at the airport. Departure tax is now included in the cost of the airline ticket.

Airport transfers

Even though some international flights arrive in Mahé before sunrise or late at night, taxis are always available at the airport (SR300 for a ride to Victoria, SR600 to Beau Vallon). It will take about 10 minutes into town and half an hour to Beau Vallon, or a little longer if there is a lot of traffic. There is a bus stop on the main road opposite the airport building. Just cross the road to get a local bus into Victoria (SR5 or SR10 for a bus with air conditioning). Buses that stop on the same side of the road as the airport are on their way to the southern part of Mahé.

Inter-island flights

Air Seychelles (*Mahé airport; domestic terminal,* 4391230; *international terminal,* 4384000; *Praslin airport; general enquiries* 4391000) operates regular, and frequent, local inter-island flights to Praslin. Flights to Frégate, Bird, Denis, Desroches and Alphonse are operated in conjunction with island owners and charters. Aircraft in use are Twin Otters and Shorts 360. The domestic luggage allowance is 15kg. Note that some of the island resorts include the transfer from Mahé in their prices but others do not, so it is advisable to check your travel arrangements carefully. The inter-island fleet has a large, brightly coloured logo on the tail with stylised hibiscus flowers and a white fairy tern.

Air Seychelles can also arrange special charter flights. The Islands Development Company has three planes that fly to the Outer Islands that have landing strips, including a daily flight to Desroches (4384640; e *ceo@idc.sc or aviation@idc.sc*).

Zil Air (*Pointe Larue;* 4375100; e *reservations@zilair.com; www.zilair.com*) can take you by helicopter to Praslin, La Digue, Silhouette, Frégate, North, Denis, Cousine, Félicité or even to other parts of Mahé. Scenic trips and gift vouchers are also available.

BY SEA

Cruise and expedition ships sometimes call at the port of Victoria in Mahé, mainly from November to April when the seas are calmer. The larger cruise ships generally only visit Mahé but passengers can be ferried to Praslin and La Digue by local vessels. Expedition cruises with smaller vessels sometimes include the outer islands in their itineraries, although this has been somewhat curtailed by recent Somali pirate activity.

Noble Caledonia 2 Chester Cl, London SW1X 7BE, UK; +44 (0)20 7752 0000; www. noble-caledonia.co.uk. Uses various small ships.

Zegrahm Expeditions 3131 Elliott Av, Suite 300, Seattle, WA 98121, USA; www.zeco.com. Uses a number of small cruise ships for expeditions around the Seychelles islands.

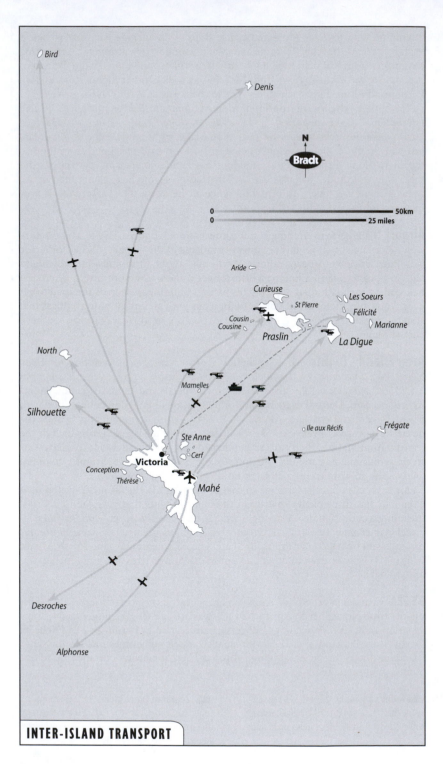

Bird

Denis

N

Bradt

| 0 | | 50km |
| 0 | | 25 miles |

Aride

Curieuse

St Pierre

Les Soeurs

Félicité

Cousin
Cousine

Marianne

Praslin

La Digue

North

Mamelles

Silhouette

Ile aux Récifs

Frégate

Ste Anne

Cerf

Conception

Victoria

Thérèse

Mahé

Desroches

Alphonse

INTER-ISLAND TRANSPORT

Yachts Visiting by yacht must be the finest way to explore the fabulous islands of the Seychelles. All visiting yachts must obtain clearance with Customs, Immigration and Health in Victoria, Mahé. Hefty tariffs previously levied on cruising yachts visiting the Seychelles appear to have been rescinded and current port tariffs for visiting yachts under 20 tonnes are in the region of SR50 per day for stays of more than ten days.

🚢 **Seychelles Port Authority** ☎4224701;
e enquiries@seychellesports.sc; www.spa.sc

HEALTH *with Dr Felicity Nicholson*

The islands of the Seychelles pose no great health threats, and probably the worst thing that could happen is sunburn or dehydration. The standard of living is generally high and there are no awful unsanitary conditions.

BEFORE YOU GO The only absolute requirement for the Seychelles is proof of **vaccination** against yellow fever when travelling from an infected area (eg: sub-Saharan Africa); it is a good idea to secure the international certificate inside your passport. If you are unable to take the yellow fever vaccine and are travelling from an endemic area, then you should carry an Exemption Certificate instead of proof of vaccination. These may be available from your GP but, if not, then from a travel clinic. However, travellers here, as elsewhere, are wise to be up to date with routine immunisations such as tetanus, diphtheria and polio (now given as the all-in-one vaccine Revaxis, which lasts for ten years) and hepatitis A. One dose of hepatitis A vaccine protects for about one year, and a booster dose at around this time will extend cover in adults for about 25 years.

Special circumstances may dictate that other vaccines are advised. For trips of a month or more typhoid vaccine should be considered. If you are intending to work in a hospital/medical setting or closely with children then hepatitis B vaccine is recommended. A full list of current travel clinic websites worldwide is available on www.istm.org/. For other journey preparation information, consult www.tripprep.com. Information about various medications may be found on www.emedicine.com/wild/topiclist.htm.

Health insurance is advisable, especially should you have to be repatriated for treatment in an emergency. Shop around to make sure that you get the best value for your money, and check the small print carefully.

IN THE SEYCHELLES

Mosquitoes There is no malaria on the islands but, at times, there can be plenty of irritating mosquitoes that can cause itchy bites. You may find sandflies on some of the beaches with washed-up seaweed and seagrasses. If they are troublesome, use an insect repellent as the bites can be very itchy and some people have a mild allergic reaction. More recently there have been isolated cases of dengue fever and Chikungunya which are 'flu-like' viruses that are transmitted by day-biting mosquitoes. It is wise therefore to use a 50–55% DEET-based repellent after first applying sunscreen.

Sunburn When visiting the Seychelles you do have to be very careful of the sun, especially if visiting from a cooler European climate. It is very tempting on your first day just to lie in the sun after all those damp, grey, wintry days. Beware! If you are not careful your holiday could be spoilt, to say nothing of later skin cancer problems.

It is wise to build up a tan slowly, using a good sunscreen with an SPF of 25 or more and a UVA of four or more stars, incrementally increasing your time in the sunshine. Wear a sunhat with a wide brim, a light cotton, long-sleeved shirt to protect your shoulders and a floaty sarong or light cotton trousers to shade your legs. Protection from the sun is not only for ladies, as men are also susceptible – especially on balding pates! If you are on an open boat wearing a swimming costume or shorts, watch your knees and the tops of your feet as they can get red and sore in no time at all. Remember that both water and white sand are reflective, an extra contributory factor to getting sunburnt. So, even if the day is overcast, lather on the sunscreen, renewing it regularly, especially if you are swimming. While snorkelling, one can also be very prone to sunburn, particularly on the back of the neck, shoulders and legs, so it's a good idea to wear a T-shirt or lycra vest.

Drinking water Water is clean and it is quite safe to drink straight from the tap on the main islands. The Rochon Dam and La Gogue Reservoir in the mountains above Victoria supply Mahé with fresh water. Food is usually well prepared and clean, and one seldom hears of upset tummies. But, as so often happens when travelling, your system can take a little while to get used to different types of food and water of different mineral content. The Creole food may be more spicy than your usual home fare. It is important to drink plenty of water to prevent dehydration in the tropical heat.

HEALTHCARE The main granitic islands have an efficient healthcare system, and are within easy reach of Victoria by air or boat. The outlying coralline islands, however, have no hospital facilities. Some may only have a resident warden with the barest emergency bandages and a bottle of mercurochrome, if you are lucky! It should not be a problem as they are right off the tourist track and none but intrepid yachties will visit them. If you are on a cruise ship, you will have your own doctor on board.

The **Victoria Hospital** in Mont Fleuri is well equipped to handle accidents and emergencies (☎ 4388000; clinic ⊕ 08.00–16.00 Mon–Fri, 08.00–noon Sat; Accident & Emergency ⊕ 24hrs). A doctor is available for consultation by tourists for a basic fee of between SR150–SR300. Some of the hotels have a nurse who is able to give medical advice, and will arrange a hospital visit if necessary. The new Anse Royal Hospital (☎ 4371222) has a clinic (⊕ 08.00–16.00 Mon–Fri) and a 24-hour emergency service. Small clinics with a nurse in attendance are dotted about Mahé, with a fee of SR100.

Praslin has a hospital at Baie Ste Anne (☎ 4232333), which charges a fee of SR200, as well as a clinic at Grande Anse. There is a small hospital on La Digue (☎ 4234255), and Silhouette has a small clinic. However, good travel insurance with adequate health coverage is still essential.

The **emergency telephone number** for fire, police or ambulance is ☎ 999.

Pharmacies It is always safest to bring enough of your own medication with you, but medicines on prescription may be obtained from the dispensary at the Victoria Hospital (☎ 4388000). There are four pharmacies in Victoria, and all operate during normal business hours and sell a small range of well-known pharmaceutical products, although anything obscure will probably not be available.

✚ **Absolue Pharmacy** Bois de Rose Av; m 2511203; e info@asdsey.com
✚ **Behram's Pharmacy** Orion Mall Bldg; ☎ 4225559; e behrampharmacy@seychelles.net

✚ **Central Point Pharmacy** Le Chantier Bldg, Francis Rachel St; ☎ 4225574; e cppharmacy@seychelles.net
✚ **Lai Lam Pharmacy** Market St; ☎ 4322336

Dentists On Praslin, a dental clinic at the hospital charges SR200 for a consultation; a private dentist, PSM Dental Clinic, is located in Grande Anse (m 2794420).

On Mahé, as well as those listed, there is a dental clinic at the Victoria Hospital (⊕ 08.00–15.00 Mon–Fri).

✚ **Dr Samsoodien Dental Clinic** Oceangate Hse, Independence Av, Victoria; ✆4224852; ⊕ 08.00–16.00 Mon–Fri

✚ **Royal Dent Pty Ltd** Room 101, Aarti Chambers, Mont Fleuri; ✆4225445; m 2511377; e sinhageorge@hotmail.com or royaldent421@yahoo.com

Optometrists There are several optometrists in Victoria. They are all able to repair spectacles, and they also sell contact-lens paraphernalia; pharmacies also sell contact-lens solutions and non-prescription eye drops.

LONG-HAUL FLIGHTS, CLOTS AND DVT

Any prolonged immobility including travel by land or air can result in deep vein thrombosis (DVT) with the risk of embolus to the lungs. Certain factors can increase the risk. These include:

* Previous clot or close relative with a history
* People over 40, but greater risk in those over 80
* Recent major operation or varicose veins surgery
* Cancer
* Stroke
* Heart disease
* Obesity
* Pregnancy
* Hormone therapy
* Heavy smokers
* Severe varicose veins
* People who are very tall (over 6ft/1.8m) or short (under 5ft/1.5m)

A DVT causes painful swelling and redness of the calf or sometimes the thigh. It is only dangerous if a clot travels to the lungs (pulmonary embolus). Symptoms of a pulmonary embolus include chest pain, shortness of breath, and sometimes coughing up small amounts of blood. Symptoms commonly start three to ten days after a long flight. Anyone who thinks that they might have a DVT needs to see a doctor immediately.

PREVENTION OF DVT
* Keep mobile before and during the flight; move around every couple of hours
* Drink plenty of fluids during the flight
* Avoid taking sleeping pills and excessive tea, coffee and alcohol
* Consider wearing flight socks or support stockings (see *www.legshealth.com*).

If you think you are at increased risk of a clot, ask your doctor if it is safe to travel.

Micock Consulting Room 104, Aarti Chambers opposite the Victoria Hospital; ☏ 4321177
Ou Linet Optics In the Codevar, Albert St; ☏ 4321993

SpecSaver Seychelles Adam Moosa Bldg, Francis Rachel St; ☏ 4224050; e specsaver@seychelles.net
Vision Care Riverside Point; ☏ 4322792; e visioncare@visioncare-sey.com

SAFETY

The Seychelles is not a crime-ridden part of the world. However, most of the larger hotels have safety deposit boxes for your valuables like tickets, cash and travellers' cheques. When out and about, use your common sense. For example, it is not wise to leave fancy, expensive camera equipment lying on the back seat of an unattended open vehicle. Neither is it a good idea to leave a handbag on the beach while you go swimming or snorkelling.

Police stations are situated in Revolution Avenue in Victoria (☏ 4288000), at Beau Vallon (☏ 4247242), Mont Fleuri (☏ 4288250) and Anse Royale (☏ 4371226) on Mahé. On Praslin (☏ 4233251), there are police stations at Baie Ste Anne and at Grande Anse. The police station on La Digue is at La Passe (☏ 4234251). Policemen wear dark blue trousers and a white short-sleeved shirt. Dial 999 for fire, police or ambulance.

WOMEN TRAVELLERS It is generally safe for women to be out on their own, and travelling on the buses is absolutely fine. Take care not to offend the local people by wearing ultra-skimpy clothes that could be misinterpreted as provocative.

HOMOSEXUAL TRAVELLERS There is no problem with gay and lesbian travellers, but it is always wise to be discreet. Homosexuality is actually illegal in the Seychelles, although there are moves in the legislature to decriminalise it. Same-sex relationships between women are legal.

TRAVELLERS WITH A DISABILITY Wheelchairs are available at the airport and at most of the larger hotels. It is advisable to notify the tour agent of any disabilities prior to travelling to ensure that the accommodation is suitable. Depending on the degree of disability, travelling in small boats could be difficult.

TRAVELLING WITH CHILDREN The Seychelles is generally a wonderfully relaxed country for children but do be aware that a few hotels do not accept children under certain ages.

WHAT TO TAKE

Not a lot! As the climate is hot all year round, light cotton clothing is the answer. Generally, a very relaxed atmosphere prevails in the Seychelles, and for women, shorts with blouses or T-shirts or a light dress are fine. Many of the hotels do not appreciate swimming costumes in the dining room, and the smarter hotels may suggest that men wear long trousers in the evening. Other than that, everything is really informal.

A wide-brimmed hat is important, as are sunglasses, plenty of sunscreen with a high sun protection factor and a general moisturising cream. Don't forget your swimming costume. Open sandals or thongs are the most comfortable footwear in a hot climate. Waterproof sandals are fine for walking on the rocks. If you are thinking of walking in the mountains, a pair of lightweight walking shoes will be adequate. A small torch is always handy, especially when negotiating the path to your chalet in the evening.

The islands are most photogenic so you will need your camera and plenty of space on your memory cards. Film is still available from photographic shops and some hotel boutiques but you may not be able to get the brand, speed or type that you prefer, so it is best to bring your own supplies if you are not using a digital camera. A polarising filter can be put to good use to cut the glare from your water shots. One-hour processing of print film is possible in Victoria. Both photographic shops in Independence Avenue in Victoria will transfer your digital images onto a CD or make prints. If you are into birdwatching, a good pair of binoculars is essential: both 10x40 and 8x32 are good choices. For snorkelling and scuba diving, the dive centres all have good equipment, which can be hired. If you wear spectacles and don't want to go to the expense of having a prescription diving mask made up, a good tip is to silicone the lenses from an old pair of spectacles onto the inside of your mask if you want to see the corals and reef fishes at their best. Still on the underwater scene, if you are planning on scuba diving, do remember to take your certification of proficiency with you.

The Seychelles uses the British-style square-pin three-point plug so if you are using any other electrical plug, it would be wise to bring your own adaptor.

The Seychelles is a civilised part of the world, so you should be able to get almost anything you have forgotten, although it might be more expensive.

MONEY

FOREIGN-EXCHANGE REGULATIONS There are no restrictions on the amount of foreign exchange brought into the country. You can change money at authorised moneychangers at Seychelles International Airport, at banks and at most of the bigger hotels; the rates are fairly standard. You are advised to use only authorised moneychangers and keep your money-exchange receipt. Travellers' cheques are not always easy to cash. ATMs in good working order are found on the three main islands of Mahé, Praslin and La Digue.

Many of the prices for hotels, car hire, taxis and ferries may be quoted in euros as well as Seychelles rupees. Payment for services may be made in any of the major currencies using cash or credit cards or Seychelles rupees. Incidental purchases in restaurants outside of hotels, shopping (excluding duty-free shops) and petrol are usually paid in local currency.

Should you wish to change rupees back into your own currency, it can be done provided you show proof of official transactions. Nevertheless, it is wise not to change too much cash in the first place; change only what you will require for petrol and incidentals.

LOCAL CURRENCY The Seychelles rupee is the currency of the islands and 100 cents constitute one rupee. Coin denominations are five, ten and 25 cents, which are bronze, and one and five rupees, which are silver. The coins each have a natural history subject on the face: five cents – a pandanus; ten cents – a tuna; 25 cents – a black parrot; one rupee – a shell; and five rupees – a coco de mer palm. The Seychelles rupee can be abbreviated as SR, SCR, R or Rs.

Denominations of the notes are SR10, SR25, SR50 and SR100. They are beautifully designed, all depicting the rich natural heritage of the Seychelles.

In October 2015, £1 would give you SR20.16, US$1 SR13.14, Australia $1 SR9.51 and €1 SR14.83.

BANKS, ATMS AND CREDIT CARDS The following banks operate in Victoria: Barclays Bank, Habib Bank, Bank of Baroda, Nouvobanq, Mauritius Commercial Bank (MCB) and Seychelles Savings Bank. Banks are open 08.30–14.00 Monday–Friday, 09.00–11.00 Saturday, and do not close for lunch. On Praslin and La Digue there are branches of Barclays Bank, MCB and Seychelles Savings Bank. ATMs are also available on Mahé, Praslin and La Digue.

Banks at the airport are open only for international flights. Use only official moneychangers. SWIFT and EFTPOS are available for international transfers.

Visa and MasterCard are widely accepted and American Express and Diners Club to a lesser extent in the larger hotels, restaurants and shops. Credit cards may not be accepted by some of the smaller establishments, so it is always wise to check first.

BUDGETING

While most of the accommodation and restaurants in the Seychelles are fairly expensive, it is possible to have a holiday on the islands without spending a vast amount of money. **Package tours** often offer the best value as they generally include flights, hotel accommodation and airport transfers. Self-catering and bed and breakfast accommodation, especially for a couple or family, can be an economical option. Camping is not permitted in the Seychelles and there are no backpacker hostels.

Buses provide an interesting and very cheap way to get around Mahé and, to a lesser extent, Praslin. They run regularly during the day with the last service at around 19.00. Over weekends and public holidays the service is reduced. The fare is SR5 or SR10 for an air-conditioned bus for any destination. Theoretically, you can go around Mahé for SR10. Bicycles can be used on Praslin and La Digue but are only recommended in certain parts of Mahé as many of the roads are very steep and narrow. The schooners operating between the islands are far cheaper options than the fast ferry or air transfers, but you do need time on your hands. The many little stores around the islands sell groceries and a great variety of sweet and savoury snacks that do very well for a light lunch (SR5–15), and an icy beer (SR30) or soft drink (SR20) bought from these shops will cost half the price of one served in a restaurant. There are also many take-away food shops and, for example, a substantial chicken curry meal will set you back about SR45. It is not necessary to buy bottled water, as tap water is quite safe to drink – simply refill your own water bottle. The beaches, snorkelling and wonderful walks on the mountains are free to enjoy.

GETTING AROUND

It is really easy to get around Mahé and Praslin by hire car or taxi. Victoria is the only town with some traffic lights! Buses are a good way to see the two larger islands and bicycles are ideal on La Digue. Travel between the islands is a cinch with efficient aeroplanes, helicopters, ferries and other boats. There are no trains in the Seychelles.

BY TAXI About 300 taxis are waiting to transport you around Mahé, a further 40 will take you around Praslin, and there are now also three on La Digue. They operate under the banner of the Taxi Operators Association (☎ *4323895*). The drivers are encouraged to attend regular meetings and talks aimed at improving their knowledge of the islands. Many of the drivers will be happy to take you on a 'conducted tour' and many of them speak English. Apart from the taxi rank in

Victoria, taxis are available at all the major hotels, at the airport when international flights arrive, and at the quayside when ferries dock. It is more difficult to get a taxi in the evening but your hotel or guesthouse will be able to arrange one for you. If you need to arrange your own taxi, call Victoria (↘ 4322279), Berjaya Beau Vallon Bay Resort (↘ 4287287) or Le Meridien Fisherman's Cove Hotel (↘ 4677000). The fares are regulated: the cost of getting from the airport to Victoria is about SR300 and Beau Vallon about SR600 and prices are frequently quoted in euros.

CAR HIRE At least 20 car-hire companies operate on Mahé including some of the well-known international names as well as many smaller, local companies. About nine car-hire companies are based on Praslin. Cars range from run-of-the-mill small cars to smart chauffeur-driven, air-conditioned, luxury cars and limousines. They are usually well maintained. You can expect to pay around €50 per day for a small air-conditioned car. To hire a car, a current driving licence is required. Your travel agent or hotel can arrange a chauffeur-driven car. For details of companies on Mahé and Praslin, see pages 81 and 125.

The Seychellois drive on the left. The speed limit in towns is 40km/h and out of town it is 65km/h except on the new east coast road on Mahé where it is 80km/h. If you see a branch from a tree lying across the road, slow down as it generally indicates some sort of hazard ahead such as a pot-hole, a breakdown or even an accident. Red warning triangles are in short supply.

BY BUS Buses are widely used by the residents and, as a ride costs only SR5, are a most economical way to get from place to place. The buses have wonderful natural air conditioning through all the open windows but they do battle up the steep hillsides at times. Some of the newer buses do have air conditioning, and these charge SR10 per ride. The bus terminus on Mahé is in Palm Street, Victoria, where detailed timetables are available. Buses run from 05.30 to 19.00 with reduced services on Saturdays, Sundays and public holidays. The bus service on Praslin is not as extensive as on Mahé but is still a useful way to get around.

INTER-ISLAND FERRIES Three large, fast, *Cat Cocos* catamarans of varying sizes link Mahé, Praslin and La Digue (*reservations* ↘ 4324843; e *reservation@catcocos. com; www.catcocos.com or* e *office@seychellesbookings.com; www.seychellesbookings. com*). The catamarans have three classes: economy class main cabin, economy class upper cabin, and business class. The crossing between Mahé and Praslin takes 45 minutes and a further 15 minutes between Praslin and La Digue. A shuttle service is provided to and from the airport at a cost of €10 per adult and €5 per child one-way.

The *Cat Rose*'s ferry also operates throughout the day between Praslin and La Digue (↘ 4232329 *or* 4232394; e *iif@seychelles.net*). Various other types of boats can be hired to get to the smaller islands and an inter-island schooner cargo service plies between Mahé, Praslin and La Digue.

ACCOMMODATION

The Seychelles is marketed as an exclusive destination, and visitors pay for the privilege of having secluded beaches and open spaces. There are no high-rise hotels or massive edge-to-edge tourist resorts lining the shores, nor are there squalid areas with fly-by-night, low-life accommodation, and camping is forbidden. Although there is no official 'star rating' system there is, generally, a good standard of

3

accommodation, ranging from large, resort-type hotels with casinos to small hotels and guesthouses. Only two hotels have over 200 rooms, and they are on Mahé, while the largest hotel on Praslin has only 88 rooms. The newer resorts or hotels favour the single villa approach which spreads the footprint over a larger area. There are also ultra-exclusive, luxurious lodges set on private islands as well as self-catering and family-run bed and breakfast establishments.

Hotel tariffs are high, and though the service is not always as efficient as it could be, there is always a smile from the laid-back Seychellois. The more exclusive lodges, however, offer unparalleled comfort and luxury with excellent service. While the Seychelles is a lovely destination for those travelling with children and most hotels generally welcome them, there are some that specifically do not cater for children.

It is very often a more economical option to take a package tour, which will usually include the flight, hotel and airport transfers. For travellers wishing to organise their own itineraries, nothing could be easier as local tour operators are most helpful. Prices quoted for accommodation in subsequent chapters are approximate as costs vary according to season and type of room.

EATING AND DRINKING

FOOD Imagine the freshest seafood, flavoured with coconut milk, garlic, ginger, limes and chillies, and cooked to perfection by chefs who know how to make a thousand different fish dishes! Creole cuisine combines the subtlety of Asian food

A TYPICAL CREOLE RECIPE: *BOUILLON BLAN*

As prepared by Philip the boatman on Aldabra

INGREDIENTS

One clean, whole fish of about 1kg	20g fresh ginger
3ml mixed herbs	Salt and pepper
5ml dried thyme	100g purple onions
3ml spice for fish	One litre water
3ml turmeric	20ml tomato sauce
20g garlic	50g fresh tomato (if available)

METHOD Cut the fish (including the head) into three or four chunks and coat with herbs and turmeric. Pound the garlic and ginger with the salt. Slice the onions and fry gently in a little oil. Add the fish, garlic and ginger, stir and add water. Simmer for about ten minutes. Add tomato sauce, and about 50g of finely chopped fresh tomato if available. Continue simmering for another ten minutes. Remove the fish and strain the soup. Remove the bones from the fish and return the flesh to the soup. Enjoy!

CHICKEN CURRY À LA SEYCHELLOISE (FOR TWO PEOPLE)

Presented by Chef Wilson Lesperance from the Coco de Mer Hotel, Praslin

INGREDIENTS

450g chicken breast (cut into cubes)
45g turmeric or 20g saffron powder
40g hot/mild curry powder
Salt and pepper

2tbsp cooking oil
100g aubergine (cut into cubes)
50g garlic and ginger paste
Two cinnamon leaves/cinnamon stick
Three curry leaves
350ml coconut milk

METHOD Marinate the cut chicken with the turmeric, curry powder, salt and pepper in a bowl. Heat the pot with cooking oil, add the aubergine and cook for two minutes, then mix in the marinated chicken, stirring with a wooden spoon and cook for another two minutes. Cover the pot and cook on a medium heat for three minutes. Add the garlic and ginger paste, cinnamon leaves, curry leaves and coconut milk. Mix well and allow it to cook uncovered until the gravy is thick and the meat tender. Finally, season with salt and pepper. Serve hot with fresh herbed rice or plain rice and a pumpkin or aubergine chutney.
Bon appétit!

with the spices of Indian cooking, all moulded by fine French flair. Rice is the staple and fish is eaten almost every day. Soup is a tasty starter and is often made from *tec-tec*, a tiny shellfish. *Bouillon blan*, a fish soup that uses a whole, small fish with loads of garlic, ginger and chilli, is a meal in itself. Salads are made with sweet, little purple onions, tomatoes and crisp *bilimbis* which resemble tiny cucumbers. Millionaire's salad used to be prepared from the heart of the rare *palmiste* palm, but now the heart of the coconut palm suffices. Curries are traditional – usually fish or octopus – and quite delicious. For something really exotic you could try the fruit bat curry which is reputed to be tasty, though not as tender as chicken. Breadfruit, plantain, cassava and sweet potatoes provide alternatives to rice. *Chatinis* or chutneys are side dishes made by grating green papaya or the local fruit known as the golden apple, which is fried with a little onion and served in fresh lime juice or vinegar with ginger and garlic. Dried fish such as shark or tuna can also be prepared this way. Little chillies are often served on the side – they can be dynamite, so try with caution! Breadfruit, with the addition of island spices and coconut milk, is also used for sweet desserts. Other desserts are prepared from coconut and bananas and are usually very sweet and sticky. Try some Seychelles recipes. We have included a simple, typical Creole dish and a recipe from the friendly Coco de Mer Hotel on Praslin.

Eating out Although take-away stalls are well frequented, eating out is expensive. Many restaurants serve excellent Creole food so tourists can get a taste of the islands. All the major hotels serve international cuisine and various speciality restaurants (Indian,

RESTAURANT CODES

Lists of restaurants in this book are ranked in decreasing order of price (based on the average price of a main course).

$$$$	€23+
$$$	€15–23
$$	€7–15
$	<€7

Italian, French and Chinese) serve really good and tasty meals. Vegetarian food can be a little difficult as a lot of fresh vegetables and salads have to be imported. Pizzas are easy to obtain and Chinese food with rice and noodles is found in some restaurants.

DRINK The national drink is the locally brewed beer, Seybrew, which, when chilled, slips down ever so easily! It is available in cans, 280ml returnable bottles or as draught in various restaurants. The brewery also makes Eku, a Bavarian lager, Celebration Brew, and Guinness is made under licence. The Seychellois drink an amazing amount of fizzy soft drinks, and fruit juices are also readily available.

TIPPING This is not expected as very often a service charge is added to the bill. However, a tip for extra-attentive service is always appreciated.

PUBLIC HOLIDAYS AND FESTIVALS

Various holidays and festivals may influence the time when you wish to visit the Seychelles – you may especially want to be there then, or you may wish to avoid them altogether! High-season times coincide with Christmas and Easter, which also coincide with the Seychelles school holidays. The list of holidays, festivals and special events which follows may help you plan your holiday.

1 and 2 January	New Year
March/April	Easter (dates vary)
1 May	Labour Day
5 June	Liberation Day
18 June	National Day
29 June	Independence Day
15 August	Assumption Day (La Digue Festival Day)
1 November	All Saints' Day
8 December	The Immaculate Conception
25 December	Christmas Day

The **Kreol Festival**, the most important in the cultural calendar, is an annual event that usually takes place at the end of October or early November, where Creole people from several nations get together and celebrate with art, music and dance. Joyful participants come from Mauritius, Rodrigues, Mayotte, Réunion, Madagascar and the Caribbean islands. A conference takes place, there are fashion shows, poetry readings, traditional games, a street procession and all sorts of school events, and many of the hotels put on special dinners featuring Creole culinary delights. A special event takes place on the beach at Beau Vallon Bay with stalls selling exotic food, like shark salad with *bilimbi* (a small local green fruit), salads from green mangoes and papaya and octopus in curry coconut cream.

The **Carnaval International de Victoria** is an exciting new Seychelles festival with many colourful floats, and beautiful people from all over the world, parading through the streets. The event takes place over three days in March and is held under the auspices of the Seychelles Tourism Board. **FetAfrik**, celebrated on Africa Day (25 May), commemorates the strong ancestral connections between the Seychelles and the continent. An annual agricultural and horticultural show is held in Mahé in June at the Sports Complex in Roche Caiman; tourism, commerce, sports, culture, food and leisure activities are showcased.

The SUBIOS (Sub Indian Ocean Seychelles) **Underwater Festival** (*www.subios. com*) caters for international underwater film and image photographers and is held in Mahé each year, usually in October. Famous international photographers and well-known speakers give presentations. Events take place on several of the islands and there is a strong associated school programme aimed at educating the youth in matters marine.

Various international game-fishing competitions, sailing and windsurfing regattas are also held annually. The **Festival de la Mer** in September includes the Beau Vallon regatta and the inter-island windsurfing race from Mahé to Praslin. For more information, go to www.seychelles.travel.

SHOPPING

The Seychelles has no big shopping malls but there is an exciting, vibrant and colourful local market filled with exotic fruits, spices and souvenirs. Eden Plaza on Eden Island has a wide variety of shops including a well-stocked supermarket, specialist shops and several restaurants. Numerous boutiques and stalls on Mahé and Praslin sell a wide variety of tempting articles, and various galleries have some superb artworks including paintings, sculpture and pottery. Classy gold and pearl jewellery, made in Mahé and Praslin, is also available. In Victoria, Antigone Trading in the Temooljies Arcade on Francis Rachel Street and at the airport and Chanterelle in Quincy Street, sell a good range of books about the Seychelles. Take home the sounds of the Seychelles with local music on CD. Support local handicrafts by purchasing handmade items like dyed batiks and woven mats and hats crafted from coconut palm leaves. Local spices and teas are Seychelles treats, and some perfumes are unique to the islands. The exotic tropical liqueur from the Seychelles, Coco d'Amour, bottled in a jar shaped like the coco de mer, is available in many boutiques. Spirit Artisanal concocts various island-style liqueurs from exotic fruits and flowers, and they are available in the market and some small boutiques. Takamaka Bay rum is also available.

It is not advisable to buy the shells and corals offered at the souvenir kiosks as most of them are taken live from the sea, if not in the Seychelles, then in other parts of the world. Turtle- and tortoiseshell artefacts should not be bought as they fall under CITES (see box, page 36). Any purchases of coco de mer products must be accompanied by the appropriate government certification.

ARTS AND ENTERTAINMENT

The Seychelles does not have a conventional programme of arts and entertainment. However, most hotels offer evening entertainment in the form of live music or traditional dancing. Various vibrant festivals take place on an annual basis and highlight Seychellois traditions. There is a small cinema in Victoria, various discos and nightclubs and a few casinos. The Seychelles is well known for its local artists and their works can be viewed at their studios or galleries.

MEDIA AND COMMUNICATIONS

TELEPHONES AND INTERNET The Seychelles operates an efficient, worldwide telephone service with direct dialling to most countries, and its international code is 248. The Seychelles has a GSM mobile-phone network service with roaming agreements for many countries; SIM cards can be obtained from **Airtel** in Victoria and at the airport (✆ *4600600;* e *airtel@seychelles.net*), or from Cable & Wireless on Francis Rachel Street (✆ *4284000;* ⊕ *07.30–16.30 daily*). It is easy to purchase airtime from the many smaller shops around the islands.

Coin and card telephones are scattered over the main islands, and you can buy phonecards from Cable & Wireless, Airtel, the post office and some of the smaller shops. Most of the larger hotels have telephones in the rooms but a high surcharge is often levied. It is much cheaper to use phonecards, which are beautifully designed and come in various units from SR30 to SR200. For directory enquiries, dial ✆ 181; most of the operators speak English.

In 2011, all telephone numbers in the Seychelles changed. Land-line numbers had the prefix number 4 added and the mobile phones which usually began with either 5 or 7 had a prefix 2 added.

MEDIA The daily newspaper, *The Seychelles Nation*, has articles in Creole, English and French. It is not available on Sundays or public holidays. *Regar* and *Le Nouveau Seychelles* are the opposition weekly papers, available on Fridays. *The People* is the ruling party's weekly publication and is in English only.

The Seychelles Broadcasting Corporation (SBC) and Paradise FM provide radio news, music and information in Creole, English and French. The BBC Indian Ocean relay station is located at Grande Anse. SBC television broadcasts news and entertainment in Creole, English and French

SPORTS AND RECREATION

The Seychellois are a sport-loving nation. The government, through the National Sports Council, encourages and promotes sport at all levels and has done much to improve sporting facilities. Some of the more popular sports include football, basketball, volleyball, swimming, athletics, cycling, bodybuilding and weightlifting. Participants representing the Seychelles take part in many international competitions and do very well for such a small nation.

There are 35 **football** teams registered with the local federation and matches are played on Thursday evenings and Saturday afternoons; big games are played at the stadium in Victoria. There is keen competition between the teams from the Indian Ocean islands, so you don't want to be on a flight with the victorious Seychelles team returning from Madagascar!

Running is also a popular pastime and sponsored runs are held from time to time throughout the year. Running up the hills is no mean feat and only advisable in the early mornings. Amongst the older generation, **dominoes** is almost the national sport, sedately played outside under the trees and on the pavements.

Sailing and other **watersports** are popular amongst the Seychellois, and training programmes aimed at young people are run from the yacht club in Victoria. An annual sailing regatta, sponsored by Eden Island, starts and finishes in the Eden Island Marina and there is a windsurfing race between Mahé and Praslin. January 2006 saw the debut of the Seychelles Sailing Cup, an international sailing event with teams from Europe and the Seychelles, organised in accordance with the International Sailing Federation rules, under the auspices of the Seychelles Yachting Association.

For the local people, **fishing** is a way of life and the sport of game fishing is developing rapidly, and every year several tournaments are held off the islands.

With all the granite in the Seychelles, **rock climbing** is an emerging sport. Indeed, in 2014, a climbing wall and zip lines were developed at Constance Ephelia in the northwest of Mahé (page 115). It's a great adventure sport open to all.

DIVING AND SNORKELLING The warm tropical waters of the Seychelles are the perfect place to explore the underwater world. But, be warned – it could spoil your other diving experiences forever! There are countless opportunities for both snorkelling and scuba diving, and the Seychelles can cater for all skill levels, from the most timid person trying on a mask for the first time to advanced divers who flinch at nothing and scour the planet for exciting dive locations.

Diving takes place all year round in the Seychelles. The best months for calm, clear water are the inter-seasonal months of April to May and October to November. When the southeast trades are blowing, visibility is usually a bit reduced but pelagic fish increase in abundance, and the wonderful whale sharks arrive. During the northwest monsoon, choppy seas may make access to some dive sites difficult, but calm days intersperse the breezy days and a spot of rain never harmed a diver! Most of the dive operators are located on Mahé or Praslin, and diving excursions to the outer islands have been somewhat curtailed owing to Somali pirate activity.

There are numerous safe snorkelling sites, and on Mahé, Sunset Beach, Northolme and Port Launay Marine Park offer easy shore access. Many of the Seychelles tour operators (page 84) offer trips that include snorkelling.

Around the granitic islands, a huge number of dive sites, mostly in the 10–30m depth range and requiring access by boat, are frequented by the various dive operators. Many can be dived during all seasons but some sites are used specifically during the southeast trades or northwest monsoon periods; others require very calm conditions. They include sites on coral reef pinnacles and drop-offs, granite boulders and tunnels, and eerie wrecks. The sites vary in the level of diving skills required, and many can also be dived safely at night. Be careful to match your choice of dives to your training and skills and, if you have not dived for a while, complete some shallow, easy dives first before taking on anything too strenuous.

Dive operators offer scuba-diving training courses under the auspices of the Professional Association of Diving Instructors (PADI), and these range from basic through to advanced, as well as various specialist qualifications. Internationally recognised certificates are issued, and a basic open-water course comprises theory lessons and pool and open-water training. The dive operators can provide full equipment rental and, in addition to single dives, offer packages of dives at different localities which are usually more cost-effective.

If you are hiring equipment, it is advisable to spend some time ensuring that it fits properly. It is important to ensure that your mask seals well, so you don't experience leaks when you are snorkelling or diving. To check this, take the mask and fit it on your face but without pulling the strap over your head; then take a deep breath through your nose and let go of the mask. If the mask stays firmly on your face the mask is a good fit. Use of open or closed fins is really a matter of choice but do be careful what you tramp on when getting in and out of the water.

It's easy to get sunburned when snorkelling in tropical waters so, in addition to applying protective sunscreen to the back of the legs it is recommended that a T-shirt or lycra vest is worn. It is also advisable to take a bottle of fresh water with you on any snorkelling or diving trip as it is easy to dehydrate in the tropics.

Dive operators

ʯ **Angelfish Dive Operations** Roche Caiman, Mahé; ☏ 4344644; e info@seychelles-charter.com; www.seychelles-charter.com

ʯ **Azzura Pro Dive** Anse La Réunion, La Digue; ☏ 4292525; e azzura@ladigue.sc; www.ladigue.sc

✔ **Big Blue Divers** Mare Anglaise, Mahé; \4261106; e bigblue@seychelles.net; www. bigbluedivers.net

✔ **Blue Sea Divers** Beau Vallon, Mahé; m 2526051; e contact@blueseadivers.com; www. blueseadivers.com

✔ **Denis Island Dive Centre** Denis; \4295999; e denis@seychelles.net

✔ **Dive Resort Seychelles** Anse la Mouche, Mahé; \4372057; e divereso@seychelles.net; www.divetheseychelles.com

✔ **Dive Seychelles/Underwater Centre** Beau Vallon, Mahé; \4247165; e divesey@seychelles. net; www.diveseychelles.com.sc

✔ **King Bambo Dive Charters** Mahé; m 2513945; e kingbmbo@seychelles.net; www. kingbambo.com

✔ **Octopus Diving** Anse Volbert, Praslin; \4232602; e octopus.seychelles@gmail.com; www.octopusdiver.com

✔ **Whitetip Divers** Paradise Sun Hotel, Anse Volbert, Praslin; \4232282; e whitetipdivers@ seychelles.net; www.whitetipdivers.com

ANGLING Big-game fishing around the islands of the Seychelles is possible all year round, and anglers troll the warm, blue waters for the likes of marlin, sailfish, tuna, wahoo, dorado, kingfish and barracuda from a wide range of charter fishing boats. Sailfish are much sought after, and the Seychelles ranks highly as an international destination for those anglers targeting these magnificent fish. Silhouette, in particular, is the favoured area for sailfishing.

Fishing charter vessels operating on the islands' waters range in size from small runabouts with outboard motors to large, luxury vessels with inboard diesel engines and all the mod cons. Those boats operating out of Mahé frequent sites such as North Island, Shark Bank, Silhouette, Hermes, D'An l'Or, Pilot Patches, Tocos, D'An Sud, Topaz Bank and Ile aux Récifs. Further afield, Denis and Bird, as a result of their location on the edge of the Seychelles Bank, offer excellent opportunities on the drop-off into the deep Indian Ocean waters. In fact, several world records for dogtooth tuna caught off Denis have been ratified by the International Game Fishing Association.

Many of the fishing boat operators promote the eco-friendly practice of tag and release, to try and ensure sustainability of the fish resources. Fly-fishing is also becoming popular, and the Seychelles is gaining a reputation as the finest venue in the world for catching bonefish, particularly at Alphonse, St François and Desroches. Some boats also offer bottom-fishing opportunities to tourists, and the reefs around the Seychelles boast an amazing variety of sought-after reef fish. Although the Seychelles reef fish stocks still appear to be in reasonable condition, cognisance should be taken of the stock collapses in many other parts of the world where fishing pressure has decimated populations of these relatively sedentary, long-lived, slow-growing species.

Fishing operators The **Marine Charter Association** in Victoria (\ *4322126*; e *mca@seychelles.net*) is the place to contact to arrange a fishing trip. Other charter boat operations include:

🎣 **Angel Tours Pty Ltd** Praslin; m 2515327; e angeltours@seychelles.net; www.angeltours.net

🎣 **Anse Royale Charters Ltd** Anse Royal, Mahé; m 2525506; e imtiaz.umarji@ thepalmseychelles.com; www.zafirahseychelles.com

🎣 **Barracuda** Praslin; m 2512298; e sybille@ seychelles.net

🎣 **Bedier & Son** Anse Volbert, Praslin; \4232192; e bedier_son@hotmail.com

🎣 **Blue Water Charters** Mahé; \4346100; e bluewater@seychelles.net; www. bluewatercharter.sc

🎣 **Corsaire Boat Charter** Anse Boudin, Praslin; \2516998; e fishingpraslin@email.sc; www.fishingpraslin.com

🎣 **Le Superbe Hirecraft (Sport Fishing)** Mahé; \4322288; e booking@ superbcharters.com

MV *Maya's Dugong* (an expedition & support vessel) Mahé; ☎ 4324026; e cruises@seychelles.net; www.ocean-odysseys.com

Ocean Girl Charter Bel Ombre, Mahé; m 2713371; e oceangirlcharter@yahoo.com

Sailfishing Charters Seychelles Mahé; m 2514468; e contact@sail-seychelles.com; www.sail-seychelles.com

Star Boat Charters Mahé; m 2510432; e starboatcharter@hotmail.com; www.seychellesstarboatcharter.com

Striker Angler's Corner, Beau Vallon, Mahé; ☎ 4247848; e striker@seychelles.net

WaterWorld Charter Providence, Mahé; m 2514735; e wworld@seychelles.net; www.seychelles.net/wworld

CRUISING Cruising, by motor boat or sailing yacht, is a superb way to explore the Seychelles, and there are various options available amongst the inner islands or even venturing further afield to the Amirantes or alluring Aldabra. The **Marine Charter Association** represents many of the charter vessels, both yachts and game-fishing boats. Their quay, with bar and restaurant in downtown Victoria (page 70), is a good place to head for if you are contemplating any sort of boat hire.

The best time for cruising is September to December, after the boisterous southeast trades recede and before the unsettled rainy northwest monsoon sets in. April and May are also good months although inter-seasonal winds can sometimes be a bit light for making passage under sail. If you plan on heading to the outer islands, be sure to allow sufficient time to get there and back as well as to enjoy your tropical island destination. For a trip to the Amirantes allow about a week, and Aldabra at least two weeks, preferably more!

The **Seychelles Yacht Club** is conveniently situated adjacent to the Marine Charter Association, and has reciprocity with several foreign yacht clubs. The club has a bar and also offers reasonably priced meals. With the development of **Eden Island** and the associated marina and facilities there is now considerable boating activity in the Roche Caiman area. In Victoria, a few small shops sell chandlery items and Max Sails is a small sail-repair loft in Mont Fleuri, on the road to the airport. Nautical **charts** are not usually in stock anywhere in the Seychelles, and anyone cruising around the islands should consider purchasing the definitive cruising guide *Seychelles Nautical Pilot* by Alain Rondeau, which describes many of the stunning anchorages in fair detail (page 203).

Cruising operators The sailing charter business has grown considerably in the Seychelles in recent years, and nowadays numerous vessels are available for bareboat and crewed sailing charters.

Mahé

Angel Fish Yacht Charter Roche Caiman; ☎ 4344644; e info@seychelles.charter.com; www.seychelles.charter.com

Silhouette Cruises Victoria; ☎ 4324026; e nick@seychelles-cruises.com or cruises@seychelles.net; www.seychelles-cruises.com. They have 4 beautiful sailing schooners in their fleet: *Sea Shell* & *Sea Pearl* plus 2 newer ships, *Sea Star* & *Sea Bird*, operating out of Victoria. Combining the romance of sail & the beauty of the islands, they offer day trips & longer cruises around the inner islands for individuals & groups. They have AC en-suite cabins & are fully equipped with dive tanks & equipment for hire. They all carry a range of watersports equipment & you can enjoy kayaking, water skiing, windsurfing, wave riding & snorkelling. 7-night cruises are offered to include a mix of relaxation, watersports & nature across the Seychelles, & a whale shark odyssey is offered in Aug & Sep with the enriching experience of learning about these enormous creatures & participating in scientific monitoring. A sporting adventure cruise is available which includes cycling, hiking, kayaking & competitive swimming around the different islands. Dedicated sea kayaking cruises can also be undertaken. Should you wish to make your own specific tour, that can also be arranged.

Sunsail Eden Island; 4346122;
e ssseychel@seychelles.net; www.sunsail.com
VPM Yacht Charter Roche Caiman;
4344719; e customerseychelles@vpm-bestsale.
com; www.vpm.fr. Offers monohulls & catamarans.

Praslin

Dream Yacht Seychelles Marina near
the jetty in Baie Ste Anne; 4232681; e info@
dreamyachtcharter.com; www.dreamyachtseychelles.
com. Offers a range of monohulls & catamarans
including the large catamaran *Indiana* which
undertakes day sailing trips.

Island-hopping Many motor boats are available for **island-hopping** day trips
and they often double up as platforms for game fishing and diving. In addition to
those available through the Marine Charter Association, Creole Travel Services also
has a selection of vessels for island-hopping including the large catamaran *Oplezir*
used for day excursions, sunset cruises, parties and dances.

Ocean Charters 4321100; e info@
oceancharters.sc; www.oceancharters.sc. Also offer
motor boats for luxury cruising.

Sunseeker Cruises m 2713425;
e info@sunseekercruisesseychelles.com; www.
sunseekercruisesseychelles.com
Water World m 2514735; e wworld@
seychelles.net

BIRDWATCHING Birdwatching in the Seychelles is a treat and there are many desirable
new ticks for your list! It is really easy to get around the main islands and, on Mahé,
hiring a car will get you to the Morne Seychellois National Park where you can look for
the Seychelles white-eye and the scops owl, both of which are notoriously difficult to
locate. It is a good idea to hire a local guide if you are serious about seeing these birds;
Gemma Jessie is an excellent choice and much more than a birding guide (*Grand Anse,
Praslin;* 2510431; e jessiegemm@yahoo.com), but also consider Lindsay Chong Seng
(4241104) or Nature Seychelles (4601100; e nature@seychelles.net). Other endemic
birds can be seen in any of the natural areas and hotel gardens with flowering shrubs.
Bird Island, with its vast seabird colonies, is easy to reach from Mahé, and arrangements
can be made at their office on the inter-island quay, Victoria (page 109).

On Praslin, the black parrot is the target species, and the best place to see it is in
the Vallée de Mai. The walk up to the shelter is often a good route to see them, but
also look out for sunbirds in the flowering trees. It is also possible to see the parrots
around the Coco de Mer Hotel or anywhere with fruiting trees. Cousin and Aride
are fabulous places to observe seabirds as you can get really close up as they are
used to visitors; both are easily accessible from Praslin (pages 167–9 and 164–7).

Aldabra is the ultimate birding destination in the Seychelles with endemic land
birds and great colonies of breeding boobies and frigate birds. Cosmoledo, too, is
an exceptional atoll to visit. Unfortunately, however, there are no tourist facilities on
either, and getting there is difficult and expensive.

Nature Seychelles with its UK partner, BirdLife International, is one of the
primary organisations concerned with research and conservation of birds and bird
reserves. The newsletter, *Zwazo,* is published twice a year. Their office is at Roche
Caiman (4601100). They are currently rehabilitating the small wetland around
their offices with excellent results as several species of water birds are now seen on
a regular basis, and they are also very involved with education and frequently have
schoolchildren taking part in projects at the centre.

The Island Conservation Society (4324607; e ics@seychelles.net) is an
organisation, formed in association with the Royal Society for Wildlife Trust,
primarily for the protection of Aride.

Fulfilling the romantic notion of getting married in the Seychelles is relatively easy to arrange, even in a hurry. Marriage ceremonies take place on Tuesday–Thursday mornings between 09.00 and 11.00 at the Civil Status Office (*PO Box 430, Victoria;* 4293613 *or* 4293604; e *info@civilstatus.gov.sc*). The legal ceremony can also be performed at your hotel or outdoors. Ceremonies can be held on any of the islands, but transportation for the official also has to be paid, so bear this in mind. Extra fees will also be incurred if the ceremony takes place after 17.00 or on a Saturday or Sunday. A church wedding without a civil wedding is not recognised as being legal and the civil ceremony must be performed before the church wedding. It is therefore ideal to plan at least two months in advance to allow for processing of the documentation but, for a fee, it can be arranged with a special licence. Couples have to be in the Seychelles for at least two days prior to the wedding, and originals or certified copies of certain documents such as passports and birth certificates are required. If either prospective spouse is a divorcee, widow or widower, the death certificate or divorce documents are also required. For those couples wishing to marry in a church, contact a local priest. Wedding banns have to be published 11 days prior to the wedding but this period can be shortened to just two days if a special licence is obtained.

Most Seychelles tour operators are able to arrange the entire wedding event for you, including organising photographic and video services, hairdressers and beauticians. Creole Travel Services (4297000; e *info@ creoletravelservices.com*) has exclusive use of an open-air site at Cap Lazare, an ideal wedding location. Many of the hotels, large or small, offer wedding and honeymoon specials and are able to arrange the entire event, including the bouquets, wedding cake and photographer. Prices range from several hundred euros to many thousands. French citizens are required to contact their embassy in the Seychelles prior to the celebration of their marriage.

BUYING PROPERTY

There are several real-estate agents who deal in property in the Seychelles, but in general, foreigners buying property need a Seychellois partner. However, **Eden Island** (4346000; e *info@edenisland.net; www.edenisland.sc*), newly created through the reclamation project and linked to the mainland by bridge, has been developed specifically for foreign investment. Extensive marinas have been established with freehold houses and apartments available for purchase by non-Seychellois. Shops, restaurants, a gymnasium and other recreational facilities are available.

Raffles Praslin (4296000; e *rafflespraslinseychelles@raffles.com; www.raffles. com/praslin*) has a section of hillside, close to the hotel on Praslin, set aside for the development of 14 free-standing luxury villas and some have already been completed.

TRAVELLING POSITIVELY

Responsible tourism can mean many different things. It is about common sense and it hardly needs to be spelt out but it is worth making a few comments. Respect for the host country's culture is high on the awareness list. It is always polite to ask if you may photograph people and, if they refuse, honour their refusal. In the Seychelles, although an easy-going, relaxed lifestyle prevails, it is not a good idea to go into town scantily clad in beachwear. The beaches and surrounds are so lovely it would be a shame to spoil them with litter even though it appears that the residents do just that at times. Rather than using bottled water, and generating landfill waste from the plastic containers, bring your own bottle and simply refill it from the tap. During dry times of the year there can be water shortages, so be mindful of not using more water than necessary in showers.

Although the Seychelles is a developing country, there is not the dire poverty one finds in other parts of the world and social services appear to be doing a good job; there are no beggars or street children, the elderly are cared for and the literacy levels are high. Supporting the local economy by using local stores and smaller independent restaurants is important.

One of the greatest areas of responsibility for tourists in the Seychelles is around conservation of the environment. It is the basis on which the country's tourism depends and generates significant foreign exchange for the country. There are codes of conduct for visiting most of the island nature reserves and they have been put in place for the protection of both wildlife and visitors. It is most clearly spelt out when visiting Cousin Special Reserve where the birdlife appears completely unafraid of humans and a respectful distance must be maintained. A similar situation occurs on Aride with the additional aspect of huge numbers of ground-nesting birds making it clearly necessary to keep to the paths to prevent the nests, eggs and chicks from being trampled.

The other sensitive areas are the coral reefs. After the bleaching in 1998, corals are slowly regenerating and it is essential to keep off them, keeping fins well away while diving or snorkelling. The old cliché 'Take only photographs and leave only footprints' still holds true, as does 'Walk slowly, talk softly'.

Part of the responsibility can be proactive and you can join, or make a donation to, one or more of the conservation NGOs. These play a vital and active part in the maintenance and running of many of the island reserves. Several organisations rely on the assistance from volunteers in the Seychelles.

If you prefer, you can become involved with an organisation that benefits children, such as the National Council for Children (*Bel Eau;* \ 4224390; e *ncc@ seychelles.sc; www.ncc.sc*).

Earthwatch Environmental Research and Volunteer Programme www.earthwatch.org.au. Get involved with teaching & working with local students. Many of the programmes are run through a support partner, usually a university or a private foundation.

Global Vision International www.gvi.co.uk. Volunteers have to be proficient PADI divers for monitoring & surveys of whale sharks, marine invertebrates, turtle nesting & much more.

Island Conservation Society www. islandconservation.net. This is a worthwhile NGO spearheading the management of Aride &, at the same time, has input in the development of other small islands.

Marine Conservation Society of Seychelles (MCSS) e info@mcss.sc; www.mcss.sc. An NGO promoting conservation of the marine environment through education & research. The main areas of research are whale sharks, turtles & corals. Volunteers are able to join any of these programmes.

Nature Seychelles Roche Caiman (affiliated to BirdLife International) PO Box 1310, Victoria; \ 4601100; e nature@seychelles.net; www.natureseychelles.org

Seychelles Islands Foundation (administering Aldabra & Vallée de Mai) PO Box 853, Victoria; \ 4321735; e sif@seychelles.net

Part Two

THE ISLANDS

TURN YOUR DREAM HOLIDAY INTO REALITY!

Welcome to the world of **Creole Travel Services**, Seychelles' most dynamic and prestigious Destination Management Company! With over 42 years of experience in the Tourism Industry, our "savoir-faire" provides you with a blend of tradition, local flair, efficiency and personalised service.

An ISO-9001 certified company, **Creole Travel Services** is run by a team of committed, creative and "passionately Seychelles" travel professionals.

OUR OFFERING GOES HAND IN HAND WITH OUR AFFILIATED COMPANIES...

"Oplezir" sailing Catamaran and its seating capacity of 80 passengers is the occasion to treat yourself to day-trip charters, romantic sunset cruises or diving escapades.

Cap Lazare Nature Reserve and its 65-hectare nature reserve and restaurant in the South of Mahe is the ideal location for weddings and exclusive events.

United Yacht Charter, Creole Exchange, Creole Air Travel, Creole Exclusive & the High-Speed **Cat Cocos** catamarans

... AND OUR EXCLUSIVE "DOMAINES" HOTEL ESTABLISHMENTS:

Le Domaine de La Reserve & **Le Domaine de L'Orangeraie**

contact us at: **info@creoletravelservices.com**

4

Mahé

Mahé is the largest island in the Seychelles. Granite hills and mountains rise steeply from the sea providing a dramatic backdrop to the irregular coastline. Mahé is 27km long, only 8km wide, and covers an area of 152km². It has a circumference of about 120km with breathtaking bays, intriguing coves and glorious long stretches of soft, white sand. Coconut palms, *badamier* and *takamaka* trees fringe the shoreline creating welcome shade and beautiful vistas.

The highest peak, Morne Seychellois, reaches up to 905m and, even on the hottest day, is frequently bathed in swirling mists. Much of the natural vegetation was destroyed in the early years of Seychelles settlement but the rich soils and high rainfall coupled with keen conservation by the Seychellois have been conducive to a remarkable recovery, and the slopes are now clad with many indigenous trees, ferns, palms and orchids.

A necklace of coral encircles this truly magnificent island, protecting and sheltering the bays and beaches. Every beach or cove of any size or importance is named *Anse*, from the French word for 'cove', and although there may be a small village with a church, school, clinic and shop, it is simply known by its beach name – Anse Royale, Grande Anse, Anse aux Pins, etc. The only town on Mahé, or the whole of the Seychelles for that matter, is Victoria, named in 1841 after the young queen of England.

Mahé is surrounded by groups of satellite islands. Closest to Victoria on the east coast are Ste Anne, Cerf, Moyenne, Round and Long islands. All these are situated within the Ste Anne Marine National Park. Thérèse and Conception are located off Port Glaud on the western side, while Silhouette and North can be seen from Beau Vallon. The newly created manmade islands of Ile du Port, Ile Persévèrence and Ile Aurore are located along the northeast shore of Mahé, north of the port of Victoria, whilst Ile de Romainville, Ile Soleil and Eden Island are south of the capital. On a clear day with good visibility, other, more distant islands like Praslin, La Digue, Mamelles and Frégate may be seen.

It is possible to drive almost all the way around Mahé, and there are only a few short stretches in the western and southern extremities with no linking roads. A good system of well-maintained roads has been developed. However, they are not without their dangers. The roads climbing the steep slopes are narrow and twisting with some hairpin bends and few, if any, shoulders. To accommodate the tropical downpours, deep channels have been constructed along the sides of the roads. But, beware: there are no protective barriers, and frequently the white or yellow lines have been worn away and are hardly visible. There is an easy-going attitude among the drivers, who will frequently stop to chat to a fellow driver or pedestrian pal, with scant regard to traffic travelling in either direction. This, combined with the tourists in their hired cars who are unfamiliar with the geography, makes for

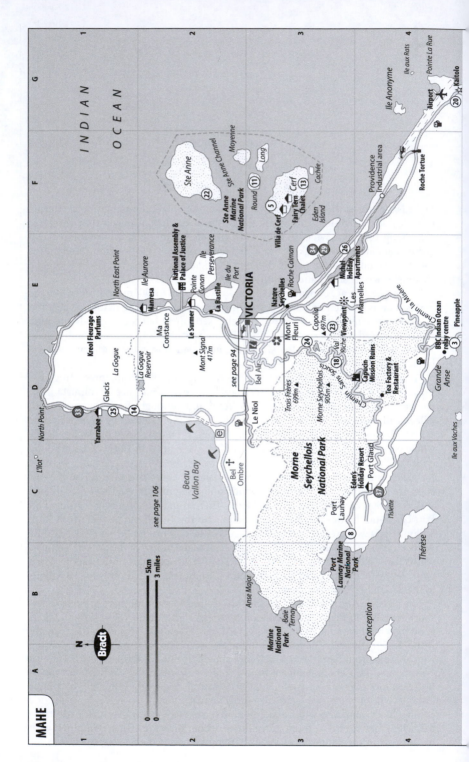

MAHE

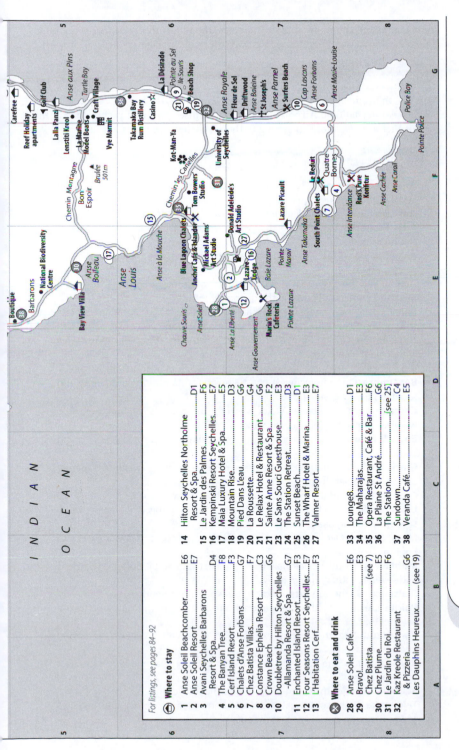

For listings, see pages 84–92

Where to stay

1	Anse Soleil Beachcomber	E6
2	Anse Soleil Resort	E7
3	Avani Seychelles Barbarons Resort & Spa	D4
4	The Banyan Tree	F8
5	Cerf Island Resort	F3
6	Chalets d'Anse Forbans	G7
7	Chez Batista Villas	F7
8	Constance Ephelia Resort	C3
9	Crown Beach	G6
10	Doubletree by Hilton Seychelles –Allamanda Resort & Spa	G7
11	Enchanted Island Resort	F3
12	Four Seasons Resort Seychelles	E7
13	L'Habitation Cerf	F3
14	Hilton Seychelles Northolme Resort & Spa	D1
15	Le Jardin des Palmes	F5
16	Kempinski Resort Seychelles	E7
17	Maia Luxury Hotel & Spa	E5
18	Mountain Rise	D3
19	Pied Dans l'eau	G6
20	La Roussette	G4
21	Le Relax Hotel & Restaurant	G6
21	Sainte Anne Resort & Spa	F2
23	Le Sans Souci Guesthouse	E3
24	The Station Retreat	D3
25	Sunset Beach	D1
26	The Wharf Hotel & Marina	E3
27	Valmer Resort	E7

Where to eat and drink

28	Anse Soleil Café	E6
29	Bravo!	E3
30	Chez Batista	(see 7)
31	Chez Plume	E5
32	Le Jardin du Roi	F6
32	Kaz Kreole Restaurant & Pizzeria	G6
	Les Dauphins Heureux	(see 19)
33	Lounge8	D1
34	The Maharajas	E3
35	Opera Restaurant, Café & Bar	F6
36	La Plaine St André	G6
37	The Station	(see 25)
38	Sundown	C4
	Veranda Café	E5

Mahé

4

79

some interesting situations. The saving grace, though, is that speeding is not often possible except along Providence Highway, the dual carriageway near the airport.

GETTING THERE AND AWAY

Mahé is the official entry point into the Seychelles. By air, one arrives at the Seychelles International Airport [79 G4], and cruise ships and yachts dock at the port of Victoria. For more on getting to the Seychelles, see pages 54–7.

ADMINISTRATIVE DISTRICTS OF MAHE

Anse aux Pins On the east coast, characterised by protective reefs and old coconut plantations.

Anse Boileau Large agricultural district on the west coast.

Anse Etoile On the coast north of Victoria overlooking the Ste Anne Marine National Park.

Anse Royale In the southeast with a long history as the original Seychelles spice gardens.

Au Cap On the east coast, this is the centre of Creole culture, and some old plantation houses still exist in the district.

Baie Lazare Near where Lazare Picault first set foot in the Seychelles in 1742; the community maintains a strong maritime tradition.

Beau Vallon On the northwest coast, this is the most popular tourist area with a magnificent beach.

Bel Air Residential area in the foothills of Trois Frères overlooking Victoria.

Bel Ombre On the northwest coast, known for its fishing community and reputed pirate treasure trove.

Cascade Located between Victoria and the airport, this is noted for its two waterfalls, imposing granite cliffs and Mont Sebert.

English River In the northern part of Victoria this is a rapidly developing district.

Glacis In the north, this is characterised by spectacular, weathered granite and secluded beaches.

Grande Anse Another agricultural district on the west coast.

Les Mamelles Located inland and south of Victoria, this is characterised by several imposing peaks.

Mont Buxton Overlooking Victoria and the east coast, this is adjacent to English River.

Mont Fleuri South of Victoria, this is home to the hospital, Botanical Gardens and several schools and colleges.

Plaisance On the outskirts of Victoria between Mont Fleuri and Les Mamelles.

Pointe Larue With the international airport, this is the gateway to the Seychelles.

Port Glaud Near the western extremity of Mahé, with a waterfall and other fine natural assets.

Roche Caiman The youngest district, located on reclaimed land southeast of Victoria.

St Louis Includes the central business district of Victoria.

Takamaka In the southwest, this is well known for its two beautiful beaches of Anse Takamaka and Anse Intendance.

BY TAXI An efficient 24-hour taxi service operates on Mahé with over 300 taxis in service. The main taxi rank is on Albert Street, Victoria, not far from the clock tower in the centre of the town (4323895) and is shaded by large, flamboyant trees.

Other taxis are based at centres around the island, and your hotel or guesthouse will be able to arrange one for you. There are always taxis to meet incoming flights at the airport at all hours of the day or night. They also meet the incoming ferries at the inter-island quay and cruise ships docking at the port. Taxis frequent the major hotels, and it is never a problem to find a taxi during the day, although you may have to telephone for one at night or early in the morning. All registered taxis display a red 'taxi' sign on the roof and the drivers wear an identification badge. There is an agreed fare structure but it is a good idea to ask the taxi driver to turn on the fare meter at the start of the trip. It should cost about SR600 for a trip from the airport to Beau Vallon, SR300 to Victoria, the *Cat Cocos* jetty, Eden Island or the Ste Anne jetty, and SR800 to the southwest of Mahé.

Drivers belong to the Seychelles Taxi Drivers Association, and though not all of them speak English very well, many of them will gladly offer to take you on a 'tour' of their island. They are generally very knowledgeable about the flora and fauna as well as the best beaches and most important places to visit.

CAR HIRE There are at least 30 car-hire companies on Mahé. Some of the larger companies have offices in town, and several have offices at the airport and are open for business when international flights arrive, but your hotel, guesthouse or local tour operator will be able to arrange car hire for you. Hire only from a licensed hire company that shows a yellow 'HV' sign on the number plate. Foreigners must be over 18 years of age and be in possession of a valid national or international driver's licence. It is advisable to take out the extra insurance cover.

There are six petrol stations on Mahé, located in Roche Caiman, closest to the centre of town, at Pointe Larue opposite the airport, in Beau Vallon on the road between Victoria and Bel Ombre, at Baie Lazare, at Anse Royale close to Kaz Kreol Restaurant and on the western side of Mahé where Chemin La Misère meets the main road. They close in the evenings before sunset, so make sure that you have sufficient fuel. Fuel costs about SR22 per litre. On Mahé, distances are not great, and you will need about half a tank of petrol for a leisurely circumnavigation. There are pay-parking zones in central Victoria and tickets can be purchased from the nearby shops. Remember to drive on the left.

Avis Norman's Car Hire 4224511; e avis@seychelles.net; www.avis.com.sc
Hertz Rent a Car 4322447; e hertz@seychelles.net; www.seychelles.net/hertz
Mein's Car Hire 4266005; e meinscar@seychelles.net

Millennium Car Hire m 2511774; e sahtime@hotmail.com
Tropicar 4373336; e tropicar@seychelles.net

BY BUS Timetables can be obtained at the central bus station on Palm Street, Victoria (4280280). Whatever destination you choose, the fare will be SR5, although some of the new buses are air conditioned and the fare on these is SR10. Do not choose peak times to sightsee as the buses will be so full of commuters that you probably will not get a good view out of the windows. Most of the buses do have bells but the old ones do not and the way to get the driver to stop is to yell '*devant*' very loudly before you need to get off. If you are unsure about where to get off, ask the person you are sitting next to, or the bus driver. Finding the desired bus at the bus station can be a little confusing, as the bus numbers do not correspond with the platform numbers. For example, to get to Beau Vallon, take buses numbered 20, 22 or 24 from platform 9. These buses all pass Beau Vallon *en route* to Glacis. Bus 20 leaves Victoria at five and 35 minutes past the hour, and bus 22 leaves Victoria at 20 and 50 minutes past the hour.

On Revolution Avenue, up the hill past Bel Air Road, there is a bus shelter, and this is a good place to catch the Beau Vallon or Glacis bus mid morning or afternoon. If you try later at peak hour, the bus will be full and simply drive by without stopping.

There are many routes to get around Mahé, and it will be best for you to consult the timetable and associated map. Most of the buses run more frequently at peak times, but the timetable states that 'times are subject to change without notice'. Once out of the town area you will find 'BUS STOP' painted in large white letters on the road at the relevant stops or a covered bus shelter.

INTER-ISLAND TRAVEL

BY AIR Air Seychelles (*Independence Hse, Independence Av, Victoria;* \ *4391000;* e *info@airseychelles.com; www.airseychelles.com*) operates a regular and frequent service to Praslin. Most of the flights to the other islands are generally included in package tours, as few, if any, cater for day visitors. Visit the office to make reservations (and see also page 55).

Zil Air (*Pointe Larue;* \ *4375100;* e *info@zilair.com; www.zilair.com*) can take you by helicopter to Praslin, La Digue, Silhouette, Frégate, North, Denis, Cousine, Félicité or even to other parts of Mahé. Scenic trips are also available, as are gift vouchers.

BY SEA
To Praslin The most efficient way to get to Praslin is on *Cat Cocos*. The three Australian-built catamarans, *Isle of Mahé*, *Isle of Praslin* and *Isle of La Digue*, regularly shuttle between Victoria, Baie Ste Anne, Praslin and La Digue. Each offers three classes of seating – economy class main cabin, economy class upper cabin and business class. The journey takes about 50 minutes. It costs €50 one-way in economy class and €65 in business class. In business class, a buffet breakfast is served in the mornings and a finger snack buffet is available in the afternoons, while a bar in the main deck lounge sells drinks and snacks. Videos are shown in both cabins, which are fully air conditioned. A shuttle service is provided to and from the airport at a cost of €10 each way per adult and €5 for a child. There is an office at the inter-island quay (*central reservations* \ *4324843;* e *reservation@ catcocos.com; www.cat-cocos-seychelles.com*), but reservations may also be made at www.seychellesbookings.com. Schedules may change from time to time depending on the season or special events so it would be wise to confirm sailing times.

To La Digue La Digue can also be reached by using *Cat Cocos* over to Praslin and then, depending on the ferry timetable, continuing on to La Digue or using the *Cat Rose*'s ferry for the short hop across to La Digue. The traditional inter-island schooners also ply between Mahé, Praslin and La Digue on weekdays and, as they are basically cargo carriers, they do not usually take passengers.

CAT COCOS SCHEDULE

Please note that this timetable is between Mahé and Praslin. The * denotes a ferry continuing to, or commencing from, La Digue and making a 30-minute stop in Praslin. Please note that the schedules may change without prior notice.

Days	Depart Mahé to Praslin & La Digue	Depart La Digue & Praslin to Mahé
Monday	07.30	07.00*
	10.30*	07.30
	12.30*	12.30*
	16.30*	13.00
	17.30	
Tuesday	07.30	08.15*
	09.00	
	10.30	12.00
	16.00*	17.30
Wednesday	07.30	07.00*
	10.30	07.30
	13.00	
	16.30*	17.30
Thursday	07.30	07.00*
	10.00	07.30
	16.30*	noon
	17.30	
Friday	07.30	08.00*
	10.00	09.00
	17.00 direct to La Digue	12.30*
	13.00	
Saturday	07.30*	08.00*
	11.30*	09.00
	16.30*	15.00
	14.15*	
	18.00	
Sunday	09.00*	07.00*
	14.15*	
	16.30*	18.00

Excursions to the islands in the Ste Anne Marine National Park can be arranged at the Marine Charter Association or through one of the tour operators. The **Marine Charter Association** is on the sea side of 5th June Avenue in Victoria. They cater for boat charter needs and from their quay you will be able to arrange a snorkelling trip to the islands of Ste Anne and Cerf. The **Seychelles Yacht Club**, next to the Marine Charter Association, is for members only, although it does have reciprocity with other yacht clubs. **Angelfish Bayside** (❦ *4345001;* e *info@ seychelles.charter.com; www.angelfish-bayside.com*) is located close to the bridge linking Mahé to Eden Island. They have a variety of yachts available for charter and can also arrange excursions to some of the islands as well as fishing and snorkelling trips.

TOURIST INFORMATION

The tourist information office is in Independence House in Victoria (📞 *4610800;* e *info@seychelles.net; www.seychelles.travel;* 🕐 *08.00–16.30 Mon–Fri, 09.00–noon Sat*), where you can pick up a good map of the main granitic islands as well as all the information you may need for getting around.

LOCAL TOUR OPERATORS If you feel like having all the arrangements made for you, any of the tour companies in Mahé will be able to set up an interesting tour which could even be a personalised trip, tailor-made to your specific needs. Your expedition could be a simple half-day tour around part of the island, a full-day island tour, a snorkelling trip, an excursion to Praslin, La Digue or one of the other nearby islands, or a scenic helicopter trip. Or you might like to hire a guide to take you on one of the mountain walks, or perhaps do an art tour and visit some of the colourful artists. Many of the tour operators have fairly routine trips on a regular basis. Good guides accompany the tours, and a delicious Creole or seafood lunch is usually part of the deal on a full day out. Shop around to see which operators are offering the tour of your choice.

Operators in Victoria

7°South Kingsgate Travel Centre, PO Box 475; 📞4292800; e 7south@7south.net; www.7south.net
Creole Travel Services Independence Av, PO Box 611; 📞4297000; e info@creoletravelservices.com; www.creoletravelservices.com. A comfortable private lounge is available at the airport. See ad, page 76.

Mason's Travel Revolution Av, PO Box 459; 📞4288888; e info@masonstravel.com; www.masonstravel.com
Select Seychelles The Docklands, Level 4, New Port, PO Box 464; 📞4298888; e info@selectseychelles.com; www.select-seychelles.com

WHERE TO STAY

Mahé offers a wide selection of large resorts, small hotels, guesthouses and self-catering establishments. At this stage there is no formal star rating allocated. All the larger hotels, and many of the smaller ones, have a watersports and dive centre, a swimming pool, satellite channel television, DVD/CD facility, IDD telephone, minibar, safe and hairdryer. Most establishments have Wi-Fi, free or otherwise. The bedrooms are generally air conditioned, but the smaller guesthouses may only have ceiling fans. Accommodation is listed according to area. As a basic guideline, a hotel with over 25 rooms is considered a large hotel and there are very few hotels offering over 100 rooms. A price code system has been used (see inside front cover) and relates to the cost of a double room, unless otherwise stated. The high end of the scale is generally an opulent island resort. Tour operators are frequently able to quote better prices and tour packages are often the most economical way to go. Often there are special offers, so do shop around for the best prices. A 15% government tax is charged on all services; it is generally included in the quoted price but it is best to check when making your reservations. Remember you will be paying for privacy and exclusivity in many cases.

VICTORIA

There are no hotels or guesthouses in the centre of Victoria.

🏠 **The Station Retreat Hotel** [78 D3] (6 rooms & 1 villa) Sans Souci; 📞4224203;

e reservations@thestationseychelles.com; www. thestationseychelles.com. A 10min drive from Victoria, this small, eco-friendly hotel set in the lush mountains offers an alternative holiday experience with a spa & yoga pavilion. Besides offering 2- to 7-day retreats, the hotel is available for anyone to enjoy a peaceful & tranquil stay away from the beaches. Homeopathic & Ayurvedic treatments are available using natural products made on the property by the owner Jenny Gilbert & can be found in their Lily Moon Health & Gift Shop under the 'Nourished by Nature' label. The restaurant with lovely views over Bay Ste Anne focuses on healthy & tasty meals (page 92). There are daily transfers to town, the beaches & mountain hikes. **$$$–$$$$**

🏠 **The Wharf Hotel and Marina** [79 E3]
(15 rooms) Providence; ✆ 4670700; e thewharf@ seychelles.net; www.wharfseychelles.com. The hotel opened in 2004 & is very conveniently situated midway between the international airport & Victoria on the east coast of Mahé. There is a 4-bedroom penthouse with all the luxuries & 15 other bedrooms, 8 with a marina view & 7 with mountain views. The beautifully appointed hotel has a marina bar, a smart restaurant (Aubergine) & a swimming pool. The marina has a slipway & berthing facilities for 60 yachts on either a short- or long-term basis. **$$$**

🏠 **Hilltop Boutique Hotel** [map, page 94]
(4 studios & 7 apts) Serret Rd, St Louis; m 2526870; e info@hilltop.sc; www.hilltop.sc. A delightful establishment adjoining the famous Marie Antoinette Restaurant & run by the same family. Available as a self-catering or B&B. A 10min walk to town & a 10min drive to the nearest beach. Airport transfers & all your tours can be arranged. **$$**

🏠 **Le Sans Souci Guesthouse** [79 E3]
(3 rooms) Sans Souci; ✆ 4225355; e sansouci@ seychelles.net. Small guesthouse located on the mountain road about 5mins' drive from Victoria & within walking distance of some fine nature trails & mountain walks. There is a swimming pool, car-hire service & guidance on various excursions. **$$**

🏠 **Mountain Rise** [78 D3] (5 rooms) Sans Souci; ✆ 4225308; e mountainrise@seychelles. sc. This old colonial house, in a large garden high on the mountainside with expansive views of the Trois Frères Mountain, has 5 spacious suites, a large swimming pool & a restaurant. Jane will look after you & dinner can be provided on request. Being higher, it can be a little cooler & has a quiet ambience. **$$**

🏠 **Bel Air Hotel** [map, page 94] (7 rooms) Bel Air; ✆ 4224416; e belair@seychelles.net; www. seychelles.net/belair. Conveniently up Bel Air Rd just 10mins from town, this family-run, small hotel

offers en-suite rooms with AC. Lunch & dinners can be provided on request. **$**

NORTHWEST
Hotels

🏠 **Constance Ephelia Resort** [78 C3]
(279 suites & villas) Port Launay; ✆ 4395000; e info@epheliaresort.com; www.epheliaresort. com. This exclusive resort is spread across a 120ha estate overlooking the Port Launay Marine Park & 2 stunning beaches. The junior & senior suites have all the creature comforts while the villas, with 2 or 3 bedrooms, have their own private pools. The lavish Presidential Villa has 3 bedrooms & private gym, pool & dining area. All accommodation has AC, Wi-Fi, CD, DVD & iPod connections. 5 bars & 5 themed restaurants serve à la carte, fine grills & international, Asian, Mediterranean & local Seychellois menus. The Shiseido Spa has an extensive treatment range. Various pools, yoga pavilion, gym, watersports, squash & tennis courts are available. The latest adventure attractions include zip lines, rock climbing & abseiling facilities (page 114). Babysitting on request; children are catered for in the kids' club (⏰ 09.00–22.00 daily). **$$$–$$$$$**

🏠 **Savoy Resort and Spa** [106 F3] (163 rooms) Beau Vallon; m 2610161; e sales@savoy.sc; www. savoy.sc. Enormous hotel located a 1min walk away from Beau Vallon Beach offers a beautifully appointed spa using Sothys products; a gym with the latest equipment; a Russian sauna & a kids' club. The Grand Savoy Restaurant is open for all-day dining; Pescado, the fine-dining seafood restaurant is open in the evenings & the Gecko Bar & Restaurant provides casual meals & a wide variety of smoothies & drinks. **$$$–$$$$$**

🏠 **Hilton Seychelles Northolme Resort and Spa** [78 D1] (40 villas) Glacis; ✆ 4299000; e reservations.seychelles@hilton.com; www. seychelles.hilton.com. This famous old hotel with a lovely ambience incorporates all the most up-to-date amenities. The luxurious wooden villas are tucked away among the lush vegetation, with glorious views of Beau Vallon Bay & the inviting infinity pool. There are several dining options: the Hilltop Restaurant, the Ocean View Bar & Restaurant & the well-renowned Les Cocotiers Restaurant, all presenting first-class dining options. The luxurious Duniye Spa offers a variety of pampering treatments. Snorkelling is easy off the lovely sheltered beach below the hotel. Best of all are the friendly, caring & efficient staff. Recommended. Named by World Travel Awards as 2015 Seychelles Leading Boutique Hotel. **$$$$**

🏠 **Berjaya Beau Vallon Bay Beach Resort & Casino** [106 E3] (232 rooms) Beau Vallon; ☎4287287; e sales@berjayaseychelles.com; www. berjayahotels.com. It is located on Beau Vallon Beach & offers a wide variety of watersports (Dive Seychelles) as well as a large swimming pool adjoining the beach. The hotel features several restaurants – fine Cantonese cuisine at Le Canton, tasty Italian fare at the Pizzeria, the Parrot Restaurant serves traditional theme dinners & the Teppanyaki offers a traditional Japanese grill. There are 4 bars & live bands regularly provide musical entertainment. The casino is well frequented by visitors & residents. The hotel also hosts the Victoria Health & Beauty Salon & a business centre with internet access. **$$$**

🏠 **Coral Strand** [106 F3] (161 rooms) Beau Vallon; ☎4291000; e Info@coralstrand.com; www. coralstrand.com. This large, older, unpretentious hotel is superbly located on Beau Vallon Bay & is ideal for families. It features a pool & several restaurants including a sushi bar & the Mahek, well known for its authentic Indian cuisine. Live entertainment is part of the scene, especially over w/ends & scheduled daily activities for children & families are available. Watersports can be arranged. **$$$**

🏠 **Le Méridien Fisherman's Cove** [106 D3] (68 rooms) Bel Ombre; ☎4677000; e reservations. fishcove@lemeridien.com; www.lemeridien.com/ fishcove. This hotel has a gracious ambience & the spacious rooms, each opening onto a sea-facing balcony or garden terrace, are beautifully decorated with mirrors reflecting the Indian Ocean. The reception area has cascading waterfalls, shop & spa & the boardwalk leading to the Sunset Pavilion offers the best views of Beau Vallon Bay. There are 2 restaurants offering seafood, Mediterranean & local cuisine. A free-form swimming pool is set on the beachfront; a floodlit tennis court & non-motorised watersports are available. **$$$**

🏠 **Sunset Beach Hotel** [78 D1] (28 rooms) Glacis; ☎4261111; e sunset@seychelles.net; www. thesunsethotelgroup.com. The hotel is located on a spectacular small rocky peninsula & takes full advantage of views in both directions across the tiny bays to lush, dense vegetation, granite boulders

& a beautiful secluded beach. The décor is most attractive with thatch & high ceilings, open-air eating facilities & a superbly sited swimming pool. The restaurant offers Creole, French & international cuisine. There is an unhurried atmosphere, palms & thatched umbrellas. Snorkelling from the beach is easy. Children over 7 years are accepted. **$$$**

🏠 **Coco d'Or Hotel** [106 F3] (27 rooms) Beau Vallon; ☎4247331; e reservations@cocodor.sc; www.cocodor.sc. In a quiet road, 5mins' walk from the Beau Vallon Beach, the rooms of this attractively refurbished hotel all have a private balcony & AC. The restaurant features Creole cuisine while snacks & drinks are served around the pool or at the Latanier Bar & pizzas are available at Uncle Will's Pizzeria. **$$**

Small hotels, guesthouses & self-catering apartments

🏠 **Augerine Small Hotel** [106 E3] (15 rooms) Beau Vallon; ☎4247257; e augerine@seychelles. sc; www.augerinehotel.com. This establishment is on the same small road as the Berjaya Beau Vallon Bay Beach Resort, almost on the beach. Each room has AC, a small fridge & en-suite bathroom. Easy access to watersports & restaurants. **$$**

🏠 **Daniella's Bungalows** [106 D3] (10 rooms) Bel Ombre; ☎4247212; e daniella@seychelles. net; www.daniellasbungalows.com. The simple but comfortable bungalows are set in a verdant garden with a small stream. Each bungalow has a private veranda & fans help to keep cool. Breakfast is served on the veranda of the main house & evening meals can be provided on request. Located on the mountainside of the main road & are only a few mins' walk from Beau Vallon. **$$**

🏠 **Treasure Cove Hotel** [106 B4] (10 rooms) Bel Ombre; ☎4295151; e treasurecove@ seychelles.sc; www.treasurecove.sc. High on the hill above the remains of the treasure hunt, this new, locally owned hotel offers friendly Seychellois hospitality, with good food & drink at the Olivier Le Vasseur Restaurant & the Baya Bar. **$$**

🏠 **Beau Vallon Bungalows** [106 G2] (12 rooms) Beau Vallon; ☎4247382; e bvbung@ seychelles.net; www.beauvallonbungalows.com. Located in the centre of Beau Vallon Bay within easy walking distance of the beach, restaurants, shops, watersport centres & the bus stop. The bungalows have a self-catering option. Meals can be served on request. **$**

Casadani [106 C4] (7 rooms) Bel Ombre; 4414036; e lloizeau@intelvision.net; www. casadani.sc. Situated on the hillside giving the best views of Beau Vallon Bay, this guesthouse is within walking distance of Marie Laure Beach & a mere 1min drive to Beau Vallon Beach with all the local amenities. Dani Car Hire & Dani Boat Charter, for fishing or snorkelling trips, will take care of all your exploring needs. **$**

Georgina's Cottage Beach Guest House [106 F1] (9 rooms) Mare Anglaise; 4247016; e georgina@seychelles.net; www.georginas-cottage. com. Good-value, no-frills guesthouse, a mere 10m from Beau Vallon Beach. The rooms are simple, each with a bathroom & a ceiling fan; 2 allow self-catering. There are restaurants, hotels & a dive centre within easy walking distance & several small shops are close by; the bus stop is outside the gate. **$**

Hanneman Holiday Residence [106 F3] (12 rooms) Beau Vallon; 4425000; e info@hannemanholidayresidence.com; www. hanneman-seychelles.com. This self-catering establishment has many options for families or groups travelling together, with a studio room & 2- or 3-bedroomed duplexes. The kitchenettes are well equipped with all modern facilities. A sparkling pool in the grounds will help to keep you cool. Only a few mins' walk to Beau Vallon Beach. Excellent reviews. **$**

Panorama Guesthouse [106 F2] (10 rooms) Beau Vallon; 4247300; e panorama@ seychelles.net; www.panorama-guesthouse.com. This small hotel is in a prime location only a few metres away from Beau Vallon Beach & close to all the amenities of the area. **$**

Rockhaven Residence [106 F1] (2 villas) Mare Anglaise; m 2584188; e evitalouis@gmail. com. Across the road from Beau Vallon Beach. This self-catering establishment has 1 villa with 1 bedroom & a 2nd with 3 bedrooms, each with a fully equipped kitchen. Small convenience stores are almost next door & fresh fish is available from the nearby roadside stall each day. Friendly Josieanne will take good care of you. **$**

Romance Bungalows [106 F2] (7 rooms) Beau Vallon; 4247732; e romance@ romancebungalows.com; www.romance-bungalows.com. This small establishment is located in the middle of Beau Vallon with all amenities a short walk away. The rooms have facilities for basic self-catering. **$**

Villa de Roses [106 F3] (8 rooms) Beau Vallon; 4247455; e vderoses@seychelles.net; www.villadesroses.net. This small, family-run guesthouse surrounded by well-tended gardens is on a quiet road just a 3min stroll from the beach. B&B & self-catering options are available. **$**

SOUTHEAST & SOUTHWEST
Hotels

Four Seasons Resort Seychelles [79 E7] (67 villas) Petit Anse, Baie Lazare; 4393000; e res. seychelles@fourseasons.com; www.fourseasons. com/seychelles. Each villa, built on stilts along the hillside, has its own veranda & plunge pool. The villas range from the top-of-the-range 3-bedroomed Royal Suite to smaller 1-bedroomed villas with all the creature comforts. Guest services are extensive & offer everything from a helicopter service to babysitting. Some villas are suitable for wheelchairs. Conference & function rooms are available. The stunning spa has an extensive menu. **$$$$$**

The Banyan Tree [78 F8] (63 villas) Anse Intendance; 4383500; e reservations-seychelles@banyantree.com; www.banyantree. com. This large & beautiful hotel has been created in the colonial, Creole style of architecture with furnishings influenced by Indonesia & West Africa. The luxurious secluded private villas are set far apart in lush vegetation overlooking Intendance Beach, either on the beachfront or higher up on the hillside. Each self-contained villa has its own pool & outside pavilion, the bedrooms are stunning & the bathrooms have wide windows facing out to sea. The central area of the hotel houses the restaurants, Saffron with Thai & southeast Asian specialities & Au Jardin d'Epices serving international & Creole cuisine. An open bar area serves a variety of drinks & snacks throughout the day. Meals can be served in the villa or on the beach. A gallery offering Banyan Tree products is available. There is a magnificent spa located in a secluded spot. Attention to detail is extraordinary with orchids & soothing scents, fine muslin drapes & glass walls. Therapists are specially trained in Thailand & India & offer a wide range of treatments, some of which can be done in your villa. There is also a well-equipped gym & small conference room. An electric buggy will take you around the sprawling resort grounds & a 4x4 will collect you from the airport. **$$$$$**

Kempinski Resort Seychelles [79 E7]
(150 rooms) Baie Lazare; 4386666; e info.
seychelles@kempinski.com; www.kempinski.com/
seychelles. This large hotel, beautifully located
against a backdrop of massive granite rocks, is
30mins from the airport & offers a wide range of
options. The 4 restaurants & bars will cater for your
every need & private dining can also be arranged.
The Casino Paradiso (⊕ 20.00–04.00 daily) has
the full range of gambling options. The Water
Sports Pavilion has snorkel gear & kayaks; tennis &
volleyball courts are available & a modern gym will
keep you fit. The kids' club (⊕ 08.00–16.00 daily)
is for children 4–12 years. **$$$$**

Maia Luxury Hotel and Spa [79 E5]
(30 villas) Anse Louis; 4390000; e reservations@
southernsun.sc; www.maia.com.sc. This luxury
resort has 4 categories of villas: ocean view, ocean
front & ocean panoramic villas as well as the
signature suites. The design is inspired by Bali with
tall, thatched roofs & shaded gazebos. Each villa
has its own infinity pool & every creature comfort
you could desire. The Tec Tec Restaurant serves
Creole & Franco-Asian cuisine; you can also dine
on the beach in fine weather, in your villa or in the
secluded dining pavilion. Enjoy the sunset at the
Pool Bar with cocktails & snacks. A Boutique Spa
with 3 treatment rooms uses La Prairie products,
which are also in all the villas. Yoga & pilates can
be practised in the meditation area. As there
are a lot of steps, the resort could be difficult for
physically disabled people. Buggies are available
for transport between the villas & the restaurant,
pool bar & spa. Children are welcome in the ocean-
front villas only. **$$$$**

**Avani Seychelles Barbarons Resort &
Spa** [78 D4] (124 rooms) Barbarons; 4673000;
e seychell@avanihotels.com; www.avanihotels.
com/seychelles-barbarons. A modern hotel with
extensive grounds in a quiet part of Mahé, it
has large spacious rooms plus ocean view suites
all with their own private terrace. A swimming
pool, tennis court, fitness centre, yoga, diving,
snorkelling & surfing are available. The hotel is
close to the start of some interesting nature walks
& guides can be arranged. **$$$**

**Doubletree by Hilton Seychelles-
Allamanda Resort & Spa** [79 G7] (30 rooms)
Anse Forbans; 4388800; e reservations@
allamanda-seychelles.com; www.doubletree3.
hilton.com. This salmon-pink, modern hotel with
imposing pillars is right on the beach in a quiet part
of Mahé. All the spacious rooms have a balcony &
face the ocean. The attractive rim-flow pool appears
to merge with the ocean. The Palms Restaurant
serves delicious international & Creole cuisine with
a good dinner buffet; the Ocean View Bar has a
tempting array of cocktails. Be pampered in the
Duniye Spa overlooking the blue Indian Ocean. The
friendly staff will see to your every need. **$$$**

Small hotels, guesthouses &
self-catering

Crown Beach Hotel [79 G6] (12 rooms)
Fairyland, Pointe au Sel; 4382800;
e marketing@crownbeachseychelles.com; www.
crownbeachseychelles.com. This new, modern,
bright & airy, locally owned hotel is 8km south of
the airport & offers all the usual amenities. It is
almost on the beach & has a pretty garden with a
swimming pool. The friendly staff go out of their
way to be helpful. **$$$**

Anse Soleil Beachcomber [79 E6]
(14 rooms) Anse Soleil; 4361461;
e beachcomber@seychelles.sc; www.beachcomber.
sc. This quiet hotel is ideally located on a small,
secluded, very beautiful beach with good snorkelling
& swimming. The road leading down to the hotel is
a bit rough but don't be put off because even a small
car will manage it. B&B & HB are offered. The hotel is
next door to the Anse Soleil Café. **$$**

Anse Soleil Resort [79 E7] (4 houses)
Anse Soleil; 4361090; e soleil@seychelles.net;
www.ansesoleil.sc. The houses used to belong to
the American tracking-station personnel & are
now owned by Andrew & Paula who run them as
a very comfortable self-catering establishment.
Conveniently close to restaurants & a large
hotel, they are perched high on the hillside
overlooking Anse à la Mouche. There are different
configurations to suit couples or families. Living
areas are comfortable with TV & music centre,
floors are shiny cool granite & the kitchens are
well equipped. Each spacious house has a private
patio & lawn. Meals can be prepared on request &
airport transfers can be arranged. **$$**

Chez Batista Villas [79 F7] (11 rooms in
5 bungalows) Anse Takamaka; 4366300;
e batistas@seychelles.net; www.chez-batista.de.
This small hotel with chalets in the lush garden is
on one of the most beautiful beaches & has the
well-known restaurant Chez Batista on the beach.

At the time of writing, 3 more suites are being constructed. **$$**

🏠 **Le Jardin des Palmes** [79 F6] (10 rooms) Anse à la Mouche; ✆4389100; e jardindespalmes@email.sc; www. jardindespalmes-seychelles.com. Situated on a hillside up a winding driveway, the attractive wooden buildings look over the bay. Each bedroom has a lounge area & space for 2 extra beds which make it ideal for a family. **$$**

🏠 **Le Relax Hotel and Restaurant** [79 G6] (15 rooms) Anse Royale; ✆4382900; e helpdesk@ lerelaxhotel.com; www.lerelaxhotel.com. Perched on a hill overlooking the lovely Anse Royale & Souris Island, the hotel is only 2mins from Fairyland Beach, one of the best snorkelling sites. The hotel offers deluxe & standard rooms each with minibar, AC, fan, TV, tea- & coffee-maker. Breakfast can be served in the room or by the pool. Also has internet, swimming pool, gym, beauty salon & body therapy centre; babysitting & secretarial services are available on request. They will go out of their way to make your stay comfortable. **$$**

🏠 **Pied Dans L'eau** [79 G6] (5 self-catering apts) Anse Royale; ✆4430100; e pdl.seychelles@ gmail.com; www.piedansleau.sc. These attractive apartments are right on the beach & close to the small Anse Royale shops, post office & bank. The kitchens are fully equipped & the bed linen of a high quality. Marie Noelle & Henk will happily give you all the assistance you need. Their restaurant, Les Dauphins Hereux, offers local & international cuisine (page 92). **$$**

🏠 **Valmer Resort** [79 E7] (24 rooms) Baie Lazare; ✆4381555; e valmer@seychelles.net; www. valmerresort.com. This self-catering establishment with its studio or 2-bedroom apartments has recently been enlarged & refurbished. The rooms come in a range of configurations; all have AC, with a good range of appliances. A daily maid service is available. Le Palmier Restaurant & La Gaulette Bar are open all day. The resort is adjacent to the Gerard Devoux Art Gallery. **$$**

🏠 **Chalets d'Anse Forbans** [79 G7] (16 rooms) Anse Forbans; ✆4366111; e info@ forbans.com; www.forbans.com. The chalets, located in a quiet part of Mahé, are spaced apart under the coconut palms in an extensive lawned garden, all face the sea & are a few metres from the beach. The bungalows are suitable for either 2 or 4–6 people. Sustainable tourism is practised

& conservation issues are important as the hawksbill turtles & their nests are monitored, their wetlands maintained & the kestrels protected. **$–$$**

🏠 **La Roussette Hotel** [79 G4] (10 rooms) Au Cap; ✆4376245; e reservations@hotel-laroussette. com; www.hotel-laroussette.com. This small hotel on the east coast is a mere 5km from the airport. The rooms are tastefully decorated each with a private veranda. The family restaurant serves good Creole cuisine. **$**

ISLAND RESORTS CLOSE TO VICTORIA

🏠 **Cerf Island Resort** [79 F3] (24 villas) ✆4294500; e info@cerf-resort.com; www.cerf-resort.com. A small boutique hotel with all the buildings created from local materials to blend into the natural surroundings. The luxurious, thatched-roofed villas are well appointed & have a gentle ambience. Spend the day & indulge in a spa treatment. Non-residents are welcome; booking essential. The restaurant '1756' has wonderful views & serves traditional Creole & international cuisine. Book for lunch or dinner even if you are not staying in the hotel. A boat shuttle is available but you must check its departure point as it varies between Eden Island & Marine Charter. **$$$$**

🏠 **Enchanted Island Resort** [79 F3] (10 villas) Round Island; ✆4672727; e eir.reservations@ jaresorts.com. A 15min boat ride from Mahé will take you to this tiny island in the Ste Anne Marine Park. The villas are beautifully appointed with easy beach access. Hotel amenities include a gym, spa, yoga pavilion, pool & a watersports centre offering complimentary mask, snorkel, fins & kayaks. International gourmet cuisine is available at the Bounty Restaurant. **$$$$**

🏠 **Ste Anne Resort & Spa** [79 F2] (87 rooms) ✆4292400; e steanne.sa@bchot.com; www. sainteanne-resort.com. Part of the Beachcomber group, this large hotel spreads across 1km of the island. The 26 Garden, 32 Tropical & 21 Pool Villas with over 200m² of living space are private & beautifully appointed with luxurious bathroom & outside gazebo. There are a further 3 Beach Villas & 4 Presidential Villas. The Royal Villa is enormous with several bedrooms & private pool. There are several restaurants: L'Abondance buffet serving an array of international dishes; the Mont Fleuri on stilts serves fine gourmet fare & the rustic Le

Robinson is set in a cove below. A spectacular infinity pool appears to merge into the sea with Mahé in the distance. A children's centre, Pti Klib, caters for the youngsters & electric buggies & bicycles are on hand for transport around the resort. Watersports including a dive centre, many forested walks & a gym are available. If you need pampering, the resort has a luxurious spa using Clarins products. Transfers from Mahé take 10mins in a covered boat & depart from a quayside near the Unity Stadium at Roche Caiman on a regular basis. Helicopter transfers may also be made as there is a helipad at the resort. **$$$$**

L'Habitation Cerf [79 F3] (14 rooms) 4323111; e habicerf@seychelles.net. Designed as a plantation house, this small hotel offers a really quiet & peaceful time on the tiny island of Cerf in the Ste Anne Marine National Park. Snorkelling & diving are available on the coral reefs around the island & the restaurant serves international & Creole meals. There is a free shuttle boat between Mahé & Cerf which takes 15mins. **$$$**

WHERE TO EAT AND DRINK

Most hotels are only too pleased to serve non-residents but, if they are full, they may not be able to accommodate extra guests, so it is really important to make a reservation beforehand. Menus are usually biased towards fresh fish and seafood with some chicken and meat, while salads and vegetables are not as prominent, as they are frequently imported. Wines are expensive with nothing available under SR300 per bottle and a local beer is about SR50 in a restaurant.

Generally, restaurants are very casual, especially the ones on the beachfront – step off the beach in your swimming gear for lunch or even dinner. Hotels are often smarter; some require men to wear long trousers, not shorts, to dinner. Usually, lunch is served between noon and 14.00 and dinner between 19.00 and 21.00. This does, however, vary by restaurant and season. The smaller cafés and restaurants that serve both lunch and dinner often close around 14.30 and reopen in the evening. Smaller roadside cafés selling snacks and soft drinks may accept cash only.

Lunchtime is take-away time and there are many small places where you can find good-value tasty Creole/Chinese food served in a polystyrene box for around SR35. Alongside icy soft drinks and beer, many of the small shops sell a range of samosas, small pies and chilli bites, as well as sweet cakes, which are ideal for an inexpensive lunchtime snack. They are made on a daily basis so are always fresh, but you are not likely to find anything left after 14.00. A price code system has been used (page 65) and relates to the cost of a main course.

Particularly recommended hotel restaurants include the beautiful **Saffron Restaurant** at the Banyan Tree with its Thai and southeast Asian specialities (**$$$$**). **Le Canton** at the Berjaya Beau Vallon Bay Resort is an excellent Cantonese restaurant (**$$$$**) and **Les Cocotiers** at the Hilton Seychelles Northolme Resort and Spa offers the finest dining under the stars serving classic Creole and international food (**$$$$**).

The following are the major restaurants; other, smaller establishments may be mentioned in the text. A 15% government tax is added on to the price and in most cases it is included on the menu price, but occasionally it is not. A 10% service charge is also sometimes added on to the bill at the end, so it is a good idea to check on what is actually included in the price, as you could end up paying 25% more than you expected.

VICTORIA *Map, page 95*

Café de L'Horlorge Corner of State House Rd & Francis Rachel St; 4323556; ⏲ lunch & dinner daily. This is a trendy meeting & eating place in Victoria. The upstairs restaurant is open on 2 sides with pleasant views of the post office & law courts & down Independence Av. A full range of snacks, drinks & meals is available & best of all, the service is fairly quick & friendly. **$$$**

✘ **Kaz Zanana** Revolution Av; ☏4324150; ⊕ 11.00–23.00 Mon–Sat. Set in a restored colonial wooden house dating back to 1915. The veranda looks into a lush tropical garden. Georges Camille exhibits his colourful artworks here. The restaurant is known as 'Pink Salt' & fresh fruit juices, light meals & delicious Creole food are available. $$$

✘ **Marie Antoinette** Serret Rd, St Louis; ☏4266222; e guytomondon@gmail.com; www.marieantoinette.sc; ⊕ lunch & dinner Mon–Sat. This well-known restaurant is situated in a beautiful wood-&-iron colonial Seychellois house, & Madame Fonseka, the owner, serves a fixed menu of traditional food in true Creole style. Reservations recommended as this is known as the best Creole restaurant in Victoria. $$$

✘ **Pirates Arms** Independence Av; ☏4225001; ⊕ lunch & dinner daily. *The* meeting, eating & drinking place in Victoria for locals & tourists alike. The bar & restaurant have an island-style atmosphere with fans whirring overhead. There is always an enjoyable buzz of activity, especially around lunchtime when tables are at a premium, particularly the ones overlooking the street. The menu is extensive including club sandwiches (*SR110*), pizza (*SR115*) & fish & chips (*SR160*); fruit juices cost SR28 & local beers from SR41. Service is more nonchalant & slower than ever so don't go there if you are in a tearing hurry or literally dying of thirst. Around the corner, the Pirates Arms has a take-away counter. Join the locals in the queue but remember it closes at 14.00. Chow mein, chicken curry or sausage & chips are around SR35–40. $$$

✘ **La Pause Restaurant** Revolution Av; ☏4373106; e contact@lapause-seychelles.com; www.lapause-seychelles.com; ⊕ 09.00–17.30 Mon–Fri. The best place in town for a smoothie, fresh juice, cakes, tarts or a crêpe. Fresh salads & burgers are a speciality. At the time of writing, cash only is accepted. $$

✘ **News Café** Trinity Hse; ☏4322999; ⊕ 08.30–17.00 Mon–Fri, 08.30–14.00 Sat. The lunchtime eating place for people working nearby. It is modern, has AC, & light meals are available. $$

✘ **Restaurant du Marche** Upper level of Victoria Market; ⊕ 08.00–16.30 Mon–Fri, 08.00–14.00 Sat. Don't expect scintillating service or an inexpensive drink; a cappuccino will cost you SR60. $$

✘ **Sam's Pizzeria** Francis Rachel St, on the 1st floor of Maison Suleman; ⊕ 11.00–15.00 & 18.00–23.00 daily. This pizzeria has been making tasty pizzas since 1999. $$

✘ **A Taste of Italy** Market St; ⊕ lunch. A tempting array of ice creams & a selection of pizzas & snacks that are ideal for a light & inexpensive lunch. $

✘ **The Butcher's Grill** Unity Bldg, Palm St; ⊕ b/fast, lunch & dinner daily. Opposite the bus station, this is a large, busy fast-food restaurant serving pizzas, burgers, Chinese food & much more with many specials. Good value. $

FURTHER AFIELD

✘ **La Perle Noire** [106 F3] Beau Vallon; ☏4620220; e eclch@yahoo.com; ⊕ 19.00–21.30 Mon–Sat. The restaurant looks a little scruffy from the outside, but tables are set on the attractive veranda or inside & the Italian/Creole food comes highly recommended. Reservations necessary. $$$$

✘ **La Plage** [106 F2] Beau Vallon; ☏4620240; e laplageresto@gmail.com; ⊕ noon–22.00 Thu–Tue. Located on the beachfront with the best sunset views over to Silhouette & North islands; tables are inside or on the patio. Inventive food by a Belgian food designer. $$$$

✘ **La Scala** [106 A4] Bel Ombre; ☏4247535; e silscala@seychelles.net; www.lascala.net; ⊕ dinner only Mon–Sat, closed in Jun. One of the best restaurants on Mahé. Owned by Italian chef Gianni Torsi & his charming wife Silvana, the restaurant is perched high on the granite rocks with great ocean views. This restaurant is famous for its fine Italian food & homemade pasta is a speciality. Off-road parking. Reservations are advisable especially if you want a special table with the best view. $$$$

✘ **Mahek Restaurant** [106 F3] Coral Strand Hotel, Beau Vallon; ☏4291000. Specialises in authentic, excellent Indian food, which is attractively served on traditional Indian antique ware. You can even join the chef in the kitchen to see how the delicious meals are prepared. Sit inside the AC dining room or out on the sea-facing terrace. $$$$

✘ **Boat House** [106 F3] Beau Vallon; ☏4247898; e richardmancienne@live.com; www.boathouse.sc; ⊕ lunch noon–15.00, buffet dinner daily. A very casual restaurant & the Creole buffet, eat as much as you like, is good value; a wide variety of local salads, vegetables & fruits are served & the barbecued fish is particularly good. $$$

✕ **Bravo!** [78 E3] Eden Island; ☎ 4346020; e bravo@seychelles.net; ☉ noon–22.00 daily. This trendy restaurant specialises in Italian food & they are famous for their square pizzas. You are welcome to arrive at this waterfront eatery in a yacht or on your jet-ski as they have their own nearby private mooring. $$$

✕ **Chez Plume** [79 E5] Anse Boileau; ☎ 4355050; e plume@Seychelles.net; www. aubergeanseboileau.com; ☉ dinner only Mon–Sat from 19.15. Situated in an attractive house serving Creole food. $$$

✕ **Kaz Kreole Restaurant & Pizzeria** [79 G6] Anse Royale; ☎ 4371680; e kazkreoleresto@gmail. com; ☉ 09.00–22.00 Mon–Sat. This open-sided, toes-in-the-sand restaurant is on the beach at Anse Royale & serves Chinese & Italian food. Service a bit slow & casual. Live music & dancing entertains guests on Sat nights. $$$

✕ **La Plaine St André** [79 G6] Au Cap; ☎ 4372010; e reservations@laplaine.sc; www. laplaine.sc; ☉ 10.00–midnight Mon–Sat. The lovely old plantation house with its wide veranda is a great place for a meal with beautifully presented, delicious food & friendly service. See special offers on the website for a combination of a meal & a tour of the adjacent Takamaka Bay Rum Distillery. Have a taste of the various rums on offer (page 111). $$$

✕ **Le Jardin du Roi** [79 F6] Anse Royale; ☎ 4371313; e brymich@seychelles.net; ☉ 10.00–16.30 daily. Once you have made a tour of the spice gardens (€8pp) & looked at the museum, try one of their fresh fruit drinks, snack on a delicious sweet or savoury crêpe or be extravagant & have a tasty spiced ice cream. The snack menu is limited but uses the spices grown on the plantation. The 3-course plantation lunch on Sun is worth trying at SCR289pp. $$$

✕ **Les Dauphins Heureux** [79 G6] Pied Dans L'eau, Anse Royale; ☎ 4430100; e piedanslo@ intelvision.net; ☉ 19.00–22.00 daily. Well-priced good Creole & international cuisine. $$$

✕ **Lounge8** Glacis; m 2746808; e lounge8@ seychelles.net; ☉ Chill Out Terrace from noon daily, Lounge8 dinner 19.30–midnight. Enjoy the stunning décor, sip a cocktail & watch the sunset followed by a really good dinner. $$$

✕ **Olivier Le Vasseur Restaurant** [106 B4] Treasure Cove Hotel, Bel Ombre; ☎ 4295151;

lunch & dinner Mon–Sat. Stunning views & blackened Cajun fish a standout in a wide-ranging menu. $$$

✕ **Sundown Restaurant** [78 C4] Port Glaud; ☎ 4378352; ☉ lunch & dinner Mon–Sat. This little restaurant is almost on the beach opposite the tiny L'Islette. Fresh seafood is the speciality here. $$$

✕ **The Maharajas** [79 E3] Eden Island; m 2811461; e rm@themaharajasseychelles.com; www.themaharajasseychelles.com; ☉ dinner only from 18.30 Mon, noon–22.45 Tue–Sun. With indoor & outdoor seating overlooking the marina, this is an excellent restaurant for authentic Indian food & a good vegetarian selection. Take-away also available. $$$

✕ **Opera Restaurant, Café & Bar** [79 F6] Anse la Mouche; ☎ 4371943; e info@opera-mahe.com; www.opera-seychelles.sc; ☉ 10.00–midnight daily. Across the road from the beach. The exotic Laguna Lounge (☉ 21.00–02.00 Fri/Sat) offers cocktails, music, live entertainment & big-screen sports broadcasts. $–$$$

✕ **Anse Soleil Café** [79 E6] Baie Lazare; ☎ 4361700; ☉ lunch daily. It is worth making the trip down the rather rough road to this rustic, palm-thatched little restaurant. It is a few steps up from the particularly lovely beach & the advantage of the sandy floor is that the tables never wobble. Seafood curry or seafood with ginger is tasty & there are ordinary things like chicken & chips, & ice cream for dessert. $$

✕ **Chez Batista** [79 F7] Anse Takamaka; ☎ 4366300; e batistas@seychelles.net; ☉ 12.30–15.30 Mon, 10.00–22.00 Tue–Sun. Their speciality is seafood with the best views of the beach & the waves from under the palm-thatched roof. $$

✕ **The Station** [78 D3] Sans Souci; ☎ 4224203; e reservations@thestationseychelles.com; ☉ 08.30–16.00 Mon–Sat, 09.00–15.00 Sun. Simple, tasty, healthy food with a vegetarian emphasis. The eclectically decorated restaurant has a tranquil feel with great views. Look for the mural design of the route map across the mountains. $$

✕ **Veranda Café** [79 E5] Barbarons; m 2600384; e verandacafeseychelles@gmail. com; ☉ 11.00–18.00 Thu–Tue. This delightful little restaurant is situated on the terrace of the Pineapple Studio & serves fresh light meals & especially good desserts. $$

✕ **Baobab Pizzeria** [106 F2] Mare Anglaise; ☎ 4247167; ☉ lunch from noon & dinner from

18.00. This casual, toes-in-the-sand pizzeria is on the water's edge at the end of Beau Vallon Beach. At low tide some tables are on the beach under the *takamaka* trees. Excellent pizzas are cooked in a huge outdoor oven & the fried fish & chips is good value. Musicians sometimes entertain the diners. $

✗ La Fontaine Restaurant & Pizzeria
[106 F2] Beau Vallon; ✆ 4248408; e rdl@intelvision.net; ⊕ 11.00–23.00 Mon–Sat. A very casual eatery close to the beach with delicious wood-fired pizzas. $

NIGHTLIFE

The Seychelles are not renowned for the nightlife, but many of the hotels have some sort of evening entertainment. There are also two popular independent nightclubs.

☆ Katiolo [79 G4] Anse Faure; ✆ 4375453; ⊕ 21.00 til early hours of the morning Wed & Fri/Sat; admission SR100. South of the airport, this is an open-air nightclub almost on the beach. Wed is no entry fee for ladies, payment is cash only; no under 18s, dress code is 'sharp' – no shorts or sneakers. Expect lively music with a Creole touch.

☆ Tequila Boom and La Faya Bar [106 E3] Bel Ombre; ✆ 4247005; m 2774117; e tequilaboomseychelles@gmail.com; www.tequilaboom.com; ⊕ 22.00–05.00 Wed & Fri/Sat. State-of-the-art sound & lighting, VIP booths have to be reserved in advance. Plays hip-hop, dancehall, reggae. No under 18s.

VICTORIA *Map, page 94*

Victoria, one of the smallest capitals in the world, nestles beneath the imposing granite mountains on the northeast side of Mahé on a ribbon of flat land edging the sheltered bay. It is an interesting little town with typical Creole-style buildings interspersed with more modern architecture. In keeping with the promotion of Creole culture, many of the new buildings follow the traditional style, and some even have a vaguely Indian influence with ornate archways and small tiles. There is a general air of prosperity, new buildings are under construction, the streets are clean, the people appear healthy and well fed, and there are no beggars. However, sometimes the shops simply do not have the specific item that you require as everything has to be imported.

Victoria is a busy commercial centre, well serviced by banks, shops and restaurants. Taxis and buses operating from the town centre provide quick and easy connections with the rest of the island. Down at the harbour, the inter-island quay has boats of all descriptions travelling to many of the islands, and the deep-water international quay provides access for large cruise ships and cargo vessels. Located between the two busy quays are the Seychelles Yacht Club and the Marine Charter Association. Unfortunately, the tuna factory is also down on the quayside and, at times, the smell from the processing strongly pervades the air.

SHOPPING There are several souvenir shops in Victoria, including **Antik Colony** on Independence Avenue behind the Pirates Arms, which sells charming local cotton and linen products. Souvenir kiosks, with only a few open for business, line **Fiennes Esplanade** and the colourful **Victoria Market** has wonderful spices and a range of souvenirs. **Kenwyn House**, an example of fine Creole architecture in Francis Rachel Street, has been beautifully restored. The ground floor houses an impressive collection of jewellery in tanzanite and diamonds while the upper floor has Seychelles goodies for sale as well as other upmarket souvenirs all advertised at duty-free prices. Paintings by local artists are on view.

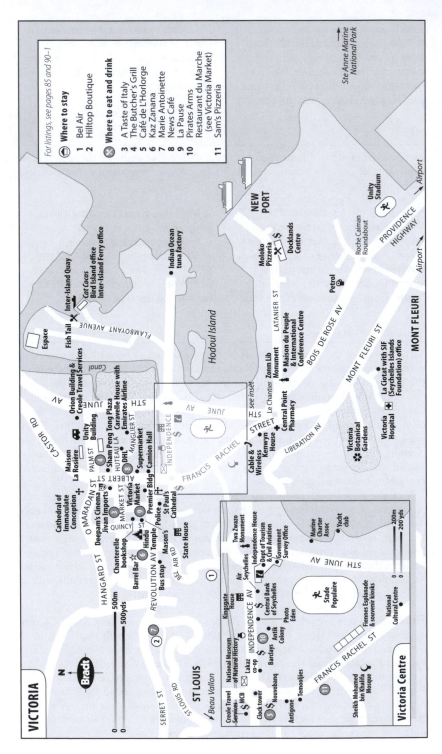

VICTORIA

For listings, see pages 85 and 90–1

Where to stay
1 Bel Air
2 Hilltop Boutique

Where to eat and drink
3 A Taste of Italy
4 The Butcher's Grill
5 Café de L'Horloge
6 Kaz Zanana
7 Marie Antoinette
8 News Café
9 La Pause
10 Pirates Arms
Restaurant du Marche (see Victoria Market)
11 Sam's Pizzeria

Ste Anne Marine National Park

NEW PORT

Unity Stadium

Airport

PROVIDENCE HIGHWAY

Roche Caiman Roundabout

Airport

MONT FLEURI

Moloko Pizzeria

Docklands Centre

Petrol

LATANIER ST

BOIS DE ROSE AV

MONT FLEURI ST

La Ciotat with SIF (Seychelles Islands Foundation) office

Victoria Hospital

Maison du Peuple & International Conference Centre

Zonm Lib Monument

Le Chantier

Victoria Botanical Gardens

LIBERATION AV

Central Point Pharmacy

Kenwyn House

Cable & Wireless

FRANCIS RACHEL STREET

see inset

5TH JUNE AV

INDEPENDENCE AV

Indian Ocean tuna factory

Hodoul Island

Inter-Island Quay

Cat Cocos Bird Island office Inter-Island Ferry office

FLAMBOYANT AVENUE

Fish Tail

Espace

Canal

Orion Building & Creole Travel Services

Caravelle House with Emirates Airline

Sham Peng Tong Plaza

HUTEAU LA

DHL

Supermarket

MANGLIER ST

ALBERT ST

JUNE AV

5TH

Unity Building

Maison La Rosière

PALM ST

Cathedral of Immaculate Conception

Deepam's Cinema

Jivan Imports

O MARADAN ST

Chanterelle bookshop

Hindu Temple

REVOLUTION AV

Barrel Bar

Mason's

BEL AIR RD

State House

Bus stop

Police

St Paul's Cathedral

Premier Bldg

Camion Hall

Victoria Market

MARKET ST

QUINCY ST

HANGARD ST

CASTOR RD

500m
500yds

N

Bradt

ST LOUIS RD

SERRET ST

Beau Vallon

ST LOUIS

Creole Travel Services

Clock tower

MCB

Nouvobanq

Antigone

Temooljies

National Museum of Natural History

Lakaz co-op

Barclays

Antik Colony

Photo Eden

Central Bank of Seychelles

INDEPENDENCE AV

Kingsgate House

Air Seychelles

Dept of Tourism & Civil Aviation

Government Survey Office

Independence House

Twa Zwazo Monument

Marine Charter Assoc

Yacht club

5TH JUNE AV

Stade Populaire

Fiennes Esplanade & souvenir kiosks

National Cultural Centre

FRANCIS RACHEL ST

Sheikh Mohamed bin Khalifa Mosque

Victoria Centre

200m
200yds

94

Between Barclays and the law court is **Lakaz Co-operative**, a small shop selling handmade curios and books. **Temooljies**, on Francis Rachel Street, is a general store and there is a small arcade next to it with a variety of shops. **Antigone** is the tiny bookshop in this arcade, with a wide selection of books dealing with the Seychelles. The new spacious branch of Antigone, **Chanterelle**, is located in Quincy Street, also with a wide range of books.

Camion Hall, on Albert Street, is a shopping arcade incorporating several outlets with a wide variety of souvenirs. **Kreol d'Or** sells beautiful, high-quality, gold jewellery incorporating many local subjects like the coco de mer palm, tortoises and dolphins. **Codevar**, a non-profit organisation promoting Seychelles handicrafts, has a shop in the arcade, and all items are genuine local crafts made from Seychelles natural products. They include bags and hats made from palm leaf fibres, coconut jewellery and ornaments, bright island-style clothing and postcards.

Beyond Camion Hall, **Seychelles Trading Company (STC)** offers all the usual supermarket fare. Foodstuffs are imported from Australia, New Zealand, Singapore, Pakistan and South Africa, so prices are generally high. **Jivan Imports**, a little further down the street opposite the **Habib Bank**, is a well-preserved old Creole-style building resounding with character. The store sells fabrics and clothing and the copious wares hang from the ceiling and line the walls. Opposite Jivan's, the **Sham Peng Tong Plaza** with the **Bank of Baroda** on the ground floor also has a variety of small shops selling a wide range of Chinese bazaar-type goods.

OTHER PRACTICALITIES

Banks Several of the major banks have branches in Mahé and the opening hours are generally 08.30–14.30 Monday–Friday, 08.30–11.30 Saturday.

$ **Barclays** Opposite the Natural History Museum on Independence Av, with a convenient ATM.

$ **Central Bank of Seychelles** The large, modern, glass-fronted building is opposite Kingsgate Hse.

BAZARS

Pop-up *bazars* (markets) occur on certain days of the week where stalls sell fresh fruit and vegetables with loads of coconuts, avocados and papayas; there are souvenirs aplenty in the form of local arts and crafts; barbecues are set up offering grilled fish, kebabs, chicken and sausages, and other local delicacies like curried octopus are available. There are always local musicians creating a lively Creole ambience. They are frequented by Seychellois who love a good party and it's a great place to mingle with the locals and get a taste of the Seychelles lifestyle. However, they are a little unpredictable, so it is advisable to check with the locals or the newspaper to see when they are on.

Bazar Labrin Bel Ombre; ⏱ 16.00–20.30 every Wed & the last Sat of the month. The stalls are under tall shady trees almost next to the beach, by the Savoy Hotel (page 85). Get a take-away & sit on the beach for a tasty, inexpensive supper!

Bazar Ovan Roche Copra, Baie Lazare; ⏱ 11.00–18.00 last Sun of the month. In the quieter part of Mahé, it has a beachy, countryside atmosphere with stunning scenery & a wide range of food to sample.

Bazar Victoria Near the clock tower in central Victoria; ⏱ 16.00–21.00 every Fri.

$ Mauritius Commercial Bank (MCB) Albert St, on the corner opposite the post office.

$ Nouvobanq Victoria Hse, corner of Francis Rachel St & State Hse Rd, diagonally opposite the post office.

Post, telephone and internet

The **post office** (🕐 *08.00–16.00 Mon–Fri, 08.00–noon Sat*) is on the corner of Independence Avenue and Francis Rachel Street opposite the clock tower and is an old, granite building. Phonecards are on sale here. It costs SR8 to send a postcard anywhere in the world and the colourful stamps depict the remarkable scenery and natural history of the islands. There is a special philately counter that sells sets of stamps for collectors (see box, below).

Cable & Wireless is close to Kenwyn House on Francis Rachel Street where telephone and internet services are available (🕐 *07.30–16.30 daily*). International and local phonecards are available. A starter pack for your mobile phone will cost SR50 which gives you SR25 of airtime and you can then add as much credit as you need.

The small, independent internet shops open up and close down a few months later so by the time you visit, the ones described might not exist anymore. However, Seychellois people are so helpful that you will soon be directed to the closest one. The prices are pretty much standard at about SR15 for 15 minutes.

STAMPS OF THE SEYCHELLES

The first post office opened in Victoria on 11 December 1861 as a sub-branch of the Port Louis post office in Mauritius. It was not until 5 April 1890 that the first set of stamps was issued in the Seychelles, and this set comprised eight stamps with values from two to 16 cents. Reportedly, parcels less than 1.5kg in weight cost two rupees and 22 cents to send by sea mail to any British destination. The Seychelles was a remote and exotic location and the stamps became valuable to collectors. To add to the rarity of the stamps there were dye changes, overprints, surcharges and value changes. Further, the value of many of the stamps was enhanced as they were only in use for a short period before they were withdrawn. As the English monarchs died, the stamp faces changed, but in some cases not until a year or more later. Edward VII's face did not appear on a Seychelles stamp until 18 months after Queen Victoria's death, and two years would elapse after his death before George V had his face depicted on a Seychelles stamp. The Silver Jubilee set issued in 1935 caused a furore when it was discovered that some stamps showed an extra flagpole on Windsor Castle! The random deviants fetched prices way above their value. The next set of stamps issued for the coronation of King George VI sold for such incredibly high prices that the government was able to fund some reclamation work in Victoria. The first photogravure pictorial stamps, depicting typical Seychelles subjects, were issued in 1938, and some of these showed errors and retouching and became sought after by philatelists.

Over the years the natural heritage of the Seychelles has been used to illustrate many of the stamps. Stamps are often issued in commemorative blocks with each set surrounded by an illustrated margin. The outer islands, Zil Elwannyen Sesel, had their own sets of stamps issued from 1980. They could be purchased in faraway places like Aldabra and Farquhar and became very valuable. The first set of these had five two-rupee stamps, each depicting a different type of coral, and the entire set joined together illustrated a coral garden.

Doubleclick (⏰ *08.00–21.00*) is situated on the ground floor of Maison La Rosière on Palm Street, not far from the bus terminal, where videos can be hired and snacks and soft drinks are reasonably priced. **Cyberwave Internet Bureau** is on Francis Rachel Street (⏰ *09.00–13.00 & 14.00–16.30 Mon–Fri, 09.00–noon Sat*). **The Net Internet Bureau** is on the ground floor of Sham Peng Tong Plaza, Albert Street (⏰ *08.00–13.00 & 14.00–17.00 Mon–Fri, 08.30–13.00 Sat*). Next door is Trinity House with **AirTel** at street level.

Photography Photo **Eden Kodak Express** is near the Pirates Arms and can download your digital photos onto a CD or make prints. **Kim Koon** is across the road in Kingsgate House and they can also make a CD and prints from your digital camera. Camera batteries and various films are sometimes available but it is wise to travel with adequate supplies of your own favourite brands. The same applies to cards for digital cameras; it is best to take all you need with you plus an extra card for your camera.

DISCOVERING VICTORIA

THE CLOCK TOWER The clock tower is the focal point of the town and stands in the middle of the important intersection of Independence Avenue and Francis Rachel Street (Francis Rachel was the first Seychellois soldier to die in the 1977 coup). The silver-painted clock is a replica of that on London's Vauxhall Bridge Road. It arrived in the port in Mahé in 1903. As the clock was being unloaded, the pendulum accidentally fell into the water and was never recovered. Although a new one was made, the clock never chimed, and seldom displayed the correct time. As a millennium treat, a new mechanism was installed, and a local businessman commented: 'Its soul is full of memories, it gave freely the time to everyone, to work, play, think or just do nothing.' The clock tower is a good starting point for setting out to explore Victoria on foot.

INDEPENDENCE AVENUE This tree-lined boulevard runs from the clock tower away from the mountain towards the ocean and it is here that banks, restaurants, travel companies and assorted shops and offices are located.

The old **Law Court** building on the opposite corner to the post office is elegantly reminiscent of the colonial era. Under the shady trees is a small statue of Queen Victoria, and on the other side of the building is a bust of Pierre Poivre from Mauritius, who was responsible for establishing the first spice gardens on Mahé. The building was closed at the time of writing as it is in the process of being renovated, and the National History Museum and the Seychelles tourist information office will be relocating there.

A little further down from the post office on the same side of Independence Avenue is the **National Museum of Natural History** (⏰ *08.30–16.30 Mon–Thu, 08.30–noon Fri/Sat; admission SR15*). It was originally the Carnegie Library and is now a national monument. The entrance steps are flanked by a replica of a large, toothy crocodile on one side and a sad-looking dugong on the other. It is a small, but interesting, museum with historical and cultural exhibits as well as several of environmental interest that inform the visitor about the various ecosystems of the Seychelles. A collection of paintings by Marianne North is on permanent display in the upstairs gallery.

If you're in need of refreshments try the **Pirates Arms** (page 91). In the nearby arcade you will find a Barclays ATM and various shops including Photo Eden, Maki

Despite a relatively short period of human settlement, extending over only two centuries, the Seychelles does have some interesting artefacts. Since the introduction, in 1980, of the National Monuments Act, which protects objects of architectural, archaeological or historical interest, about 30 structures have been proclaimed as national monuments. In fact, in terms of the act, any building, grave, or structure erected or used before 1900 must remain undisturbed. Most of the declared national monuments are located on Mahé, though the Roman Catholic churches on La Digue and Praslin, the plantation houses on Silhouette, Farquhar and La Digue, and the doctor's house on Curieuse, are on the list. The granite boulders at L'Union Estate on La Digue are the only natural feature to be declared a national monument.

The original Stone of Possession, initially placed on the hillside in present-day Victoria by the French in 1756, is now lodged in the National Museum. It did, however, survive an unsolicited round trip to Europe when a visiting French general took it away to present it to the Paris Museum. Also in the National Museum is the small original statue of Queen Victoria which was unveiled in 1897 to mark her diamond jubilee. A replica is located above the Jubilee Fountain, in front of the Law Court building which dates back to 1887.

The State House and the cemetery in its grounds where several colonial administrators are buried also constitute national monuments. The most prominent tomb is that of the last French commandant, Queau de Quincy, who died in 1827. Other national monuments in Victoria include St Paul's Anglican Cathedral, the priests' residence at the Catholic Cathedral of the Immaculate Conception, the Bel Air cemetery, the Botanical Gardens, Freedom Square, La Bastille, the Maison du Peuple, the bust of Pierre Poivre and the Bicentennial Monument (Twa Zwazo) with its three crescents symbolising the African, Asian and European origins of the Seychellois people.

Probably the best-known monument is the Victoria clock tower, which was intended as a memorial to Queen Victoria. However, as the Seychelles became a Crown Colony within a few weeks of its unveiling in 1903, the clock tower has become more accepted as a symbol of the gradual advance of the Seychelles to independence than a memorial to a dead queen. It regularly gets a coat of silver paint!

selling T-shirts, and Antik Colony which sells classy Seychellois cotton and linen clothing. Public toilets are located in the arcade behind the Pirates Arms.

Capital City across the road houses the BMI and Barclays banks as well as a moneychanger on the ground floor. **Kingsgate House** contains several travel-related companies including 7°South, Kenya Airways and Bunson Travel. **Independence House** is the large building on the corner of Independence Avenue and 5th June Avenue that houses a variety of offices, shops and the Seychelles tourist information office, although this is moving to the Law Court. The Government Survey Office that sells topographic maps and the Air Seychelles booking office are also located here. At street level there is a small fountain, and a snack counter that sells samosas, sandwiches, pies and soft drinks. Upstairs there are several government offices including tourism and civil aviation.

The white **Bicentennial Monument** on the roundabout at the intersection of Independence Avenue and 5th June Avenue is known locally as **Twa Zwazo** ('Three

Birds') and symbolises the unity of the Seychellois heritage – Africa, Asia and Europe. The enormous sculpture is the work of Lorenzo Appiani, an artist of Italian descent. **Oceangate House**, a large office block near the roundabout, accommodates the social service departments and a dental clinic. It also has the 777 Amusement Centre with bar and 190 slot machines (⏰ *10.00–02.00 daily*).

Independence Avenue continues beyond the roundabout towards the sea (keep left after the Amusement Centre) and passes the **Indian Ocean tuna factory** *en route* to the inter-island quay, from where the schooners and *Cat Cocos* catamarans depart.

THE INTER-ISLAND QUAY *Cat Cocos* (see pages 63 and 82–3), various inter-island schooners and MY *Pegasos* depart from this quay. Mason's Travel and Creole Travel Services are represented here and there are booking offices for the ferry as well as for Bird Island Lodge, from where you can make your reservation to visit this amazing seabird breeding colony. Taxis usually await the arrival of *Cat Cocos* from Praslin. A spacious casual restaurant, Fish Tail, at the quayside offers light meals, snacks and a variety of drinks. It's a good place to sit and wait for your ferry.

Beyond the quay, a new road continues to the latest developments on part of the reclaimed land. A large pink building, Espace, houses the headquarters of the Seychelles Tourism Board and Creole Travel Services, among others.

5TH JUNE AVENUE This wide road, built on reclaimed land, links the two roundabouts of Twa Zwazo and Le Chantier. Overlooking the harbour by the **Marine Charter Association** (page 70) is a somewhat scruffy-looking restaurant and bar which is buzzing on Friday nights! Taxi boats for several island resorts use the jetty for transfers. **Hodoul Island** is a tiny piece of land in the middle of the yacht basin, covered in casuarina trees and egrets. It is named after Jean François Hodoul, a 17th-century corsair.

The **National Cultural Centre** is a grand-looking building on the right before the roundabout. The entrance is in Francis Rachel Street (page 101).

Le Chantier roundabout has a striking monument with four huge, white sailfish rising out of a fountain. The French name is a reminder that this was once a boatbuilding yard on the shoreline. Several roads lead off this roundabout.

CHEMIN LATANIER This is the road leading down to the **New Port**, the deep-water harbour where visiting cruise ships and other large vessels moor. The **Maison du Peuple** on the right-hand side of Chemin Latanier is a modern building housing the offices of the Seychelles People's Progressive Front. Dominating the gardens in front is a large statue of a man, arms held high, escaping from a broken chain. Recently transplanted from its original home on 5th June Avenue, it is the **Zonm Lib Monument** celebrating freedom and liberation from colonialism. The adjoining **International Conference Centre** has a main auditorium that can seat up to 600 delegates, while the various smaller rooms can handle 150 to 225 delegates. For bookings contact the Ministry of Local Government, Sports and Culture (*PO Box 92;* ✆ *4324353;* e *iccs@seychelles.net*). Nearer the port is the STC depot, fire station and the bright-orange **Docklands Centre** which houses a supermarket, ATM, Moloko Restaurant and pizzeria. Island Trading and Seychelles gift shop are located around the corner especially for passengers and crew of cruise vessels.

AVENUE DE BOIS ROSE AND PROVIDENCE HIGHWAY Avenue de Bois Rose is a relatively small road leading off Le Chantier roundabout and becomes Providence Highway; this is the quickest way to the airport (page 109).

The Botanical Gardens were started in 1901 by Paul Rivaltz du Pont. As director, he made two sorties to the East where he collected many specimens for the gardens. They were chiefly crop plants but he also brought back many ornamental shrubs and trees. The gardens became part of the Department of Agriculture and du Pont became Director of Agriculture. In this position he was able to maintain his interest in the gardens until he retired in 1934 after making a significant contribution to the botanical knowledge of the Seychelles.

The 6ha park, besides being a retreat from the bustle of Victoria, has a fascinating array of plants and houses the Ministry of Health and the Department of Environment. There is an impressive collection of tropical palms, including the six Seychelles endemic species. A group of bottle palms are on the left near the entrance and Pritchard palms and coco de mer palms flank the long driveway. A cluster of endemic screw pines (*Pandanus hornei*) is at the top end of the gardens close to the cafeteria, which seems to be continually under renovation! Several streams trickle down the hillside and the lawn at the top of the drive leads to a pond with huge-leafed *Alocasias* and water lilies. The cannonball tree (*Couroupita guianensis*) has pink flowers on the tree trunk, and the large round fruits resemble cannonballs. Nutmeg, cinnamon and allspice trees are dotted about, and there is also a small collection of trees from Aldabra. An orchid house, now in a state of neglect, at the top end of the gardens houses a collection of exotic orchids from all over the world. A large pen is home to a group of giant Aldabra tortoises.

See if you can find the plaque commemorating the environmental time capsule that was buried in the gardens on 3 June 1994 and is due to be opened in 2044. Two other monuments can be found; a stone bench dedicated to Mr P R Du Pont and a Japan–Seychelles Friendship Monument.

CHEMIN MONT FLEURI This road also leads off Le Chantier roundabout, and is the road to take to the hospital and the Botanical Gardens. The road continues through residential areas to the airport, and beyond to the south of Mahé. **National House**, on the upper side of the road, houses some government offices. **Liberation Avenue** is a narrow, little road winding up the mountainside of Victoria, and which meets up with Bel Air Road leading to Chemin Sans Souci. A private dental clinic is almost opposite this junction.

The **Botanical Gardens** (☏ *4670558; ⊕ 08.00–16.00 daily; admission SR100*) have a good selection of Seychelles indigenous plants as well as numerous introduced species. A map of the gardens, which includes a list of most of the plants, is available at the entrance kiosk next to the car park. Various souvenirs are available and this is a good place to pick up leaflets describing the various walks on Mahé. This is one of the best places to photograph both male and female coco de mer palms as they are out in the open and in good light. Notice the large coco de mer planted by HRH Duke of Edinburgh during his brief visit to the Seychelles in 1956. Further up the gentle slope is a large pen housing a collection of Aldabra tortoises, but it will cost you an extra SCR50 to feed them inside their enclosure. The offices of the Department of Environment are located in the Botanical Gardens. Toilets are on the left of the main path towards the top of the driveway. A colony of fruit bats roosts in the tall trees behind the closed cafeteria building.

Victoria Hospital, next to the tranquil gardens, has modern facilities to cater for most health problems (pages 57–8). **Aarti Chambers**, an office block, is opposite the entrance to the hospital. La Ciotat Building, in front of the hospital, houses the offices of the **Seychelles Islands Foundation (SIF)**, which can be found on the ground floor (☏ *4371735*; page 136).

FRANCIS RACHEL STREET
This road connects the centre of town with Le Chantier traffic circle. On the corner is a large multi-storey pink building housing a dental clinic and the **Central Point Pharmacy** (⊕ *08.00–18.00 Mon–Fri, 08.00–14.00 Sat; after hours* ☏ *4225574*). **Kenwyn House** (*www.kenwynhouse.com*) is on the left if you are walking from Le Chantier towards town, and is a wonderful example of a typical colonial Creole house built in about 1868. Now a national monument, it has been painstakingly renovated and has become a duty-free shop selling beautiful jewellery, mainly diamonds and tanzanite and with an interesting display showing the relative sizes of famous diamonds. A shop selling sophisticated Seychelles souvenirs is located upstairs and paintings by Seychellois artists are on display on both levels. Cable & Wireless, with public telephones and internet access, is conveniently located next door.

The **National Cultural Centre** (⊕ *08.30–16.30 Mon/Tue & Thu/Fri, 09.00–13.00 Sat; admission free (SR15 for foreigners)*) has an impressive façade facing 5th June Avenue but the main entrance to this imposing, modern brick and glass building is in Francis Rachel Street. It houses the national, public and reference libraries, national archives and an art gallery. The **National History Museum** is currently closed and is being relocated to the old Law Court on the corner of Independence Avenue and Francis Rachel Street. It has a variety of artefacts of historical interest including the Stone of Possession, which was originally placed on the island as a formal act by France in 1756 as well as photographic portraits of all the British governors of the Seychelles.

Souvenir kiosks line the right-hand side of the road along the tree-shaded **Fiennes Esplanade**, which was once on the seafront. Only a few are operating, but there you will find colourful *pareos* and shirts, hats made from coconut fibre, and all sorts of other knick-knacks. Resist buying the shells as many are not sustainably harvested out of the sea and many are not even from the Seychelles. Behind the kiosks, on a lane leading to 5th June Avenue, is a row of boutiques, the Carrefour art gallery and a small café. **Stade Populaire** is also located behind the kiosks as is a pay car park. This stadium is the venue for large events like football matches, holiday parades and school sports events.

The **Sheikh Mohamed bin Khalifa Mosque** is opposite the kiosks, and there are still a few typical old, iron, Creole-style buildings with little, shuttered windows jutting out of the high-pitched roofs. Maison Suleman, Qatar Airways, Temooljies, Antigone bookshop and Sam's Pizzeria are all located in this area of Victoria.

The large building on the corner of Francis Rachel Street and State House Road is **Victoria House**, home to Nouvobanq (with ATM and foreign exchange). Upstairs is a restaurant, Café de L'Horlorge (page 90), which looks over the clock tower onto Independence Avenue; light snacks and full meals are available. Over the road is **Creole Travel Services** with helpful staff who can arrange a wide variety of tours in Mahé and the other islands.

STATE HOUSE ROAD
This small road leads up to **State House**, the home of the president, which is closed to the public. A square granite building located near the driveway entrance to the house was inaugurated by Sir Ernest Bickham Sweet-

Escott in 1902, and was utilised as offices for the various governors until 1934. After that it was used by government departments, and served as the National Library for many years before becoming a museum and then, later, the Appeal Court. It was being renovated at the time of writing.

From the car park in State House Road, a walled alley leads into Revolution Avenue between the police station and the Anglican cathedral. It crosses the St Louis River and you can often see cattle egrets and green-backed herons fishing in the clear waters.

ALBERT STREET Named after Queen Victoria's husband, this street is a continuation of Francis Rachel Street on the other side of the clock tower. To discover more of Victoria continue along Albert Street in a northerly direction, passing the Ministry of Finance and Mauritius Commercial Bank (with ATM). **Freedom Square**, the large grassy area behind the taxi rank, was formed during the avalanche of 1862 when part of the St Louis hillside slid onto Victoria, killing 75 inhabitants. It was originally known as Gordon Square, after Sir Charles Gordon of Khartoum fame, and the present name came into use after the political rallies that were held there during the revolutionary period of the mid 1970s. A convenient small parking area is located behind the taxi rank, though is usually jam-packed.

Almost next to the taxi rank you will find the **Seychelles Trading Company (STC)**, a fairly large supermarket with a wide range of groceries. **Camion Hall** is a shopping arcade next to the taxi rank full of souvenir shops and a bureau de change. Opposite is the **Premier Building** with several floors of offices. On the ground floor, with an entrance in Revolution Avenue, is the popular Love Nut Nightclub. Further along, after the Market Street and Huteau Lane traffic lights, is the fascinating Jivan Imports, a colourfully painted shop in the authentic, old Creole style filled with fabric hanging from the rafters, soft furnishings, clothes, souvenirs and postcards. It is reported to be one of the oldest buildings in Victoria. **Deepam's Cinema**, the only one in Mahé, is a little further along the road. On the other side of the road are Baroda and Barclays banks (with ATMs) and Trinity House (with News Café upstairs).

HUTEAU LANE Huteau Lane leads off to the right, via a series of bends and a name change, to 5th June Avenue. **Da Ciro Pizzeria** and the **DHL offices** are found here before Huteau Lane becomes Manglier Street. On the left, approaching 5th June Avenue, a large building, **Caravelle House**, houses many offices including the Seychelles International Business Authority (SIBA), the Seychelles Investment Bureau (SIB), Emirates Airlines and a branch of the MCB, with ATM.

MARKET STREET This is the heart of town where the residents do their daily shopping. It is largely closed to traffic and always bustling with activity. The clothing and music shops are here, and if you want some local Creole music, look out for CDs by Jean Marc Volcy or Jany Letourdie who are two of the local stars. Coin and card public telephones are located in the middle of this pedestrian walkway. **Sunstroke Shop** with the **George Camille Gallery** upstairs have a collection of colourful clothing in pure silks and cottons. The paintings on display are generally in brilliant, vibrant colours depicting fish and birds as well as the life of the Seychellois.

The **Victoria Market** was rebuilt and opened again in June 1999. It is still known as the Sir Selwyn Selwyn-Clarke Market, named after the last British governor of the Seychelles in the late 1940s. The colourful market has a distinctly oriental look about it, with a bright turquoise pagoda-style roof and red supporting columns with splashes of yellow and dark blue. An enormous mango tree shades the central square, while frangipani trees with fragrant white flowers scent the air. On the lower level, the fish market has a wide selection of fresh fish including *ton* (tuna), *makrou dou* (mackerel), *vyey* (groupers), *zob* (jobfish), *karang* (trevally) and *bourswa* (snappers). There are always several cattle egrets, locally known as *Madanm Paton,* hanging around the fish, hopping on the counters, and doing a good job of cleaning up all the bits and pieces. Stalls with colourful vegetables, tropical fruits, exotic herbs and tantalising spices are spread out under umbrellas in the central part of the market and even flow out into the street. Spices are very important in Creole cuisine. Fresh ginger and turmeric (often labelled saffron) are readily available, bottles of hot chillies add a dash of colour, and cinnamon quills and vanilla pods complete the exotic mix. If you can find it, the pure vanilla essence distilled on La Digue is a gourmet's delight. Still on the lower level, Rosie's Flower Shop sells sprays of orchids and huge bunches of fragrant roses out of galvanised buckets. Upstairs are some tiny shops selling touristy things like colourful *pareos*, paintings and coconut lamps with shades made out of coconut fibres. It is an excellent place to collect gifts and souvenirs. There is also a small café upstairs from which you can observe the hustle and bustle of the market; Saturdays are particularly frenetic!

OLIVIER MARADAN STREET At the end of Albert Street there is an intersection, with Olivier Maradan Street leading off to the left. The stone **Catholic Cathedral of the Immaculate Conception** which was built in 1900 is located here. The grand, almost Spanish-looking building to the left of the cathedral is the priestly residence and is a national monument.

PALM STREET At the Albert Street intersection, Palm Street leads off to the right towards the bus station. Doubleclick internet café and the S&D Supermarket selling fresh meat and vegetables can be found on the ground floor of Maison La Rosière on the left, just beyond the intersection. Palm Street eventually meets up with the continuation of 5th June Avenue (with a traffic light, the only one in the Seychelles!). **Orion Building** on the corner houses Behram's Pharmacy, Seychelles Savings Bank (with ATM) and a very large supermarket. This is a busy part of town, particularly during peak hours. On the right, the large, new, pink multi-storey Unity House extends almost the length of the street and houses an eclectic mix of businesses; a pharmacy, Vision Care, Doubleclick money exchange, Lifestyle shop and The Butcher's Grill Restaurant (page 91).

BENEZET STREET This is a short alley behind the market that connects Revolution Avenue with Market Street. The **PRG Boulangerie** (🕐 *08.30–16.00*) is a popular place, and at lunchtime you can hardly get inside this bakery as so many people crowd in to buy their favourite snacks – they are usually sold out by 14.00. Pizzas, quiches, fish and vegetable samosas, sandwiches, rolls and sweet coconut cakes are all available.

REVOLUTION AVENUE This is the beginning of the main road going over to Beau Vallon and starts at the Albert Street intersection (with traffic lights!). Up the hill is a good place to catch the bus to Beau Vallon or Glacis – but not at peak times, when it won't stop. The first building on the left is the **Anglican Cathedral of St Paul**. It was built in 1857 and, over the years, the small church was enlarged and became a cathedral in 1973. It was completely rebuilt and the new cathedral was consecrated on 25 April 2004. It has lovely stained-glass windows depicting Seychellois life.

The **police station** is located adjacent to the alley that runs from Revolution Avenue to State House Road. **Mason's Travel** is located diagonally opposite, and a maze of Indian shops can be found in a passageway leading off the street next to Mason's. The Bel Air Road leads off to the left. The Barrel Bar discotheque (⊕ *21.00–03.00 Thu–Sun*) is opposite the bus shelter, as is Kaz Zanana 'Pink Salt' Restaurant and gallery (page 91). This attractive wooden building is owned by the artist, Georges Camille, whose works are on permanent exhibition and are for sale. Marie-Antoinette Restaurant (page 91) is further up the hill on the right as Revolution Avenue curves to the left to become St Louis Road.

QUINCY STREET Leading off to the right from Revolution Avenue is the one-way Quincy Street with the brightly painted **Arul Mihu Navasakthi Vinayagar Hindu Temple** (⊕ *06.00–noon & 17.00–21.00 daily*) on the left and next to it the new **Quincy Mall**. On the right, the Creole Spirit Building houses the air-conditioned **Chanterelle bookshop**, with an excellent selection of Seychelles literature. Stop to look at the stunning, stained-glass door at the entrance to the building. There is a convenient parking area here which is next to the side entrance to the market.

HALF-DAY WALK For details of a half-day walking tour of Victoria, see page 117.

DISCOVERING MAHÉ   *Map, pages 78–9*

Mahé is an island of secluded beaches, long stretches of glistening, white sands and tiny, picturesque coves fringed with tall trees, shady palms and framed by impressive granite boulders. Take the opportunity to explore them and find your own patch of paradise for the day. Soak up the sun-kissed feeling, cool off in the inviting clear, blue water and savour the delights of the underwater world. At certain times of the year, seaweed and seagrasses may be washed ashore on some of the beaches. It is usually cleared away but, if not, try another secluded cove.

Don't be lulled into thinking that only the beaches of the Seychelles are to be enjoyed. Take a walk in the mountains, experience the profusion of luxuriant forest greenery, look at plants that exist nowhere else on earth, and be enticed to reach the summit to gaze upon the perfect panorama. If you are after action and not romantic seclusion, a number of resorts offer thrilling watersports and other activities.

Mahé with its luscious beauty is a magnet to artists of all persuasions so visit a sculptor's studio or an artist's gallery and take home a lasting and valuable memento. In between the sun, sand and exploring there will be time to try the local Creole cuisine at a range of restaurants and local stalls. Wherever you go on Mahé you will never feel swamped by huge numbers of tourists, nor will you be trapped in lengthy traffic jams although the locals do complain about 'the traffic'.

THE NORTHWEST From Victoria, a road follows the coast around the northern tip of Mahé, a circular route of 20km. However, the quickest way to Beau Vallon is to travel along Revolution Avenue and over to the other side on St Louis Road.

St Louis Road continues from Revolution Avenue and swings to the left, passing the Marie-Antoinette Restaurant (page 91) and the insignificant Serret Road. The Chinese embassy is an impressive white-and-blue-tiled building a little further along on the left in the St Louis area. The narrow road with several hairpin bends passes through residential areas enveloped in lush, tropical vegetation, and there are expansive views across Victoria to the islands in the Ste Anne Marine

National Park. The road descends steeply to Beau Vallon with a petrol station on the left.

Before this, a dark, forested road branches off to the left and ends at **Le Niol** where little houses are hidden amongst the trees. The Russian embassy is located on this road and, from there, a very narrow road actually winds round the hillside and connects with the Sans Souci Road – an interesting route to bypass Victoria if you are not afraid of heights!

Beau Vallon and around (*Map, page 106*)

As the road descends towards Beau Vallon, it forks at the police station with the left side leading to Bel Ombre and the right to Beau Vallon and Glacis. Beau Vallon Beach is a glorious 3km crescent of gleaming, white sand fringed with *takamaka* trees and coconut palms, and defined by chunky granite boulders at each end. The idyllic bay is sheltered from the southeast trades. Hotels, guesthouses, restaurants, dive centres and souvenir shops nestle in the verdant vegetation, and all share the view of Beau Vallon Bay and the enticing Silhouette Island on the horizon. It is easy to reach the beach from both the Bel Ombre and Glacis roads.

The **Bel Ombre road** leads off to the left in a westerly direction. Several hotels are on the seaward side of the road and a few guesthouses are situated on the hillside. A large residential area spreads out on the slopes away from the beach. There is a community centre, a large health centre, a lovely old church and cemetery, a few shops and a tiny harbour used by local fishermen and increasingly by tourist operators.

Berjaya Beau Vallon Bay Beach Resort and Casino (page 86) is the first hotel on the right after the road divides. Live bands perform here regularly and there is a large swimming pool in the gardens adjoining the beach. Dive Seychelles is located here, and the **Augerine Small Hotel** (page 86) is down the same road, on the right.

The grounds of the brand new, sprawling Bel Ombre Hotel spread to **Le Méridien Fisherman's Cove**, a large hotel with a gracious ambience and lovely views across the bay (page 86). The area beyond the hotel is Bel Ombre ('lovely shadow'). The **Tequila Boom Nite Club** [106 E3] (⏲ *22.00 until late Sat/Sun*) and **La Faya Bar** [106 E3] (⏲ *18.00 until late daily*) are located nearby. There are several small accommodation establishments in this area, including **Bel Ombre Holiday Villas**, **Daniella's Bungalows** (page 86) and **Marie Laure Suites**. On the hillside, the **Casadani Hotel** (page 87) probably has the best views of the bay and also offers a car-hire service.

The picturesque Bel Ombre fishing harbour, with its colourful collection of small fishing craft, has been expanded to the west to incorporate new facilities for the artisanal fishing fleet. The transfer vessel for Hilton Labriz on Silhouette departs from here.

A short way further along is the **remains of a local treasure hunt** [106 B4]. It is reputed that Le Vasseur, the notorious pirate of the 17th century, stashed away fabulous, plundered treasures in this area. The Cruise-Wilkins family has spent vast sums of money excavating around the rocks and surrounding shore, but to no avail. Le Vasseur's treasure trove still awaits discovery.

Building on this theme, the lime-green **Treasure Cove Hotel** (page 86) has recently opened on the slopes above the site with the **Olivier Le Vasseur Restaurant** (page 92) offering stunning views across the bay.

The road continues along the coast with several small general dealers, houses, a church, a school and a community centre. If you are staying in self-catering accommodation, call in at Harold's store as he has a wide selection of essential goodies. **La Scala Restaurant** (page 91), although looking a bit shabby, is one of Mahé's better

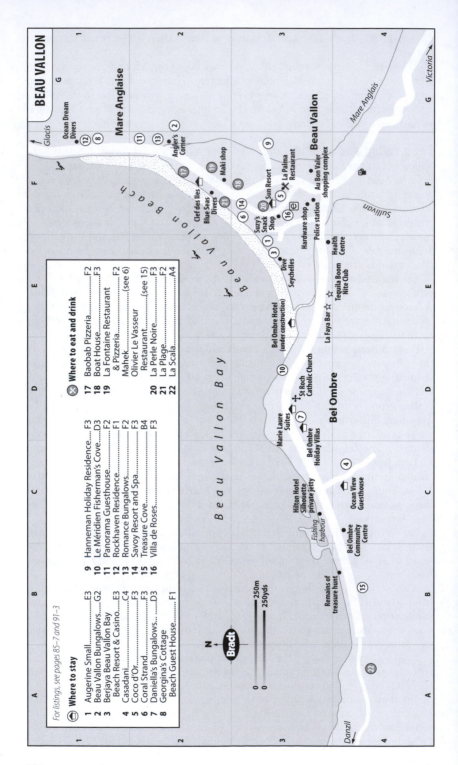

BEAU VALLON

Mare Anglaise

Beau Vallon Beach

Beau Vallon Bay

Bel Ombre

Beau Vallon

Mare Anglais

Victoria

Danzil

Bradt

Grande Soeur must have one of the loveliest beaches in the Seychelles (RS/STB) page 141

W&ONDERFUL
SEYCHELLES

top left   **Many of the islets within the Aldabra lagoon are** *champignons* — **limestone formations with a flat surface and a slender stalk** (LM) page 187

above left & right   **Within Praslin National Park, the Vallée de Mai is cool and shady and home to over 4,000 coco de mer palms** (GL/STB) pages 132–6

below   **Miniature paradise of Ile St Pierre, midway between Praslin and Curieuse, with a topknot of palms and a tiny beach only at low tide** (LM) page 172

top right Together with the surrounding ocean, the island of Curieuse forms the Curieuse Marine National Park, home to many endemic and indigenous plants and creatures (RS/STB) pages 170–2

right The Dauban family mausoleum on Silhouette is a copy of the Eglise de la Madeleine in Paris (LM) page 159

below Creole architecture is common on La Digue; this building in La Passe is typical of the bygone era (LM) page 150

top The Carnaval International de Victoria is an annual event with visitors from all over the world taking part in the festivities (CS/S) page 66

middle Local artworks are on display at the Café des Artes in Anse Volbert, Praslin (LM) page 140

bottom Mahé is home to workshops where replicas of historic ships are made using naval plans (S/A) page 110

above The three crescents of the Twa Zwazo bicentennial monument in downtown Victoria symbolise the African, Asian and European origins of the Seychellois people (LM) pages 98–9

right Exuberant dancing to live music is *de rigeur* during the Kreol Festival, held every year to celebrate traditional aspects of Creole life (IB/A) pages 24–5

below A roadside stall at Anse Boudin, Praslin, where you can pick up a T-shirt or a cold drink (LM) page 140

top left

Red-footed boobies (*Sula sula*) perch in mangrove trees on Cosmoledo (LM) page 41

middle left

The magpie robin (*Copsychus seychellarum*) an iconic bird of Seychelles that faced extinction but can now be found in small numbers on several islands (GL/STB) pages 38–9

below

A white fairy tern (*Gygis alba*) taking a fishy morsel to a nearby chick — these can be found on nearly all of the Seychelles islands (RS/STB) page 40

bottom

Coconut crab (*Birgus latro*) (LM) page 196

above Wright's gardenia (*Rothmania annae*) is endemic to Aride and has beautiful fragrant flowers and a small round fruit (LM) page 165

right The carnivorous endemic pitcher plant (*Nepenthes pervillei*) only grows on the granitic mountain slopes of Mahé and Silhouette (P/S) page 30

below The coco de mer palm (*Lodoicea maldivica*) has both a male plant (pictured right; SF) and a female plant with flowers and nuts (pictured left; LM) pages 134–5

above Snorkellers like these two off Bird Island are often rewarded with wonderful underwater sights (LM) pages 175–7

left Semicircle angelfish (*Pomecanthus semicirculatus*) among colourful soft corals are frequently encountered when snorkelling or diving (TB/STB) page 46

below Whale sharks (*Rhincodon typus*) spend a few months of the year in Seychelles waters, and these gentle giants can sometimes be seen on dive expeditions (TB/STB) page 48

restaurants, and is perched high above the road with fabulous sunset views through the tall palms. Parking for their clients is available off-road. The Bel Ombre bus route terminates at the restaurant and from here the road narrows, becoming quite steep as it continues as Danzil Road. There are a few houses and Batman Studio (complete with tame fruit bat!) before the road peters out. Two walks commence at this point: one is to Anse Major and the other is the Mare aux Cochons walk (page 119).

If you travel back to the police station and turn left, you will discover the rest of Beau Vallon. The **Au Bon Valer shopping complex** [106 F3] is located on the right and houses several shops as well as a supermarket, internet café and Barclays ATM. On the left, a narrow signposted road leads to the Coral Strand Hotel and the beach.

Nearby, **Villa de Roses** (page 87), a charming bed and breakfast and self-catering establishment, is set in pretty well-tended gardens. **Coco d'Or**, a small hotel (page 86), is only about 100m from the beach and houses La Palma Restaurant and Uncle Will's Pizzeria. **Suzy's Snack Shop** [106 F3], a little further on, is an excellent place to stop for a quick cold beer or an icy soft drink and a local snack, although it does not seem to have any pattern to its opening times – you are in luck if it is open. On the other side of the road you will find the **Sun Resort** which has the Sun Coco coffee bar and take-away, and further on, **La Perle Noire Restaurant** (page 91), which has a good reputation. There are several small car-hire companies located in this area including Millennium and Sylvie's. The **Coral Strand Hotel** (page 86) has undergone major refurbishment and now sports the Riva Boutique and Coral Asia Sushi Restaurant, as well as its well-established **Mahek Restaurant** (page 91) which specialises in Indian cuisine.

From the Coral Strand, the road narrows to become a paved pedestrian walkway alongside the beach through to the main road towards Glacis. All the fun of Bazar Labrin (see box, page 95) takes place here on Wednesdays and the last Saturday of the month from about 16.00 until 20.30 with freshly barbecued fish and local delicacies, lively music and many craft stalls. A few souvenir stalls are there throughout the week.

To continue your discovery of Mahé, you will have to backtrack to the main road near the police station and turn left. From here, the road to Glacis sweeps down towards the shore through lush forest. The enormous **Savoy Resort and Spa** (page 85), completed in 2014, occupies a large area on the right, and their Pescado and Grand Savoy restaurants are open to the public, as is the **Gecko Bar**. Opposite and up the hill is **Hanneman Holiday Residence** (page 87).

The main road then swings right along the coast and, as you reach the shoreline, stop to enjoy glorious Beau Vallon Beach. Fine white sands stretch out in both directions and Silhouette and North islands grace the horizon. Bel Ombre and Danzil are away in the greenery to the left, and Glacis is behind giant rocks on the right. Several shops and restaurants are found here. Almost on the beach, is **La Plage Restaurant** (page 91) with some tables on the sunny patio and the best views of the lovely bay and the two islands on the horizon. Over the road, the **Boat House** (pages 91–2) serves a remarkable evening Creole buffet with plenty of fresh fish and is also open for lunch. Next to this are several establishments including a Maki shop selling T-shirts and **La Fontaine Restaurant** which serves excellent pizzas (page 93). **Blue Seas Divers** [106 F2] operates out of a shop next to the **Baobab Pizzeria** (pages 92–3), a rustic restaurant with sandy floors and a large pizza oven. In fine weather and at low tide, tables may be put out on the beach. **Clef des Iles**, with four apartments, is located next door and **Teddy's Glass-Bottom Boat** (4261125; m 2511125; e teddysgbb@yahoo.com; prices start at €40) has a stand near here offering full- and half-day trips in his glass-bottomed boat. It is an easy way to admire the underwater world without getting wet. He will also take you snorkelling and swimming and offers a beach barbecue on the full-day tour. Over the road, **Angler's Corner** [106 F2] sells fishing tackle and offers fishing trips.

Next comes the area known as Mare Anglaise, where the Mare Anglaise River enters Beau Vallon Bay. **Romance Bungalows** (page 87) are tucked into the hillside across the road from the beach and offer bed and breakfast and self-catering options, and **Beau Vallon Bungalows** and **Panorama** (pages 86 and 87) provide bed and breakfast accommodation. **Georgina's Cottage Beach Guest House** (page 87) is a little further down the road next to the bus stop and has recently been refurbished, and the **Rockhaven Residence** (page 87) is at the end of Beau Vallon Beach. Further along the road you will find two small general stores that sell everything from beer to toiletries. **Ocean Dream Divers** [106 F1] have a smart office on the right-hand side of the road. Further on, there is the conspicuous **Big Blue Divers** (page 71) with the adjacent Anse Norwa self-catering holiday home, Divers Lodge B&B and Le Petit Payot guesthouse.

Glacis From here on, the area is known as Glacis (*glacis* is the name for the great, weathered granite slopes), and you will see mostly residential properties, a few small grocery stores and a few hotels.

Hilton Seychelles Northolme Resort and Spa (pages 85–6) has been completely rebuilt to the highest luxurious standards, retaining only the name as a reminder of its exciting past. It is one of the older hotels on Mahé with a history of colourful clients including writers and film stars like Ian Fleming, Noël Coward and David Niven; there is now even a secluded Ian Fleming beach! It has several restaurants open to the public including the fine-dining Les Cocotiers Restaurant and the Hilltop Restaurant with glorious views over the bay. Nearby, the **Sunset Beach Hotel** (page 86) is lovely after upgrading, and snorkelling directly from the beaches of these two hotels is easy.

The road hugs the rocky coastline and the scenery is gorgeous with the mountains, secluded beaches and turquoise water. **Yarrabee** self-catering establishment [78 D1], the **Bliss Hotel** and **Lounge8** (page 92) are located on the sea side of the road. At the northernmost tip of Mahé there is a tiny island, l'Ilot, which is no more than a bundle of rocks. North Point is a relatively undeveloped part of Mahé as the *glacis* hillside is steep and inhospitable. Once the terrain flattens out, Villa Koket self-catering apartments, the National Institute of Health and Social Studies and several small stores are located to the right.

Kreol Fleurage Parfums [79 E1] (\ *4241329;* e *info@kreolefleurage.com; www. kreolfleurage.com*) is well worth a short visit. Four specially blended perfumes are created here from ingredients typically found on the Indian Ocean islands, namely ylang ylang, vanilla, cinnamon and patchouli. The perfumes are bottled in tiny glass *flaçons*, beautifully encased in Seychelles hardwood, either *bois noir* or *calice du pape*. They are available from some boutiques as well as the airport duty-free shops. Their Monsoon range consists of a variety of neatly packaged island spices as well as an attractive Seychellois cookbook. Opposite the small **Manresa Hotel** [79 E2] a steep, rough road, only for intrepid explorers, leads up the mountain and across to Glacis. The **La Gogue Reservoir** [78 D2], which was opened in 1979, and used to store excess water from the Rochon Dam, is found here.

Continuing south towards Victoria, this area is known as Anse Etoile and there is a large shopping centre, police station, Golden Moon and Lucky House Chinese restaurants, and the Calypha Hotel. At Ma Constance, the changing face of Mahé is clearly visible as the land reclamation islands and several imposing wind turbines become very obvious. **Le Surmer Hotel and Restaurant** [79 E2] is located at Pointe Conan and at the roundabout, the road left leads to one of the new islands, **Ile Perseverance** [79 E2], which has been developed as a housing estate with amenities and an international school. The imposing new parliament building, **Lasanble Nasyonal Sesel (National Assembly)** and the **Palais de Justice** are prominent landmarks.

Returning to the main road, the northwest loop approaches the English River residential area of Victoria with good views across to Ste Anne Marine National Park. A shabby-looking national monument, **La Bastille** [79 E2], is near the town and houses some of the national archives.

THE SOUTHEAST To explore the southeast of Mahé, leave Victoria at Le Chantier and travel south along **Avenue de Bois Rose** as it links into **Providence Highway**, the only dual carriageway in the Seychelles. It has a speed limit of 80km/h and is about the only time you can get into fifth gear! The surrounding area is reclaimed land, and was named **Roche Caiman** after the crocodiles that used to inhabit the lagoon before the settlers arrived. The fairly new housing estate of the same name is conveniently situated for people working in town. A modern petrol station with car wash (even open on Sundays) is located near the roundabout with a large fountain. Adjacent is the Unity Sports Stadium and a road between them leads to the Ste Anne Resort jetty for transfers to the hotel.

A bit further along the highway, there is a small bird sanctuary incorporating some remaining mangroves near the offices of **Nature Seychelles** [79 E3] (☏ 4601100; e *nature@seychelles.net; www.natureseychelles.org*; ⊕ *08.00–16.00 Mon–Fri; admission to Roche Caiman Sanctuary SR25 for foreigners*), a vibrant NGO headed by Nirmal Jivan Shah that deals with a range of diverse conservation issues and environmental education. Their Heritage Garden is a quiet place to wander around and see the local plants; the birdlife can also be interesting.

Along Providence Highway most of the development can be seen on the sea side of the road, as a shallow lagoon runs the length of the road on the landward side. At the next traffic circle, the large, newly developed **Eden Island** with a multitude of striking red roofs is linked to the mainland by a wide bridge. **Angelfish Bayside** has a small marina, offices for North Island, a dive centre and Angelfish, Dream and Sea Stream yacht charters. Once over the bridge, the full extent of the new housing and 100-berth marina at Eden Island becomes apparent. **Eden House** is a central feature with a host of shops, restaurants and service centres. These include the Boardwalk Bar, Bravo Restaurant, Maharajahs Restaurant (page 92), yacht chandlers, Water World Yacht Charter, the Moorings and Marine Cat Sey. There is now also the vast Eden Plaza with underground parking, hosting many shops including a well-stocked supermarket, bottle store and spas, as well as the Porto Cervo and Le Belle Epoch restaurants.

Back on Providence Highway, and set a little way off the road, is the **Wharf Hotel and Marina** (page 85) which offers sophisticated accommodation as well as a slipway and berthing facilities for 60 vessels. Heading towards the airport the distinctive red-roofed **Church of St Andrew** can be seen on the right above the lush green vegetation of Cascade. At the La Providence roundabout (with the antler-like monument) it is possible to turn right to get to Chemin Mont Fleuri. The light industrial area of Providence continues on the left and eventually the highway meets up with Chemin Mont Fleuri at the **Roche Tortue traffic circle** [79 F4] near the airport.

An alternative route to begin exploring the southeast is to drive along the Mont Fleuri Road from Le Chantier roundabout, past the Botanical Gardens and the Victoria Hospital. This road continues through an old part of town and a short distance beyond the hospital on the Mont Fleuri Road is the **Sunrise Hotel** [79 E3].

The **Seychelles Institute of Teacher Education** and the international school are conspicuous, as is the very large **People's Supermarket**. To the right, Chemin La Misère leads over to the west coast of Mahé and the south coast road continues towards the airport.

Lying rotting in the mud near the road is the rusty hulk of a wrecked schooner, *Isle of Farquhar*, once the supply ship to the outer islands. **Michel Villas and Apartments** are well appointed, but a little far for an easy walk into town. Behind these is the national monument of **Château des Mamelles**, an imposing house built in 1804 for the corsair Jean François Hodoul, and now privately owned. **Seybrew**, the local brewery and soft drink manufacturer, occupies both sides of the road. Its products are excellent, being made with the sweet waters from the mountains.

Dotted throughout the mainly residential area are many small shops and car-hire companies and a new road with bridge off to the right connects to the La Providence roundabout on Providence Highway. The attractive red-roofed Church of St Andrew, built in 1884, nestles into the mountainside. On the sea side there is a mangrove-lined lagoon. At the tortoise-shaped rock (Roche Tortue) the road meets up with Providence Highway just before the airport. There is a petrol station and a bus stop opposite the entrance and the Air Seychelles head office building has a spectacular tiled logo.

Further south, near the imposing Jean Bosco Church, the bright yellow **Sacos Sun Apartments** are on the sea side of the road. Numerous small supermarkets, hairdressers and shops line the street and the Ile Soleil, land reclaimed from the sea, is apparent. Residential and commercial development for the island is planned for Seychellois citizens only. **Katiolo** [79 G4], at Anse Faure, is the hottest disco in town (a *katiolo* is a small wooden boat very like a pirogue). **Carefree Guesthouse & Restaurant** [79 G5] (⊕ *noon–22.00 daily;* $$) and the small hotel **Château Bleu** are nearby.

Anse aux Pins The **Seychelles Golf Club** [79 G5] (✆ *4376432;* e *sgc@seychelles. net*), 5km south of the airport, is the only one on Mahé. The nine holes are set under swaying coconut palms with a dramatic backdrop of dark granite mountains. Nine holes will cost you SR300 and 18 holes SR500, a golf cart will cost you SR50 and a caddy SR150. There are numerous other holiday apartments and guesthouses along this stretch of coastline including **Reef Holiday Apartments**, **Lalla Panzi**, **La Roussette** (page 89) and **Jemalah Apartments**.

The **National Institute for Creole Development**, also known as the **Lenstiti Kreol** [79 G5], is situated in a lovely old house, Maison St Joseph, and has been established to promote the Creole culture of the Seychelles. Schoolbooks and children's books are now being printed in Creole and these are displayed in the foyer. A Creole library is also housed there, and includes many books on the Seychelles heritage, both in French and English. The old house, was built by Mr Jumeau in the typical, grand French colonial style.

The Indian consulate is near the **Craft Village**, also known as **Domaine de Val des Près** [79 G5] (⊕ *09.00–17.00 Mon–Sat*) and consists of a series of small Creole bungalows. Each has its own speciality handicraft and some function as workshops where you can watch the craftsmen at work. **La Marine Model Boats** [79 G5] (✆ *4375152*) welcomes visitors to its workshop where they build models of old sailing boats. Using naval plans, replicas are made in the finest detail but because of the time-consuming nature of the business they are not cheap. For a fee, they will gladly pack and ship them around the world for you. There's also the beautifully renovated plantation house, **Vye Marmit** [79 G5].

Further south at La Plaine St André is the **Takamaka Bay Rum Distillery, Bar and Restaurant** [79 G6] (🕐 *10.00–midnight daily*), where it is well worth doing a rum tour and tasting. The restored plantation house functions as a classy restaurant with veranda seating and well-presented, tasty meals; highly recommended (page 92).

From here onwards, the road is very close to the coast and Devon Residence, the Europe slot hall **casino** [79 G6] (🕐 *14.00–02.00*) and Castaway Fishing Lodge are all on the landward side. **La Désirade**, **La Villa Dorado**, the new **Crown Beach Hotel** (page 88), the expanded **Le Relax** (with restaurant; page 89) and Au Fond de Mer View Apartments are situated at Pointe au Sel on the northern end of Anse Royale.

Anse Royale Anse Royale is the next embayment on the route to the south, and during the northwest monsoons offers a sheltered and protected curve of beach suitable for swimming. It is a bustling centre with shops, petrol station, a new hospital, school, university campus, police station and a large community hall. South of the town is the photogenic old (1889) **St Joseph's Church** [79 G7], close to the beach.

Anse Royale is one of the few areas on Mahé with a reasonable amount of flat and fertile land, and there are some flourishing market gardens in the area. It was at Anse Royale that the first spice gardens were started in 1772 under the orders of Pierre Poivre from Mauritius. Cinnamon, nutmeg, cloves and pepper were the main crops. The entire plantation was destroyed a few years later, when the French garrison officer guarding the secret spice garden set fire to all the plants when he mistakenly thought an approaching ship was English, and about to take command of the island. By the time it was discovered to be a French vessel, all the trees had been burnt.

The long curve of Anse Royale has many small, shaded beaches and secluded coves sheltered by huge granite boulders, making it an ideal place for exploring and having a picnic. As you approach Anse Royale there is a group of rocks near the shore leading to Ile Souris. Snorkelling here is good, but do be aware that at times there can be a fairly strong current running between the coast and the little island and there are no lifeguards.

Kaz Kreol (page 92), opposite the police station, is a beachfront pizzeria that also serves seafood, and on occasions, there is live music with dancing – watch the press for details. The modern Southern Investment Building on the sea side houses the **Pied Dans L'eau apartments** and **Les Dauphins Heureux Restaurant** (pages 89 and 92), plus the **Beach Shop**, which offers snorkelling, PADI diving courses and gear hire. Next door is **Trésores des Iles**, a small shop selling souvenirs, sunblock and swimming gear, and a branch of MCB, with bureau de change and ATM.

The **University of Seychelles** [79 F6] was established in 2010 and the Anse Royale campus is quite large. At the entrance it features a statue of Plato (created by Tom Bowers) and there is a plaque commemorating the inauguration by HRH Princess Anne and James Michel on 29 November 2010. On the corner of the road leading to the university, there is a complex with Barclays Bank and ATM, small shops and boutiques. After the community centre, the Chemin les Canelles leads to the right and across the island (page 116).

Towards the south of Anse Royale are the **Fleure de Sel** and **Driftwood self-catering establishments** [79 G7]. At Anse Parnel, the **Surfers Beach Restaurant** (🕐 *noon–22.00 daily*) provides a friendly welcome and parking area off the narrow road from which to watch the local surfers tackling the waves. Further on, at Cap Lascars, the imposing, salmon-coloured, multi-storey **Doubletree by Hilton Seychelles-Allamanda Resort & Spa** (page 88) contrasts sharply with the blue ocean. Their spacious Les Palmes Restaurant welcomes visitors for lunch and dinner, where you can enjoy the friendly ambience of the cool interior or the stars at night on the lovely deck.

Anse Forbans One of the undeveloped and very quiet parts of Mahé, Anse Forbans or Pirate's Bay was named on the earliest maps, and was apparently one of the bays used by the 17th-century pirates. You can easily imagine a pirate boat being careened on this beach. **Chalets d'Anse Forbans** (page 89) are self-catering and set in large gardens with lawns and coconut palms. A small bumpy track behind the chalets leads down to the Anse Marie-Louise Beach that is regularly frequented by the local Seychellois for picnics and parties.

THE SOUTH After the Anse Forbans Chalets, the road swings away from Anse Marie-Louise and continues inland for about 1km to the village of **Quatre Bornes**. Turn left near the police station at a somewhat indistinct junction to get down to Anse Intendance, Police Bay and the southernmost point of Mahé.

Anse Intendance This must be one of the loveliest and most unspoilt bays of Mahé. Have a picnic under the shady trees and look out for the graceful white-tailed tropicbirds. Note that during the southeast trades, the currents can be dangerous for swimmers. There is a boutique and take-away before the well-signposted road to the right that leads to the luxurious and refined **Banyan Tree Hotel** (page 87). Enjoy the best Asian food at the Saffron Restaurant or indulge in their well-appointed health spa.

Continue southwards on the concrete road past **Rosi's Pure Konfitir** [79 F8] (last place for refreshments) towards Anse Corail and Pointe Police where there are the deserted remains of the old police buildings. The narrow road extends for some distance into the Southern Seas wilderness area, a wild stretch of coastline with small, unprotected bays, steep hillsides, rivers and lush vegetation. At the time of writing there was no development there whatsoever.

THE SOUTHWEST To explore the southwest go back to Quatre Bornes, turn left and proceed to Anse Takamaka, passing the Anse Takamaka View self-catering chalets. The turn-off to **Le Réduit**, a small seafood restaurant [79 F7] (✆ 4366116; ⊕ lunch & dinner daily), is clearly marked and the narrow, windy road to it ends at the secluded **South Point Chalets** [79 F7].

Anse Takamaka This is yet another fabulous, secluded, white, sandy beach fringed with palms. It takes its name from the tall, shady takamaka trees. Take care when swimming, as the waves and strong currents can be dangerous at times. Recent incidents indicate that it is unwise to leave valuables on any of the beaches in this area.

Chez Batista Villas (pages 88–9) at the southern end of the bay overlook the beach, and their attractive restaurant specialises in Creole food. At the northern end of the bay, the restaurant of the **Lazare Picault Hotel** [79 F7] is open daily for lunch and dinner.

Baie Lazare Continuing close to the coast, you will reach Baie Lazare which is a horseshoe-shaped bay facing south bounded by Pointe Maravi and Pointe Lazare. Good waves entice surfers to this area. The newly built **Valmer Resort and Art Gallery** (page 89) are on the landward side of the main road, with comfortable, upmarket self-catering apartments. The gallery exhibits and sells the works of artist Gerard Devoud, whose vibrant paintings are bright and colourful, depicting different facets of local life. Originals and prints are available and they will be carefully wrapped in protective sleeves for travelling.

Creole Travel Services owns a 65ha nature reserve at Cap Lazare with a palm-thatched Creole-styled village with a range of amenities ideal for weddings, corporate and group functions.

The road continues northward and opposite the conspicuous St Francis Church and cemetery there is a convenient petrol station (⊕ *07.00–19.30 Mon–Sat, 08.00–11.30 Sun*) with ATM on the left. **Donald Adelaide's Art Studio** [79 E6] (⊕ *09.00–18.00 Mon–Sat*) is located next to the police station. He is inspired by nature and sells his large colourful paintings and prints from his studio. The red Frangipani Café run by friendly Phare and Sarah can provide a light lunch and ice creams (⊕ *09.00–16.00 Mon–Sat*). The Anse Soleil road on the left leads to a range of hotels, restaurants and shops, the first of which is the new **Kempinski Seychelles Resort** (page 88) set in a huge garden amongst granite rocks and water features. Nearby, the **Anse Soleil Resort** (page 88) comprises several houses and is set in pretty gardens with lovely views of mountains and the sea.

The road continues on to **Andrew Gee's Art Studio** and the associated **Maison Soleil self-catering villa**. He specialises in silk paintings and his colourful works are on sale here, as well as in various outlets in Victoria and the duty-free shop at the airport. A little further down the road is the enormous new **Four Seasons Resort and Spa** (page 87) with villas on stilts hewn into the hillside. Follow the steep road down the hill and veer right to reach the **Anse Soleil Café** (page 92), a rustic, palm-roofed beach restaurant with a relaxed ambience. Enjoy the sand under your toes and dine on fresh seafood; open from noon – no reservations – first come, first served! Keeping to the left, the road ends in a shaded parking area serving Soleil car hire and the small, quiet **Anse Soleil Beachcomber Hotel** (page 88), situated right on the beautiful Anse Soleil Beach, fringed with coconut palms and great granite boulders and good for swimming.

Opposite Andrew Gee's Art Studio, a steep, narrow road leads down to the shores of **Anse Gouvernement** – a great place for a picnic. Along this road, Antonio Filipini has his **sculpture studio** at **Maria's Rock Cafeteria** [79 E7] (☏ *4361812;* ⊕ *10.00–21.00 Wed–Mon*), a great place for children with an old pirate boat for them to play in. The self-catering establishments of **La Rocaille** and **Lazare Lodge** are also nearby [79 E7].

Anse aux Poules Bleues

On the left at Anse aux Poules Bleues is **Michael Adams' Art Studio** [79 E6] (⊕ *10.00–16.00 Mon–Fri, 10.00–noon Sat*), one of the best-known artists in the Seychelles, and his work can be seen adorning book covers and calendars. Palms and thick, creeping vegetation engulf his intriguing old Creole-style building. Much of his work has been reproduced as prints, which are available here together with paintings by his son and daughter. Still in Anse aux Poules Bleues, **Pineapple Studio** [79 E5] (⊕ *10.00–16.00 Mon–Fri*) is on the sea side of the road, a busy little craft factory producing hand-decorated towels, T-shirts and *pareos*, wooden placemats, coasters, trays and coconut craft. The items are available in the boutique here and in many places around the islands.

Anse à la Mouche

Anse à la Mouche is a sweeping shallow bay with warm and sheltered waters. Apparently, Captain Lazare Picault made the first landing here in 1742, under orders from Bertrand François Mahé de Labourdonnaise, the French governor of Mauritius. The bay is named after a ship that ran aground there in 1812. There are several self-catering establishments and restaurants in this area, such as the **Anchor Café & Islander Restaurant** [79 F6] (⊕ *11.00–21.00 Mon–Sat*) which is a good place for a sundowner and smoked fish, and the **Blue Lagoon Chalets**, set in spacious grassy gardens with Palm Car Hire and Dive Resort Seychelles nearby. The conspicuous **Laguna Lounge** and **Opera Restaurant** (Munich to Mahé!) (page 92) offers a range of fare including pizzas. **Chemin les Canelles** leads off to the right, a little beyond the Opera Restaurant, and traverses the island from Anse à la Mouche to Anse Royale (page 116). The small, family-friendly **Les Jardin des Palmes Hotel and Restaurant** (page 89) is on the hillside overlooking Anse à la Mouche Bay, but it is almost completely hidden in the palm forest.

Anse Louis is the next sheltered and beautiful beach, where you will find the exclusive **Maia Luxury Hotel and Spa** (page 88) with Balinese-type, tall, thatched roofs sticking out above the natural treeline. Security is very strict and casual visitors are not encouraged.

Anse Boileau

This is the next bay along the west coast route, and has a police station, fire service, school, various shops and supermarket. Chemin de Montagne is the road off to the right and it winds its way over to the other side of the island (page 116). Some self-catering establishments are located around the shores of the bay, as is the little restaurant **Chez Plume** (page 92). Continuing on, the **Bay View Villa** is on the seaward side of the road and has a commanding view of Anse Boileau, and the 17ha National Biodiversity Centre was inaugurated in July 2014. The aim is to develop a centre preserving the endemic biodiversity of the Seychelles. A plant nursery has already been established selling plants and flowers to the public and, in the future, visitor facilities will be made available. Further along the road is the large Green Acre vegetable farm.

Grande Anse

This is a dramatically beautiful bay with a backdrop of high granite mountains highlighting the soft, silvery sands and turquoise water. Occasionally, the sandflies are bad, and at times there can be a strong undertow. The large Méridien Barbarons Hotel has now been taken over by **Avani Seychelles Barbarons Resort and Spa** (page 88), and the **Pineapple Boutique**, which sells items from the Pineapple Studio (page 113), and the recommended **Veranda Café** (page 92) are on the opposite side of the road. The conspicuous towers of the **BBC Indian Ocean relay station** are near the junction with **Chemin la Misère** (page 116), and on the corner is a petrol station, shop and ATM. The Seychelles Agricultural Agency is active in the area and there are many market gardens as well as Lydie's curio shop selling some local souvenirs, Island's Café and the Artisanal Cafétaria.

Port Glaud

Although conspicuous, the sprawling, multi-storey **Berjaya Mahé Beach Resort** was still closed at the time of writing. **Chemin Sans Souci**, heading off to the right, is an important road connecting Port Glaud to Victoria (page 115).

Eden's Creole Restaurant [78 C4] (⊕ *noon–21.00, with Sun buffet*) is next to **Eden's Holiday Villas** which are set in lush, tropical forest close to beautiful beaches and good snorkelling. Nearby, the **Sundown Restaurant** (page 92) serves fine seafood, and over the road, Dame Rose's grocery and souvenir shop is a long-standing establishment. **L'Islette**, a small islet a short way offshore, can be reached by foot at low tide.

Port Launay

The **Constance Ephelia Resort** (page 85) spreads out through the mangrove forest and hillside at the entrance to the **Port Launay Marine National Park**. The Specialised Multi Adventure Company (SMAC) (☎ *4395180;* e *office@*

smacadventures.com; www.smacadventures.com) has set up a series of eight zip lines running through the forest as well as a rock climbing adventure. All equipment is provided and these exciting escapades make a great change from all the water-based pursuits. Although they are based at the Constance Ephelia Resort, their activities are open to all, not only hotel guests. The bus route bypasses the resort and ends at the popular beach; thereafter, the road narrows and continues past tiny beaches protected by many granite boulders. It is fabulous to snorkel directly off the beach in the crystal-clear waters but parking the car can be a challenge as the road is very narrow. The road ends at a private property which was once the premises of the Seychelles Youth League.

ROUTES ACROSS MAHE

Chemin Sans Souci The Sans Souci Road from Port Glaud through the mountains to Victoria is one of the most scenic drives on Mahé and for much of the way you will be driving through the **Morne Seychellois National Park**. The tall trees are a mixture of indigenous *takamaka* and *bwa rouz*, with introduced cinnamon, mahogany, *bwa zonn* and the feathery-leaved, flat-crowned albizia. *Philodendron* vines creep up many of the trees. The **Tea Factory** [78 D4] is only about 4km from Port Glaud (✆ *4420347;* ◷ *07.00–noon Mon–Fri*). Tours are available but it is advisable to phone to check before you go. Tea production began in 1966, and the neatly tended tea bushes are visible along the roadside. It is possible to purchase some of the delicious, fragrant SeyTé (Seychelles tea) that is produced in five different flavours – vanilla, cinnamon, orange, mint and lemon. The associated cafeteria appears to open only intermittently. The Morne Seychellois walking trail (page 119) starts about 250m up the hill from the car park at the tea factory.

The **Capucin Mission Ruins** [78 D4] are a reminder of the slave trade as a school was built here by members of the London Missionary Society for the children of slaves set free during the British anti-slavery campaign in the 19th century. It was then known as Venn's Town and operated from 1875 to 1889. Marianne North, the artist, stayed here during her sojourn in the Seychelles in 1883. Today, you will see only the moss-covered ruins. A shelter was built when Queen Elizabeth II was entertained to tea during a state visit and it is now a popular picnic area. From this remarkable vantage point, one can see over the tea estates and way down to the southwestern parts of Mahé, and may even see white-tailed tropicbirds flying over the green hills.

The **Station** (page 84), located on the right with stunning views over the Ste Anne Marine Park, is the only homeopathic healing centre in the Seychelles. It offers accommodation, retreats and a shop selling homeopathic lotions and potions made on site in their small natural products factory. They also have a lovely café which is worthwhile stopping at for a cup of tea or light snack (page 92).

Val Riche is 4km further on and a signpost indicates the start of the scenic Copolia walk (page 119). The National Park Authority is on the left, and this is the beginning of the Trois Frères walk (page 119).

Bel Air is a residential area on the outskirts of Victoria and there are several diplomatic homes including the American embassy, which housed Archbishop Makarios during his year of exile. It is called '1776' and is a privately owned national monument.

Continuing along the Bel Air Road you'll come to **Mountain Rise** (page 85), a quiet and secluded small hotel, and the **Bel Air Hotel** (page 85), a family-run establishment. A little further on is **Thoughts Stained Glass Studio** and the oldest cemetery in Mahé where some interesting characters are buried. Look carefully to find the grave of the corsair Jean François Hodoul.

The Bel Air Road descends to an intersection with Revolution Avenue. If you decide to drive into Liberation Avenue instead of continuing into Bel Air there is a panoramic viewpoint where you can see the islands in the Ste Anne Marine National Park – Eden, Ste Anne, Cerf, Moyenne, Long and Round. The avenue meets up with Mont Fleuri Road on the south side of Le Chantier roundabout.

Chemin la Misère
This is another scenic road that winds through mountains and forests from Grande Anse to Victoria. Characterised by numerous hairpin bends, the views from the route are spectacular.

The **Seychelles Tourism Academy** has opened in what used to be the American tracking station. Rebuilding has commenced to make this a superior training academy and, already, many graduates are employed throughout the Seychelles. Near the top are the La Misère School and the Faire View area where the rich and famous now live. On the steep descent, there are panoramic views of Baie Ste Anne, and the map at the specially constructed **viewing point** [79 E3] (with parking!) enables a good appreciation of the east coast of Mahé and the nearby islands, including the manmade Eden Island with its extensive luxury housing and marina.

A bit further down the hill in La Louise residential area are the Chili Bar and steakhouse plus various shops including the conspicuous Fresh Cut Butchery where Chemin la Misère meets the Roche Caiman fountain-adorned roundabout.

Chemin de Montagne
This road crosses the southern part of Mahé from Anse Boileau to Anse aux Pins. The Bon Espoir Cable & Wireless radio communications centre is situated high up in the mountains, from where radio links are made to all the outlying islands as well as to ships at sea.

Chemin les Canelles
This interesting road winds over the mountain from Anse à la Mouche to Anse Royale. **Tom Bowers' Studio** [79 F6] (⊕ 09.00–17.30 Mon–Sat) is well marked, where Tom and his charming wife Ellen will welcome you to his outdoor sculpture studio home to his beautiful creations surrounded by lush vegetation, hundreds of Madagascar fodies and a menagerie of dogs. Located nearby are the **Evergreen** and Bois Calou self-catering chalets.

A bit further on there is the **Kot-Man-Ya** exotic flower garden [79 F6] (ℂ 4371190; ⊕ 08.00–17.00 daily; admission SR150) where retired ambassador, Marc Marengo, who is passionate about his plants, will guide you through his jungle-like property brimming with more than 60 varieties of colourful heliconiums, anthuriums and orchids. There are also several large tortoises.

Le Jardin du Roi [79 F6] (ℂ 4371313; ⊕ 10.00–17.30 daily; admission SR110), the first spice garden in the Seychelles, is reached via a small road located next to the Roch Richard-Low retailer. Follow the road up the hill past the Koko Grove chalets for about 2km. These spice gardens and restaurant are well worth a visit and the entrance fee enables you to undertake a self-guided tour. Besides cinnamon, cloves, nutmeg, vanilla, lemon grass, allspice and pepper there are many medicinal plants under cultivation. There are several enormous coco de mer palms, and many other fine examples of indigenous plants. A small museum allows fascinating glimpses into the agricultural past, and the views over the eastern part of Mahé are lovely. The restaurant (⊕ lunchtime daily) has a small but tasty menu but it is not the cheapest place (page 92). If you feel like really splashing out, try one of their homemade spice-flavoured ice creams – vanilla, cinnamon, clove, mint, nutmeg or lemon grass. There is also a small shop where souvenirs, spices, rum and coconut nougat can be purchased.

Full- and half-day tours are usually arranged for passengers by the cruise-ships' agents in Mahé. These are generally good value as the local guides provide many interesting insights to the Seychellois way of life. However, it is sometimes really nice to escape from organised tours and do your own thing, be it walking, taking a taxi or hiring a car for a drive around parts of Mahé. Taxis are readily available when cruise ships dock, and local tour agents on the quayside are able to arrange car hire very easily. There are several public telephones located close to the pier if you prefer to make your own car-hire arrangements.

HALF-DAY WALKING TOUR Setting off from the ship, head straight inland to the port exit and customs point. Walk up Chemin Latanier to Le Chantier roundabout, which is easily identified by the four white sailfish pointing skywards. Turning left into Chemin Mont Fleuri, you can visit the **Botanical Gardens** (page 100). It should take about 15 minutes to get there from the ship. Half an hour will allow a quick tour through the gardens, though you may prefer to linger longer. If shopping is high on your agenda, the Botanical Gardens could be missed out, allowing more time to concentrate on the market, shops and souvenir stalls.

Return to Le Chantier and proceed along Francis Rachel Street. Call in at **Kenwyn House** for a taste of upmarket goods; not all are Seychellois-made, but enjoy the ambience. From here, walk along the right-hand side of the road which will be cooler under the trees, and allowing you to browse the stalls on the **Fiennes Esplanade**. After the silvery-coloured clock tower, stay on the left side of Albert Street and turn left into Market Street to visit the **Victoria Market** (page 102); note that it closes at 14.00 on Saturdays and is closed on Sundays.

Return to Albert Street and browse around **Codevar** for handmade crafts. If time is against you, take a taxi from the nearby rank and return to the ship. If you still have plenty of time, however, walk down Independence Avenue, which leads off towards the sea at the clock tower. Try out the **Pirates Arms** (page 91), the local watering hole. If you are short of time or feeling the heat, this is a good place to pick up a taxi for the return trip to the ship but, if you can manage another 20-minute walk, continue to the **Twa Zwazo** roundabout and turn right into 5th June Avenue. You will pass the Marine Charter Association and the yacht club on your left. After the imposing **National Cultural Centre** building you will be back at Le Chantier roundabout; turn left into Chemin Latanier to return to the docks.

HALF-DAY DRIVING TOURS By doing some creative negotiating, it *might* be possible to hire a car for a half-day period. This would give the option of doing an organised half-day excursion followed by a short time to explore Mahé on your own.

North and central option (*2–3hrs round trip*) The north and central part of Mahé provide an easy and interesting route. Follow the map and drive along the northeastern coastal road. Drop into **Kreol Fleurage Parfums** (page 108) for a quick stop and then continue around North Point, through Glacis and on to **Beau Vallon Bay**. There are many places to park the car in the vicinity of the Boathouse Restaurant if you wish to do some exploring on foot, and a walk along the fine curve of **Beau Vallon Beach** (pages 105–6) is an excellent way to take some exercise after being on board ship for a few days. You can then meander on to one of the hotels like **Coral Strand**, **Berjaya Beau Vallon Bay Beach Resort**, or **La Plage Restaurant** for refreshments, before going back to the car to continue exploring.

Drive up to the junction at the police station, turn right and wend your way to **Bel Ombre** (page 105), keeping a lookout for the treasure excavations. The road ends at Danzil, so return to the police station and take the road over to Victoria. As you round the hairpin bends enjoy the spectacular views of Baie Ste Anne and the port (with your ship) way down below.

Sans Souci and the west coast option (*4hrs round trip*) For a scenic tour

through mountains, forests and along part of the west coast, try the **Chemin Sans Souci** (page 115) leading from either Bel Air Road or Liberation Avenue. Wind your way through the **Morne Seychellois National Park** and stop at **The Station** (pages 84–5) for coffee and a snack before continuing to the **Capucin Mission Ruins** for superb views. Pass the **Tea Estate and Factory** (page 115) with a basic restaurant, before descending to **Port Glaud** on the west coast. Turn right to explore some of the beautiful, small beaches in the **Port Launay Marine National Park**. As the road reaches a cul-de-sac you will have to return to Port Glaud the same way and then continue southwards along the coast past Avani, a good place for refreshments. Explore the village of **Grande Anse** and then turn inland at **Chemin la Misère** for a spectacular drive over to the eastern side of Mahé. At the junction with the main south coast road, turn left and, in no time, you will be back at Le Chantier roundabout and your ship.

FULL-DAY DRIVING TOUR With a full day on your hands, the possibilities are endless and depend on your personal preferences. The southern part of Mahé has the most interesting variety of beaches, restaurants and art studios. Timing will depend on how long you linger at any of the sights or swim and lounge on the beach; it could take from 09.00 to 17.30.

Drive out of Victoria and pass the airport. At **Anse aux Pins** stop in at the **Craft Village** for **La Marine Model Boats** (page 110). Take in some snorkelling at Anse Royale or simply find one of the secluded beaches and enjoy the sand, sun and surf. Drive across to Anse Intendance or Anse Takamaka (page 112), and between there and Anse à la Mouche you will find many delightful restaurants serving fine seafood and Creole lunches. This is also the art centre of Mahé with many studios and galleries, such as those of **Michael Adams**, **Tom Bowers** or **Donald Adelaide** (pages 113, 116 and 113), all open to the public. Follow the west coast road, stopping for a walk or a swim on any of the lovely beaches; take care as they can be boisterous during the southeast trade winds. The most scenic route back to Victoria is over the Chemin Sans Souci, where you can enjoy the panoramic views from the **Capucin Mission Ruins**. The road has many twists and turns as it descends into Victoria, and evening views over the bay are particularly lovely as the lights come on in the town and port.

WALKS ON MAHE

Walking is a great way to discover Mahé. Trails have been laid out in different areas of the **Morne Seychellois National Park** and there is a short trail along part of the northwestern coastline. The Department of Environment has published small leaflets describing the walks and they are available at the Botanical Gardens entrance office, or Antigone bookshop (pages 101 and 95). Each one has a good map and description of the trail, and they are filled with interesting information about the plants and wildlife that you will encounter *en route*. As it can become hot around midday it is a good idea to walk in the early morning, but if you do walk in the afternoon be aware that the equatorial sun sets quickly and darkness falls before you know it. Remember to wear comfortable walking shoes, a hat, use sunscreen and take plenty of water to drink. An umbrella can be used as a sunshade and is great in a sudden tropical shower. It is not wise to do these walks alone; it is always better to go in a group or, best, go with a local guide, especially if you do a mountain walk. Jacques Barreau, a trained forester (4242386), and Basil Beaudouin (m 2514972) offer guided walks on the island.

DANZIL TO ANSE MAJOR (*3hrs round trip; easy*) This trail begins at the end of Bel Ombre and follows the coast to a secluded little beach. A great deal of this trail lies within the Morne Seychellois National Park. The noisy chattering birds you are very likely to encounter are the Seychelles bulbuls, and pure-white fairy terns and white-tailed tropicbirds can be seen flying along the coastline.

LES TROIS FRERES (*2hrs round trip; moderate*) The three peaks overlook Victoria, and the views from the top are magnificent, but it is a steep climb from the Sans Souci Forest Station to the summit. The Forest Station is about 5km from Victoria on the Sans Souci Road. You may park your car there, and follow the trail marked with yellow paint blobs. At the beginning of the route you will notice many introduced plant species like cinnamon, cocoplum and vanilla. Two endemic *Latanier* palm species and a *Pandanus* are common a little higher up along the path.

VAL RICHE TO COPOLIA (*2–3hrs round trip; moderate*) This walk starts on the Sans Souci Road about 6km from Victoria. There is a signboard on the left on a bend in the road, and it is just possible to squeeze your car off onto the narrow verge to park. There is a bus stop nearby, though buses are infrequent. The tree-shaded trail is marked with yellow paint. Upon reaching the *glacis* at the top, you will see the endemic pitcher plants growing in the shallow soil. Stunning views of the east coast of Mahé and the Ste Anne Marine National Park are the rewards for the climb. There have been some muggings here recently and guards are stationed at the start of the walk, so if you don't have a guide, it's a good idea to ask one of the guards to accompany you.

TEA FACTORY TO MORNE BLANC (*1hr one-way; moderate*) This route in the Morne Seychelles National Park begins on the Sans Souci Road about 11km from Victoria, 250m up the hill from the Tea Factory car park. It's best done in the morning as the first bit is steep and not shaded. The mist forest has many unique species, and is an indication of what the islands used to look like before man arrived. Look out for the minute endemic frog (*Sooglossus gardineri*) which makes a surprisingly loud chirping sound and lives in the leaf litter. Again, the superb views across to Conception and Thérèse islands and the northern tip of Mahé, from the summit, are just rewards for the sweat up the hill.

EXCURSIONS TO SATELLITE ISLANDS

NEAR VICTORIA There are several small islands around Mahé which are well worth visiting. Closest to Victoria are the six islands in the middle of the **Ste Anne Marine National Park**, namely Ste Anne, Cerf, Long, Round, Moyenne and Ile Cachée. All marine life is protected in the park and there is worthwhile snorkelling although the coral is still showing signs of damage.

Ste Anne Ste Anne, the largest of the six islands, and only 4km from Victoria, was the site of the first settlement in the Seychelles. The first motley group of settlers arrived on 12 August 1770 from Mauritius to start growing vegetables and spices. Since then, Ste Anne has been home to a whaling station, which operated from 1832 to 1915, a World War II gun battery, and a fuel storage depot which is still in use. A navigation light is situated on the highest point of the island, Mont Ste Anne, at 205m. This little island, 2km long and 1km wide, has two beaches that are important nesting sites for the endangered hawksbill turtle. The 87 villas of the **Ste Anne Resort** (page 89) are spread along the two main beaches. This five-star resort has all the luxury amenities including fine restaurants and a health and beauty centre. Various walking trails have been laid out on the forested island and day visitors can apply for access through the hotel reception.

Cerf This island is a little smaller than Ste Anne, with the highest point being 108m. It was named after the ship *Le Cerf*, captained by Nicholas Morphey who, in 1756, claimed the Seychelles for France. About 40 people live on Cerf where there are two chapels, one Catholic and one Anglican. People wishing to visit the island can arrange to do so with the hotel they will be visiting, or with a local tour operator. There are several accommodation options on the island. **Cerf Island Resort** with 24 luxurious villas (page 89) has the well-known '1756' Restaurant and an amazing helipad with 360° views; a great spot for a sundowner. **L'Habitation Cerf** (page 90) offers ten beachfront rooms and **Villa de Cerf**, a bright and airy new small hotel, has four spacious rooms. There are also two **Fairy Tern self-catering chalets**. The beaches are lovely and your hotel will advise the best and closest snorkel spots. The old paths around, and across, the island have not been maintained and are almost impossible to locate in the dense undergrowth. Complimentary transfers are available between Mahé and Cerf Island if you are staying on the island.

Ile Cachée This treasure island, as the name implies, lies southeast of Cerf. It is uninhabited and only about 2ha in size.

Long Long Island is closed to the public. It was once a prison and there is now an unfinished small resort.

Round The island was originally a leper colony with dwellings for the patients, a house for the nurse, a chapel and a small prison. The island has been taken over by the Dubai-based Jebel Ali International Hospitality Group, and the luxurious Enchanted Island Resort has been built with ten villas, each with its own infinity pool (page 89).

Moyenne When Brendon Grimshaw, a retired newspaper editor, bought the 9ha island in 1971 it had been deserted for 60 years. The first visitors to Moyenne were no doubt pirates and, despite stories of vast treasures being left on the island, it appears that none has been unearthed. The first known owners of the island were a very young couple, Melidor Louange and Julie Chiffon who, in 1850, somehow acquired Moyenne and lived there for 42 years. They sold it to wealthy Alfred d'Emmerez de Charmoy in 1892. An Englishwoman from Berkshire, Miss Emma Wardlow-Best, lived on the island from 1899 to 1911.

It took Brendon Grimshaw nearly a year to clear a path around the island, and he subsequently re-established many indigenous trees and shrubs, including Wright's gardenia and the coco de mer. The birdlife has flourished and a hundred giant

Aldabra tortoises can be found under the shady bushes. It takes about 45 minutes to walk along the path, and the ruins of the two old houses and some very old, possibly pirate, graves can be seen. Brendon Grimshaw died in 2012 and is buried here too. The island is now a national park, the smallest in the Seychelles. Day visitors are welcome and trips can be arranged through any of the tour operators or your hotel. The channel between the northern side of Moyenne and Ste Anne is one of the prime snorkelling sites in the marine park.

OFF THE WEST COAST

Thérèse This uninhabited 70ha island lies opposite Port Glaud and the Berjaya Mahé Beach Hotel (closed at the time of writing). A fabulous reef, excellent for snorkelling, runs along the main beach of the island. There are stunning views of Mahé from the top of the hill. Day trips to Thérèse can be arranged from private boat owners at Port Glaud or Beau Vallon.

Conception Conception rises steeply out of the sea, and has little or no beach, making landing there very difficult; consequently it has never been inhabited. It lies a little south of Cap Tiernay off the Port Launay Marine Park, and has some tremendous dive sites at the northeastern end. Covering an area of about 60ha, it has a wealth of undisturbed natural vegetation. Recently, a healthy population of the rare little bird, the Seychelles white-eye, has been rediscovered on Conception. Ornithological research is being carried out with some difficulty owing to the rugged terrain of the island.

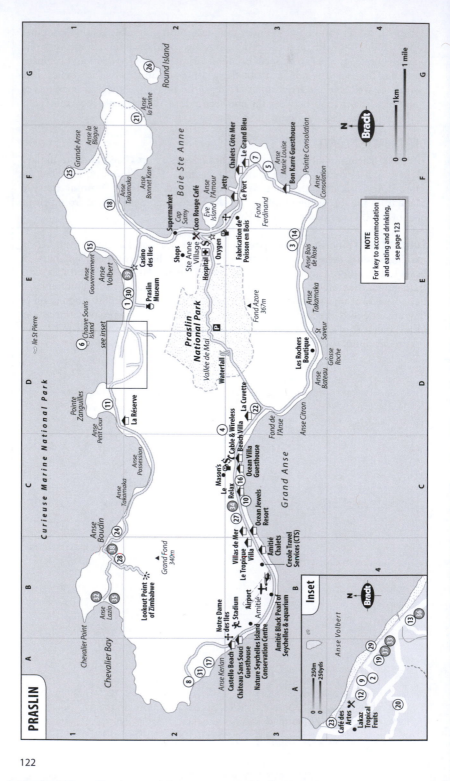

PRASLIN

Curieuse Marine National Park

Chevalier Point

Chevalier Bay

Anse Lazio

32
35

Anse Boudin

38
28

24

Grand Fond
340m

Lookout Point
of Zimbabwe

Anse Takamaka

Anse Possession

Anse Petit Cour

Pointe
Zanguilles

La Réserve
11

Ile St Pierre

Chauve Souris
Island

6

see inset

Praslin Museum
1 30

Casino
des Iles

39

Anse
Volbert

Anse
Gouvernement

15

18

Grande Anse

25

F

Anse la
Blague

21

Round Island

26

Baie Ste Anne

Supermarket

Cap
Samy

Coco Rouge Café

Eve
Island

Village

Shops
Ste Anne

Hospital
Oxygen

Fabrication de
Poisson en Bois

Anse
l'Amour

Jetty Le Port

Chalets Côte Mer
7 Le Grand Bleu

5
Anse
Marie Louise

Bon Karré Guesthouse

Pointe Consolation

Anse
Consolation

Fond
Ferdinand

3 14

Anse Bois
de Rose

Fond Azore
367m

Anse
Takamaka

Les Rochers
Boutique

St
Saveur

Grosse
Roche

Anse
Bateau

Praslin
National Park

Vallée de Mai

Waterfall

La Cuvette
22

4

Cable & Wireless
Beach Villa

Mason's

Le Relax
27 34

10

Ocean Villa
Guesthouse

16

Ocean Jewels
Resort

Fond de
l'Anse

Anse Citron

Grand Anse

Villas de Mer

Le Tropique
Villa

Amitié
Chalets

Creole Travel
Services (CTS)

Notre Dame
des Iles

Stadium

Airport

Amitié

Amitié Black Pearl of
Seychelles & aquarium

Nature Seychelles Island
Conservation Centre

Château Sans Soucl
Guesthouse

Castello Beach
Guesthouse

17

Anse Kerlan

31

8

NOTE
For key to accommodation
and eating and drinking,
see page 123

N

Bradt

0   1km
0   1 mile

Inset

Anse Volbert

N

Bradt

0   250m
0   250yds

Café des
Artes

23

Lakaz
Tropical
Fruits

12

9

2

20

29

19 37 33

13 36

Praslin

The lovely island of Praslin, home of the coco de mer palm, has a gentle, unhurried pace and an ambience of quiet tranquillity. Long stretches of fine, white sand framed by palms and shady *takamakas*, or small, secluded coves bounded by granite boulders, characterise this strangely shaped island surrounded by coral reefs. An assortment of islands lie beyond the coral reefs like chunks of emeralds in an azure sea. Mahé, 45km away to the south, is hazy in the distance; Aride, the seabird sanctuary, lies 16km to the north; and enchanting La Digue is located a mere 4km to the east. Curieuse, off to the northeast, is surrounded by its marine park and Ile St Pierre is a jumble of rocks lodged between Praslin and Curieuse. Cousin, an island bird reserve, and privately owned Cousine, lie to the west. Round Island, at the entrance to Baie Ste Anne, and Chauve Souris, a tiny clump of tree-covered rocks just 500m off Anse Volbert, complete the assorted satellite islands.

Areas of great natural beauty surround Praslin and the romantic 'island of palms' is the only place on earth where you will see coco de mer palms growing in magnificent profusion. The tall, elegant female coco de mer palm produces a huge seed, astonishingly shaped like a female belly and thighs, and the taller male palm has a remarkably phallic-looking flowering catkin. As can be imagined, these erotic shapes have resulted in the perpetuation of many myths and legends.

The first recorded visit to Praslin, when it was covered in virgin equatorial hardwood and palm forests, was made by Lazare Picault in 1744, and he gave it the

PRASLIN
For listings, see pages 127–31

Where to stay

1 Acajou	E2
2 Berjaya Praslin Beach Resort	A4
3 Black Parrot Suites	E3
4 Britannia	D2
5 Le Château des Feuilles	F3
6 Chauve Souris Island Lodge	D1
7 Colibri Guesthouse	F3
8 Constance Lémuria Resort	A2
9 Côte d'Or Lodge	A4
10 Dhevatara Beach	C3
11 La Domaine de la Réserve	D1
12 Le Duc de Praslin	A4
13 L'Hirondelle	B4
14 Hotel Coco de Mer	E3
15 Hotel L'Archipel	E1
16 Indian Ocean Lodge	C3
17 Islander	A2
18 Iles des Palmes Eco Resort	F1
19 Laurier Eco	A4
20 Mango Lodge	A4
21 New Emerald Cove	G2
22 Palm Beach	D3
23 Paradise Sun	A4
24 Raffles	C1
25 Rocky Bay Villa	F1
26 Round Island	G2
27 Villa des Alizés	C3
28 Villa Manoir	B1
29 Village du Pêcheur	A4
30 Les Villas d'Or	E2
31 Villas du Voyageur	A2

Where to eat and drink

Berjaya Pizzeria	(see 2)
32 Bonbon Plume	B1
The Britannia	(see 4)
33 Café de Luca	A4
34 Café Le Monde	C3
Capricorn	(see 17)
35 Le Chevalier	B1
36 La Goulue	B4
Laurier	(see 19)
37 Pirogue Restaurant & Bar	A4
38 PK's@Pasquerie Restaurant & Gastropub	B1
The Pond	(see 10)
39 Tante Mimi's	E2

name of Ile de Palme. Marion Dufresne, leading an exploratory expedition from Mauritius in 1768, named the island Praslin, after Gabriel de Choiseul, Duc de Praslin, the French minister of marine affairs.

Although a large amount of the original forest has disappeared as a result of fires and deforestation, there is still a valley where the remarkable palms are protected and flourish – the Vallée de Mai, a World Heritage Site. There you can enjoy the majestic splendour of the forest and see all six of the endemic palm species of the Seychelles plus an array of other trees and plants. The nearby island of Curieuse and the newly created special reserve of Fond Ferdinand in the south of Praslin are the only other places where coco de mer palms can be found growing naturally. Praslin is not only famous for the palms but it is also home to the rare endemic black parrot, and though these birds are never easy to find, they can be seen in any of the natural areas on the island.

Praslin, an island floating in quiet beauty, is second in size to Mahé, being 12km long and nowhere more than 5km wide. The highest granite summit, Fond Azore, reaches 367m. Most of the 8,600 people living on the island have tourism-related jobs. Agriculture and fishing are also important aspects of life on Praslin. The village at Baie Ste Anne, less than 2km from the jetty, has a few small shops, banks, post office, school, church and a hospital.

GETTING THERE AND AWAY

BY AIR Ile de Palme Airport in Amitié on the northwestern side of the island must be one of the most attractive airports in the Indian Ocean region, with typical Creole architecture, water features, palms and sculptures. There is a restaurant, the Touchdown Café, offering good-value light snacks, plus tour operators, car-hire companies, ATMs and public telephones. Part of the road past the airport has been washed away over the years and a sea wall has been constructed to protect the road as it continues in a northerly direction along Anse Kerlan.

Air Seychelles operates a regular and frequent service to Praslin from Mahé using 20-seater De Havilland Twin Otters. Flights shuttle between Mahé and Praslin every 15 minutes during peak times and less frequently otherwise. The flight takes only 15 minutes and costs about €88, one-way. Timetables are available at Praslin airport (✎ 4284666) or at the Air Seychelles office in Mahé (✎ 4391000; page 82).

Zil Air also has a helicopter service to and from Praslin and a representative at Praslin airport; all enquiries and reservations can be made at the central office (✎ 4375100).

BY SEA *Cat Cocos*, the fast catamaran ferry, takes less than an hour to travel between Victoria harbour on Mahé and Baie Ste Anne on Praslin. For details of times, prices and how to buy tickets, see pages 63 and 83.

There is a regular ferry service over to La Digue on the *Cat Rose*'s catamaran, which takes 15 minutes and costs €15 one-way or €30 for a return. As this can be quite a busy service, it is wise to reserve your seat with the Inter Island Ferry (✎ 4232329 or 4232394; e iif@seychelles.net; www.seychelles.net/iif). Check-in is 15 minutes prior to departure. Cash and major credit cards are accepted.

The harbour is a hive of activity with schooners and ferries plying between Praslin, Mahé and La Digue arriving and departing regularly, as well as the *Cat Cocos* ferry with up to 350 passengers at a time. Private charters for birdwatching, deep-sea fishing and pleasure cruising also use the harbour. There is a small covered waiting area, generally quite crowded, where you can shelter from the elements and buy snacks. There are card and coin public telephones. The *Cat Cocos* booking office, Seychelles Tourism Board, Mason's Travel and Creole Travel are also in the building on the jetty. As part of the large dredging and reclamation project that has taken place, a marina for yachts has been built. There has also been a development project on Eve Island to increase port facilities at Baie Ste Anne.

GETTING AROUND

Praslin has a good road around most of the perimeter of the island, as well as one crossing the island from Baie Ste Anne to Grande Anse. In the north, there is no road between Anse Lazio and Anse Kerlan, only a few tracks and paths. In the southeast, a narrow tar road connects the main Côte d'Or road to Anse La Blague.

BY TAXI Taxis are available at the airport and at the jetty. All the hotels are able to arrange for a taxi service but, if a taxi is required in the evening or early morning, it is advisable to book in advance. Expect to pay about €35–40 for a transfer between the airport and Anse Volbert. A private car transfer arranged through a hotel could cost about €110.

CAR HIRE There are several car-hire companies on Praslin and the hotels or guesthouses will arrange to use the nearest one. It is advisable to make your booking in advance.

🚗 **Austral Car Rental** Côte d'Or; 📞 4232015; e austcars@seychelles.net; www.australcarhire.com
🚗 **Century Car Rental** Grand Anse; m 2524600; e centurycars@seychelles.sc
🚗 **Grand Bleu Rent-a-Car** Anse Kerlan; 📞 4233660; m 2510640; e grandbleucars@seychelles.sc
🚗 **Prestige Car Hire** Grande Anse; 📞 4233266; e prestige@seychelles.sc

🚗 **Steppe Car Hire** Cap Samy; m 2525044; e steppe@seychelles.net; www.steppecarhire.com
🚗 **Sun Cars** Anse Kerlan; m 2593002; e info@suncars-seychelles.com
🚗 **United Car Rental** Grand Anse; m 2510637; e united@seychelles.net

CAT ROSE'S SCHEDULE

The schedule is subject to change, so be sure to check the times.

Days	Depart Praslin	Depart La Digue
Monday/	07.00	07.30
Tuesday/	09.00	09.30
Thursday	10.00	10.30
	11.45	12.15
	14.30	15.30
	16.00	16.30
	17.15	17.45
Wednesday	07.00	07.30
	09.00	09.30
	10.30	12.15
	11.45	
	14.30	15.30
	16.00	16.30
	17.15	17.45
Friday	07.00	07.30
	09.00	09.30
	10.00	10.30
	11.45	12.15
	14.30	15.30
	16.00	17.00
	17.45	18.15
Saturday	07.00	07.30
	09.00	09.30
	10.00	10.30
	11.45	12.15
	13.00	14.00
	14.30	15.30
	16.00	17.00
	17.45	18.15
Sunday	10.00	10.30
	12.30	14.30
		15.30
	16.00	17.00
	17.45	18.15

BY BUS There is a regular bus service on Praslin. Bus 61 travels between the jetty terminus and Anse Kerlan; this is a way to get to and from the airport, though it is not a very frequent service, operating half-hourly at peak times and hourly at mid morning and mid afternoon. Bus 62 travels from the airport along the coastal road past Pointe Consolation to the southwest through Baie Ste Anne village and along the west coast to La Réserve towards Anse Lazio terminating at Villa Manoir. This is not a frequent service either, and is mainly for schoolchildren. For more information ☏ 4233899. You might or might not get a sensible answer.

BY BOAT Boats are a great way to see this lush island from a different perspective. Creole Travel Services has the large sailing catamaran *Oplezir* and Mason's has *Catalina*, and both leave from the jetty in Baie St Anne. Various other vessels can be chartered for trips around Praslin and to neighbouring islands (pages 70–1).

On the beach at Anse Volbert, local Praslinois run taxi boats and tout various trips to the satellite islands in a range of vessels. Negotiate with exuberant and friendly Gianni Barra (m *2879185; www.wowislandcharter.com*) in his open-air office for a boat suitable for your needs.

BICYCLE HIRE It is difficult to find decent bikes to hire on Praslin, though some of the hotels might be able to provide them. It is quite hilly in places, especially the new road leading to Anse Lazio, so you may prefer to hire a car. Also, do not forget the high humidity and heat so, if you do find a bike, remember to take plenty of water and the usual sunscreen and a hat. Mario's Bike Hire (m *2564062*) is located at Anse Volbert and bikes are €10 per day. Remember to check the brakes, gears and seat height before setting off.

TOURIST INFORMATION

TOURS ON PRASLIN Any of the main Seychelles tour operators will be able to take you on a tour around Praslin. **Creole Travel Services** has hospitality desks at the major hotels and their office is near the entrance to the airport (☏ *4233223*). Private transfers and chauffeur-driven, air-conditioned vehicles are available; Desmond is a gem! **Mason's Travel** is located at Grande Anse (☏ *4233211*) and **7° South Travel** has an office at the airport (m *2515485*). All the hotels, guesthouses and self-catering establishments will be able to arrange any tours or boat excursions for you.

Bois Mare Nature Guide (☏ *4232936*; m *2513370*; e *boismare@gmail.com*) is a small independent company run by Victorin Laboudallon. Gemma Jessie (☏ *2510431*; e *jessiegemm@yahoo.com*) is another excellent guide living on Praslin, and Nadi Camille (m *2525478*; e *nadimcamille@gmail.com*) offers nature walks on Praslin as well as La Digue. It is a good idea to take a nature guide with you on any of the walks as their insights and knowledge about the paths, plants, birds and frogs will considerably add to your pleasure and understanding.

 ## WHERE TO STAY

Most of the hotels on Praslin have good facilities and many fall into the luxury category with prices to match. The larger hotels usually feature a watersports and dive centre and have a swimming pool or two. The cost will vary according to the season and type of room; some establishments are open to a certain amount of negotiation. Tour operators are frequently able to quote better prices and tour packages are often the most economical way to visit the Seychelles. The bed and breakfast and self-catering options are a more economical way to see the island, and as they do not have the extensive amenities of the larger hotels, they may give more of a local feeling. They can, however, make arrangements for you with the local boatmen, taxis and guides at a generally cheaper rate than a large hotel. Self-catering is usually the least expensive way to go.

LARGE HOTELS

🏠 **Raffles** [122 C1] (86 villas) Anse Takamaka; 📞 4296000; e praslin@raffles.com; www.raffles.com/praslin. The 1- & 2-bedroom villas of various configurations each with their own pool are laid out on the hillside overlooking gorgeous bays & island vistas, & there are also some beachfront villas. 6 bars & restaurants with many wining & dining options are available as well as a 24hr butler service; 13 treatment pavilions at the Raffles Spa are ready to pamper you; the Sugar Palm Kids' Club will ensure the youngsters are entertained & a state-of-the-art gym will help to keep you fit. There are also possibilities to purchase your own 3-, 4- or 5-bedroom villa in the residential section. **$$$$$**

🏠 **Constance Lémuria Resort** [122 A2] (115 rooms) Anse Kerlan; 📞 4281281; e resa@lemuriaresort.com; www.lemuriaresort.com. This award-winning hotel is the largest on Praslin, set in spacious, well-manicured grounds around a superb 18-hole Marc Farry golf course. There are 3 restaurants, 4 bars, tennis courts, swimming pools & 3 lovely beaches. The health & fitness centre uses Shiseido products & has a wide range of treatments. The Turtle Club (🕐 *09.00–21.00*) caters for children between 4 & 12 years. They have 88 villa-type junior suites, 8 senior suites & 8 private pool villas, all finished in sumptuous luxury. The Presidential Suite is more like a private hotel with its own beach, exclusive staff, chef & security & is separated from the main hotel by a small river. A helipad is available for helicopter transfers. Member of Relais & Châteaux. **$$$–$$$$$**

🏠 **La Domaine de la Réserve Hotel** [122 D2] (40 rooms) Anse Petite Cour on the northwest side of Praslin; 📞 4298000; e resa@lareserve.sc; http://domainedelareserve.sc/en. The hotel, now under new ownership, has been refurbished in a relaxed colonial style & is situated on a sheltered, secluded beach with good swimming & snorkelling. It has an impressive pool & bar as well as an attractive restaurant on a jetty serving Creole, European & Chinese food. **$$$$**

🏠 **Acajou Hotel** [122 E2] (52 rooms) Côte d'Or; 📞 4385300; e acajou@seychelles.net; www.

acajouseychelles.com. Completely refurbished & opened in early 2015 with 14 deluxe rooms, 16 superior rooms, 14 standard rooms, 2 family rooms & 2 self-catering apartments, each with 2 bedrooms set in pretty gardens & almost on the beach. The Starfish Restaurant is open daily for hotel residents & visitors; Les Boucaniers offers intimate dining with Creole flair. A rim-flow pool, gym & a massage treatment room are available. A photovoltaic solar project keeps the hotel in power. **$$$**

🏠 **Hotel Coco de Mer** [122 E3] (52 rooms) Anse Bois de Rose on the southern coastline; 📞 4290555; e cocodeme@seychelles.net; www.cocodemer.com; see ad, page 204. The Hotel Coco de Mer is located on a narrow terrace with a small stretch of beach separating it from the exclusive Black Parrot Suites & Spa. Each room has its own private patio or balcony enjoying great sea views. The Hibiscus Restaurant serves breakfast, lunch & dinner with a special Creole buffet with Seychellois music & dancing twice a week. A casual restaurant is located at the pool where complimentary afternoon tea is served. The hotel has a gym, library & besides the usual watersports you can enjoy a relaxed sundowner in the gazebo over the water. The small private beach is best at low tide & a free service also transfers guests to Anse Lazio for the morning. The family owns the steep hillside behind the hotel & the fascinating Jean-Baptiste Nature Trail has been created, allowing guests to walk through fine pristine forest with wonderful views across Praslin. A natural history guide will accompany you; a small, informative, well-illustrated booklet is also available from the office. Look out for the young coco de mer palms growing in the garden. This family-run hotel provides outstanding, friendly service & real value for money. **$$$**

🏠 **Hotel L'Archipel** [122 E1] (32 rooms) Anse Gouvernement; 📞 4284700; e archipel@seychelles.net; www.larchipel.com. This hotel is located at a lovely beach near Anse Volbert at the end of a private road along a lush hillside. Peppermint-coloured L'Archipel offers a gracious ambience, a pool & fine cuisine from 2 restaurants. All the suites & rooms are very spacious & each has its own large veranda & sea views. No facilities for travellers with disabilities. Shorts are not permitted in the cocktail lounge & bar after 19.00, or in the restaurants for dinner. Free sports include a daily boat trip for snorkelling, canoes & windsurfing. **$$$**

🏠 **Le Duc de Praslin** [122 A4] (34 rooms) Anse Volbert; ✆4294800; e leduc@seychelles. net; www.leduc-seychelles.com. Situated in an exotic orchid garden. The rooms & bathrooms are extremely spacious, decorated in lovely vibrant colours. Located a 1min walk away from Côte d'Or Beach, the Duc de Praslin has 3 restaurants & 2 bars including the colourful Café des Artes right on the beach. There is a spa with massage treatment rooms. **$$$**

🏠 **New Emerald Cove** [122 G2] (42 rooms) Anse la Farine; ✆4232323; e emeraldcove@runbox.com; www.emerald.sc. The hotel is accessible only by boat, making it the ideal island getaway. The rooms are situated in chalets set among the tall coconut palms & lawns. The picturesque Hibiscus Restaurant serves international & Creole cuisine. Snorkelling off the beach is a good option & there are lovely paths through the forest adjoining the hotel. They specialise in weddings & can arrange everything for you. **$$$**

🏠 **Paradise Sun Hotel** [122 A4] (80 rooms) Anse Volbert; ✆4293293; e paradise@seychelles. net; www.paradisesunhotel.com. Situated at the end of Côte d'Or, it features a large, open, feet-in-the-sand restaurant & bar almost on the beach. The French Creole-style chalets have all the usual amenities including tea- & coffee-making facilities & the louvered doors open onto a private veranda facing the sea. **$$$**

🏠 **Berjaya Praslin Beach Resort** [122 A4] (79 rooms) Anse Volbert; ✆4286286; e bpbres@ berjayaseychelles.com; www.berjayahotels-resorts.com. The chalets are set around a swimming pool amidst coconut palms in a lush tropical garden which leads down to the protected beach where there is a pizzeria. Facilities for travellers with disabilities. **$$**

🏠 **Côte d'Or Lodge** [122 A4] (37 rooms) Côte d'Or; ✆4232200; e vacanza@seychelles.net; www. igrandiviaggi.it. These bungalows are scattered around a large, shaded garden with direct access onto the most gorgeous beach looking out towards Chauve Souris Island. Accommodation is offered on an FB basis. Daily activities as well as evening entertainment are organised. **$$**

🏠 **Indian Ocean Lodge** [122 C3] (32 rooms) Grande Anse; ✆4233324; e reservations@ indianoceanlodge.com; www.indianoceanlodge. com. Rooms have a nice veranda & views of the lush gardens. Situated on the long beach on the western side of Praslin, a central large thatched restaurant offers local & international cuisine. **$$**

SMALLER HOTELS

🏠 **Black Parrot Suites** [122 E3] (4 rooms) Anse Bois de Rose on the southern coastline; ✆4290555; e cocodeme@seychelles.net; www. cocodemer.com. The Black Parrot Suites & Spa is the exclusive, adults-only part of the Hotel Coco de Mer (page 127). The rooms are set around a clifftop pool with bar. The Waterfront Spa is ingeniously crafted among beautiful granite boulders & the 3 treatment rooms have stunning sea views. **$$$$**

🏠 **Le Château des Feuilles** [122 F3] (9 rooms) Pointe Cabris; ✆4290000; e info@chateaudefeuilles. com; www.chateau.com.sc. This classy hotel is located high above the ocean amid lush tropical vegetation & pink granite boulders & has stunning views to the nearby islands. The rooms are well appointed with all mod cons. A spectacular jacuzzi is situated high up on a headland with an amazing 300° view. The château has a private helipad enabling guests to fly to & from Mahé or to visit the neighbouring islands. Visits can be arranged to 100ha Grande Soeur Island which is exclusively for the use of hotel guests over w/ends. Enjoy a lunchtime BBQ, snorkelling & swimming at one of the most beautiful beaches in the Seychelles. Grand Soeur is a 20min boat ride from Praslin or 5mins by helicopter. Children over 8 years of age are accepted. Member of Relais & Châteaux. **$$$$**

🏠 **Dhevatara Beach Hotel** [122 C3] (10 rooms) Grande Anse; ✆4237333; e dbh. reservations@dhevatara.com. This beautifully designed hotel with spa & attractive water features is almost on the beach. The 5 Garden View suites & 5 Ocean View suites are luxuriously decorated, & there is fine dining in the Pond Restaurant. **$$$**

🏠 **Village du Pêcheur** [122 A4] (19 rooms) Côte d'Or; ✆4290300; e village@seychelles.net; www.thesunsethotelgroup.com. This small hotel was originally built by the sculptor Lourenzo Appiani. It is in a great location right on the beach in the heart of the activity of Côte d'Or. A library, internet, souvenir shop & massage rooms are available for guests. The attractive restaurant with tables in the sand specialises in seafood & is open to the public. Children over 12 are accepted. **$$$**

🏠 **Britannia Hotel** [122 D2] (12 rooms) Grand Anse; 📞 4233215; e britannia@seychelles.net. Close to the village of Grand Anse & 500m from the beach. The rooms are sparkling clean but the décor is a little dated; all have the usual amenities: AC, TV, hairdryer, coffee- & tea-making equipment. The Britannia Restaurant is highly recommended for its seafood & Creole meals. **$$**

🏠 **Colibri Guesthouse** [122 F3] (13 rooms) Pointe Cabris, Baie Ste Anne; 📞 4294200; e colibri@seychelles.net. Located high on the hillside, the simple rooms have a rustic feel & have fantastic views across Baie Ste Anne to Round Island & La Digue; the sunrises are worth getting up for. Evening meals can be provided & everyone sits at a long table to enjoy the Creole seafood fare. **$$**

🏠 **Islander Hotel** [122 A2] (5 rooms) Anse Kerlan; 📞 4233224; e islander@seychelles.net; www.islander-seychelles.com. This has bungalows set in a garden with beach frontage & an excellent Capricorn Creole restaurant. Hospitable Miette Godley will ensure you have a pleasant stay. **$$**

🏠 **Palm Beach Hotel** [122 D3] (16 rooms) Grande Anse; 📞 4290290; e palmbeach@seychelles.sc; www.palmbeachseychelles.com. This hotel has views over to Cousin & Cousine islands. Ground-floor rooms are suitable for people with disabilities with direct access to the beach & swimming pool. The restaurant serves Creole & international dishes. **$$**

GUESTHOUSES & SELF-CATERING APARTMENTS

🏠 **Mango Lodge** [122 A4] (11 rooms) Côte d'Or; 📞 4232077; e mango@seychelles.net. Self-catering establishment perched on a ridge high above the beach. It offers a penthouse with 2 en-suite bedrooms, 5 individual chalets & several other rooms. As the lodge is up a long & steep road it is advisable to have a car. If you are considering a long holiday, prices may be negotiable. They have a connection with Sagittarius Watersports. **$$$**

🏠 **Rocky Bay Villa** [122 F1] (4 rooms) Pointe Josephine, Anse la Blague; 📞 4237411; e reservations@seychellesparadisevillas.com. This large, multi-level house is the dream design of 3 men including an artist, who let their imaginations run wild. Paintings & murals adorn the walls & the 4 bedrooms each have a balcony. The dining area, with a natural waterfall & stunning views opens

onto a deck with steps leading down into the sea, but no beach. There is a fully equipped kitchen & a starter pack of food & drink is supplied on arrival. The manager can arrange the shopping, organise a cook, taxi, car or boat rental for you. The villa is right at the end of a narrow winding road & a car would be essential. **$$$**

🏠 **Laurier Eco Hotel** [122 A4] (13 rooms) Côte d'Or; 📞 4232241; e laurier@seychelles.net www.laurier-seychelles.com. Recently rebuilt, this hotel prides itself on environmentally friendly practices & has single & family rooms. Well-established restaurant & shaded off-road parking. **$$**

🏠 **L'Hirondelle** [122 B4] (11 apts) Cote d'Or; 📞 4232243; e hirondel@seychelles.net; www.hirondelle-seychelles.com. Completely renovated & enlarged in 2014, these bright, airy, blue-&-white apartments are available for self-catering only, though breakfast can be supplied. Well positioned close to the hub of Anse Volbert. **$$**

🏠 **Les Villas d'Or** [122 E2] (12 rooms) Anse Volbert; 📞 4232777; e villador@seychelles.net; www.seychelles.net/villador. This establishment is located close to the casino. The spacious, well-appointed villas with all the creature comforts are spread out around the garden ensuring privacy. Guests may request breakfast & dinner, which will be served in your villa. **$$**

🏠 **Villa des Alizés** [122 C3] (3 villas) Amitié; 📞 4237411; e reservations@seychellesparadisevillas.com. In a pretty garden, close to the beach & the airport. Ideal for children. Well-fitted kitchens but you can also hire your own Seychellois chef to cook a special meal. Can arrange excursions. **$$**

🏠 **Villas du Voyageur** [122 A2] (2 villas) Anse Kerlan; m 233161; e info@villasduvoyageur.sc; www.villasduvoyageur.sc. Nestled amongst stunning pink granite rocks, each villa has 2 bedrooms & a large living area. Ideal for families & golfers as it is adjacent to the beach & Lemuria golf course. Friendly Natalie & her menagerie will ensure you have a comfortable stay. **$$**

🏠 **Iles des Palmes Eco Resort** [122 F1] (18 bungalows) Anse Takamaka; m 2783051; e islands@seychelles.net; www.beachbungalow.sc. The 1–3-bedroom bungalows are located along a quiet beach near the heritage treasure trail. The larger bungalows are ideal for families. As it is some distance from shops, it would be advisable to have your own car. There is a pool, bar & La Buse Restaurant. **$–$$**

Villa Manoir [122 B1] (2 rooms) Anse Boudin; ☏4232161; e villamanoir@seychelles.net. An inexpensive, simple, self-catering option at the junction of the road up to Zimbabwe. Anse Lazio is about a 20min walk away. **$**

SATELLITE ISLANDS

Round Island [122 G2] (4 villas) ☏4671600; e round@seychelles.net or reservations@7south. net. A 10min boat ride from Baie Ste Anne, this tiny exclusive boutique hotel offers all the creature comforts in 3 luxurious, 2-bedroom villas & a 3-bedroom island mansion. **$$$$$**

Chauve Souris Island Lodge [122 D1] (5 rooms) ☏4232003; e vacanze@seychelles.net. This tiny island floating on the clear turquoise sea is only a few mins by boat from Côte d'Or Beach. The buildings are almost hidden by the lush green vegetation & granite boulders. A real hideaway with quirky open-air architecture. Included are all meals. Watersports & diving facilities are available at Côte d'Or Lodge. **$$$**

✕ WHERE TO EAT AND DRINK

As in Mahé, menus are biased towards seafood. Generally, lunch is served between noon and 14.00 and dinner between 19.00 and 21.00; this does, however, vary by restaurant and season. The smaller cafés and restaurants that serve both lunch and dinner often close around 14.30 and reopen in the evening. Many of the small shops sell icy soft drinks and beer as well as a range of samosas, small pies, chilli bites and cakes which are ideal for an inexpensive lunchtime snack. They are made on a daily basis so are always fresh and you are not likely to find anything left after 14.00. Many of the local eateries are in the form of take-aways. It is a good idea to find out where the Pralinois eat – you just have to get there before they do!

THE NORTHEAST: ANSE VOLBERT TO ANSE LAZIO

✕ **Tante Mimi's Restaurant** [122 E2] Casino des Isles, Anse Volbert; ☏4232500; ⊕ dinner only. Located above the casino, this large, smart restaurant serves a wide variety of food & their authentic Creole dishes are good. **$$$$**

✕ **Bonbon Plume** [122 B1] Anse Lazio; ☏4232136; ⊕ lunch 12.30–15.00 daily, dinner can be arranged by request for a group of 10 or more. Located under the palms on the famous beach. Fresh seafood is their speciality. **$$$**

✕ **Laurier Restaurant** [122 A4] Laurier Eco Hotel, Anse Volbert; ☏4232241. Located in the hub of the tourist part of Praslin, this establishment has a casual open-air restaurant serving a Creole buffet & the fresh fish is really good. Some nights, guests are entertained to live music. **$$$**

✕ **Le Chevalier Restaurant** [122 B1] Anse Lazio; ☏4232322; ⊕ 08.00–15.00 daily. Serves fresh seafood, curry as well as light snacks & sandwiches. A most extensive souvenir shop is located next to the restaurant. **$$$**

✕ **Café de Luca** [122 A4] Anse Volbert. This gelateria has been expanded into a small restaurant offering a limited menu. **$$**

✕ **La Goulue** [122 B4] Côte d'Or; ☏4232223. A relaxed open-air type of café on the main road at Côte d'Or serving lunch & dinner with the best fish & chips & curry chicken. **$$**

✕ **PK's@Pasquerie Restaurant & Gastropub** [122 B1] Anse Boudin; ☏4236242; e pk61@ seychelles.net. Overlooking the Curieuse Marine Park, this good-value restaurant is open all day with a small but select menu & range of drinks. **$$**

✕ **Pirogue Restaurant & Bar** [122 A4] Anse Volbert; ☏4236677; ⊕ 08.30–23.00 daily. In the heart of the touristy part of Praslin, this large airy restaurant has a comprehensive menu. **$–$$**

✕ **Berjaya Pizzeria** [122 A4] Berjaya Praslin Resort, Anse Volbert; ☏4286286. Conveniently near the beach with a fair selection of pizzas. **$**

THE SOUTHWEST: GRAND ANSE TO ANSE KERLAN

✕ **Café Le Monde** [122 C3] Amitié; ☏4781121; ⊕ lunch & dinner Mon–Sat. Thatched, airy restaurant with Creole & international menu plus pizza. **$$$**

✕ **The Pond Restaurant** [122 C3] Grande Anse; ☏4237333. Delightful, small restaurant set amidst water features & historic memorabilia at the Dhevatara Beach (page 128). **$$$**

✕ The Britannia [122 D2] Grande Anse; ☏4233215; ⏱ evenings only except Sun. Has a reputation for good Creole food. $$

✕ Capricorn Restaurant at the Islander Hotel [122 A2] Anse Kerlan; ☏4233224. Fine Creole fare & the best nougat coco! $$

NIGHTLIFE

As in Mahé, there is little nightlife other than what is available in the hotels. Some of the hotels do have live bands performing from time to time.

☆ **Oxygen** [122 E2] Baie St Anne; m 2512300; ⏱ 22.00–04.00 Fri/Sat; admission SR75pp, no under 18s. Has an intense party atmosphere that the local youngsters love. Smart casual.

OTHER PRACTICALITIES

The major banks have branches or ATMs at the three main centres on Praslin, namely, Baie Ste Anne, Grande Anse and Anse Volbert. There are post offices, petrol stations, police stations and grocery stores at Baie Ste Anne and Grand Anse. The hospital is at Baie Ste Anne.

DISCOVERING PRASLIN

The unhurried pace of life on Praslin is a holidaymaker's dream – beautiful beaches, good snorkelling, many restaurants and the majestic Vallée de Mai to explore. Seaweed can be washed ashore at certain times of the year; it generally gets cleared away but, if not, there are always beaches on the other side of the island to discover. There is not much nightlife although some of the hotels have live entertainment with local bands and singers.

Four routes can be followed to discover the central, western, southern and eastern parts of Praslin.

CENTRAL PRASLIN: BAIE STE ANNE TO GRANDE ANSE VIA VALLEE DE MAI The crowded **jetty** [122 F3] is a buzz of activity during the arrival and departure of the ferries. The ticket sales office is located here and the Seychelles Tourism Board, Creole Travel Services and Mason's Travel have offices to assist tourists with any queries. There is a money exchange, snack shop and even a tiny shop for purchasing the last must-have souvenirs from Praslin.

A long, low wooden building at the beginning of the jetty houses the offices of Hawksbill Dive Centre and Dream Yacht Seychelles (☏ *4233281;* e *info@ dreamyachtcharter.com; www.dreamyachtcharter.com*), which is associated with a small private marina. Catamarans, monohulls and motor boats are available for charter and provide a picturesque entrance to Praslin. On the hillside, the Baha'i Centre overlooks the jetty.

From the car park and bus terminus at the Baie Ste Anne jetty the road hugs the coast into the village. Immediately on the right is **Le Port Guest House and Boutique** [122 F3] (☏ *4232262*), where the owner is usually found hard at work with her sewing machine producing colourful, handmade clothing, which is also for sale in some hotels. Praslin Slipway and Engineering is a little further on and one can generally see a range of vessels undergoing repairs in the shipyard. **Amir's mini market** is on the right with the **Organibar and take-away** close by [122 F3] (⏱ *08.30–20.30 daily*). On the left, Mr Albert Durand's **Fabrication de Poisson en Bois** [122 F3] (m *2594248*) has a workshop oozing scruffy old Seychellois character, where he makes wooden fish, turtles and boats and welcomes visitors. The road continues towards the village past residential properties, shops and boutiques.

The conspicuous **Baie Ste Anne Church** with its really tall palm trees is on the sea side of the road with the **Vijay International School** adjacent to it. A convenient petrol station ($\oplus$ *06.00–20.00 daily*) is on the left, but check as sometimes it might close early on a Sunday. The road passes the police station, the Kannus office complex and the Baie Ste Anne Supermarket with the Oxygen Night Club upstairs, before reaching the village proper with a series of shops, general dealers and a large A-frame building housing a gym and internet café. A branch of Barclays [122 E2] ($\oplus$ *08.30–14.30 Mon–Fri, 08.30–11.30 Sat*), with ATM, is on the corner of the road leading to the Vallée de Mai.

A bridge to the right links the manmade Eve Island, covered in casuarina trees, to the mainland. There is a primary school on the island, a fuel depot and a substantial cargo wharf for schooners and barges to unload goods. Numerous boats are moored in the lagoon between Eve Island and Praslin.

To proceed to the Vallée de Mai and Grande Anse, turn left at the intersection in the village. Nouvobanq, with a bureau de change ($\oplus$ *08.30–14.00 Mon–Fri, 08.30–11.30 Sat*), is located on this road in a fairly modern building which also houses the offices of several social services and a small post office with public telephones. The green-roofed hospital is on the right, the library on the left and the road climbs slowly uphill past some residential properties until it enters the **Praslin National Park** through a green tunnel of forest, where the National Park Authority Office is located to the left. Tall trees, palms and screw pines line the roadside, creeping vines adorn the tree trunks and there is also a large scar of bare red earth as a result of a landslide in 2014. About 2km from the village, the bus stop, car park, bicycle racks and entrance to the **UNESCO World Heritage Site of Vallée de Mai**, home of the coco de mer, are reached. This is a must-see attraction; details can be found below.

About 500m beyond the park entrance, the picturesque waterfall made famous in the painting by Marianne North can be glimpsed through the foliage on the right-hand side of the road. Unfortunately, there is nowhere to park a car to view this famous waterfall; you simply have to walk along the narrow road. Marianne North was a wealthy Englishwoman and talented artist with a great pioneering spirit. During her travels around the world, she spent some time in the Seychelles in 1883, and did 45 fine watercolour paintings of the islands, including some of Praslin and the coco de mer, some of which can be seen in the Natural History Museum in Victoria.

The road descends to the west coast at Fond de l'Anse. The road to the left leads southwards to Anse Consolation and the road to the right goes along the coast of Grande Anse to the airport and Anse Kerlan.

Vallée de Mai [122 D2] ($\oplus$ *08.00–17.00 daily; admission SR340, inc fact-filled pamphlet & map; guides available for SR100pp in a group*) The UNESCO World Heritage Site of Vallée de Mai is a tiny enclave of 20ha within the Praslin National Park, and is home to some 4,000 coco de mer palms.

At the entrance there is a souvenir shop selling books, jewellery and curios pertaining to the coco de mer. Should you wish to purchase one of the extraordinary double nuts, be sure that it has the official certification papers with it, as they are necessary for the exportation of the coco de mer. Appealing to the romantic tourist market, an alcoholic liqueur Coco d'Amour is prepared and sold in a bottle resembling the double nut. Toilets are located behind the shop and storage lockers

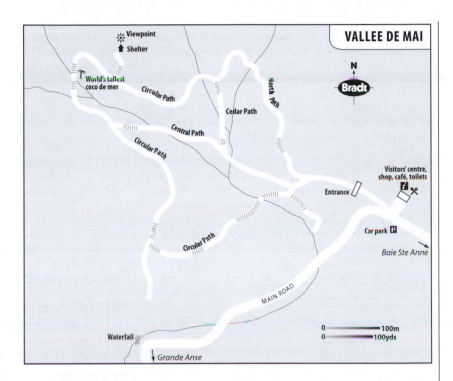

Viewpoint
Shelter
World's tallest coco de mer
Circular Path
Cedar Path
North Path
N
Central Path
Circular Path
Visitors' centre, shop, café, toilets
Entrance
Car park
Baie Ste Anne
Circular Path
MAIN ROAD
0 — 100m
0 — 100yds
Waterfall
↓ *Grande Anse*

are available. A cafeteria, **Kokosye** (⊕ *08.00–16.30 daily*), sells snacks, light meals and soft drinks.

Also at the entrance is a thatched shelter showing a detailed map of the area and there are usually a few coco de mer nuts with surrounding husks and flowers displayed on a bench. Pick up one of the nuts to feel the incredible weight.

The well-maintained paths are clearly marked and easy to follow. In some places they are a little steep with steps, and there are boulders as stepping stones across the streams. The shortest circular route of approximately 1km will take about an hour, allowing plenty of time to stop and examine all the interesting things described on informative plaques placed at various points along the way. Three hours are needed to complete the full north-to-south circular route, which includes a visit to the rustic shelter on the northern extremity. From there, the expansive views across the park give an idea of what the entire island must have looked like in its pristine state.

The palpable silence of the forest is likely to be broken by the friendly chattering of Seychelles bulbuls and, if you are lucky, by the noisy whistling calls of a black parrot. If there is a breeze, the other noise will be the clashing of the huge leaves of the coco de mer. Don't let a little shower of rain put you off visiting the Vallée de Mai as there is a special magic to visiting the valley in the rain. The enormous, thick, corrugated leaves of the coco de mer are like giant umbrellas, keeping you relatively dry as they channel the water down the gutter grooves of the leaf stems right down to the base of the trunk. Directly after rain is the most likely time to see the jewel-green female tree frogs, as well as the elusive tenrecs, rummaging around in the leaf litter looking for waterlogged insects.

The biodiversity of Vallée de Mai By a stroke of luck, the Vallée de Mai escaped any kind of degradation and remained a virtually virgin forest until the

1930s when the owner decided to beautify the valley and planted ornamental, fruit and spice trees to create a botanical garden. The government acquired the land in 1948, and started a programme to remove these alien plants and encourage the natural vegetation to regenerate. Cinnamon and allspice trees can, however, still be seen and there are a number of introduced jackfruit trees dotted about. Creeping vines of *Philodendron* and vanilla can be found in profusion, especially near the entrance. Further in, however, the forest is imbued with a pristine, primordial atmosphere.

Huge pre-Cambrian granite boulders are randomly scattered throughout the Vallée de Mai and weathering processes are responsible for leaving smaller rocks broken and jumbled together on the valley floor. Streams burble down the hillsides; freshwater crabs have burrows in the banks of the streams and shrimps live in the clear waters. Lichens, algae and mosses colour the rocks, and tiny ferns peep out from between the boulders. The low plant clinging to the edge of many of the pathways is known as gecko foot (*Salpiglossus*) and, according to folklore, has medicinal properties. Orchids, tree ferns, bird's nest fern (*Asplenium nidus*) and a variety of other epiphytic plants adorn many of the endemic trees and palms. Spectacular *Pandanus* screw pines add to the botanical mélange thriving in the Vallée de Mai.

All six species of palms (*latannyen*) endemic to the Seychelles grow in the reserve but the tall, erect coco de mer is the most spectacular, towering above them

COCO DE MER

Coco de mer (*Lodoicea maldivica*) belongs to the Borassaidae subfamily of the large palm family. It is dioecious, meaning that the male and female flowers are on separate plants. The male palm, which reaches a maximum height of about 30m, towers over the female palm which attains only about 24m. The mature, green, heart-shaped fruit is about 46cm long, and can weigh as much as 20kg, making it the heaviest seed in the plant kingdom. The male catkin can be as thick as a person's arm and roughly 50cm long. It bears small, yellow, fragrant flowers much loved by geckos and slugs. The female inflorescence bears five to 13 flowers covered by hard, round, brown bracts on a zigzag axis. Usually only one of the three ovules in each flower develops into a bi-lobed nut. Occasionally, however, a tri-lobed or even a quadri-lobed nut may be produced. Usually only three to five fruits on each female inflorescence develop and the fruit takes about seven years to reach maturity on the mother plant. During the maturation period a soft jelly develops inside the nut and, by the time the nut is fully mature, the jelly has become a very hard white kernel. The palm takes at least 25 years from germination until it bears fruit.

When the smooth, green coco de mer nut has fallen to the ground, it lies dormant for about six months as the outer husk disintegrates to expose the hard, rough-textured, dark brown nut. The shoot containing the embryo arises from the sinus between the two lobes, and probes into the soft ground before sending down a taproot and lateral roots. It takes almost two years from germination to the emergence of the first leaf. When the protective sheath splits, the enormous leaves on long stalks grow to a span of almost 6m. One of the intriguing aspects about the stability of this tall palm is the tough and fibrous bowl which forms at the base of the trunk. It is about 50cm in diameter and 20cm deep and is perforated by the numerous spreading adventitious roots, which ultimately support the tall

all. One of the most useful and important palms is *Phoenicophorium borsigianum*, known by its Creole name of *latannyen fey*. It has broad, undivided leaves and is used extensively for thatching. A roof properly thatched with these leaves will last for 20 years. The most noticeable things about *Verschaffeltia splendida* or *latannyen lat* are the sturdy prop-roots at the base of the trunk that support this tall palm. In the adult palm, the broad leaves appear shredded but they are not separate leaflets as in the coconut palm. Both *latannyen lat* and *fey* have sharp, black spines protecting the first two leaves of the young plant, so do not take hold of them. *Nephrosperma vanhoutteana* or *latannyen milpat* has leaves divided into smaller leaflets like the coconut. It gets the Creole name from the rippling leaves said to look like a walking millipede. Red berries are borne on a long straight spike, easily visible between the leaves. The *palmiste* or *Dekenia nobilis*, named after the famous Belgian explorer Baron von der Decken, is characterised by flowers that look like long strings of hanging spaghetti. *Roscheria melanochaetes*, or *latannyen oban*, which reaches a height of about 7m, is the smallest palm and has a slender trunk. It prefers shady spots and the leaves are red in young palms and dark green in the adult.

Other distinctive plants sharing the valley are the various *Pandanus* or screw pine species. Tall plants with a plethora of stilt roots to support them, they do vaguely resemble the palm family. Very often, though, the leaves have a serrated edge and appear thorny. Horne's pandanus (*Pandanus hornei*) has a single trunk

and heavily laden tree. Even after the palm has died and decayed, the bowl can remain for up to 60 years and many can be seen along the paths in the park.

MYTHS AND MYSTERIES OF THE COCO DE MER Before 1768, no-one knew the origins of the erotically shaped double-lobed nuts that were occasionally found on the faraway shores of India, Sri Lanka and the Maldives. They were named sea coconuts, and were believed to be the fruits of enormous trees that grew underwater in the great central whirlpool of the oceans. The mystical nuts were intricately carved and inlaid with precious gems, gold and silver and were the prized possessions of kings and rulers – some can be seen in the great museums of Europe. Besides its reputation of having aphrodisiac properties, the kernel of the coco de mer, decayed or otherwise, was believed to be a cure for many ailments and an antidote to poisons.

Barre, a surveyor with the Marion Dufresne expedition in 1768, brought the fabulous mysterious nuts to the attention of the world. He found the nuts in the forests of Praslin, and took them back to Mauritius where Pierre Poivre, the botanically minded quartermaster, realised what they were. *Voilà*, the secret of the coco de mer was out! General Charles Gordon visited Praslin in 1881 and was convinced that the coco de mer was the 'tree of knowledge'. He wrote extensively on his fanciful hypotheses, and contemplated that he had found the original Garden of Eden in the islands of the Seychelles.

Even today the Seychellois have some charming romantic fables about the mysterious palm. Because the male towers so protectively over the female it is reputed that, on nights when the moon is full, the male moves over to the female and they make love. No-one has ever reported on this phenomenon, because, as the story goes, if you witness it, you will be turned instantly into a black parrot!

supported by a tight cone of stilt roots, and a crown of leaves. The Seychelles pandanus (*Pandanus sechellarum*) has so many thick prop-roots that it is difficult to see which is trunk and which is root. *Pandanus* fruits are usually round or oval with many segments.

Two magnificent endemic trees are *Dillenia ferruginea*, known as *bwa rouz*, and *Northea hornei*, the *kapisen*. The scientific name of the *kapisen* honours both Marianne North, the artist, and John Horne, the botanical director of the Pamplemousse Gardens in Mauritius.

Walking along the paths, you have to be very observant to see some of the small creatures that dwell in this remarkable palm forest. The bright green tree frogs (*Tachycnemis seychellensis*) usually rest flattened against palm leaves, and you often see their shadows at eye level on the underside of the leaf. It is a good idea to use binoculars to examine the male catkins of the coco de mer as both the chunky bronze-eyed geckos (*Aeluronyx seychellensis*) and the slender green geckos (*Phelsuma*) are often seen amongst the flowers. Keep an eye on the forest floor for the brown Seychelles skink (*Mabuya seychellensis*). Amongst the molluscs, the endemic Praslin snail (*Pachnodus praslinus*), with a twirled and pointed shell, and the large *Stylodonta studeriana* snail are usually found on the coco de mer. The white slug (*Vaginula seychellensis*) particularly favours the flowers on the catkin of the male coco de mer.

The enigmatic bird of Praslin is the black parrot. It is, in reality, a dark chocolate-brown and is closely related to the Vasa parrots of Madagascar. They tend to move about in small family parties, whistling and calling to each other as they search out their favourite ripe fruits. They are likely to be heard before they are seen. Also commonly seen in the forest are Seychelles blue pigeons and noisy Seychelles bulbuls. At the beginning of the walk into the palm forest are some *takamaka* trees; when these are flowering, it is easy to see the Seychelles sunbirds feeding off the sweet nectar.

THE WEST COAST: GRANDE ANSE TO ANSE KERLAN VIA THE AIRPORT

Grande Anse Grande Anse has a lovely curved beach which, though sometimes covered in washed-up seaweeds and seagrasses during the southeast trades, is popular. Looking out beyond the beach, the islands of Cousin and Cousine seem to float upon the ocean. A thriving settlement spreads out along the shore of the bay with hotels generally positioned along the beachfront and shops on the inland side of the road.

Palm Beach Hotel, Long Beach Apartments in **House 2000** and **La Cuvette** are among the first in a series of accommodation establishments along this stretch of coastline. Kato Noir Restaurant, Sunset take-away, Island Pizzeria and Breeze Garden with take-away, bar, internet and bureau de change can supply your every need. After the St Matthew's Church, the **Britannia Hotel and Restaurant** (page 129) is located a short way up a small inland road.

Grande Anse is a busy area with a variety of services including a police station (✆ 4233251) and a health centre. Seychelles Savings Bank, MCB Seychelles and Barclays Bank, each with a bureau de change, are represented. Mason's Travel, the jewellery shop Kreol d'Or and Pradiso Cinema are all located in the large pink and grey granite Pension Complex. In the town, there are also several boutiques and souvenir outlets including Island Style, Janessa and Treasure Island, as well as hairdressers on both sides of the road.

Beyond Cable & Wireless is the petrol station (⊕ *06.00–20.00 Mon–Sat, 08.00–noon Sun*), but it is wise to ensure you have sufficient fuel during the day as opening times are apt to change. The line of hotels continues with **Beach Villa, Indian Ocean Lodge** (page 128), **Ocean Villas** and **Le Relax Beach Resort** which are all, literally, right on the beach. The classy **Dhevatara Beach Hotel** (page 128) with its bougainvillea-fringed roof garden and **Pond Restaurant** (page 130) is a new addition. Over the road is **Café le Monde** (page 130). Barakouda Boutique supplies fashionable clothing for both men and women. **Villas des Alizés** (page 129), **Villas de Mer, Ocean Jewels Resort, Le Tropique Villa** and **Amitié Chalets** are all set in lovely gardens close to the beach. The countryside flattens out beyond here with tempting views across to Cousin and Cousine islands.

Amitié Black Pearl of Seychelles [122 B3] (✆ *4233987;* e *prof@seychelles.net; www.blackpearlseychelles.com*) is on the sea side of the road opposite the airport. It includes a small **aquarium** (⊕ *09.00–16.00 Mon–Fri, 09.00–noon Sat; admission SR50 adults, under 12s are free*) with giant clams and several species of reef fishes that can be viewed in shallow tanks. The rare black pearls are farmed off Praslin and Linneys of Australia crafts the pearls into fine jewellery, which can be purchased at the boutique. Creole Travel Services have their offices next door, near the entrance to the airport.

Anse Kerlan The **Island Conservation Centre of Nature Seychelles** [122 B3] (page 109) is located on the landward side of the road next to the **new stadium** [122 B3], which promotes the conservation of Cousin Island, particularly with respect to turtles, birds and coral restoration, and welcomes visitors. After the picturesque **Notre Dame des Iles Chapel** [122 B3], a road to the left leads to the Seychellois-owned **Chateau Sans Souci** with **Cordon Bleu Restaurant, Red Dragon Chinese Restaurant** and **Kokoriko Disco**. A little further, the statue-adorned **Castello Beach Hotel** has beach frontage. Back on the road north, one finds Mas Supermarket and Happiness Bakery with a range of breads, cakes and pies.

The Islander (page 129) with beach frontage comprises 14 self-catering chalets, with Capricorn Creole Restaurant (page 131) in the same premises. Nearby are Souvenir des Iles and a small shopping centre housing the Praslin Souvenir Boutique and a general dealer selling everything from bread, beer, veggies and tinned goods to toothpaste and maybe a few coconuts. A narrow road on the seaward side leads to **Anse Kerlan Beach Chalets** and **Cap Jean Marie Chalet**. At the end, nestled amongst the pink granite rock and adjacent to the golf course, are the two spacious **Villas du Voyageur** (page 129).

Exclusive **Constance Lémuria** (page 127), a five-star hotel with a host of amenities pandering to every creature comfort, is the largest on Praslin and boasts the only 18-hole golf course in the Seychelles. Non-residents are welcome to play 18 holes for SR1,900 – fees include use of clubs and a golf cart. The gate is guarded and no-one is permitted to enter unless a prior arrangement has been made. If you feel like having a sundowner or dinner there, don't just drop in as you must make a reservation beforehand.

From this part of Praslin there are no roads over to the eastern side, only a series of tracks and walking paths to Anse Lazio, many of which are difficult to locate.

THE SOUTH COAST: GRANDE ANSE PAST POINTE CONSOLATION TO BAIE STE ANNE From Grande Anse southwards the coastal road traverses some of the most stunning parts of Praslin. Beautiful and undeveloped, with tiny, wild beaches and clear water of the most unbelievable hues – this is what the Seychelles is all about. Anse Citron is followed by Anse Bateau and a clump of granite rocks known as Grosse Roche, where **Les Rochers Boutique** [122 D3] and boat charter are found. In some places, at intervals along the road, there are small parking bays where it is possible to stop the car to admire the vistas that have the islands of Cousin and Cousine sandwiched between the sky and the sea in the distance. Coral reefs fringe the shore, but the shallow waters are not particularly good for swimming.

After Anse St Saveur, the road climbs a little towards the **Black Parrot Suites** and **Hotel Coco de Mer** (pages 128 and 127), a fine establishment with welcoming staff, wonderful hospitality and real black parrots in the natural vegetation surrounding the hotel. At Anse Consolation, look out for the limestone reef in between the granite boulders as the road swings to the left and continues past the **Bon Karé Guesthouse** [122 F3] (4322057). On the left is the entrance to the 122ha Ravin de Fond Ferdinand Nature Reserve where guided walks are offered (pages 140–1).

From its location at the top of the hill the luxurious **Le Château des Feuilles** (page 128) has a commanding view of the ocean. **Chalets Côte Mer**, **Le Grand Bleu Villa** and **Colibri** (page 129), three separate guesthouses, can be found down a very steep and narrow concrete road, but do not be put off – they are there, high on the hillside of Pointe Cabris with great views. The steep road with several sharp, hairpin bends and stunning views of Baie Ste Anne, continues down to the jetty.

THE EAST COAST: BAIE STE ANNE TO ANSE LAZIO VIA ANSE VOLBERT Instead of taking the left turn towards Vallée de Mai in Baie Ste Anne village, follow the road along the curve of the bay where the result of the reclamation project is visible. In the bustling village there is the red, corrugated-iron church, plus various merchants, general dealers, supermarkets, public telephones and the local eatery, **Coco Rouge Café** [122 E2]. The ISPC supermarket, which offers a wide range of imported goods, is on the sea side of the road and opposite you'll find a series of small self-catering establishments.

The eastern peninsula of Praslin extends to form a horseshoe providing shelter and protection to the beautiful natural harbour of Baie Ste Anne, now blemished by the land reclamation project. The very sheltered little bays of Anse Takamaka and Bonnet Kare can be found tucked in amongst the great granite boulders tinged with pink. Accessible only by boat, the **New Emerald Cove Hotel** at Anse la Farine (page 128) is located on the tip of the eastern peninsula looking out over Baie Ste Anne. Round Island is a short distance off the coast.

Although the main road swings left to Anse Volbert, one can continue towards Anse La Blague on a concrete road proceeding through wooded slopes with glimpses of the sea through the vegetation. **Iles des Palmes Eco Resort** (page 129) has large bungalows set in sprawling gardens along the beach at Anse Takamaka with views across to Baie Ste Anne. The resort has a pool, bar, La Buse Restaurant and an old copra house. The narrow, uneven road winds past the historical cinnamon distillery ruins over to the other side of the peninsula to Anse La Blague and, although it looks a bit rough, the smallest car can manage it. There, you will find the newly refurbished Villa Anse La Blague. An insignificant-looking road leads off to the left and if you fend your way through the thick vegetation you will eventually reach the large and imposing, pink **Rocky Bay Villa** (page 129), which is at the end of the track. There is now no option but to turn around, so cross the peninsula again and return to the main road leading to Anse Volbert and Côte d'Or.

A narrow road on the right-hand side of the main road leads to **L'Archipel** (pages 127–8), a hotel on the hillside with splendid views of Ile St Pierre and Curieuse and overlooking the secluded beach of Anse Gouvernement. This area is very sheltered during the southeast trades and greatly enjoyed by the local Praslinois.

Back on the main road is the grand-looking **Casino des Iles** [122 E2] (⊕ *19.30–03.00 Mon–Sat, noon–03.00 Sun, slots room ⊕ noon–02.00 daily, casino tables 20.30–03.00 daily*), which entices patrons by providing free transport from their hotels (℡ *4232500*). The exclusive **Tante Mimi's Restaurant** is upstairs (page 130).

Anse Volbert This is a fine 2km-long stretch of beach along the Côte d'Or coastline with many accommodation options available and a good selection of small shops and restaurants. All the hotels and guesthouses will arrange excursions to other islands as well as snorkelling, scuba diving or fishing expeditions. The first accommodation is **Les Villas d'Or** (page 129), located in pretty gardens, and the **Acajou Hotel** (page 127) is a little further on. Over the road, the little **Praslin Museum** [122 E2] (⊕ *09.00–17.00 daily; admission €10*), run by Steve Esther, offers insights into the lost traditional way of life in the Seychelles, medicinal plants and ethno-botany. After this, there is a stretch of woodland before reaching the more touristy part of Praslin, where the new, imposing **Cote D'Or Footprints** luxury chalets are on the sea side of the road. **La Goulue** Creole restaurant (page 130) is conveniently situated on the left and **L'Hirondelle guesthouse** (page 129) is a little further on.

At the fork in the road, a branch of MCB, with ATM, will be able to attend to your banking needs; a small supermarket and a couple of telephones are nearby. Keeping to the beach side at the fork, the first shop is the **Café de Luca** which also serves ice creams (page 130). Nouvabanq and Barclays ATMs, **Pirogue Restaurant** (page 130), Treasure Island Boutique, Louis Bedier Charter and Aquatic Store, Maki shop and the Côte d'Or souvenir boutique line the road.

Set back from the road is the yellow **Laurier Eco Hotel and Restaurant** (page 129), offering a good-value Creole buffet and easy off-road parking. Across the road, **Village du Pêcheur** (pages 128–9) and **Rosemary's Guesthouse** are located practically on the beach. Tantalising views of the tiny island of Chauve Souris can be glimpsed through the palm trees. The road ends at the **Berjaya Praslin Beach Resort** (page 128) which has all the amenities of a large hotel, and on the beach side of the cul-de-sac is the **Berjaya Pizzeria** (page 130) and **Octopus Diving** (page 70) alongside.

Returning to the fork, the road then continues parallel to the beach but behind the resorts. The first small road to the right goes down towards the beach and is lined with residential properties and a few guesthouses including the **Villa Bananier** and

Côte d'Or Chalets. Le Duc de Praslin Hotel (page 128) is set in a pretty garden filled with orchids and bright bougainvilleas. At the end of this road you will find the gaudy Café des Artes with bar. Sagittarius Watersports operate from the beach.

Back on the main road, a steep paved road to the left climbs the hill passing several residential homes before reaching Mango Lodge (page 129), perched high on the hillside with the most stunning views on Praslin. On the sea side of the main road there is another large hotel, the Paradise Sun (page 128), which is beautifully situated on a lovely stretch of beach. Whitetip Divers (page 70) is also on the beach, just beyond the hotel. Over the road is a rustic stall, Lakaz Tropical Fruits [122 A4], which extends back amongst the granite rocks. Here, Keven and Katy prepare fresh fruit juices and can rustle up Creole-style seafood meals. The road which has looped behind the hotels now reaches the coast at Anse Petite Cour where La Domaine de la Réserve Hotel (page 127) is located, boasting a remarkable restaurant built on stilts over the water.

From the coastline of Anse Possession one has great views of Curieuse, only a little way offshore. Anse Possession has historical connections, as Marion Dufresne placed a Stone of Possession there in 1768, claiming Praslin for France. A string of self-catering establishments line the bay, and in stark contrast, the lofty concrete villas of Raffles (page 127) expand over two hillsides from Anse Takamaka to Anse Boudin. The road has been diverted around behind the resort and offers commanding views. A walking and bike track does, however, follow the coastline.

PK's@Pasquerie Restaurant (page 130) is located on the hillside overlooking Curieuse and prawns are the owner's speciality. At Anse Boudin there is a large church, good snorkelling and the rustic, Rasta seaside Cabanne offering juice and souvenirs. Further on, there is the unpretentious Villa Manoir (page 130) with a small café. A secondary road heads inland up the hill to Zimbabwe [122 B2] and, although public access ends at the closed gates, the road continues to the radio communication antennae at the summit. A sunset trip up here is fabulous with panoramic views of Mahé, Silhouette and North islands to the south and Curieuse, Aride, La Digue and many of the smaller islands to the north and east.

The coastal road eventually descends to Anse Lazio, a breathtakingly beautiful, secluded beach with good snorkelling and swimming. It is often described as the most beautiful beach in the Seychelles, with a long stretch of silvery sand framed by granite boulders. Unfortunately, in 2011 there were two shark attacks in quick succession, and, as a result, a shark-exclusion net has been put in place to provide a safe swimming area. Lifeguards are on duty and the tourist police maintain an obvious presence to prevent petty theft. Almost on the beach you'll find Bonbon Plume (page 130), a feet-in-the-sand restaurant, shaded by some remaining *takamaka* trees, coconut palms and umbrellas. A large thatched shelter is a haven in a sudden tropical downpour. Le Chevalier Bar and Restaurant (page 130) is on the other side of the parking area, and Elna's Boutique, adjoining the dining area, is crammed full of souvenirs of every description.

WALKS ON PRASLIN

FOND FERDINAND The paths and boardwalk take you among the lovely forested slopes of this 122ha reserve. Guided walks (*SR125pp inc the guide*) are offered through the indigenous vegetation up to a viewpoint (at least 100 steps!) taking about 2 hours up and down. It can be very hot for the fairly steep climb so make sure you have water with you and preferably do it in the early morning. Black parrots are often sighted in this area and the views over Baie St Anne are gorgeous.

ANSE GEORGETTE To visit one of Praslin's most beautiful little beaches, walk along the golf course at Lemuria and find the path leading down to the beach. Best to get full directions and all the details from Lemuria. It is a little hilly and will take about 20 minutes. Once you get there you may well have the beach all to yourself. Be aware that the currents can be strong with large waves at times and there are no lifeguards or mobile phone coverage. There are no facilities so remember to take a snack and plenty of water with you. Get permission from Lemuria (page 127) a day in advance as limited numbers are allowed on this beach at one time. You can, of course, arrive by boat, anchor offshore and take your tender to land on the beach.

EXCURSIONS TO SATELLITE ISLANDS

Praslin is ideally situated as a springboard to the many surrounding islands. There are several options: trips that incorporate several islands in a day; one island per day; or else plan to spend a few days on La Digue, less than 30 minutes away by ferry. All the hotels and guesthouses will be able to make arrangements for you or, if you prefer, go to one of the larger tour operators. Depending on the weather, landing on some of the smaller islands can be tricky, as none has a jetty. Many of the excursions include snorkelling and, even though snorkel gear is promised, it is wise to check it thoroughly before you take off. Several of the neighbouring islands are nature reserves and most have no overnight accommodation except for La Digue. For more details, see *Chapter 7*, page 157.

COUSIN ISLAND SPECIAL RESERVE (⊕ *09.30–noon Mon–Fri*). This bird sanctuary island welcomes visitors, and each visit lasts approximately two hours. As the birds are completely unafraid of people and are breeding most of the year round, a strict behaviour code is in place for both visitors and management. The landing fee of €35 will usually be included with the cost of the excursion. See pages 167–9.

ARIDE Aride is a bird reserve surrounded by a marine protected area. It takes about 90 minutes to get there from Praslin and the cost will depend on the number of people using the boat. It is open to visitors Monday to Friday. The landing fee is €35 and will probably be included in the cost of the boat journey. See pages 164–7.

CURIEUSE Curieuse can be easily visited on a day trip and any of the Praslin hotels or tour operators will be able to arrange an excursion. See pages 170–2.

ILE ST PIERRE This islet is no more than a clump of rocks with a few palm trees on top, but it is a very good snorkelling spot and is easily accessible by boat from Anse Volbert. It is often combined with a day excursion to Curieuse. See page 170.

LES SOEURS AND ILE COCOS Grande Soeur has one of the most beautiful beaches in the Seychelles and day trips can be easily arranged with charter boats operating from Baie Ste Anne or Anse Volbert. The excursion is frequently in combination with a snorkelling trip to Ile Cocos. See pages 172–4.

Praslin EXCURSIONS TO SATELLITE ISLANDS

5

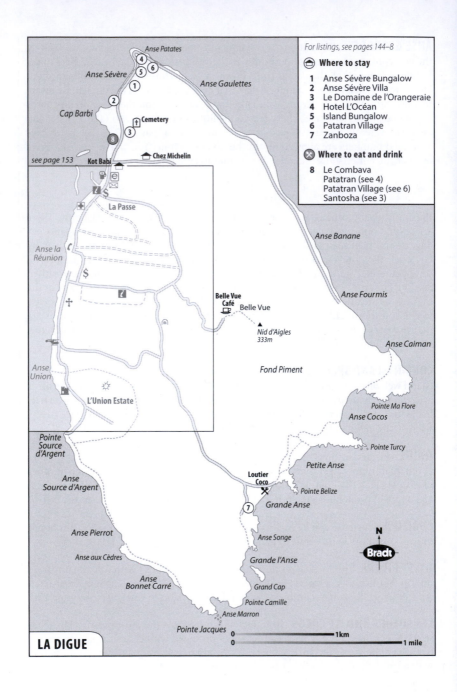

see page 153

For listings, see pages 144–8

🛏 **Where to stay**

1 Anse Sévère Bungalow
2 Anse Sévère Villa
3 Le Domaine de l'Orangeraie
4 Hotel L'Océan
5 Island Bungalow
6 Patatran Village
7 Zanboza

❌ **Where to eat and drink**

8 Le Combava
Patatran (see 4)
Patatran Village (see 6)
Santosha (see 3)

Anse Patates
Anse Sévère
Anse Gaulettes
Cap Barbi
Cemetery
Chez Michelin
Kot Babi
La Passe
Anse la Réunion
Anse Banane
Anse Union
Anse Fourmis
Belle Vue Café
Belle Vue
Nid d'Aigles 333m
Anse Caiman
Fond Piment
L'Union Estate
Pointe Ma Flore
Anse Cocos
Pointe Source d'Argent
Pointe Turcy
Anse Source d'Argent
Loutier Coco
Petite Anse
Pointe Belize
Grande Anse
Anse Pierrot
Anse Songe
Anse aux Cèdres
Grande l'Anse
Anse Bonnet Carré
Grand Cap
Pointe Camille
Anse Marron
Pointe Jacques

N

Bradt

0 _____ 1km
0 _____ 1 mile

LA DIGUE

6

La Digue

La Digue, with its dramatic, sculptured granite rocks and exquisite beaches, is a laid-back, inviting island in the sun. It lies 50km northeast of Mahé, 4km east of Praslin and is the fourth largest of the granitic islands. The 10km² island is almost completely encircled by coral reef and has no natural harbour. A jetty has been built at La Passe on the west coast and, recently, a breakwater has been constructed to provide more shelter, particularly during the northwest monsoons. The island is about 6km long, a little over 3km wide, and rises up to 333m at Nid d'Aigles, 'Eagles Nest', the highest peak.

Marion Dufresne, in his ship *La Digue*, made the first recorded discovery of this picturesque island in 1768, and the French took formal possession of it in 1771. Amid the lush vegetation, streams and swamps, the worst thing the early settlers had to contend with was the crocodiles, and they were soon eradicated along with the tortoises. The birdlife managed to cling on to a precarious existence, and the rare black paradise flycatcher is still present in low, but increasing numbers.

Coconut palms, magnificent white beaches, few shops, plenty of bicycles and a couple of ox carts all add up to a totally relaxed island-style way of life. At L'Union Estate copra is still processed in the old-fashioned way using an ox to turn the grinding wheel for extracting the coconut oil. Boats are built and repaired using traditional methods, and nobody is ever in a hurry. There are some lovely examples of Creole architecture nestling amongst the lush vegetation. Most of the 2,700 residents are involved in the tourism industry, others are fishermen and some are boat builders. On La Digue you will find small, welcoming guesthouses, coconut and vanilla plantations, art studios and the most seductive beaches. Although the public telephones may not always work, the ferries do arrive and depart on time. Over the years there has been increasing development on La Digue and, when the morning ferry arrives, it can be rather congested at the jetty. Recently, there has been a proliferation of vehicles on the island, which is somewhat disconcerting on the narrow roads.

GETTING THERE AND AWAY

BY AIR Zil Air (4375100; e book@zilair.com; www.zilair.com) provides helicopter services to La Digue from Praslin or any of the nearby islands. For four passengers from Praslin to La Digue, it costs approximately €869.

BY SEA The usual route is to take *Cat Cocos* from Mahé to La Digue via Praslin, which takes about 90 minutes, and a return trip costs approximately €128 in economy class and €158 in business class. There are only one or two of these direct crossings scheduled each day and reservations may be made at the online site at www.seychellesbookings.com or by emailing e reservation@catcocos.com. See page 83 for the timetable.

Throughout the day, there are also easy connections from Praslin to La Digue with one of the *Cat Rose*'s ferries (*reservations* ✆ *4232329*). This crossing takes less than 30 minutes and a return ticket costs approximately €30. For details on times and how to book, see pages 63 and 125.

Inter-island cargo schooners also ply the seas between La Digue, Mahé and Praslin and sometimes there is space for passengers to enjoy this unique experience. The schooner takes about 3 hours from Mahé, and in rough weather the rolling motion may cause some *mal de mer*. Boats of various descriptions may also be chartered in Mahé in order to make your own voyage of discovery to La Digue.

GETTING AROUND

The best way to get around this small island is by **bicycle**, and some of the hotels and guesthouses offer one as part of the deal. If they don't, or you are only on La Digue for the day, there are several hire companies near the jetty, including Michelin Cycles (m *2588890*), J&J (m *2591908*) and J&P (m *2514653*), as well as Tati's in La Passe. All charge around SR125 a day, and it is advisable to check the seat height, gears and brakes before setting off. There are now some taxis on the island and, if you are in a group, it is possible to find an open truck to take you around; enquire at the STB Tourist Information Office on the jetty. It is also quite easy to walk around, though you will need more time if you explore on foot.

A few **ox carts** are still available for transport around the island, but these are gradually being phased out and replaced by less rustic, open-sided **lorries**. Local guides including Robert Agnes (m *2525357*; e *sunnytrailguide@gmail.com*) and Rondy Payet (m *2590368*) are also available to show you around their island. They charge between €35 and €55 per person for a hike.

TOURIST INFORMATION

The STB Tourist Information Office (✆ *4234393*; ⏰ *08.00–16.30 Mon–Fri*) is at the jetty and they can give you plenty of local information. The jetty is the hub of La Digue and banks, the post office, the police station and local tour operators are all located close to it. Guesthouses and hotels are spread out from the northern end of the island to L'Union Estate in the south with several establishments a short distance inland.

WHERE TO STAY

There are only two largish hotels on La Digue; the other accommodation consists of a variety of small hotels, guesthouses and self-catering establishments. Most of the guesthouses have a typically relaxed Creole atmosphere and will provide delicious homemade meals on request. They can also arrange bicycle hire, snorkelling and diving trips as well as excursions to many of the nearby islands.

HOTELS

🏠 **Le Domaine de l'Orangeraie** [map, page 142] (55 chalets) Anse Sévère; ✆ 4299999; e reservations@orangeraie.sc; www.orangeraie.sc. An excellent hotel with the spectacular Eden Rock Spa perched high above the beach with views across to Praslin. 20 Garden Villas are close to the beach in a pretty garden, 31 larger Villas de Charme are spread up the steep hillside, together with 3 more luxurious Villas de Charme Elégance, & a large, ultra-luxurious Villa Présidentielle that accommodates 6 guests. The Combava (à la carte) & Santosha (buffet) restaurants & 2 pool bars provide a wide variety of dining options. Guests are transferred from the jetty by electric golf carts, which are also used to get you between your villa on the hillside & the dining/reception area, & complimentary bicycles & snorkelling gear are available. **$$$$**

La Digue Island Lodge [153 A3] (69 rooms) Anse la Réunion; 4292525; e reservation@ ladigue.sc; www.ladigue.sc. This is the original hotel on the island & has gardens opening out onto the beach. There is a big swimming pool with a bar & delicious Creole food is served in the restaurant. A range of accommodation is available, including rustic A-frame chalets & the old, yellow Creole planter's house built in 1900 (now a national heritage building). The bijoux spa has a menu of treatments on offer. Pro Diving Centre (*4292535*) can arrange your diving expeditions & is located near the swimming pool. Accommodation at L'Union Estate Chalets can also be arranged. **$$$**

Le Repaire Boutique Hotel [153 A2] (9 rooms) Anse la Réunion; 4234332; e reservations@lerepaireseychelles.com; www. lerepaireseychelles.com. New, beautifully appointed hotel on the beach with a good restaurant. Excellent reviews. **$$$**

Château St Cloud [153 C2] (29 rooms) Anse la Réunion; 4234346; e stcloud@seychelles.net; www.seychelles.net/stcloud. The former vanilla plantation house is high on the hillside & is a 10min walk down to the beach. The hotel, with a friendly, family atmosphere, is set in a large garden surrounding a refreshing pool. Matriarch Miriam St Ange will greet you with warmth & hospitality. The restaurant prides itself on serving excellent Creole cuisine. **$$**

Hotel L'Océan [map, page 142] (8 rooms) Anse Patates; 4234180; e hocean@seychelles. net; www.hotelocean.info. This small hotel is located at the northern tip of La Digue close to Anse Sévère & Anse Patates. The rooms have AC & each has a private balcony. The Patatran Restaurant serves tasty island food sometimes with local musicians in attendance. Check that the service charge & government tax is included in the price of the food or drink. **$$**

Patatran Village [map, page 142] (28 rooms) Anse Patates; 4294300; e patatran@seychelles.

net; www.patatranseychelles.com. The hotel is set on the hillside overlooking the ocean with splendid views to Cocos, Les Soeurs & Félicité islands. A tiny, secluded beach between massive granite boulders is below the hotel. There is a variety of rooms, some of which are ideal for families. A stylish new reception, dining area & swimming pool together with several new rooms have been constructed on the sea side of the road. **$$**

GUESTHOUSES

Bernique Guesthouse [153 C2] (5 rooms) La Passe; 4234229. A small, very friendly family-run establishment on the inland road & a 10–15min walk from the jetty. Rooms are cleaned daily & a good b/fast is served on the terrace. Find the 2 giant tortoises in the garden. **$$**

Birgo Guesthouse [153 C2] (8 rooms) La Passe; 4234518; e birgo@seychelles.sc. Bungalows set in a large tropical garden with a swimming pool. 5min walk from the beach. **$$**

Calou Guesthouse [153 C2] (5 rooms) La Passe; 4234083; e calouguesthouse@gmail. com; www.calouguesthouse.com. Klaus is the owner of this simple but friendly establishment set a little way back from the beachfront. Each recently refurbished room has a fridge & a veranda. There is a small, shaded pool & internet access. Delicious, inventive Creole-style cuisine is enjoyed around a communal table; non-residents are welcome for dinner but bookings are required. German atmosphere & many guests return repeatedly. **$$**

Chez Marston [153 B2] (5 rooms) La Passe; 4234023; e mars@seychelles.net; www.chezmarston.com. A typical Seychellois establishment run by Marston Saint Ange & his family. It is close to the beach & the jetty, has a large restaurant & is ideal for an informal holiday. **$$**

Le Relax Beach House [153 A4] (4 rooms) Anse la Réunion; 4234433; e marketing@ lerelaxhotel.com. Bright, spacious rooms & a lovely sea-facing veranda for the tasty meals. **$$**

Rising Sun Guesthouse [153 B3] (5 rooms) Anse la Réunion; 4234017; e risingsunghse@ seychelles.net. Well located, with the Vev Reserve almost across the road, a supermarket around the corner & about 2mins' walk to the Réunion Beach. Caters for families & homecooked Creole dinner can be ordered. **$$**

Sitronel Guesthouse [153 C2] (4 rooms) La Passe; 4234230. About 1km from the jetty, this relaxed guesthouse has spacious rooms & Madame Guy provides a Creole dinner in the garden restaurant. **$$**

🏠 **Bamboo Lodge** [153 C1] (10 rooms) La Passe; ☎ 4234155; e tournesol@seychelles. net. Located conveniently close to the beaches, this guesthouse is situated in a pretty garden. The restaurant serves good Creole food & there is free internet. **$**

🏠 **Pension Michel** [153 B3] (7 rooms) Anse la Réunion; ☎ 4234003; e pm@seychelles.net; www. pensionmichel.sc. This is conveniently located close to the Vev Reserve, supermarkets & beaches. It has a restaurant with a good reputation, & booking is essential. Good value. **$**

🏠 **Sunshine Guesthouse** [153 A2] (4 rooms) La Passe; ☎ 4234033; e judemg@hotmail.com. Small guesthouse on the beachfront. **$**

🏠 **Villa Authentique** [153 C2] (7 rooms) La Passe; ☎ 4234413; e villauthentique@seychelles. net. Mrs Ah Kong runs this guesthouse in a garden setting. It is close to the jetty & beaches. The bar is open all day & fishing trips can be arranged. **$**

🏠 **Zerof Guesthouse** [153 C3] (4 rooms) Anse la Réunion; ☎ 4234067; www.zerofguesthouse. com. Located near flycatcher nature reserve, this has an associated restaurant & bar. **$**

SELF-CATERING The price codes listed in this section are per room or bungalow per night for 2 people.

🏠 **L'Union Estate Chalets** [153 A6] (4 chalets) L'Union; ☎ 4234240; e reservation@ladigue.sc; www.ladigue.sc. The chalets are set under the palms in the estate & close to Source d'Argent Beach. Guests may use all the facilities at La Digue Island Lodge. The spacious chalets have well-equipped kitchenettes. **$$$** for 4 people

🏠 **Etoile Labrine** [153 B5] (10 rooms) L'Union; ☎ 4235140; e info@etoile-labrine. com; www.etoile-labrine.com. The rooms are in bungalows set along neat paths & tidy gardens filled with tropical flowering plants. All the en-suite rooms have an outside shower, AC & fans. The airy dining room serves breakfast & dinner. Their own boat, *Labrine*, is available for snorkelling, fishing & sunset cruises. **$$**

🏠 **Fleur de Lys** [153 A2] (4 bungalows) Anse la Réunion; ☎ 4234459; e fleurdelysey@yahoo.com; www.fleurdelysey.com. All the attractive, spacious,

colonial-style bungalows have well-equipped kitchens for self-catering. Mary & Ron Henry, your friendly hosts, will be able to arrange all your excursions. **$$**

🏠 **Island Bungalow** [map, page 142] (2 bungalows each with living room & bedroom) Anse Sévère; m 2514975; e islandbungalow@ email.sc. Mary-Anne & Fred will warmly welcome you & can provide meals on request. They can also arrange visits to the nearby islands of Cocos & Grande & Petite Soeur. **$$**

🏠 **Paradise Flycatcher Lodge** [153 A4] (4 bungalows) Anse la Réunion; ☎ 4234422; e mcdurup@seychelles.net. Spacious bungalows 2mins' walk from the beach. Offer self-catering options and a restaurant featuring Creole fare. Non-residents are welcome but booking essential. **$$**

🏠 **Petra's Guesthouse** [153 C2] (3 rooms) La Passe; ☎ 4234302; e petra@seychelles.sc. One of the least expensive options. Modest rooms are inside the owner's house so you get a truly Seychellois atmosphere. Kitchenette available but the owner can prepare meals for you. Fishing charters are available on their boat *Belle Petra* (page 155). **$$**

🏠 **Anse Sévère Bungalow** [map, page 142] Anse Sévère; ☎ 4247354; e clemco@seychelles.net. Located close to the beach, this 2-bedroom cottage is ideal for a quiet Robinson Crusoe-style holiday. **$**

🏠 **Anse Sévère Villa** [map, page 142] Anse Sévère; ☎ 4235009; e ansesevere@seychelles.net. Large 4-bedroom villa located close to the beach, ideal for a large family. **$**

🏠 **Casa de Leela** [153 C3] (8 rooms) Anse la Réunion; ☎ 4234193; e casadeleela@seychelles. sc; www.casa-de-leela.bplaced.net. These nicely decorated bungalows & apartments are located in a cool, shady garden with plenty of tall trees & is a short distance from the beach. **$**

🏠 **Kot Babi Villa** [153 B1] (4 rooms) La Passe; m 2514338; e babi@seychelles.sc. Near the jetty in a tropical garden with views over to Praslin. A private veranda for each room. Babi is a great Creole chef & will happily prepare a tasty dinner for you. **$**

🏠 **La Digue Self-Catering Apartments** [153 A3] (6 apts) La Passe; ☎ 4123521; e ladigueself@seychelles.net. Apartments upstairs in the new, as of 2015, Mills Complex. Nicely furnished, each with a private veranda & a small, but well-equipped, kitchenette, close to beaches & shops. Available on a self-catering, B&B or HB basis. **$**

⌂ Oceane [153 B1] (4 rooms) La Passe; **m** 2511818; **e** oceaneselfcatering@seychelles.net; www.oceane.sc. Near the jetty, set back from the beach along a small road. All the mod cons you will need to be comfortable. Excellent reports. **$**

⌂ Pension Hibiscus [153 B3] (5 rooms) Anse la Réunion; ☎4234029; **e** jealicel@seychelles.net. A small establishment in landscaped grounds that offers B&B or self-catering options. Close to the beach. **$**

⌂ Pension Residence [153 C1] (6 bungalows) La Passe; ☎4234304; **e** chezmich@seychelles.

net; www.seychelles.net/chezmich. Choice of self-catering or B&B. The spacious bungalows are close to the beach, each with a veranda. **$**

⌂ Tannettes Villa [153 C3] (5 rooms) La Passe; ☎4234039. Double-story villa located at the end of the track from the beach close to La Vev Reserve. **$**

⌂ Zanboza [map, page 142] (3 rooms) Grande Anse; ☎4234776; **e** wilfrid@seychelles.net. Located in the southeastern, more rural part of La Digue. **$**

✕ WHERE TO EAT AND DRINK

Many of the smaller guesthouses have restaurants and will happily provide meals on request. It is necessary to book in advance as they are really simple, family-run establishments that serve traditional Creole meals usually featuring fresh fish. Generally, lunch is served between noon and 14.00 and dinner between 19.00 and 21.00. This does, however, vary by restaurant and season. A government tax is payable and usually included with the price as is a service fee but occasionally they are excluded from the menu price so it is a good idea to ask if it is not clearly stated on the menu, you could end up paying 25% more for a meal or a drink.

✕ Le Combava at Le Domaine d'Orangerie [map, page 142] ☎429999; ⊕ lunch & dinner daily, closed Wed night. A superior fine dining à la carte restaurant situated on the rooftop terrace with a great ambience & excellent food. Expensive, but spoil yourself. Reservations essential. **$$$$$**

✕ Le Repaire Hotel Italian Restaurant [153 A2] Anse la Réunion; ☎4234332; www. lerepaireseychelles.com; ⊕ b/fast, lunch & dinner. Authentic Italian restaurant in the new hotel. **$$$**

✕ Le Veuve Restaurant at La Digue Island Lodge [153 A3] Anse la Réunion; ☎4292525. This has a high, thatched roof & feet-in-the-sand ambience, & offers a fine Creole buffet. **$$$**

✕ Patatran Restaurant [map, page 142] Hotel L'Océan, Anse Patates; ☎4234180; lunch & dinner daily. The restaurant has great views of the ocean & a good reputation for its spicy Creole fare. Guests can sometimes enjoy live music. The dining tables are beach-life showcases with all manner of shells & seaweed on display. **$$$**

✕ Patatran Village Restaurant [map, page 142] Anse Patates; ☎4294300. The restaurant of the hotel with the same name has lovely views through the palms over the ocean. Good selection of wines. **$$$**

✕ Santosha Restaurant at Le Domaine d'Orangerie [map, page 142] Elegant restaurant with a delicious, diverse themed buffet for dinner. **$$$**

✕ Fish Trap [153 B2] La Passe; **m** 2512111; **e** ladigueself@seychelles.net; ⊕ 07.30–23.00 daily. Opened in Jun 2015, this is the largest stand-alone restaurant in La Digue owned by Seychellois brothers. Located on the beachfront, it is bright & airy in blue & white with a seaside theme showing plenty of fish traps & shells. Specialising in fresh seafood. **$$–$$$**

✕ Chez Marston Restaurant & Bar [153 B2] Anse la Réunion; ☎4234023; ⊕ 08.00–22.00 daily. A large, casual Creole restaurant. The menu is expansive, catering for all tastes. It features a salad bar, coffee, cakes, wines, & even a special La Digue pizza. **$$**

✕ Lanbousir [153 A6] ⊕ 09.00–17.00 daily. Casual open-air restaurant selling welcome cool drinks & light meals, along the path leading to the Source d'Argent Beach. Fresh fish is especially good & well priced. **$$**

✕ Loutier [map, page 142] Grand Anse; **m** 2514762; ⊕ 08.00–17.00 for drinks only, lunch 12.30–15.00 daily. This is the only restaurant on the east side of the island, with a palm frond roof

& a lively ambience only a little way off the beach. A generous Creole buffet lunch is served including curried octopus & a large grilled fish. $$

✕ **Zerof Restaurant & Bar** [153 C3] Anse la Réunion; ☎ 4234439; ☉ lunch & dinner. Take-away available. $$

NIGHTLIFE

La Digue is even quieter than Praslin, but the locals frequent **La Noche Disco and Chill Down Bar** at La Passe [153 B1] (☉ *22.00–04.00 Fri/Sat, 16.00–22.00 Sun*), where there is a cafeteria and snack bar, dance floor, pool tables, table football, darts and a large flat-screen TV which shows sports and some movies. The **Jugglers Inn Casino and Fun Park** [153 B1] are right next door.

OTHER PRACTICALITIES

The police station (☎ *4234251*) is in La Passe, next to the post office [153 B1] (☉ *08.00–16.00 Mon–Fri, 08.00–noon Sat*). Creole Travel Services has an office at La Passe [153 B1] (☎ *4234411*), as does Mason's [153 B2] (☎ *4234227*). Shops have the usual Seychellois opening times (☉ *08.00–16.00 Mon–Fri, 08.00–11.30 Sat*), but these may vary a little by opening and closing later – some may even close at lunchtime as it is, after all, a laid-back little island with a slow pace.

BANKS
$ **Barclays** [153 B3] Anse La Réunion; ☎ 4234148; ☉ 08.30–14.30 Mon–Fri, 08.30–11.30 Sat
$ **MCB** [153 B2] La Passe; ☎ 4234560; ☉ 08.30–11.30 & 12.15–14.30 Mon–Fri
$ **Nouvobanq** [153 B2] La Passe; ☎ 4235032; ☉ 08.30–14.00 Mon–Fri, 08.00–11.00 Sat
$ **Seychelles Savings Bank** [153 B2] La Passe; ☉ 08.30–14.30 Mon–Fri

DISCOVERING LA DIGUE

Cycling is a great way to get around the island although, in hot weather, it can be a bit of a slog to get over to Grande Anse on the eastern side. At the jetty, and along the road, there are several bicycle-hire shops; remember to check the tyres, gears and brakes before you set off. It is advisable to take plenty of water to drink, a hat and sunscreen when you head out on your travels. Maps and local information can be obtained from the **tourist office** [153 B1] at the jetty.

Start exploring the beautiful little island from the jetty. Several routes can be followed but, basically, they cover the coast to the north, the coast to the southwest, across the island to Grande Anse, and inland leading up the hill to Nid d'Aigles.

THE NORTH: LA PASSE TO ANSE PATATES AND ANSE GROSSE ROCHE From **La Passe jetty,** turn left at the **Port Authority** building which houses *Cat Cocos*, 7° South Travel, Le Kazye, an internet bureau, public toilets and several souvenir kiosks. The post office, police station and bakery are on the other side of the road and there are sometimes a couple of ox carts in the vicinity with the patient beasts waiting in the shade. A large STC supermarket, fire station with shiny new fire truck and a petrol station reflect the changing face of La Digue. Jugglers Inn Casino and Fun Park (☎ *4234500*) with roulette, slot machines, arcade games and a bar are on the left, with La Noche Disco and Chill Down Bar next door (see above). A small road leads inland to a group of local guesthouses including Oceane, Beryl's, MaryAnne's, La Passe and Vanilla.

There are lovely views of Praslin through the trees and, with boats lying on the beach, there are some good photographic opportunities. Look out for the white fairy terns roosting in the *takamaka* trees. There is an old planter's house on the right hiding behind an enormous banyan tree. **Kot Babi Guesthouse** (page 146) and Moonlight Beach Villa with the ground-floor Eau Claire de Lune Restaurant are located nearby.

The road swings away from Cap Barbi and, on both sides of the road, is the imposing new Balinese-style **Le Domaine de l'Orangeraie** (page 144). The pool, bars and Le Combava and Santosha restaurants are on the seaward side and the thatched chalets spread up the steep hill commanding magnificent views and total privacy. A little further on, one can see the cemetery, complete with glistening white tombstones. The road curves round beautiful Anse Sévère to the northern point of La Digue and there are several little stalls selling drinks, souvenirs and handmade jewellery on the way. **Island Bungalow** (page 146), **Anse Sévère Bungalow** (page 146), and the bright yellow **Anse Sévère Villa** (page 146) provide self-catering accommodation adjacent to the lovely beach.

Around the point, the gloriously situated **Patatran Restaurant** (part of the small **Hotel L'Océan**; page 145) has stunning ocean views and serves delicious Creole-style food. It is open for lunch and dinner every day and the tables have inset glass cases exhibiting shells, seeds and other flotsam and jetsam. **Patatran**

VANILLA

Vanilla was used to flavour the *xocoatl*, the chocolate drink of the Aztecs. The Spanish conquistadors took it back to Spain, giving it the name *vainilla* from the diminutive of the word for pod – *vaina*. Although there is an indigenous variety of vanilla growing on some of the Seychelles islands, it is the orchid, *Vanilla planifolia*, native to Mexico, which is propagated to produce the flavourful pods.

Vanilla is a creeping vine with a fleshy stem no thicker than a thumb, and aerial roots that cling to the host tree. The leaves are thick and firm and the flowers are pale green. As there are no natural pollinators for vanilla on the Seychelles, each flower has to be pollinated by hand which is a very delicate job performed with a small stick. After successful pollination, the long, bean-shaped seed pods develop and can reach their full length of 20cm within four to six weeks, attaining maturity nine months later. When the bases of the thick, fleshy pods turn yellow, they are picked by hand and immediately plunged into a cauldron of boiling water. Thereafter the pods, now chocolate-brown, are placed on drying racks in the Seychelles sunshine. It takes about four months for the curing process to be completed. The soft, pliable pods, filled with hundreds of pinprick-sized seeds, are then sorted according to length, and neatly tied into bundles with raffia strands.

On La Digue, pure vanilla essence is extracted from the pods and this is sold in the Victoria Market. The flavour and bouquet of the real thing are sublime and a gourmet's delight. In addition to the usual culinary uses of vanilla essence, there are many delightful uses for the pods themselves. Several pods placed in a jar of sugar will impart a wonderful vanilla flavour, as will a pod in the teapot or in the coffee filter. A couple of pods soaking in a bottle of white rum add a distinctive flavour and colour – add a measure of this to chocolate sauce for something memorable!

Village Hotel and Restaurant (page 173), set into the hillside, is only a little way down the road and the rooms, each named after a flower, have magnificent views of Marianne, Félicité, Ile Cocos and Les Souers from their balconies. There is reasonable snorkelling off the beach but the area can be susceptible to large swells and strong currents, especially during the northwest monsoon. The road continues along the northeast coast towards Anse Grosse Roche and beyond. Your heart may sink at the appearance of sand that looks like it might bring your cycle ride to an abrupt end, but do press on. Your efforts will be rewarded with fewer and fewer people around.

THE SOUTHWEST: LA PASSE TO ANSE SOURCE D'ARGENT

To explore the southwest of La Digue, turn right at the jetty after the tourist information centre. There are some small shops selling postcards, souvenirs, snacks and cool drinks as well as a convenient ATM and a branch of MCB (page 148). Mason's Travel and Creole Travel Services have offices here separated by the Seychelles jewellery shop, Kreol Or. Around the corner, there is a small take-away next to La Digue internet and video shop ($\oplus$ *09.00–19.00 Mon–Sat*). The **Tarosa** [153 B1], an open-air cafeteria and bar, sells icy drinks and light snacks. Service is slow, but why hurry? Next door, there is a small kiosk for **Trek Divers** (m *2513066*) and **Tati's Bicycle Hire** [153 B2] and repair shop offers bicycles at SR125 per day. Over the road, in the yellow Kazaz Safran Building, you'll find a Nouvobanq with ATM (page 148), and Vanille boutique selling *pareos* and coconut souvenirs. The conspicuous new La Passe Pension House accommodates various social services and has an upstairs boutique. The Seychelles Savings Bank and ATM (page 148) is nearby. The large wooden building flying the Seychelles flag houses the district administration, the social centre and the library. From here on, the road to the south is characterised by a tunnel of tall, shady *badamier* trees.

The **Logan Hospital** [153 A2] is on the sea side of the road, and was named after Sir Marston Logan, Governor of the Seychelles between 1942 and 1947. A small road leads inland through a new housing estate to **Orchid Apartments** [153 B2] ($\curvearrowright$ *4234023*) and **Petra's Guesthouse** (page 146). **Chez Marston Guesthouse and Restaurant** (page 145) is on the left and a little further on is Cabanon de Laura, a small boutique. Next to the **Maki** clothing shop is **Lionel's Bicycle Hire** ($\curvearrowright$ *4234026*). Near Cable & Wireless is **Fleur de Lys** (page 146), a charming self-catering establishment and the brand new **Marie-France Apartments** ($\curvearrowright$ *4234018*). A track on the left eventually leads to **Tannettes Villa** (page 147). There are some really old, traditional Creole houses in this part of La Digue, their balconies and verandas overflowing with pot plants, and the attractive **Sunshine Guesthouse** (page 146) occupies one of these. The new boutique hotel **Le Repaire** (page 145) with Italian restaurant sits on a prime beachfront position.

Anse la Réunion, a dazzling white beach, runs all the way from the jetty to L'Union Estate. On the rocks beyond the beach is the La Digue Cross, which was erected in 1931 by a Swedish priest to commemorate those who had perished while attempting to land on the island. Glimpses of Praslin through the trees over the turquoise sea are spectacular. Terns and waders are often seen on this part of the beach, especially from December to February.

The road swings to the left and there is the large (for La Digue!) **Gregoire's** [153 B3] building which has accommodation and a supermarket stocking everything from building materials to delicious hot pastries. In the same building a pizzeria with take-away ($\oplus$ *11.00–14.30 & 18.00–20.00 daily*) offers pizza and pasta dishes and Barclays Bank has a branch and ATM. A road off to the left leads to **Pension**

Michel and **Pension Hibiscus** (page 147) and several self-catering establishments. **La Digue Island Lodge and Spa** (page 145) is on the right behind a fence, though you have to proceed past the hotel to La Réunion Road and then double back for 50m to reach it. The Pro Diving Centre (📞 *4292525*) can be found close to the swimming pool in the hotel grounds. Quick's Boutique, the imposing, wooden Emerald Villa (m *2513445*) and a mini market are near the entrance to the hotel. A bit further on, the new, bright and airy **Le Relax Beach House** (page 145) has beach frontage with self-catering villas over the road.

Continuing southwards along the road to Source d'Argent, La Digue school and the **Church of the Assumption** [153 A4] are on the left. On 15 August, Assumption Day, La Digue celebrates with a joyous festival commencing with a procession and mass followed by music and dancing, art exhibitions and stalls selling food and drink. Everything comes to a standstill as La Digue has a party and welcomes visitors from the other islands.

Le Surmer self-catering chalets and Benjamine's Guesthouse are next to the church. The **Barbara Jenson Studio** [153 A4] (🕐 *10.00–18.00 Mon–Sat*) is always worth a visit, and features original work by this versatile artist. She uses watercolour, gauche, acrylics and does pencil and charcoal drawings of landscapes, Creole scenes and portraits. Nearby is a rustic boatyard with several vessels in various stages of disrepair. As you approach L'Union Estate, the road divides and the left fork heads inland and joins the road leading over to the east coast and Grande Anse. A short distance up this road there is a sports field. The Zil Air **helipad** [153 A4] is almost on the beach on a piece of open ground shortly before the road divides.

The right fork leads to the old coconut plantation of **L'Union Estate** [153 A5] (🕐 *07.00–17.00 daily; admission SR125*), where copra is still being produced using traditional methods. The old calorifier, or drying shed, is fuelled from the discarded husks and, after the thick white coconut meat has been dried, the patient old ox will turn the grinding wheel to extract the coconut oil. Try some sweet coconut water and taste as much fresh coconut as you like. A small shop sells coconut products (soap, oil and candles), as well as vanilla beans and, if you are lucky, some real vanilla essence. A couple of other small stalls may also sell vanilla and coconut products.

Moving on through the estate, there is the beautiful old plantation house built of the local hardwood and thatched with palm leaves. It has been restored to its former glory, and is used by the president as a holiday house. Behind the old house and bounded by spectacular chunks of granite is a pen with giant Aldabra tortoises. Along the path towards the beach there are vanilla vines supported on poles. The vanilla pods ripen around September when they are treated, cured and put out to dry in the sun. Beyond the vanilla is a marshy area with some mangroves next to a small river. Chinese bitterns can sometimes be seen skulking among the vegetation, and this area is known for *tortues-soupapes*, or terrapins.

Closer to the beach is the boat yard, with boats up on blocks being repaired and new ones being built. Located within the grounds of the estate, very close to the beach, are the **L'Union Estate Chalets** (page 146) which offer self-catering accommodation. Along the small path leading from the estate to the beaches is a rustic restaurant, **Lanbousir** (page 147) (the same name as the nearby stream), selling cold drinks, Creole meals, snacks and souvenirs.

Wind your way through the palms, *badamier* trees and great granite boulders which characterise the dramatic landscape of the next few beaches. Note the enormous palm spiders with their incredibly strong webs spanned between the rocks. Stalls selling locally made beads and handicrafts can be found along the path and you may even be able to purchase freshly squeezed fruit juice.

The first wonderful beach is **Source d'Argent**, one of the most photogenic beaches in the world. From here, there is a series of small beaches and enticing coves framed by enormous boulders: Anse Pierrot, Anse aux Cèdres and then Anse Bonnet Kare. Coconut palms bow over the white sands and the crystal-clear, turquoise water beckons. Several Hollywood movies have been filmed on these beautiful beaches. At very low tide you may be able to walk around the southern rocks of Pointe Jacques to Anse Marron. But remember that you have to return while the tide is still low, otherwise you might be stuck till the next low tide and have to spend a very uncomfortable time perched on the rocks. Snorkelling is best at high tide though you have to swim out beyond the seagrass beds. Be careful of the currents as the tide recedes.

GRANDE ANSE: ANSE LA REUNION TO GRANDE ANSE VIA THE FLYCATCHER RESERVE

From the jetty take the route to the south but instead of turning towards La Digue Island Lodge, turn left, away from the sea, and proceed along La Réunion Road. On the left side of the road there are some small shops, and on the right is the beginning of the **La Digue Vev Reserve** [153 B/C 3/4] (⏰ *08.00–16.00 Mon–Fri; admission free*). *Vev* is the Creole name for the black paradise flycatcher, and this special reserve has been established as a safe haven for these endemic birds. The Royal Society for Nature Conservation established the 21ha reserve in 1987 for the protection of this single species. The small resource centre at the entrance to the reserve provides information about these endangered birds. An educational initiative at the local school has taught the children to value these rare and beautiful birds, instead of shooting them with catapults. From the road, a short, flat path leads to the interior of the reserve. The forest consists mainly of *takamaka* and *badamier* trees. Listen for the whistling calls of the flycatchers as they flit amongst the trees, and see if you can spot a delicate nest of soft lichens and leaves bound together with spider webs gently swaying at the end of a branch. A walk through the reserve will take about 30 minutes but you may want to spend more time observing the fabulous flycatchers. Recent counts have indicated an increase in the number of birds in the reserve (250), possibly because of the removal of habitat elsewhere on the island.

Over the road is the **Rising Sun Guesthouse** (page 145), two boutiques, the Gala Takeaway and the **Casa de Leela Guesthouse** (page 146). The multi-functional **Zerof Guesthouse, Bar and Restaurant** (page 146) with boutique and take-

ANSE LA REUNION

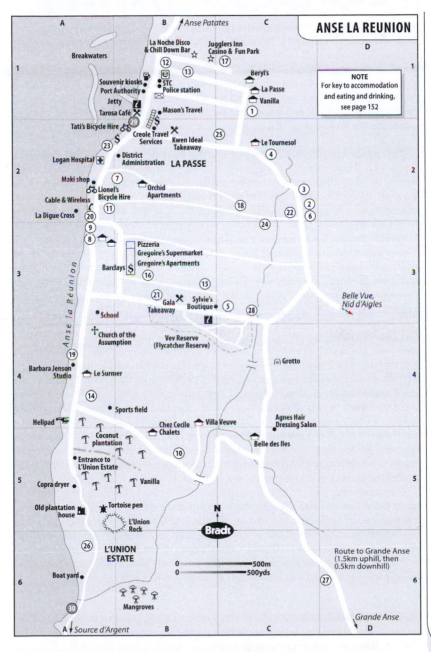

NOTE
For key to accommodation
and eating and drinking,
see page 152

Anse Patates

La Noche Disco
& Chill Down Bar

Jugglers Inn
Casino & Fun Park

Breakwaters

Beryl's

Souvenir kiosks
Port Authority
Jetty
Tarosa Café

STC
Police station

La Passe
Vanilla

Mason's Travel

Tati's Bicycle Hire

Creole Travel
Services

Kwen Ideal
Takeaway

Le Tournesol

Logan Hospital

District
Administration

LA PASSE

Maki shop

Lionel's
Bicycle Hire

Orchid
Apartments

Cable & Wireless

La Digue Cross

Anse la Réunion

Pizzeria
Gregoire's Supermarket
Gregoire's Apartments

Barclays

Belle Vue,
Nid d'Aigles

Gala
Takeaway

Sylvie's
Boutique

School

Church of the
Assumption

Vev Reserve
(Flycatcher Reserve)

Grotto

Barbara Jenson
Studio

Le Surmer

Sports field

Agnes Hair
Dressing Salon

Helipad

Chez Cecile
Chalets

Villa Veuve

Coconut
plantation

Belle des Iles

Entrance to
L'Union Estate

Copra dryer

Vanilla

Old plantation
house

Tortoise pen

L'Union
Rock

N

Route to Grande Anse
(1.5km uphill, then
0.5km downhill)

L'UNION
ESTATE

Boat yard

Bradt

0   500m
0   500yds

Mangroves

Source d'Argent

Grande Anse

away, is a bit further on. The restaurant specialises in Creole food and is open for lunch and dinner.

At the T-junction, turn right into the road coming from Château St Cloud. The **grotto** [153 C4], on the left, is a natural recess or overhang of huge granite rocks forming a cave, which has an effigy of the Virgin Mary. This is the point from where the Feast of Assumption procession begins after an open-air mass on 15 August each year. The **Agnes Hair Dressing Salon** [153 C5] (m *2715656*) is also located here, and **Belle des Iles** self-catering guesthouse [153 C5] (☏ *4234252*) is a little further along the way. Soon after, near Roche Bois, is a road on the right going down to Villa Veuve Hotel, Etoile Labrine (page 146), Chez Cecile self-catering chalets, L'Union Estate and the southern end of Anse la Réunion. Continue on the Grande Anse road, which is fairly steep in parts, for about 2km. Most of this rural way is in deep shade among great boulders, streams and some small farms. The **Zanboza** (page 147) self-catering establishment and a colourful fruit stall, which prepares blended juices from seasonal fruits of your choice, are located along the way.

The dramatically beautiful beach of Grande Anse lies before you. It can be wild, rough and dangerous as the huge waves crash in from the Indian Ocean. Body surfing in the shore breakers can be exhilarating but, because of the dangerous currents, it is not recommended for genteel bathing. Take time to look around – you may well see white-tailed tropicbirds flying about, as well as enormous, harmless fruit bats with furry faces, also known as flying foxes. A rustic beach restaurant **Loutier** (page 147) operates daily at Grande Anse. From Grande Anse there is a track leading westwards to Anse Songe and, if you can find it, another track behind the marshes leads to Petite Anse and Anse Cocos. It is possible to continue over the headland to Anse Caiman and, from there, a long walk will take you up the wild and remote east coast past Anse Fourmis and Anse Grosse Roche right up to Anse Patates.

THE INLAND ROAD From the jetty at La Passe, just after the shops, a road leads directly away from the sea. This can best be described as the accommodation road as here you will find many little places to stay. Closest to the pier is **Villa Authentique** (page 146), a family guesthouse. The well-stocked B&M Store is nearby, then fairly close together are **Bamboo Lodge**, **Calou**, **Birgo** and **Bernique** guesthouses (page 145), followed by Maria's Store selling clothes, bicycles and other hardware. **Sitronel Guesthouse** (pages 145–6) is on the lower side of the road (sometimes spelt Citronelle). A little further on you get to **Château St Cloud** (page 145), an old planter's house, which has been extensively renovated into a small hotel. It has a superior restaurant with an excellent octopus curry! There are several small shops a bit further on, and this is the part of the island to see some typical old La Digue houses.

Continue along and the next road that leads off to the left is the start of the walk up to **Belle Vue** and **Nid d'Aigles**, the highest point on La Digue. The walk is steep but the phenomenal views of La Digue, Praslin and other islands are superb. Follow the concrete road up the hill and when it forks, keep left. The Belle Vue Café, *en route*, sells the coldest Cokes on La Digue! The walk takes about 2 hours up and down.

Back at the Belle Vue junction, you could follow the road down to the flycatcher reserve and back to Anse la Réunion or continue on to Grande Anse.

EXCURSIONS FROM LA DIGUE

If you are staying on La Digue it is easy to take the regular ferry across to Praslin for the day. If you go in the morning there will be sufficient time to visit the Vallée de Mai and return in the late afternoon.

La Digue is the ideal place from which to set off on a trip to the small neighbouring islands of Ile Cocos, Félicité and Les Soeurs. The waters surrounding these little islands are good for snorkelling and several boats offer half- or full-day trips. As Ile Cocos is a national park, and Félicité is privately owned, passengers usually go onshore at Grand Souer where a delicious beach barbecue can be included in the full-day trips. Boats can take you to both Ile Cocos and Félicité for offshore snorkelling only (pages 172–4).

Nevis Ernesta (m *2515557*; e *nevisernesta@gmail.com*) will charge about €55 per person for a half-day snorkelling trip to Ile Cocos and Félicité; a full day of snorkelling around three islands plus a barbecue at Grand Soeur will cost about €110 per person, as will a full day to Ile St Pierre and Curieuse plus a barbecue at Curieuse.

Lone Wolf (m *2570344*; e *lonewolf@seychelles.net*), La Fidelite (m *2512233*; e *lafidelite@seychelles.net*), Kaya Charters (m *2608955*), Belle Petra (m *2716220*; e *petra@seychelles.sc*), and other small boats are available for trips and some will also take you on fishing expeditions. Booking can easily be made through the tourist office, Mason's, Creole Travel Services or your hotel reception.

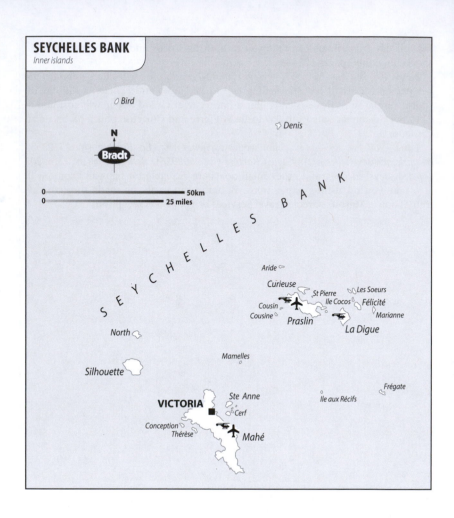

SEYCHELLES BANK
Inner islands

N
Bradt

0 _____ 50km
0 _____ 25 miles

○ Bird

◇ Denis

S E Y C H E L L E S   B A N K

Aride ▭

Curieuse

St Pierre   ◇ Les Soeurs
Cousin   ✈   Ile Cocos ◇ Félicité
Cousine ◇   **Praslin**   Marianne
          La Digue

North ◇

Mamelles
         ○

Silhouette

                                    Frégate
                          Ile aux Récifs ○

VICTORIA   Ste Anne
               ◇ Cerf
Conception ◇   ✈ **Mahé**
Thérèse

7

Other Inner Islands

The inner granitic islands of the Seychelles Bank encompass Mahé, Praslin, La Digue and a host of smaller satellite islands. Silhouette, North, Mamelles and Frégate islands, which are closest to Mahé, as well as Aride, Cousin, Cousine, Curieuse, Ile St Pierre, Félicité, Les Soeurs, Marianne and Ile Cocos, which are nearer to Praslin and La Digue, will be covered in this chapter. In addition, Bird and Denis islands, which are coralline in origin, and found on the northern edge of the Seychelles Bank, will be discussed. The status of the various islands differs, as some are set apart as nature reserves, some are privately owned with exclusive guest lodges, and others are a combination of both. A very encouraging aspect of the privately owned islands is the strong conservation ethic the owners foster.

SILHOUETTE

From Beau Vallon on Mahé, the familiar shape of this island is a silhouette against the sunset. The green and verdant isle rises out of the encircling coral reef to Mont Dauban at a height of 740m. It is almost round, roughly 5km in diameter, and covers an area of 20km². Because of the protective nature of the surrounding reef, landing on Silhouette has never been easy, and this has guarded the island from overdevelopment and exploitation. It is probably the most densely vegetated island in the Indian Ocean, and its higher slopes and summit are clad in largely undisturbed, pristine forest with a high level of endemic flora and fauna. The Anse Mondon Valley is exceptionally rich in its biodiversity with many rare Seychelles hardwood trees, shrubs and orchids. Silhouette has a population of a mere 130 inhabitants. The pace of life on Silhouette is slow: there are no roads, no motor cars, only one tractor and some electric buggies at Labriz Hotel, no police station and only one small shop selling essentials.

The Dauban family from Mauritius were the first settlers to arrive on Silhouette at the end of the 19th century. They gradually acquired the entire island and a thriving farming community developed.

Coconut and cinnamon plantations were established on the fairly level plateau at about 500m, patchouli was grown for the perfume trade, fruit trees supplied the local market and, by the 1950s, the population had increased to around 1,000. However, after the crash in the world copra market most of the workers drifted back to Mahé. There is a small jetty at La Passe on the east coast, which is the site of the largest settlement, the Hilton Seychelles Labriz Hotel Resort and Spa, and La Belle Tortue apartments and restaurant.

GETTING THERE AND AWAY Guests staying at either the Hilton Seychelles Labriz Resort and Spa or La Belle Tortue will be transported by fast boat from Bel Ombre,

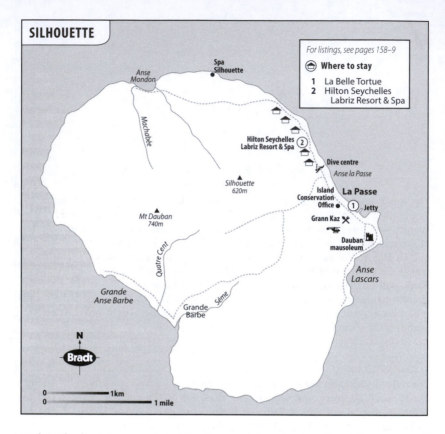

For listings, see pages 158–9

🛏 **Where to stay**

1 La Belle Tortue
2 Hilton Seychelles
    Labriz Resort & Spa

Mahé. The boat is covered and the journey takes about an hour (transport and payment will be arranged when booking). Alternatively, a helicopter transfer can be arranged through Zil Air (📞 *4375100*; e *book@zilair.com; www.zilair.com*).

For anyone wishing to do a day trip, your hotel, guesthouse or local travel agent might be able to arrange a return boat ride from Mahé to Silhouette. At the time of writing, though, there were no organised day excursions. If you do manage to secure a boat trip, it would be wise to confirm that the Labriz or La Belle Tortue can accommodate you for lunch.

🛏 WHERE TO STAY AND EAT *Map, above.*

🛏 **Hilton Seychelles Labriz Resort and Spa** (110 villas & 1 presidential villa) 📞 4293949; e selbz.info@labriz-seychelles.com; www. seychelleslabriz.hilton.com. This 5-star hotel comprises 110 villas spread along a magnificent fine, silvery beach with rich, tropical, indigenous forest stretching up into the mountains. The presidential villa is in its own private oasis. The units are beautifully designed with simple, uncluttered lines & finished with fine hardwoods. All have LCD television with DVD player, outdoor shower, AC & Wi-Fi (though this can be a little

slow). There are 17 luxurious, spacious pool villas, 9 facing the ocean & 8 looking towards the gorgeous granite mountains, each with its own private pool & garden. The 63 beach villas are slightly smaller & are tucked into the beachfront vegetation & the 30 garden villas are scattered around the grounds of the property. Spa Silhouette is set among the picturesque, granite boulders. The main dining room, Café Dauban, with floor-to-ceiling glass doors & windows, presents sumptuous buffets for breakfast & makes an ideal location for light lunches & casual dinners. Grann Kaz, the old plantation house & Dauban family home in days gone by, has been tastefully renovated & now serves Creole cuisine dinners several times during the week. Portobello, with its minimal but exquisite décor featuring the outdoor pools & tropical vegetation, specialises in the finest Italian cuisine. It also boasts an extensive, temperature-controlled wine cellar. Sakura, which is close to the beach, is influenced by Japanese design. The 'show kitchen' specialises in the freshest grilled seafood while the lakeside pavilion offers teppanyaki. Do make sure you visit the restrooms! Bar Lo Brizan, close to the beach, is an open-air cocktail lounge & La Pizzeria, near the swimming pool, is open all day. However, should you wish to dine in romantic splendour in your own pavilion or villa you only have to call the hotel staff. Labriz is the ideal honeymoon spot & special packages can be arranged. Marriage ceremonies can also be performed (see box, page 73). Even though it is

a large hotel, all the public areas are so spacious that you will never feel crowded. Bicycles are available & children are welcome, with the Jungle Fun Kids Club to keep them occupied. The hotel was awarded the 2015 World Travel Awards Indian Ocean's Leading Resort & Spa & Seychelles Leading Spa resort. $$$–$$$$$

🏠**La Belle Tortue** (6 rooms & suites) 📞4325335; e contact@labelletortue.com; www. labelletortue; see ad, page 156. Accommodation is split across 3 villas. In addition to the rooms, there are 2 suites & 1 private villa, & breakfast is part of the deal. Remember, there are no grocery shops on the island so if you need extra food it is best to bring it with you. The beachside location is great & the Belle Tortue Restaurant can provide all your meals, including picnics. The chef has a fantastic reputation. The amenities of the nearby Hilton hotel are available at the current rate. $$$

WHAT TO SEE AND DO As there are no roads or cars, the only way to explore the island is to walk. There are several **paths** as this is how the residents get from one side of the island to the other. However, it is essential that you arrange with the hotel to have a qualified guide with you as some of the paths are not always clearly marked in places, and the granite rocks can be slippery and a little dangerous. Near the jetty, the old Planter's House or **Grann Kaz**, which was built by August Dauban in the 1860s, has been renovated and restored to its former glory, and now serves as a restaurant for Labriz.

The path from the jetty over to the west splits into two, with one ending at Jardin Marron and the other going all the way over to **Grande Barbe**. You will need a whole day to enjoy the delights of this walk, which is steep and arduous in parts, but well worth the exertion as it passes through forests with sandalwood, ferns, orchids and pitcher plants. Look out, too, for the endemic stick insect, recently rediscovered by a team of Oxford undergraduates. Take plenty of insect repellent as the mosquitoes can be very annoying. Once on the western side at Grande Barbe there is a church overlooking a glorious beach. The Séme River enters the sea at Grande Barbe.

From La Passe a path leads to Anse Mondon on the northern shore. You can walk to Anse Lascars from here too, passing Pointe Ramasse Tout and Anse Cimitère. Look out for the small shrine perched high on the rocks. The **Dauban family mausoleum** is located near Pointe Ramasse Tout, home to a classic old edifice that is a copy of the Eglise de la Madeleine in Paris and was created to resemble marble – a recent coat of paint hides the rust marks.

The **Eco Centre** at Labriz has a five-star PADI dive centre and pool for teaching beginners. It also has the only decompression chamber in the Seychelles, as well as Nitrox. If you are already a trained diver, remember to bring all relevant certificates. There are good snorkelling and diving spots around Silhouette. Fishing trips can be arranged through the hotel.

Between November and March, birdwatching can be exciting as many migrants stop over on the island and, from time to time, it may be possible to see crab plovers, whimbrels, greenshanks and Eurasian oystercatchers to name but a few.

Silhouette is an island of great importance for its natural history (93% is under conservation) and has recently been taken over by the Islands Development Company to run it as a nature reserve, but to date, they have done little to implement this. The **Silhouette Island Conservation Society** has a small office near the jetty (m *2714488*; ☉ *08.00–noon & 14.00–16.00 Mon–Fri*), and they can inform you about their latest projects on the island.

NORTH ISLAND

North Island lies almost 5km north of Silhouette and 30km north of Mahé. It covers an area of 210ha and reaches a rocky height of 214m. It has four superb beaches, framed by massive granite slabs and palm trees.

North Island had been in the Beaufond family since it was first awarded to Madame Celerine Beaufond in 1826. Like most of the Seychelles islands, it had large colonies of breeding seabirds, which contributed considerable guano that was mined and sold for fertiliser. The island later became a coconut plantation but, after the collapse of the copra industry, it was sold. It remained as a farm but became overgrown with many alien plants. Cattle, goats and pigs became feral and cats and rats proliferated, decimating birds and other animals.

The potential for tourism and restoration of the island was recognised when it was bought in 1997. The aim was to remove the alien plants and animals, restore the natural balance of the island and create a small, exclusive lodge in harmony with the environment. An extensive rat eradication programme was carried out to make North Island one of the few rat-free islands in the Seychelles and an area of land was cleared for construction of the lodge. Impressive indigenous plant nurseries were established and over 100,000 plants of 73 species were grown from seed. At least half of these have been planted out already and the reintroduction of some of the rare and endangered Seychelles bird species is underway. In July 2007, 25 Seychelles white-eyes were introduced from Conception. These tiny birds have settled down well, are singing happily and are breeding.

A resident ecologist and a marine biologist work closely together, running conservation programmes on all aspects of the environment. Hawksbill and green turtles nest on the beaches and, now that rats have been exterminated, the hatchlings stand a better chance of survival. A turtle monitoring and tagging programme is running in collaboration with others in the Seychelles. Tropicbirds are returning to nest, and kestrels and sunbirds have been sighted.

GETTING THERE AND AWAY The island is exclusively for lodge residents and no day visitors are permitted. Transfers from Mahé are by helicopter and take 20 minutes. It is also possible to transfer by boat, which takes about an hour; this will be arranged when you make your reservations and priced accordingly.

WHERE TO STAY AND EAT

🏠 **North Island Lodge** (11 villas) ☏4293100; e info@north-island.com; www. north-island.com. This exclusive lodge was opened in Jul 2003 & all the buildings are on the eastern side of the island. The lodge was built using craftsmen from Africa, Zanzibar & the Seychelles, creating a fusion of cultures & architectural styles to produce a 'Robinson Crusoe-styled luxury paradise'. It takes barefoot luxury into another realm with stunning sensual designs & an aura of sophisticated, stylish calm created by the use of weathered wood, velvet cushions, glass, thatch & coral. The lounge, bar & dining room are open-air spaces under high thatch that flow on to a large deck & the beach. Ponds & waterfalls lend a tranquil ambience &

an enormous rimflow swimming pool sweeps along the granite curve of the hillside, shaded by palms & forest vegetation. The North Island Gym & Spa is located above the pool & the luxurious treatment areas take full advantage of the stunning views. A full range of holistic treatments & massages is available for your indulgence either in the spa or in your villa.

Secluded, self-contained villas face the sunrise & all have areas of over 400m². Each villa consists of a spacious bedroom, an indoor lounge where extra guests can be accommodated & a lounge & dining area under a thatch cover on a deck with a swirling plunge pool & *sala* (a thatch-covered daybed) leading down to the beach. The main bedroom has a huge bed, separate dressing area & bathroom complex more like a spa with an oversized bath. A separate well-equipped kitchen enables the chef to prepare & serve gourmet meals in your villa & each villa has a butler attending to all your needs.

On arrival, once the formalities are over, each guest is met by the executive chef who discusses the 'no menu' concept & plans the meals with each person. Guests may eat in the dining room, on the beach or in their villa. The majority of the vegetables are grown in organic gardens on the island (with the surplus exported to other islands), the fish could not be fresher, & many local plants are used in the preparation of the gourmet food. The executive chef is passionate about food & has the knack of knowing exactly how to mix different flavours & textures using unexpected ingredients. This lodge won the Indian Ocean's Leading Green Resort 2014

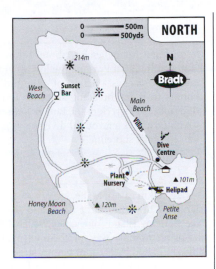

and took 3rd best in the world in Condé Nast Traveller's 2014 awards. All meals & drinks are included (except for premier drinks on the special reserve list), as is scuba diving, snorkelling, sea kayaking, fly-fishing, catamaran sailing, mountain bikes, walking tours, use of the library & gymnasium & all the government taxes & service charges. As part of their giving something back to Seychelles philosophy, the lodge is closed to guests for a week every 2 years & a group of about 30 underprivileged children are hosted in the guest villas. The programmes include a great deal of outdoor environmental activities as well as getting the children involved in the kitchen creating their own food & experiencing a taste of luxury. **$$$$$**

WHAT TO SEE AND DO North Island has an unhurried, tranquil atmosphere and the combination of seclusion, location, accommodation, services and facilities provides the epitome of sophisticated, yet simple, luxury. There is a range of activities for guests and many of these take advantage of the superb natural environment.

Walks with the resident ecologist are recommended as he will enthusiastically tell you all about the island, the indigenous plant nursery and the management strategies in place to restore the environment. Participate in the various **watersports** like sailing, kayaking, scuba diving and snorkelling or visit the health spa and indulge in one of their treatments.

Take your buggy to the western side of the island to the **Sunset Bar** and watch the sun go down while the barman creates a special cocktail to celebrate the day. Sit under the stars and see how many constellations you can find. Best of all, revel in the sheer beauty of the island and applaud the owners for their far-sighted dreams to create such a special sanctuary for guests and nature.

MAMELLES

Uninhabited Mamelles lies about 15km northeast of Victoria, Mahé, and about 30km southwest of Praslin. The lowish granitic island, a mere 1.5km long by about 1km wide, reaches a height of 42m and there is a lighthouse on the summit. It is home to many breeding seabirds and its silhouette on the horizon is always noticeable. The wreck of the tanker *Ennerdale*, which dates from 1970, lies in close proximity, and is a favoured dive site. It is not possible to land on Mamelles due to its steep rocky shoreline.

FREGATE

Frégate, 56km east of Mahé, is a privately owned island with an exclusive resort. The island reaches a height of 125m and massive slabs of *glacis* dominate the plateau. Like so many islands of the Seychelles, Frégate also saw removal of endemic trees and plants to make way for coconut plantations. Nowadays, although the island is still dominated by coconut palms, large areas of woodland have been rehabilitated with a variety of indigenous trees including *takamakas*, *badamiers*, palms and screw pines. Sadly, many of the mighty sandragon trees have died as a result of a fatal wilt disease that has attacked the species throughout the Seychelles. Indigenous trees have been planted in their place and are growing fast.

The efforts of the conservation team on Frégate are famous for the recovery of the endangered magpie robins. The smart black-and-white birds had declined to a critical number of only 24 but the total population now stands at around 100, with almost half on Frégate. When the numbers started increasing, some were relocated to Cousin, Cousine and Aride. It is also one of the few islands supporting

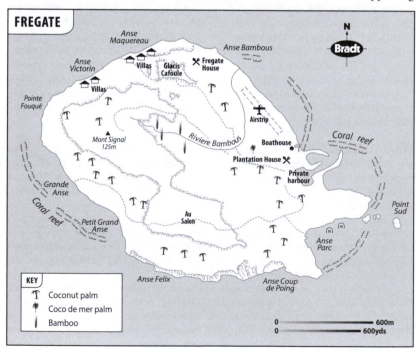

a population of the Seychelles fody, which are now so numerous they even come into the restaurant to share in the breakfast crumbs. Some of the rare Seychelles white-eyes have been relocated to Frégate and are thriving. Much of the success of the rehabilitation process has been due not only to the replanting of hundreds of indigenous trees and plants, but also to the extensive rat eradication programme and the construction of an impressive rat-proof fence around the harbour area.

Remarkably, Frégate is the only known home of a strange insect, the 4cm-long giant tenebrionid beetle (*Pulposipes herculeanus*). This weird but harmless creature has long legs and rough bumpy wing cases but cannot fly. Small groups of these beetles can be seen on tree trunks around Frégate. A small herd of reintroduced Aldabra tortoises has an easy life on this beautiful little island. The juvenile tortoises are held in captivity until they are sufficiently mature to be released among the free herd.

Frégate is also famous for its stories of Arab sailors and pirate treasure which are fuelled by a few scattered ruins, some ancient graves, an old well and some interesting artefacts discovered on the island. Lazare Picault made the first recorded visit to the island in 1744 when he sailed from Mauritius via Chagos on his second exploratory expedition. He named the island Frégate, after the stately frigatebirds which occur in the area. Other early explorers noted the presence of giant tortoises, turtles and dugongs as well as the absence of crocodiles. Hawksbill and green turtles still haul up on to the beaches of Frégate to lay their eggs. Countless noddies and white fairy terns breed on the island and large fruit bats can also be seen hanging in the trees.

A team of about 120 people is responsible for maintaining the island, protecting the habitat and nurturing the critically endangered species that have found refuge on Frégate, as well as running the hotel, the marina and looking after the plantation, plant nurseries and vegetable gardens.

GETTING THERE AND AWAY The island is for the exclusive use of the resident guests and day visitors are not permitted. Transfers to the island are organised by Frégate Island Private directly by Twin Otter plane, helicopter or boat. The flying time from Mahé to Frégate is approximately 20 minutes and the cost will be discussed when booking.

WHERE TO STAY AND EAT

Frégate Island Private (16 villas & Banyan Hill Estate) Reservations can be made through the worldwide reservations office; +27 21 557 0366; e reservations@fregate.com; www. fregate.com. This establishment is the epitome of a luxurious eco-getaway with beautifully constructed, widely spaced villas giving the feeling of total seclusion & privacy. A central reception area, adorned with fresh flowers & Michael Adams paintings, houses the main restaurant, Pirates Bar, boutique & library. The architecture captures the essence of Indonesia using African hardwoods, marble flooring & Balinese *alang-alang* roof thatching. There are 2 freshwater swimming pools surrounded by granite boulders below the restaurant. The old plantation house has been given a facelift & now hosts a restaurant & museum with artefacts of historical interest as well

as a shell collection. The Rock Spa, sited high on a hillside in spectacular natural surroundings, offers an exclusive range of retreat packages based on over 140 different ingredients growing all over the island. There is an on-site apothecary & a Zen & yoga garden with meditation coves.

Most of the 16 private villas are spread along the northern granite cliffs of the island commanding magnificent views of palms, turquoise ocean & distant islands & are positioned to ensure that privacy is guaranteed. Each has an infinity pool, private terrace with a jacuzzi, & is attended to by a certified butler. 2 villas designed with children in mind stand on sheltered meadows, & the Castaways Club has been designed to enhance their island experience with outdoor activities & nature conservation programmes taking place over the Christmas & Easter holidays. Banyan Hill Estate, which includes 3 separate villas for 6 people, lies high above the plateau on a secluded peninsula with stunning views over the island & the ocean & offers privacy & exclusivity.

Frégate House offers a daily gourmet menu featuring the chef's selection of local produce at its peak, & the Plantation House serves authentic Creole cuisine. This historical building evokes memories of the early settlers & is a wonderful venue for open-air dining, but is closed seasonally owing to bird nesting. Casual drinks & snacks are offered in the Pirates Bar & Anse Bambous Beach Bar. The island's own plantation & hydroponics guarantee that guests can enjoy fresh fruit & vegetables every day.

Rates are per villa per night on FB with a minimum of 3 nights' stay (except in high season). All non-alcoholic drinks are included. For an exclusive occasion, you can even hire the entire island. **$$$$$**

WHAT TO SEE AND DO Take advantage of all the seclusion and relax with room service to your villa or indulge in unique dining experiences at various locations around the island. If you venture out you could spend a few hours rejuvenating in the Rock Spa, take tea in the well-stocked library, or play a game of tennis. Have a romantic candle-lit dinner on the beach, lunch in the Tree House high up in the largest banyan tree on the island, or indulge in the freshest sashimi on a sunset cruise.

It is a great experience to take a **buggy** to explore the island and discover the secluded beaches and enjoy some of the spectacular lookout points; watching the sunset from Mont Signal is particularly impressive. For the ultimate romantic experience flip the 'Private' sign at Anse Macquereau, walk down the steps to the stunning little beach, and you will be undisturbed – loungers and a daybed are there for your convenience.

Frégate Island Private has its own **marina** with a fleet of boats including kayaks, small sailboats, yachts, catamarans, and motor yachts for deep-sea fishing and excursions. Scuba diving can also be arranged.

Shaded paths lead throughout the island and there are ten different **nature walks** along the coast or straight through the tropical jungle where guests can explore the island's interior and discover the fauna and flora. The tour to **Mont Signal**, a 125m-high granite rock is particularly rewarding and a range of other walks can be arranged. The island's own plantation and hydroponics guarantee that guests can enjoy fresh fruit and vegetables every day.

For children six to 12 years of age, the **Castaways Club** has been designed to enhance their island experience with outdoor activities and nature conservation programmes taking place over the Christmas and Easter holidays.

ARIDE

Aride Island Nature Reserve (*c/o GPO Grande Anse, Praslin;* \ *4321600;* e *aride@ ics.sc; www.arideisland.com*) is a special nature reserve and is the most northerly of the granitic islands, lying 10km north of Praslin and 50km northeast of Mahé. The only beach on Aride faces south, which makes landing here very tricky when the southeast trades are blowing, and this, in fact, protected the island from colonisation until 1851. Only 1,500m long and a little over 500m wide, Aride has majestic granite cliffs rising steeply from the shoreline to the highest point, Gros la Tête, 134m above sea level.

The Chenard family owned the island for over a century and during the copra production era a large amount of natural vegetation was cleared to make way for coconut palms. It was declared a private nature reserve in 1970 when copra production ceased. Christopher Cadbury then purchased the island in 1973 on behalf of the Royal Society for Nature Conservation, now the Royal Society for

Wildlife Trust (RSWT). In 1975, it was declared a Special Nature Reserve by the Seychelles government, and in June 2004 the responsibility for Aride was transferred to the Island Conservation Society (ICS). The lease has been linked to conservation and management goals set out by the RSWT and it is expected that the ICS is improving the management of the island. One of the most alarming problems facing Aride is poaching, with turtles and sooty tern eggs being targeted as well as illegal fishing in the marine reserve. It is hoped that, with a local organisation in control and continuing education, poaching will diminish and there are hopeful signs. Most of the coconut palms and fruit trees have been removed and the natural vegetation is rapidly regenerating. An island warden, his staff and research officers and volunteers are the only people living on Aride, amounting to about ten people.

In the western Indian Ocean, Aride is second only to Aldabra in its importance as a seabird breeding colony. Ten species of seabirds, plus a variety of land birds, nest on the 73ha island. It is a haven for two special plant species: the endemic Wright's gardenia (*Rothmannia annae*), found growing naturally in the wild only on Aride, and the creeping Aride peponium (*Peponium vogelii*). The island lies within a marine protected area and is partly surrounded by coral reef. Hawksbill turtles come ashore to lay their eggs from October to February, but it is possible to see them swimming around the island at any time.

GETTING THERE AND AWAY   Boat departures are from Praslin and any of the tour operators or hotels and guesthouses on Praslin or Mahé can make the necessary arrangements to visit Aride. The island is closed to visitors from May to September because of the strong wave action. Should you wish to make your own arrangements with a local boat owner the following can be recommended:

Bedier & Son Côte d'Or; 4232192; m 2513840; e bedier_son@hotmail.com
Indigo Seychelles Grand Anse, Praslin; m 2515676; e info@indigoseychelles.com

Kevin L'Esperance's boats Paradise Sun Hotel, Côte d'Or; m 2521137

The boat trip takes about 90 minutes; on approaching Aride, look out for an outcrop of granite known as Booby Island, so named because of all the red-footed boobies

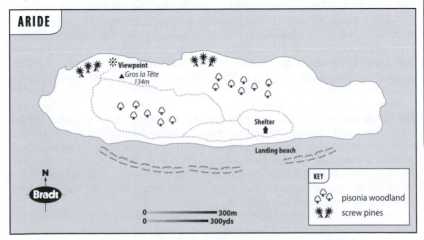

that used to nest there. Getting closer to Aride you may notice a swirling mass of hundreds of thousands of sooty terns circling and displaying above the island. They start congregating in March prior to nesting there during June and July. Note that the huge, black creatures with broad wings flying around the island are not buzzards but giant fruit bats. Although the beach looks heavenly it is not always easy to land there, as there are sometimes sneaky little side swells to contend with. As there is no jetty, a rubber inflatable boat will always transfer passengers from the larger boat to the beach. It is strongly advised to ensure that all cameras and valuables are safely secured inside a watertight bag as you will probably get wet.

WHAT TO SEE AND DO On Aride there is no airstrip, road or accommodation for visitors although the helipad is a recent addition. A shelter with tables and benches has been constructed on the beach and is perfect for a barbecue, which are occasionally arranged. There are a couple of toilets behind the shelter. A series of **well-marked paths** lead from there to the interior of the island, and Seychellois guides, informative and conversant in English, French and Creole, must accompany the visitors. It is essential to keep to the paths, as shearwaters nest underground and, if you stand on the soft roof of a burrow, you are likely to squash eggs, a chick or a brooding adult, and possibly sprain your ankle. The guides will conduct the tour through the settlement area where some fruit trees and coconut palms still grow. Look out for Wright's gardenia, a small tree with creamy white, bell-shaped, fragrant flowers that produces a hard, green, shiny fruit resembling a lemon (hence the Creole name *bwa sitron*). While still on the flat coastal plateau, keep an eye out for the Seychelles warbler, one of the conservation success stories of the Seychelles, which was resurrected from the brink of extinction. The ground is literally covered with two species of skinks: the slender Seychelles skink and the larger, fatter Wright's skink. These harmless lizards devour birds' eggs with relish. Green and bronze geckos can often be seen in the vegetation, and further up the slopes there is an abundance of harmless, shiny giant millipedes which are black with orange legs.

The path to the summit veers away from the coast and, although mostly in the shade, it can be quite a slog. On the way, white-tailed tropicbirds will often be encountered nesting on the ground, and the speckled, downy chicks are trusting and fearless. A simple granite memorial plaque honouring the late Christopher Cadbury is located a little way up the hillside walk. Pause here for a moment to savour the unique features of this small granitic island. Breathtaking views from the top will be worth the uphill sweat. The crystal-clear, deep-blue sea melts into the horizon. To the north, Denis is a dot in the distance, while to the south, on a clear day, there is a superb panorama of all the granitic islands. Stately frigatebirds with long, tapering wings and deeply forked tails appear to hang effortlessly in midair above the lookout point. Sooty terns and noddies swirl around and may even perch in the surrounding Balfour's screw pines growing between the granite boulders.

Birds are prolific on Aride with about 1.25 million seabirds nesting on the island. The ten species of breeding seabirds include six species of terns with numbers fluctuating widely from year to year depending on food availability: up to 360,000 pairs of sooty terns; 16,000 pairs of brown noddies; 6,500 white fairy terns; as well as bridled and roseate terns. An estimated 170,000 pairs of lesser noddies breed on Aride, choosing the *Pisonia grandis* trees in which to make their seaweed nests. The trees have very sticky seeds that sometimes get entangled in the birds' feathers, rendering them flightless and resulting in death.

There are approximately 32,000 tropical shearwaters and 18,000 wedge-tail shearwaters breeding on the island, but they are seldom seen as the adult birds spend the daylight hours far out to sea, only returning at dusk or later. Shearwater burrows are difficult to locate as they are often concealed under rocks or tree roots. Both species of tropicbird, red-tailed and white-tailed, breed on Aride. Frigatebirds breed only on Aldabra but many, especially juveniles, spend the non-breeding season in the granitic islands, roosting on Aride. Numbers can reach over 3,000 in November.

The relocation of the highly endangered magpie robins onto Aride has not always been a success as many of the birds died in the early stages of the project. However, in 2007, with improved land-management techniques, the magpie robins are now thriving and there are at least 22 birds on the island in five distinct territories, and young are successfully being raised. Other land birds include the Seychelles warbler, moorhen, barred ground dove, blue pigeon and turtle doves. Aride is also a good spot for migrant birds. A wide variety, ranging from waders to unexpected species like the Jacobin cuckoo, Antarctic skua, Eleanora's falcon and even a hobby, have been recorded. Turnstones, common sandpipers and whimbrels frequent the shoreline and spotted flycatchers are seen among the trees from time to time. Early records show that before most of the natural vegetation was cleared to make way for coconuts, black parrots, the black paradise flycatcher and the Seychelles fody were all resident on Aride.

A **day tour** could include a walk around the island with Aride Island staff followed by a beach barbecue and snorkelling. You could even bring your own picnic lunch and drinks. The landing fee is €30 per person and €15 for children and it is often included with the cost of the boat transfer. Aride is open to visitors 10.00–15.00 Sunday, Monday and Wednesday. Between May and September the strong trade winds make landing on the island difficult or even impossible. Zil Air may be able to land you there on the recently constructed helipad.

COUSIN

Located in a marine protected area, this small 27ha granitic island, encircled by a coral reef, is another conservation success story. Like the other granitic islands, it too had most of the natural vegetation cleared to make way for the production of copra and some cotton, thus almost eliminating the endemic birds and plants. Green and hawksbill turtles, captured by the thousand for their ornamental shells and meat, were almost wiped out, and sooty tern egg collecting totally obliterated the breeding colony of these birds.

However, in the early 1960s, when a bird count revealed only 29 Seychelles warblers left in the entire world, the World Wildlife Fund, with financial assistance from Christopher Cadbury, collected enough money to purchase Cousin for the Royal Society for Nature Conservation as a sanctuary for birds and other animals. The island was further protected when it was declared a Special Reserve by the Seychelles government in 1974. The island now falls under the management of Nature Seychelles. Much of the alien vegetation was gradually removed and the recovery of the natural vegetation has been remarkable. While it is still possible to see introduced plants like coffee and cotton, the mixed woodland of pisonia and tortoise trees (*Morinda citrifolia*), as well as beach crest plants, has regenerated with vigour. As the natural vegetation was restored, the numbers of Seychelles warblers increased dramatically. Birds have been relocated to Aride, Frégate and Cousine and there are now hundreds of warblers warbling away on all four islands. This species has now been downlisted to endangered on the Red Data List, a magnificent achievement for a group of dedicated people on a tiny island. Magpie robins have

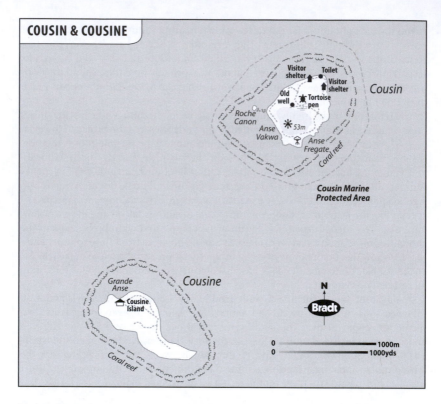

been relocated to Cousine and Denis and they too are thriving with an annual increase in the population.

This island bird sanctuary is a popular tourist destination with about 600 visitors per week. It is also playing an important role in science, as local and international students are involved in studies on different aspects of botanical, ornithological and marine research.

GETTING THERE AND AWAY Boat trips generally depart from the beach at Anse Volbert, Praslin, and arrangements can be made with any of the Praslin tour operators. There is a €35 landing fee per person which will be included in the price of the tour. As there is no jetty, passengers will be transferred from their boat to the island in a small boat, zooming right up onto the beach. Although it is generally a much more sedate landing than at Aride, ensure that all cameras and valuables are secure in a watertight bag. There is no overnight accommodation on Cousin. The island is open to visitors (⊕ *09.30–12.30 Mon–Fri*) but is closed on weekends and public holidays. The management of Cousin welcomes visitors, reaches out to local people through awareness and educational programmes, undertakes to protect the rich biodiversity, and maintains the reserve as a heritage for all mankind. There is a strict tourism code of ethics for Cousin put in place to protect the apparently fearless bird populations as well as the visitors.

WHAT TO SEE AND DO An attractive shelter for visitors is located on the beach near the landing site with some information about the biodiversity of Cousin. A staff member gives visitors a short talk about the work being done on the island

and explains the rules. Flash photography is forbidden, as is swimming, collecting shells and picnicking. The nesting birds appear completely fearless and, although it is easy to approach them, it is imperative that they are not disturbed – never try to touch them.

Knowledgeable and informative guides will accompany you around Cousin on the wide **paths**, pointing out important and interesting aspects of the island. The walk takes about an hour and a half; it is mostly flat but there is a raised area of rocky granite in the centre which rises to a height of 53m above sea level. Nesting amongst these rocks are tropical and wedge-tailed shearwaters. With no rats or cats, ground-nesting birds flourish on Cousin. White-tailed tropicbirds and their unguarded, fat, speckled chicks are easily seen on the ground near the path, usually close to a tree trunk or rocky boulder. Lesser noddies nest in huge numbers – there are up to 100,000 pairs on Cousin. Brown noddies, white fairy terns and bridled terns all use the little island for breeding and roosting purposes. Many waders feed on the sandy beaches of Praslin during the day but return to their overnight roosts on Cousin. Turnstones, though, spend their days on Cousin feeding under the trees as well as on the beaches and rocky shores, and frequently go over to Booby Island for the night roost.

The most endangered of all Seychelles **birds** is the magpie robin, but more than 30 are alive and well and rearing young on Cousin, and these handsome black-and-white birds are easily seen rummaging among the leaf litter for grubs. It remains to be seen whether they will have the same outstanding recovery success as the Seychelles warbler has had. The Seychelles fody, locally known as the *tok-tok,* is found only on Cousin, Cousine, Denis and Frégate. The Madagascar fody, bright red in breeding colours, is a common inhabitant of most of the Seychelles islands. The two species can thus be seen together on Cousin.

Cousin is not only an important bird sanctuary but the lovely sandy **beaches** are also favoured and important nesting sites for the hawksbill turtle. They are vigorously protected and monitoring and tagging programmes continue. Several reintroduced Aldabra tortoises wander around freely on Cousin, seeking out the shade in the noonday sun. As on Aride, there is an abundance of skinks and geckos.

COUSINE

Cousine, a privately owned island nature reserve, lies 6km off the west coast of Praslin and covers an area of 25ha. The sister island to Cousin, it has similar topography. A conservation team manages the island, and their mission is 'to promote and practise nature conservation and our aim is to share this philosophy with our guests'. All profits from tourism are put directly back into conservation efforts on the island. It is home to five species of endemic birds, and many thousands of seabirds breed on the island. It boasts the remarkable status of having no alien or introduced mammals.

GETTING THERE AND AWAY Guests use a helicopter for the transfer from Mahé or Praslin and costs will be arranged when you book. Day visitors are not catered for.

 WHERE TO STAY AND EAT

Cousine Island (4 villas) \ 4321107; m 2713418; e reservations@cousineisland.com; www.cousineisland.com. The spacious villas built in the old, French colonial style are positioned to ensure maximum privacy & are only about 30m from the beach. Each has AC, a private veranda, jacuzzi & kitchenette, with fridge, coffee maker & minibar. IDD telephone, satellite TV, DVD & a mini sound system complete the range of amenities. The dining room, Gecko Bar, lounge & well-stocked library are situated in a pavilion overlooking a freshwater swimming pool. Fine international cuisine is served with an emphasis on fresh seafood. A small spa, the Beach House Wellness Retreat, uses exclusive & luxurious products from Ligne St Barth. Weddings & honeymoons are specially catered for. Book all 4 villas & have the island to yourselves. There is a minimum stay of 3 nights but during the peak season from around 20 Dec to 10 Jan, a minimum of 7 nights is required. Children under 15 years of age are not catered for. Rates include FB (all drinks except selected wines on the reserve list), snorkelling & guided walks. There is a complimentary foot massage when you arrive. $$$$$

WHAT TO SEE AND DO There is no nightlife or organised entertainment, but the conservation officer is available to take guests around and explain the interesting aspects of the island. Magpie robins have been successfully relocated to Cousine and there are 39 individuals on the island. The Seychelles warbler is also abundant, and this is one of the three islands where the Seychelles fody can be found. In July 2007, 20 endangered Seychelles white-eyes were relocated to Cousine from Conception Island, and they appear to have settled into their new home quite happily. Other endemic birds are the blue pigeon and the Seychelles sunbird. Breeding seabirds include white fairy terns, tropicbirds, noddies and shearwaters. Both green and hawksbill turtles clamber onto the beach to lay their eggs, and with some luck they can be observed between September and January. It may also be possible to see the tiny hatchlings emerge and make their way down to the sea. An indigenous tree-planting programme is in progress and guests may participate if they wish. The solitude, beautiful beaches and views over to Praslin, Cousin and Aride are to be savoured.

CURIEUSE

Curieuse, located only 1km from the northern tip of Praslin, is dominated by rugged sculpted granite. Curieuse Peak reaches a height of 172m. The island is about 3km long and about 2km wide. The marine park extends from the Anse Boudin shores of Praslin to surround Curieuse and the islet of St Pierre. The mangrove forests, sandy beaches, rocky shores and coral reefs form part of the marine park. Hawksbill turtles come ashore to nest during the northwest monsoons and are frequently seen while snorkelling.

Curieuse is the only other island, apart from Praslin, where a few coco de mer palms can be found growing in the wild. Many were destroyed in the successive fires that have plagued the island over the years, and bare patches of red earth can still be seen through the vegetation. Because of the red soil, Curieuse was originally known as Ile Rouge or Red Island until 1768 when Marion Dufresne renamed the island after his ship, *La Curieuse*. With careful management and tree-planting programmes, the island is recovering and looks green and lush in many places.

In 1833, a leper colony was established on Curieuse and the ruined remains of the village lend an eerie atmosphere to the southwest coast around Anse St José. Windows, doors and roofs have all gone and the remains of the stone buildings are covered in moss, creeping vines and other invading plants. Great *badamier* and *takamaka* trees cast dark shadows over the deserted colony that faces onto a most beautiful beach – at least the sufferers had wonderful vistas across to Praslin to help cheer them up.

A herd of about 250 giant Aldabra tortoises was relocated onto Curieuse with the aim of having a breeding colony outside of Aldabra. However, many have been poached and numbers are down to about 100, though they are breeding well now. The hatchlings are kept in enclosures until they are five years old, when they are released into the wild and allowed to roam and forage freely. Black parrots can sometimes be heard whistling and calling, but they are not common and are difficult to spot.

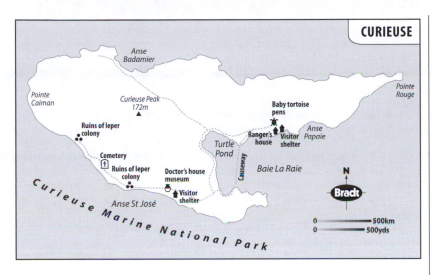

CURIEUSE

Anse Badamier

Pointe Caiman

Curieuse Peak 172m ▲

Pointe Rouge

Baby tortoise pens ★

Ruins of leper colony

Ranger's house

Visitor shelter

Anse Papaie

Cemetery ⊕

Ruins of leper colony

Doctor's house museum

Visitor shelter

Turtle Pond

Causeway

Baie La Raie

Anse St José

N

Curieuse Marine National Park

Bradt

0 ————— 500km
0 ————— 500yds

GETTING THERE AND AWAY Day trips can be arranged from most of the hotels on Praslin, and boat departures are from Anse Volbert. Arrival on Curieuse is either at Anse St José or on the beautiful beach of Baie la Raie. A snorkelling visit to Ile St Pierre is often included in the day outing.

WHAT TO SEE AND DO On arriving at **Baie la Raie** you will clearly see the remains of a long causeway across the western inlet. This was constructed to serve as a turtle holding pen where captured turtles could be kept until they were transported to the market in Mahé. In places, the wall has crumbled and broken and access across it is not possible. Early in the morning, before it is too hot, visitors are often welcomed onto magnificent Baie la Raie by a couple of giant tortoises taking a walk on the beach. The smooth, gleaming white beach is bounded by some of the most spectacular grooved granite rocks in the Seychelles.

There is a substantial **shelter** for visitors that can accommodate a cruise ship full of people, and toilets are located nearby. Visitors can walk around the tortoise nurseries in this part of the island, and there are always groups of adults to be found on the closely cropped grass in this area. Sometimes a coconut falls down and crashes onto an unsuspecting snoozing tortoise leaving a slightly cracked and dented carapace. They seem to survive this without any panel beating! March is tortoise mating season and their loud ringing groans echo around the island. The eggs hatch about two months later and the ever-vigilant staff collect many of the soft-shelled creatures to protect and rear until they are truly able to fend for themselves. There are usually a few specimens of coco de mer nuts to look at on a bench near the warden's office. Swimming and snorkelling are allowed off this beach. At low tide the bay is very shallow and hardly deep enough for swimming; the seabed is covered with seagrass which is not particularly exciting for snorkelling. When the tide comes in it is easy to swim out to the reef where the marine life is much more diverse.

The warden or one of his staff may take visitors on a guided walk. Starting at the visitor shelter, the path leads around the edge of the bay, often a great place to see some marine life close up. On occasions there are groups of squid near the surface, bonefish and blacktip reef sharks which cruise in the shallow waters, and the occasional sightings of hawksbill turtles are a treat. Batfish, scissortail sergeants

7

and many other colourful reef fish are easily seen in the clear waters. Mangroves line the shoreward edge of the old turtle pond and, at low water, many of the mangrove dwellers and wading birds will be on the exposed mud amongst the root systems of the trees. It is a lovely walk, partly on a **boardwalk** through mangroves and partly on sand. Near the beginning of the walk is a collection of black granite rocks looking like foreboding Rodin creations with inland views over swampy ground. Further on, there is a bit of a climb on an easy path with a lookout point giving great views across Baie la Raie. While walking across the sandy patches, notice the large crab burrows and look out for the beach hibiscus, a common tree in this area. The bright, golden-yellow flowers turn reddish-brown as they mature, and the nectar is much loved by Seychelles sunbirds. Littered on the mud floor among the mangrove roots are the long, spiralled brown whelk shells, which make wonderful homes for hermit crabs when their owners die. From this point it takes about 20 minutes to walk over the low saddle to the old doctor's house and visitors' shelter at Anse St José.

Day trips will often begin at **Anse St José** near the **doctor's house museum**, a large colonial villa that housed the doctor during his visits to the colony, which has been renovated and now houses a museum with a few posters describing the history and the natural heritage of the Seychelles. A path runs close to the beach in a northwesterly direction past a little staff house. Scattered ruins can be seen at intervals on either side of the cemetery. A barbecue generally takes place at Anse St José near the little museum where a thatched shelter, tables and benches make for a cheerful rustic dining area, perfect for eating the scrumptious, freshly grilled, Creole-style fish.

A clearly marked path from the shelter to Baie la Raie links up with the boardwalk that has already been discussed. It is an easy walk from here to see the tortoise sanctuary on the other side. Two hours will allow plenty of time for the return walk and a good look at the tortoises. Allow more time for swimming and snorkelling or arrange for the boatman to collect you from this side. When travelling by boat between Anse St José and Baie la Raie, look out for groups of coco de mer growing on the rocky hillside.

ILE ST PIERRE

'Miniature paradise' could be another name for this enchanting islet. Gloriously sculpted pink and grey granite arises from the clear, turquoise water and a perfect, tiny beach is exposed at low tide. The fairy-tale islet has a tiara of emerald-green palms. Regular boat trips are made to Ile St Pierre from Anse Volbert on Praslin and arrangements can be made through any of the hotels. Although there are a couple of palms, there is very little shade and no fresh water on the island. It is advisable to take plenty of sunscreen and water as well as snorkelling gear. Landing on the rocks at high tide can be a bit of a wobble, so ensure that all valuables are well protected in a watertight bag. Underwater, the dazzling colours of the reef fish complete the picture of a miniature island paradise.

FELICITE, LES SOEURS, ILE COCOS AND MARIANNE

FELICITE Félicité, a small, rocky, granite island, 227m high and 275ha in extent, lies 4km northeast of La Digue. There is a beach on the protected southwest side of the island where small boats can land.

⌂ **Where to stay and eat** The accommodation on this island is in the process of renovation.

What to see and do The snorkelling around the island is reasonably good with many of the corals slowly regenerating.

LES SOEURS These two little islands lie about 3km north of Félicité and offer relatively good diving and snorkelling.

The larger, eastern island, Grande Soeur, rises to a rocky height of 113m and covers an area of 100ha. It is only about 200m wide in the middle and there are several walks around the island. Much of the natural vegetation is interspersed with coconut palms but it is the massive grey granite boulders which dominate this island. Boats land on the western beach, which is also the best snorkelling side of the island. The silvery-white eastern beach, framed by sculpted granite rocks and fringed with palms, must be one of the most beautiful in all of the Seychelles. A small community lives here raising their chickens and ducks and living off fresh fish and coconuts. The island is for the exclusive use of guests from Château des Feuilles, Praslin, during the weekend but is open to visitors during the week. Excursions to this 'Robinson Crusoe' retreat, which often include a beach barbecue, can be arranged by most of the tour operators on Praslin and La Digue.

The western island, or Petite Soeur, attains a height of 105m and is separated from its big sister by a deep channel. It is a clump of granite rocks with sparse vegetation scattered around it.

ILE COCOS This small island, located between Félicité and Les Soeurs, was closed to the public for about ten years as much of the coral had been damaged. It is now part

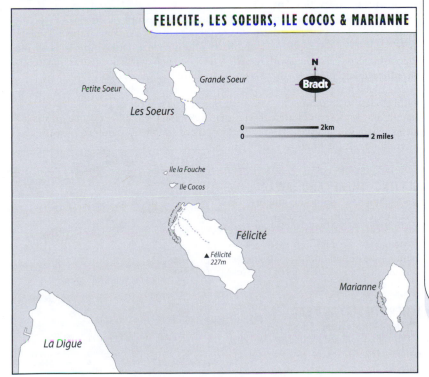

FELICITE, LES SOEURS, ILE COCOS & MARIANNE

7

of a marine protected area with a warden in charge, and it is open for day visitors. In spite of the heavily damaged coral, snorkelling can be rewarding with turtles and a fair selection of reef fish to be seen.

MARIANNE Marianne is about 4km east of Félicité and the granite rocks rise up to about 129m. A little beach on the southwest side allows access in calm weather only. Marine life around this island is particularly rich and diving and snorkelling are good.

DENIS

Denis, on the most northerly part of the shallow Seychelles Bank, lies about 95km north of Mahé. This privately owned island is only 2km long and, at most, 1.5km wide, and covers an area of 120ha. It is an emerald-green, flat coral island edged by white beaches with coral reefs protecting the southern side. Denis de Trobriand, master of the *Etoile*, was the first to discover the island in 1773; he claimed it for France and gave it his name. It suffered the same fate as many of the other islands as, firstly, guano mining was undertaken, followed by the development of coconut plantations. Since then, a rat eradication programme has been successfully carried out and a large number of indigenous trees planted. Several species of endemic birds are slowly being reintroduced and Denis now has a thriving population of Seychelles fodies and warblers. Magpie robins and the beautiful black paradise flycatcher have also been successfully introduced by Nature Seychelles and Birdlife UK with the help of funds from the Disney Worldwide Conservation Fund.

A lighthouse was erected in 1910 to warn passing ships of the hazards of the shallow area close to the northern side of the island. The remains of the old village include an abandoned prison, a cemetery and a chapel. Denis runs a small but successful farm in keeping with its self-sufficiency policy which ensures that guests have the freshest produce. There is even an old vanilla plantation.

The island was purchased by a German industrialist in 1976 and he proceeded to build chalets to accommodate guests in his own little piece of paradise. Denis was acquired by Mickey and Kathleen Mason in 1999 and the island now operates as the ultimate tropical getaway with the philosophy of simplicity, comfort, pleasure and relaxation with the finest hospitality in the Creole tradition.

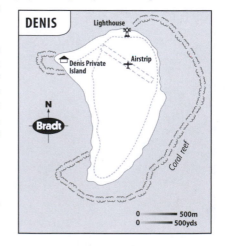

GETTING THERE AND AWAY There are scheduled domestic flights on Twin Otters from Mahé airport every day except Wednesday and these are arranged in conjunction with Denis Island accommodation. Otherwise, charter flights and helicopter transfers can be arranged to suit your schedule.

WHERE TO STAY AND EAT
Denis Private Island (25 cottages)
4295999; e reservation@denisisland.com; www. denisisland.com. The cottages are scattered along 2 beaches. Their motto is 'no keys, no phones, no

worries', but internet is available only if absolutely necessary. The restaurant serves excellent cuisine using the fresh farm produce. There are all sorts of special offers so do check out the website or talk to your travel agent. Weddings & honeymoons are a speciality (page 73). Rates are FB. **$$$$**

WHAT TO SEE AND DO A lattice of paths criss-crosses the lush, green island and it is impossible to get lost. Watersports are a major feature of Denis, and it is a favoured spot for big-game fishermen as the Seychelles Bank plummets steeply down to a depth of 2,000m near the island. World records for dogtooth tuna have been set here and marlin, sailfish, tuna and barracuda are plentiful. Snorkelling and diving are particularly good. There is a floodlit tennis court, guided nature walks and billiards for an indoor, out-of-the-sun, pastime.

The 50 island inhabitants live in a tiny village earning their living working in the hotel or on the farm and small coconut plantation.

BIRD

Remote Bird Island, another privately owned sandy speck in the ocean, lies 105km northwest of Mahé on the edge of the Seychelles Bank. It is, in fact, the most northerly island in the Seychelles, being a mere fraction closer to the Equator than Denis. It covers only 70ha of land, is 1,500m long and 750m wide. Very little is known of the early history of Bird but the first recorded visit was in 1771 when the master of *The Eagle* charted the island. In 1808, a French privateer, *Hirondelle,* with 180 people on board, was wrecked on the reef and the survivors remained on the island for three weeks while they constructed a raft, before sailing to Mahé. Bird was originally called Ile aux Vaches ('Island of Sea Cows'), after all the dugongs that grazed on the prolific seagrasses in the clear waters. They have become extinct but the island is still sometimes referred to as Ile aux Vaches and it appears on many maps as such. In 1896, guano was already being mined on the island and 17,000 tonnes were removed between 1900 and 1905. At the end of that phase, coconuts were planted for the copra industry. The present owner bought the island in 1967, an airstrip was cleared, and a small tourist lodge was developed. He declared the island a wildlife sanctuary in 1986 and the lodge was upgraded. Over the years, the lodge has been enlarged and upgraded but it remains a delightful, unpretentious hotel with a blend of hospitality, relaxation and simplicity in a natural environment.

GETTING THERE AND AWAY Any of the tour operators on Mahé will be able to arrange a visit to the island. Alternatively, the Bird Island office at the Inter-Island Quay, Victoria, will make all the necessary arrangements. Air Seychelles flights, in small aircraft, depart from the domestic airport, take about 30 minutes and are arranged in conjunction with the accommodation. Guests are met on the grass runway by the friendly island managers and are taken to the reception area where they receive an informative and passionate talk about the island. A motor-boat trip from Mahé to Bird takes about 8 hours.

 WHERE TO STAY AND EAT

🏠 **Bird Island Lodge** (24 bungalows) 🔌4323322; e thelodge@birdislandseychelles.com; reservations: 🔌4224925; e reservations@birdislandseychelles.com; www.birdislandseychelles.com. The spacious, comfortable bungalows are located close to the beach & are a short walk away from the reception & dining areas. A relaxed & informal atmosphere prevails & the staff are exceptionally friendly & obliging. Excellent food is usually served buffet-style using fresh fish, &

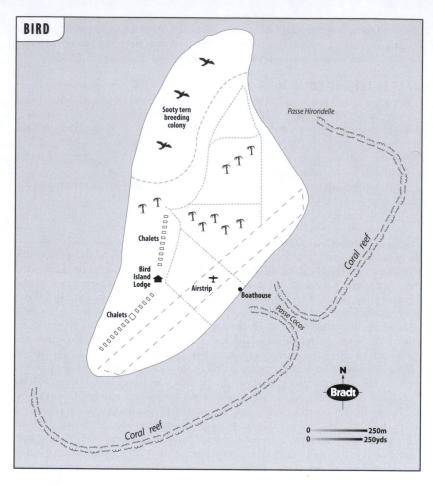

vegetables grown on the island. There are no bright lights at night that might interfere with the habits of the wildlife & there are no TVs in the bungalows to detract from the natural sounds. The reception area has a small boutique with several good natural history reference books. The airy rooms have ceiling fans but no AC, & with such beautiful beaches, who needs a swimming pool? It is refreshing to find a down-to-earth hotel without the 5-star trappings. Rates are FB. **$$$**

WHAT TO SEE AND DO Bird, as its name implies, is for the birds, and they are the main tourist attraction of the island. Walking paths traverse the island and reveal a variety of natural and introduced plants. Guests are free to wander anywhere around the nature reserve on easy and well-marked sandy paths. Besides, it is such a small island you could never get lost!

About 800,000 pairs of **sooty terns** breed there during the southeasterly trade wind season. Their first 'wide awake' calls are heard as early as mid-March when they start gathering prior to nesting. Great noisy masses of terns swirl over the island like a low, hazy cloud and by June they are laying their eggs. The sooty tern colony is at the northern end of the island, reached by walking along the beach and following the sign inland. A small raised platform enables guests to have a good view over the nesting ground without disturbing the birds.

As the Seychellois consider their eggs a great delicacy, they used to be gathered in vast quantities, thereby causing the sooty tern numbers to decline. Now, with a conservation ethos on the island, and only a controlled number of eggs (around 3%) harvested annually, the terns are no longer threatened and the Seychellois are delighted to have an annual supply of tern eggs.

Rats have been eradicated from the island, and the infestation of 'crazy ants' that plagued the birds, especially the chicks, has been brought under control. Large numbers of lesser and brown noddies are quite fearless and take no notice of the hotel guests. This is the best place to see these two easily confused species close up. White fairy terns are in abundance and many waders frequent the beautiful beaches. Madagascar fodies are also common. In February 2006, 33 Seychelles sunbirds were introduced onto Bird Island. They soon paired up and are breeding well, having truly adapted to their new home.

Besides the birds, 24 giant **Aldabra tortoises** live out a quiet life, roaming wherever they please, even grazing the airstrip. The largest tortoise in the world, Esmeralda, lives on the island and when he was weighed by the Royal Zoological Society in 1980, he broke the scales at 303kg and is reputed to be around 240 years old! Two yellow-and-black radiated tortoises from Madagascar, called Jeremy and Jermina, can also be found wandering around.

Both **green** and **hawksbill turtles** use the sandy beaches for their nests, which are closely monitored by staff, together with interested guests, under a programme initiated by Dr Jeanne Mortimer. It is a great thrill for guests to see the hawksbill turtles laying their eggs during the day between October and January, and also a special treat to see the tiny turtle hatchlings making their way to the open ocean. As many as 13,000 turtle hatchlings can emerge in one season (pages 35–7).

The northern tip of the island projects out to sea as a long exposed sand spit, which is good for observing wading birds. The spit changes size and shape with the monsoons. Snorkelling inside the reef reveals the vast seagrass beds with frequent sightings of grazing turtles as well as many small tropical fishes. Currents can be strong around Passe Cocos and Passe Hirondelle, but some buoys indicate safe areas. The management will advise on the best snorkelling spots and masks and fins are available to hire through the reception. With the edge of the Seychelles Bank just beyond the northern point of the island, **deep-sea fishing** is excellent with sailfish and tuna amongst the regular catch. Boat tours can be arranged at the hotel reception and dolphins and occasionally whales are seen around the island. This excursion is a lovely way to experience the island from another perspective and gives the understanding of just how remote this island is.

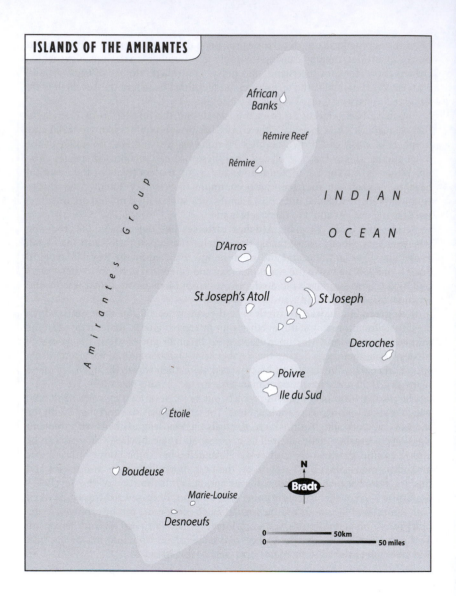

ISLANDS OF THE AMIRANTES

African Banks

Rémire Reef

Rémire

INDIAN

OCEAN

Amirantes Group

D'Arros

St Joseph's Atoll

St Joseph

Desroches

Poivre

Ile du Sud

Étoile

N

Bradt

Boudeuse

Marie-Louise

Desnoeufs

0   50km

0   50 miles

8

Outer Coralline Islands

The outer islands of the Seychelles, scattered across a vast area of the western Indian Ocean, are isolated groups of coral islands, hundreds of kilometres from anywhere. The Amirantes, a string of about ten islands, are the closest to Mahé; Alphonse consists of three islands; the Farquhar group is made up of two atolls; and Plat and Coëtivy are two far-flung islands, neither of them near to any other part of the Seychelles. Many of the outer islands are surrounded by coral reefs with shallow lagoons protecting some of the most fabulous beaches imaginable. The islands are not on regular shipping routes and though many are uninhabited others may have a small staff of contract workers on the still-active coconut plantations. Some of the islands are being developed as exclusive getaway tourist destinations.

After the colonisation and exploitation of the granitic islands of the Seychelles in the late 18th century, it did not take long for people to spread to the outer islands. The first concessions were granted around 1815, and work was usually done for the absentee landlords by slave labour, with a *commandeur* or overseer in charge. Rich guano deposits were mined, fish and turtles were exploited, and sooty tern eggs were collected by the thousand. Cotton and a little maize were grown before coconut palms were planted on the islands. The plantation system was created and it remains today as Seychellois island managers and contract workers live out a lonely existence far from the gregarious lifestyle of Mahé. Most of the islands are owned by the government, and are managed by the parastatal Islands Development Company.

Airstrips have been built on some of the islands, but for the others, the only contact with the outside world is the radio-telephone and the supply ship, which calls about every two months. The eagerly awaited ship delivers mail, fuel and provisions and brings new staff to the islands to relieve those whose contracts have expired. It is possible to visit these far-flung islands by yacht and permission has to be obtained from the Islands Development Company in Mahé. Should you arrive without permission it is unlikely that you will be permitted onto the islands. Note that the maps used in this text should not be used for navigation purposes.

Activity by Somali pirates has curtailed sailing to these lovely outer islands. It is advisable to check with all authorities before you set sail into these waters.

THE AMIRANTES

The Amirantes Bank has ten islands, several shoals and many submerged reefs, which are strung out between 5° and 6°S. African Banks, in the north, is about 250km from Mahé, and Desnoeufs, the most southerly, is about 135km further south. The main islands in the group are Rémire, D'Arros, St Joseph's Atoll, Desroches, Poivre, Etoile, Boudeuse and Marie-Louise. This remote group of islands was discovered by the Portuguese navigator, Vasco da Gama, on his second voyage to India in 1502.

They were subsequently known as Ilhas do Almirantes after the famous admiral. It is possible that 17th-century pirates used the quiet lagoons and sandy beaches for shelter after marauding sprees, but it is more likely that they came to grief on the treacherous reefs surrounding many of the islands. In fact, voyaging among the outer islands reveals many latter-day shipwrecks. Funnels and bulkheads loom out of the breakers crashing onto the coral reefs and sometimes, on still and calm days, they appear as mirages hovering on the ocean surface.

DESROCHES Desroches, a sandy cay on the rim of a submerged nearly circular atoll, is a long, narrow, flat island, 6km long, 1km wide, covering an area of about 320ha. The island, covered in coconut palms and casuarina trees, is 230km south of Mahé and approximately 16km east of the main Amirantes Bank. Desroches was named after François Julien Desroches, Governor of Mauritius from 1767–72. The exclusive Desroches Island resort is located on the western side of the island and there is an airstrip within easy walking distance. A lighthouse, located at the northeastern end of the island, is now nothing more than a rusty edifice almost hidden among the dense vegetation. The northern part of the island is run as a coconut plantation and farm, and there is a settlement on the northern shore. The first coconut plantations were started in 1875 and copra was processed for decades. Fresh vegetables from the farm are sold to the resort and salted fish and recyclable materials are sent to Mahé.

This is the ultimate get-away-from-it-all island. The only noise you are likely to hear above the ocean waves is the gentle cooing of the little barred ground doves. There are long stretches of dazzling white beaches with sheltered swimming on the northern shore. The southern shore, which is a favoured spot for fly-fishing, is guarded by a wide reef that almost dries at low tide. During the northwest monsoons, hawksbill turtles clamber onto the beaches to lay their eggs above the high-tide mark, and it is possible to see them during the day. A few giant Aldabra tortoises roam freely around the island seeking out deep shade in the heat. As mosquitoes lurking in the undergrowth can be a nuisance, ensure that you have plenty of insect repellent. Seabirds are often seen feeding in the quiet waters of the lagoon, and turnstones, usually associated with the shore, frequent the grassy areas under the coconut palms.

Getting there and away There are five flights per week from Mahé (*45–60mins*) and they will be arranged in conjunction with accommodation at the lodge. The baggage allowance is 15kg per person.

Where to stay and eat

Desroches Island (48 suites & villas) resort: ☎ 4229003; reservations: ☎ +27 82496 4570; e bookings@desroches-island.com; www.desroches-island.com. This all-inclusive resort has 18 beach & 12 luxury beach suites, decorated in a blend of island style & modern comfort, & each with their own private pool. Each has IDD telephone, satellite TV, DVD players, tea- & coffee-making facilities & a private patio very close to the beach. The 3-, 4- & 5- bedroom beach villas & the exclusive Madame Zabra Villa are located along the Madame Zabra Beach a little distance from the main hotel. They are fully self-sufficient with every luxury imaginable, including fully fitted kitchens & swimming pools. The main dining venue, Hideaway, serves really delicious international gourmet & innovative Creole-style cuisine with an emphasis on the freshest seafood. More casual meals are served in the relaxed, feet-in-the-sand, beach restaurant near the pool. The L'Amirantes bar is a casual meeting place with an extensive wine list. The resort has various special offers for couples getting married or on honeymoon. Desroches is an all-inclusive experience. **$$$$–$$$$$**

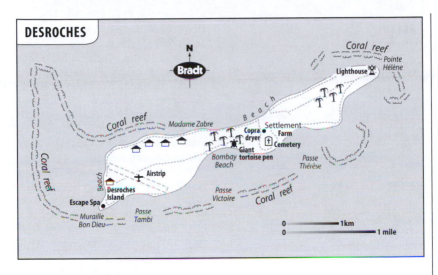

What to see and do Bicycles are available and it is possible to walk or cycle around most of the island on flat easy paths. Look for the life-sized driftwood sculpture of Jonah and the Whale, visit the coconut plantation, the old cemetery and see the rescued tortoises in a huge enclosure. You may even be able to adopt one of them so enquire at reception. Keen birdwatchers should bring binoculars as migrant birds often stop over on Desroches on passage migration. There is an air-conditioned beachfront gym, floodlit tennis court, a library, a boutique and some indoor games. The Escape Spa has a range of treatments in a quiet location.

All **water-based activities** can be arranged by the Cast–A–Way centre; canoes, surfboards, stand-up paddle boards, windsurfers and pedalos are available. The island is well known for its good scuba diving on the reef drop-off known as the Desroches Drop and there is a well-equipped PADI dive centre. Snorkelling too, can be very rewarding. Desroches is well situated for big-game fishing and the island has several boats to cater for different fishing adventures. Fly-fishing is a daily activity from November to April when the seas are very calm. Guests can be taken across to the lagoons of St Joseph and Poivre for bone-fishing. For some though, the 14km of unspoilt beaches are the perfect getaway.

POIVRE Poivre, about 40km west of Desroches, consists of two sandy cays, a shallow lagoon and many reefs. It is close to the eastern end of the Amirantes Bank and about 270km southwest of Mahé. This uninhabited island, covered in coconuts and casuarinas, was named after Pierre Poivre, the quartermaster on Mauritius who was instrumental in setting up the spice industry in the Seychelles in the late 1770s. Excursions to Poivre can be arranged through Desroches Island resort.

ETOILE AND BOUDEUSE These two sandy cays, 30km apart, are located southwest of Poivre. Uninhabited, both are bird reserves with large numbers of sooty terns nesting on them.

MARIE-LOUISE AND DESNOEUFS Marie-Louise and Desnoeufs, about 10km apart, are the southernmost islets of the Amirantes group, roughly 325km from Mahé, with each island a small settlement. Marie-Louise, no more than a sandy cay with a

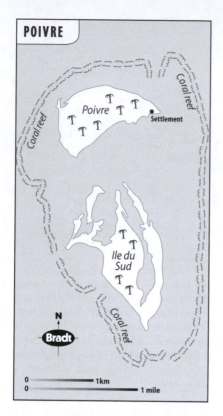

POIVRE

Poivre

Settlement

Coral reef

Coral reef

Ile du Sud

Coral reef

N

Bradt

0   1km
0   1 mile

clump of casuarinas, covers an area of about 500m². It is encircled by a coral reef, and landing there is hazardous because of rough surf and hidden wrecks. Failing to live up to its name, the surveying ship *Alert* ran aground in 1882, and in 1905 a steamer sank in the anchorage. Desnoeufs covers an area of 35ha and is an extraordinary sooty tern colony.

In the breeding season, May to early August, the sky above the island is a seething, hovering mass of hundreds of thousands of these black-and-white birds. The sound of them calling almost eclipses the roar of the surf. A large part of the colony has been set aside as a sanctuary, but the remainder is officially harvested and crates of the fragile eggs are transported back to the market on Mahé. It is a tricky manoeuvre to hoist the boxes of eggs on board the supply ship from the tiny boat, rocking and rolling in the heavy swells of the southeast trades. Again, there are no tourist facilities whatsoever.

AFRICAN BANKS African Banks is made up of two small, very low islands joined by a sand spit and coral reef, covering an area less than 1km². It has low beach crest bush, a couple of coconut palms, a derelict fishermen's hut and is uninhabited except for thousands of seabirds.

REMIRE Rémire, lying on a small reef, is a sandy, oval island of about 1km². It has a landing strip for light aircraft and is inhabited by the workers on the coconut plantation and vegetable gardens. Rémire was also known as Eagle Island. It was stripped of its guano before coconuts were planted. There is a simple four-bedroomed guesthouse available through the Island Development Company (*IDC*; ◊ *4384640;* e *ceo@idc.sc*).

D'ARROS AND ST JOSEPH'S ATOLL These islands, about 1km apart, are privately owned. **D'Arros** is an oval, sandy cay perched on a flat reef and was named after Baron d'Arros, marine commander on Mauritius in 1771. Although most of the island is covered in coconut palms, there is a significant portion of natural coastal forest with *Guettada*, *Morinda* and *Terminalia* species dominating. Birdlife is notable with about 480 Seychelles fodies and 260 Madagascar fodies; both common and lesser noddies breed on the island. The enormous robber crab (*Birgus latro*) is widespread on the island but most abundant on the south coast. A small research station supports work on turtles and corals. D'Arros is under new ownership of the Save the Seas Foundation, and the entire atoll has been declared a special nature reserve to preserve its unique biodiversity. Part of D'Arros is provisionally being set aside as a RAMSAR site. The island is now rat-free and much of the alien vegetation is being removed and replaced by endemic plants.

St Joseph's Atoll consists of a ring of eight islets surrounded by submerged coral reefs with St Joseph's Island the largest and easternmost of the group. There is very little natural vegetation left, coconut palms being the dominant trees. A large population of approximately 19,000 breeding pairs of wedge-tailed shearwaters nest on one of the smaller islets. Grey herons as well as black-naped and crested terns are to be found on some of the islets.

THE ALPHONSE GROUP

The Alphonse group of islands lie on a separate bank south of the Amirantes Bank at 7°S and 400km from Mahé. They were named after Chevalier Alphonse di Pontirez, the commander of a French ship, *Le Lys*, which visited the island in 1730.

ALPHONSE Alphonse, a sand cay on the rim of a circular atoll which is exposed at low tide, is a small, flat, triangular-shaped island covered in coconut palms. There are paths and a road that weave through the coconut plantation and you can see the plantation manager's shabby old house. Two sides of the island extend to embrace the large, sheltered lagoon and it makes an ideal holiday escape. Alphonse frequently experiences less rain than the granitic islands, especially during the northwest monsoons. Small boats can enter the lagoon only at high

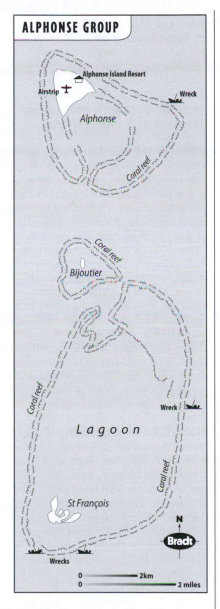

tide through the southwestern channel. Shipwrecks lie on either side of the lagoon and bear testimony to the strong currents and shallow reefs hiding beneath the clear turquoise water. *Dot*, a French coal steamer, ran aground *en route* to Réunion in 1873, and on the other side is the wreck of the *Tamatave*, grounded in 1903.

GETTING THERE AND AWAY The 1-hour flight to Alphonse will be arranged with IDC Aviation in conjunction with the resort. Flights depart from Mahé on a Saturday morning and return from Alphonse on the same afternoon; the cost is US$1,300 return. The luggage allowance is strictly 15kg.

WHERE TO STAY AND EAT

Alphonse Island Resort (16 A-frame chalets & 5 villas) 📞 4229030; e info@alphonse-island. com or reservations@alphonse-island.com; www. alphonse-resort.com. All the chalets & villas are located along the beach & there is a spacious reception, dining & bar areas as well as a large pool. The restaurant offers delicious, inventive, Creole cuisine with plenty of fresh fish & produce from the island & picnics can be arranged. The resort is generally closed between May & Sep, the windy period, but if a group of 6 or more request to stay there it can be arranged. Alphonse is primarily a fishing & diving resort, but any non-fishing or diving members of the party are well taken care of. **$$$$**

WHAT TO SEE AND DO Besides relaxing by the pool and soaking up the sun there are a surprising amount of things to do on Alphonse. **Birdwatching** can be interesting as many migrating birds visit the island and Amur falcons, Oriental pratincoles, Madagascar lesser cuckoos and white and grey wagtails have been seen. Walking along the shore of the lagoon or snorkelling from the beach can also be fascinating with all sorts of wonderful creatures to be seen in the intertidal zone – look out for the large crabs! Take a bicycle around the island under the shade of tall coconut palms. It is also great fun to have a picnic lunch on the expansive sand flats with feet in the water and big umbrellas for shade.

The main attraction is the fly-fishing in the lagoon around St François and the record is 50 fish species caught on fly in one week. Barbless hooks are used and great care is taken of the fish before being released. The fishing and diving packages are for seven nights from Saturday to Saturday; however, should you wish to stay longer that can be arranged with flights on Wednesdays. If you wish to use your own charter plane, that too can be organised. Conservation levies of US$175 for fishing, US$70 for diving and US$70 for staying on the island for a week are to be paid in cash on the island. The concession is limited to 12 rods only and the fishing season is early October to late May. Diving is also a great attraction with outstanding drop-offs in the area and excellent coral, with a great diversity of reef fish.

BIJOUTIER AND ST FRANÇOIS These two tiny gems, both adorned by a topknot of coconut palms, are set in a coral reef separated from Alphonse by a deep channel. Bijoutier is only 5km south of Alphonse and it takes less than an hour to walk around it. St François, a small atoll, 17ha in extent and with shallow lagoons, is a further 7km south and is regarded as the best fly-fishing destination in the world. It is also an important bird area as hundreds of crab plovers gather there during the non-breeding season with over 1,200 recorded at one time. These small islands are uninhabited, but picnics here can be arranged through the Alphonse resort. Remember, though, there is little shade.

THE FARQUHAR GROUP

Providence and Farquhar are two atolls 60km apart lying on the Farquhar Ridge at 10°S. Exquisite and remote, each island is surrounded by sandy cays, sheltered lagoons, shallow coral reefs and clear, deep turquoise water.

Although there are plans afoot, no tourist facilities currently exist on either of these islands but both have settlements and active coconut plantations run by the Islands Development Company (IDC). Once the copra is dried, it is bagged and transported to Mahé aboard the supply ship which calls every two months. Agriculture plays a minor role with only a few cows and pigs being reared for local use. Fishing is an important feature of these outer islands, with several vessels working in the area.

GETTING THERE AND AWAY Tourists can visit these islands by sea, on their own yachts or by chartering vessels from one of the boat-charter facilities in Mahé (pages 71–2 and 83). It is important to obtain permission from the Islands Development Company in Mahé if you wish to go ashore. There are no tourist facilities but, if you are staying at the Farquhar guesthouse, it is possible to charter a flight through IDC. During the period when the southeast trades blow from May to September, the sea is often extremely rough.

FARQUHAR ATOLL Farquhar is the most important of the 11 islands that make up the Farquhar Atoll. The atoll is ear-shaped with most of the islands on the eastern rim of the atoll. It has one of the most beautiful and sheltered lagoons in the Seychelles. Sparkling clear water,

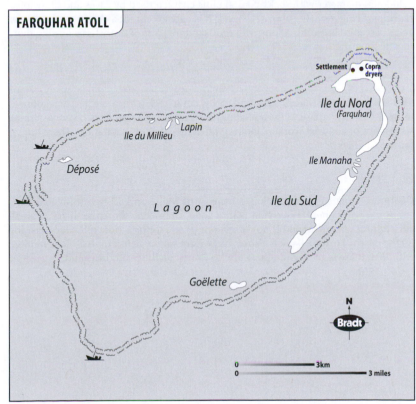

8

wide coral reefs and shimmering, silvery beaches make Farquhar a tantalising island. There is an airstrip with a heart-shaped sign that says 'Welcome to Farquhar'. The picturesque settlement and copra-drying sheds are surrounded by coconut palms, casuarinas and *badamier* trees. A large number of sooty terns breed on the small island of Goëlette. Many of the surrounding islets and reefs are littered with shipwrecks, and there are great hulks of rusting metal visible, especially when the tide is low. Snorkelling and scuba diving are good, particularly in November and April, and the best time for fly-fishing is between early October and late May.

Where to stay and eat There is a guesthouse owned by the Islands Development Company (*6 rooms;* ↘ *4384640;* e *ceo@idc.sc*) which is available in the fly-fishing season, if you want to go diving or just chill out. It is not a plush five-star establishment with gourmet food; just a simple house with a lovely, spacious veranda. Three meals a day are provided and a small shop sells soft drinks and beer.

PROVIDENCE Providence Atoll is about 710km from Mahé and comprises Providence Island in the north and some banks at the southern extremity of the atoll. Landing on Providence is a hazardous procedure because of the surrounding shallow reef and heavy surf. Over the years there have been many ships wrecked in the vicinity. A handful of contract workers run the coconut plantation.

ST PIERRE St Pierre, 30km to the west of Providence, is a circular raised atoll 1,200m in diameter with rocky coastal cliffs characterised by caves and blowholes, reaching a height of 10m above sea level. It is bare except for a clump of casuarinas, and is a seabird breeding colony with thousands of pairs of sooty terns nesting there during June and July.

PLAT

This tiny platform island, surrounded by coral reef with a sheltered lagoon, is located 140km south of Mahé and about 200km east of Desroches. There is a small settlement of contract workers looking after the coconut plantation. There are no tourist facilities.

COETIVY

Coëtivy is situated about 290km southeast of Mahé and 170km from Plat. It is 10km long and about 1km wide with a long, unbroken shoreline. It has a small agricultural settlement and is now used as a prison for first-time offenders. Fishing off the nearby Fortune Bank is also an important source of fish for the Mahé market. Although there is an airstrip, there are no tourist facilities on the island.

9

The Aldabra Group

The Aldabra group is made up of Aldabra, Assumption, Astove and Cosmoledo. It is roughly 460km from the northern tip of Madagascar, 600km from the East African coast and over 1,000km from Mahé. The remote atolls were once covered in thick vegetation, home to hundreds of thousands of tortoises, nesting place for millions of breeding seabirds, and each year vast numbers of marine turtles laid their eggs in the soft sand on the seashore. This idyllic state lasted until the late 1800s when the islands suffered the same exploitation as that which occurred on all the other Seychelles islands. Concessions were granted to private individuals who cleared much of the natural vegetation on Assumption, Astove and Cosmoledo to make way for cotton, sisal, guano mining and, later, coconut plantations. Because of the harsh terrain of Aldabra, only small areas were cleared and planted with coconuts, but turtles and tortoises were heavily exploited there as well as on the other three islands.

Naturalists undertook many collections during the 19th and early 20th centuries, but it was only after 1960 that the first comprehensive scientific surveys of the Aldabra group were undertaken. Aldabra nearly became an air-force base in 1967 and, subsequently, the Royal Geographical Society and other institutions became involved in studying the natural history of the Aldabra group. Aldabra was declared a UNESCO World Heritage Site in 1982 and the islands, the lagoon and the surrounding reefs are now protected areas.

There are no tourist facilities on any of the islands, and they are not on the general tourist route except for the occasional expedition-type cruise ship or live-aboard dive boat that may call at these out-of-the-way islands. They are visited regularly by the supply ship from Mahé, which calls at the outlying islands about every two months, delivering food, fuel and mail. Scientists are able to use the supply ship to get to these remote areas. Note that maps used in this text should not be used for navigation purposes.

ASSUMPTION

Assumption is surrounded by a narrow, fringing reef and covers an area of 11km² with a series of sand dunes on the southeastern shores attaining a height of 30m. There is a gap in the reef on the northwestern side of the island with a beautiful, long crescent of beach lining the bay. A dilapidated concrete pier stretches into the sea opposite the small settlement at the southern end of the bay. There are a few houses and a string of little huts under the coconut palms surrounded by colourful flowers and lime trees growing in profusion. At the edge of the sea a few graves, some of which are crumbling into the ocean, are shaded by casuarinas.

Assumption has a landing strip and it is mainly used as a connection to Aldabra for visiting scientists and staff changes (the 27km journey across to Aldabra

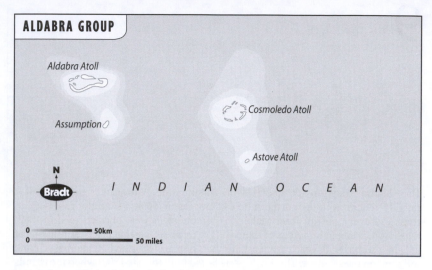

ALDABRA GROUP

Aldabra Atoll

Cosmoledo Atoll

Assumption

Astove Atoll

N

Bradt

I N D I A N   O C E A N

0 _____ 50km
0 _____ 50 miles

has to be made by boat). Only about half-a-dozen people live on the island and they maintain the runway and the communications station. There is no tourist accommodation. The interior of the island is rough, coral limestone covered in low, scrubby bushes. In the past, the main activity was guano mining, and when that came to an end in 1948, coconut plantations were set up to produce copra. With the denudation of the natural vegetation came the demise of the birdlife. Abbott's booby, once breeding on Assumption, is now confined to Christmas Island, further east in the Indian Ocean. Today, introduced Mozambique serins mix cheerfully with the noisy Mauritian red-whiskered bulbul, and the ubiquitous crows. Abbott's sunbird is also resident. During the years of exploitation, green and hawksbill turtles were hunted and now very few come to the island to lay their eggs. The slow, lumbering giant tortoises have also been wiped off the island.

ASTOVE

Located at 10°S, Astove is the most southerly of the Seychelles islands. It is a small, uninhabited atoll of 6km² embracing a shallow lagoon with only one opening to the sea. An airstrip has recently been completed and a small rustic fishing camp has been developed by the Islands Development Company and opened in mid 2015, with basic accommodation for six people in single rooms each with an en-suite bathroom. Bookings can be made through Alphonse (\ +27 82 748 7290; e *reservations@alphonse-island.com*). One guide is provided for two anglers (page 184). A reef with deep, spectacular drop-offs surrounds the island. This is an excellent diving and snorkelling spot with caves and overhangs creating amazing underwater scenery teeming with colourful reef fish and turtles. History books tell tales of many shipwrecks on the treacherous reef. In 1760, a Portuguese ship, *Dom Royal*, laden with treasures and slaves, ran aground. The captain and crew tried to reach the East African coast on a raft and were never seen again, while the slaves were left to their own devices on the atoll. Several ships from Mauritius went to try to capture the slaves but were beaten off by the fierce and wild castaways. It was not until 1796 that a ship from Mahé finally captured some of the slaves, but it, too, was wrecked, with all on board ending up in a watery grave.

Like Assumption, Astove was exploited for its guano, followed by copra production. Tumbled-down ruins of a few houses, copra-drying sheds and stagnant water tanks are all that remain of the thriving little establishment that in 1968 was run by about 40 people.

The vegetation is impenetrable and the overgrown path from the old settlement to the lagoon is sometimes impossible to locate, but with new tourist accommodation this will no doubt change. Large, black-and-white, bird-wing butterflies are common, and the mosquitoes are a terrible menace. They will descend upon you in droves, so, if you are ever to land on Astove, take gallons of repellent and wear long-sleeved shirts and long trousers. Abbott's sunbirds, white-eyes and the Madagascar cisticolas feast on these insects.

COSMOLEDO

Mysterious, wild and uninhabited, Cosmoledo's buildings are in ruins and overgrown plantations of coconuts and sisal are reminders of the past exploitation of this remote atoll. Cosmoledo comprises a dozen small islands encircling a huge, shallow lagoon that almost dries at low tide. The largest island is crescent-shaped Menai at 2.5km², where there are several disintegrating buildings, a cemetery and the remains of a once productive coconut plantation. The other islands, some still unsurveyed, are Grande Ile (also known as Wizard Island), Ile du Nord, Ile Nord

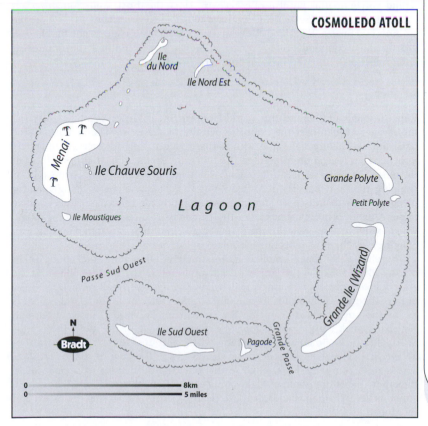

COSMOLEDO ATOLL

Ile du Nord

Ile Nord Est

Menai

Ile Chauve Souris

Grande Polyte

Petit Polyte

L a g o o n

Ile Moustiques

Passe Sud Ouest

Grande Ile (Wizard)

N

Bradt

Ile Sud Ouest

Pagode

Grande Passe

0   8km
0   5 miles

Est, Ile du Trou, Goëlette, Grande Polyte, Pagode, Ile Sud Ouest, Ile Moustiques, Ile Baleine and Ile Chauve Souris.

The largest breeding colony of sooty terns in the Seychelles can be found on Cosmoledo, with over a million pairs nesting on the sandy islands. Three species of boobies – red-footed, brown and masked – also nest on the islands and small flocks of crab plovers can be seen feeding on the exposed coral flats at low tide at certain times of the year. Grey herons, a variety of terns and some remarkable passerines make their home on the islands. There is an endemic, resident population of Abbott's sunbird and their shining, jewelled, prismatic plumage provides flashes of colour as they dart among the vegetation. Taxonomic research is currently being carried out on the sunbirds and Madagascar white-eyes. Madagascar cisticolas are also commonly seen in the scrubby vegetation and can be seen flying between the tiny, vegetated clumps of *champignon* (sharp, pitted and strangely shaped limestone, from the French word for mushroom) in the lagoon.

At high tide it is possible to ride in a flat-bottomed boat through parts of the lagoon, but there are many uncharted rocks and it is only in the two principal channels that there is any depth of water. Many fish become trapped as the tide recedes, and it is easy to see eels and parrotfish quietly waiting in the shallow pools for the tide to rise. Excellent snorkelling and diving are to be found off some of the reefs, particularly off Menai Island.

Successful rat-eradication programmes were carried out on Grand Ile and Grand Polyte in 2007 but it is only recently, since the threat from Somali pirates has decreased, that research workers have returned to the islands to monitor the seabirds and turtles. The Islands Development Company is planning on building an airstrip and accommodation for conservation workers to continue the monitoring and protection of the wildlife from poachers.

ALDABRA

Rugged, rough and remote, this World Heritage Site wilderness atoll has survived the ravages of man over the centuries because of these very characteristics. The harsh and arid nature of the atoll, with its sharp, jagged, limestone terrain and thick, impenetrable vegetation, prevented the full-scale exploitation that beset most of the other Seychelles islands. Although it is not, and never has been, on any regular shipping routes, it was first recorded on early Portuguese charts in 1509, and it is highly likely that discovery by Arab seafarers preceded this date. The evocative name Aldabra probably stems from the Arabic word *Al-Khadra* meaning green, which could be a reference to the green-based cloud that can sometimes be seen hanging over the atoll, reflecting the colour of the vast interior lagoon.

The elliptically shaped atoll is approximately 34km long and about 14km across, which makes it the largest raised coral atoll in the world. The rim of the atoll is broken by four channels which link the massive, shallow lagoon to the ocean. The four islands thus formed are Grande Terre or Main Island, which is by far the largest; Picard, hosting the settlement; Polymnie, the smallest; and Malabar, which runs straight along the northern edge of the atoll. The islands of Aldabra make up an area of 154km², which accounts for almost one-third of all the Seychelles land territory. The lagoon inside the ring of islands is 11km across and 27km long, big enough so that one cannot see over from one side to the other. The entire island of Mahé could easily fit inside the lagoon. The lagoon contains several small islands, namely, Ile aux Cèdres, Ile Michel, Ile Esprit and Ile Moustiques.

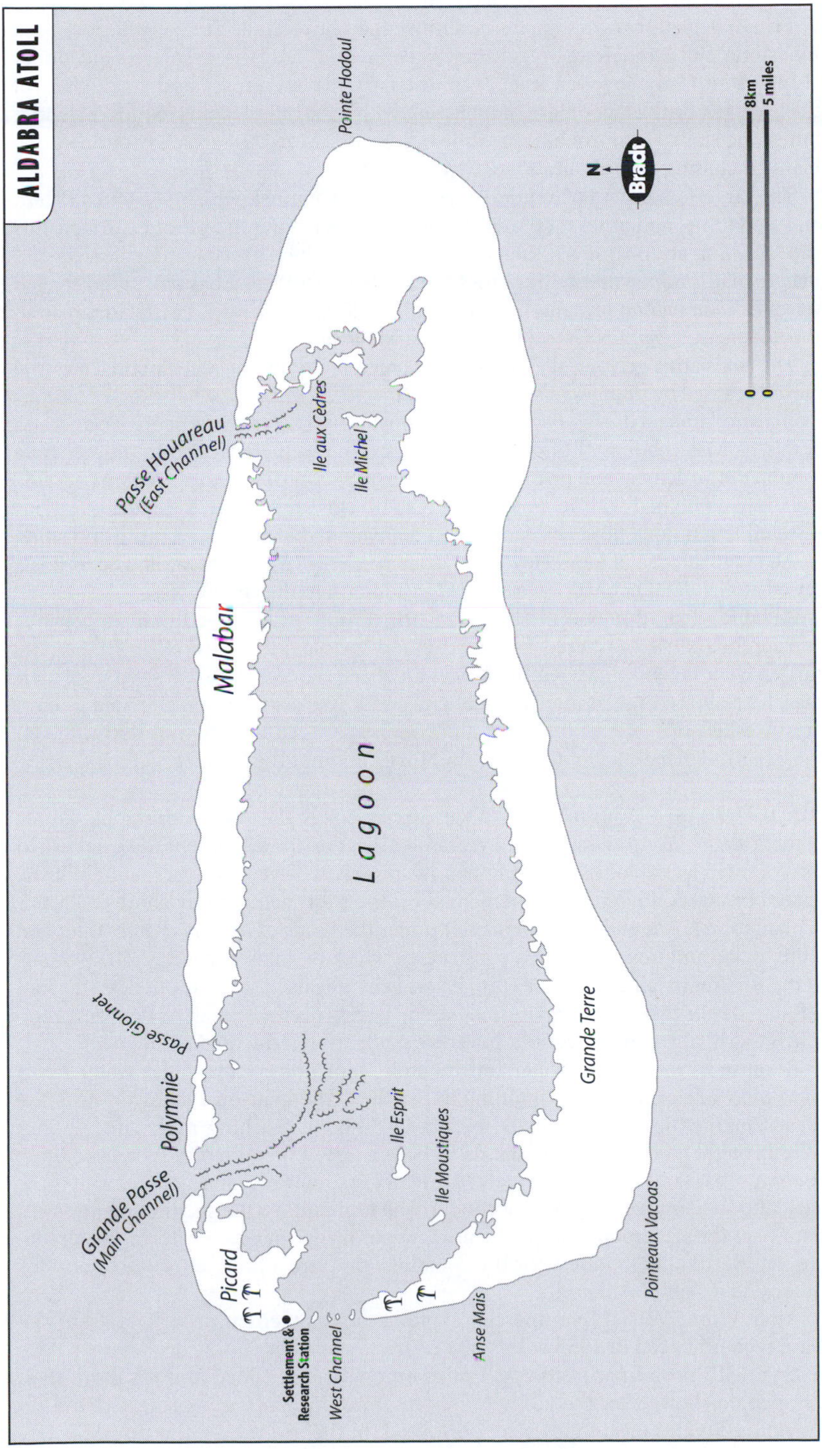

Pointe Hodoul

Passe Houareau
(East Channel)

Ile aux Cèdres

Ile Michel

Malabar

L a g o o n

Passe Gionnet

Polymnie

Grande Terre

Grande Passe
(Main Channel)

Ile Esprit

Ile Moustiques

Picard

Pointeaux Vacoas

Settlement &
Research Station

West Channel

Anse Mais

N

Bradt

8km
5 miles

0

0

Fringing platform reef encircles almost the entire atoll. The jagged, fossilised limestone cliffs undercut by constant wave action, and the desolate sand dunes rising up to 15m above sea level, form the barrier between sea and land. Many of the islets inside the lagoon are *champignon* with a flat, tabular surface and a slender limestone stalk. Some are barren while others are covered in a variety of flowering plants including orchids and mangroves.

The largest channel is Grande Passe, or Main Channel, which separates Picard and Polymnie, and at least 60% of the lagoon water flows in and out through this gap, running at up to seven knots at spring tides. There are about eight islets and many small *champignon* lying across the entrance to West Channel, and a ragged series of *champignon* protects the entrance of Gionnet Channel. Passe Hoaureau in the northeast separates Grande Terre from Malabar.

The fascinating geological past of Aldabra reveals alternating marine and terrestrial periods caused by changes in sea level when the polar oceans froze during the various ice ages and melted during periods of warming. Fossilised remains of giant clams and corals, as well as bones of birds and reptiles, can be seen embedded in the substrate around the settlement and on the more inaccessible parts of the atoll. Aldabra's oceanic isolation, combined with its links to Africa and close proximity to Madagascar, has resulted in a unique flora and fauna with many endemic species – quite astonishing for so small an area of land. However, Aldabra is very large for an atoll, and as it is a raised atoll, inland habitats have evolved in addition to the coastal ones.

Aldabra, like the other islands in the group, was leased out to various entrepreneurs who gathered fish, turtles and tortoises there to sell in Mahé. The turtles were taken in vast numbers to satisfy the market as turtle soup and their meat was all the rage in international cuisine. It was also very fashionable to have 'tortoiseshell' ornaments, hair clips and combs; the 'tortoiseshell' was derived from the beautiful, hard shell of the hawksbill turtle and not the tortoise.

HISTORY In 1878, Admiral W J L Wharton carried out the first hydrographic survey of the Aldabra group and it was ten years later that the first settlement was established for commercial exploitation of the natural resources. Over the years, although the lessees changed, the settlement remained on the west-facing sandy shore of Picard. A plantation house and office were built under the shade of huge *badamier* trees and a tiny wood and iron chapel was constructed which is still in use today. The remains of the two-room jail can also be seen. It was generally used to allow offenders to cool off for a day or two after tempers had flared, usually over a woman or because of too much toddy (the potent alcoholic beverage made from fermented palm juice).

Because of the lack of water on the atoll, enormous, rectangular water tanks were built adjacent to each building. Near the settlement on Picard towards the West Channel lie the remains of an old turtle-bone crushing mill. Turtle bones were brought from the other islands to be processed on Aldabra. At a later time, coconuts, sisal and cotton were planted, but because of water shortages none of these agricultural ventures was very successful. The remnants of the coconut plantations, both near the settlement and on the northwestern edge of Grande Terre, are all that are left. But thank goodness for the coconuts; they are a little bit of fresh food for the resident staff of Aldabra.

After World War II, commercial exploitation was temporarily halted but the lease recommenced in 1955 with some restrictions. Aldabra was declared a nature reserve with no human settlement allowed on Grande Terre and no more than 200 people allowed on the atoll at any one time. All biota was protected and no introduced plants or animals were permitted. In the mid 1960s, the Royal Society of London conducted a series of expeditions to Aldabra to study the marine and terrestrial ecosystems.

The effects of the Cold War were felt even in such isolated places as Aldabra. The British created a new political entity known as the British Indian Ocean Territory with the queen signing the annexure documents on 8 November 1965. Included with Aldabra were the Farquhar group, Desroches and the Chagos archipelago. The rationale for this was to establish an Anglo-American air-force base in the Indian Ocean. After much military research, it was decided to undertake this ambitious project on Aldabra. Construction of the long runways would have involved clearing much of the natural vegetation and getting rid of the nesting frigates and boobies. However, it was around this time that the ecological importance of Aldabra was being fully realised, and the battle was on between the military and the ecologists. Science won the day – the air-force base was subsequently built at Diego Garcia and Aldabra survived. The Royal Society bought the lease in 1970, stopped all exploitation, and built a research station. In 1980, the station was handed over to the Seychelles Island Foundation, which continues to administer the atoll as a conservation and research area under the patronage of the President of the Seychelles. Aldabra was declared a Special Reserve in 1981 and proclaimed a UNESCO World Heritage Site on 19 November 1982. The brass plaque commemorating this momentous occasion bears the words 'Aldabra, wonder of nature, given to humanity by the people of the Republic of Seychelles'. A truly fitting accolade for the most majestic, and ecologically intact, raised coral atoll on the planet.

THE SETTLEMENT The World Heritage Site of Aldabra is uninhabited except for a handful of dedicated people who maintain the research station and continue the scientific programmes. There are generally between six and 12 people living at the settlement on Picard. A warden is in charge of the atoll, the staff, the researchers and ongoing scientific monitoring. Mechanics, boatmen, rangers and field workers handle the chores associated with running the station and carry out the daily monitoring required for the scientific programmes. From time to time, visiting scientists from various universities and research institutes may stay on Aldabra for extended periods of time, completing scientific surveys and research. The current monitoring includes demographics of turtles, tortoises and white-throated rails, the seabirds that nest on the atoll.

There is an office block with a small laboratory and a library, a communal lounge with a large, covered veranda and a small accommodation block for visiting scientists. The island staff live in an assortment of houses around the research station. Workshops, a large solar panel depot and back-up generators keep the station running smoothly. There is no shop as such but sometimes there is a small selection of books and Aldabra T-shirts for sale to visitors.

NATURAL HISTORY The inhospitable and sometimes desolate interior of Aldabra is home to thousands of giant tortoises, and turtles haul themselves out onto the beaches to lay their eggs. Aldabra is the last outpost of the small white-throated rail, the only flightless bird left in the Indian Ocean. The great colonies of frigatebirds and red-footed boobies nesting in the tall mangrove trees in the lagoon are remarkable. The rich botanical diversity is notable for its endemic species and is of great interest to botanists.

Turtles Hunted to extinction on so many islands, green and hawksbill turtles find a last refuge on Aldabra, which is one of the few conserved nesting grounds in the

Indian Ocean. Almost every night during the southeast trades, female green turtles come ashore onto the sandy beaches to lay their eggs in the soft sand above the high-tide mark. First, using her front flippers, a great body pit is dug. Then, using her rear flippers, she will excavate a nest chamber into which she deposits up to 120 soft-shelled, round eggs. Two to three months later the tiny turtle hatchlings will clamber out of the soft sand and make the hazardous journey down to the water. Pied crows, sacred ibis, hermit and ghost crabs make a quick snack of the little critters as they run the gauntlet to the water. When the survivors eventually reach the sea, they then encounter the ever-present sharks and other fish predators. Natural mortality is thus high, and only a very small percentage actually survive to adulthood.

Hawksbill turtles nest on the protected sandy shores of the inner lagoon and will come up during the day from October to January to lay their eggs. The young hawksbill turtles spend a lot of time in the quiet protected areas around the mangrove stands as there is plenty of food and they are safe from predation (page 36).

Tortoises There are only two places in the world where giant tortoises still occur naturally: the Galápagos Islands in the Pacific, and Aldabra. The Aldabra population of about 100,000 is much greater than that of Galápagos. These great, lumbering herbivores are easily seen around the Picard settlement grazing on the short turf. The tortoises are generally shy and on being approached will hiss and retreat into their shells, except, that is, for one very large and friendly tortoise near the settlement that loves having his neck stroked! In the noonday sun, they will hide under the buildings and in the dense vegetation around the settlement. If they do not reach shade in time they stand the very real danger of quietly baking in their shells. The bleached, white carapaces seen in the more remote areas are testimony to those that succumbed in this way (page 35).

Birds Three of the four endemic species of land birds can easily be seen on Aldabra. The white-throated rail is the last of the flightless birds left in the Indian Ocean – the dodos and solitaires all met a sorry end in the hunter's pot. The rail can be seen on Picard, Polymnie and Malabar, and the other two endemic species, the Aldabra drongo and the Aldabra fody, can be seen around the settlement, as indeed can the rail, since its successful relocation. The Aldabra brush warbler was last seen in 1983 and its status is thus uncertain. Other birds like Madagascar kestrels, sacred ibis, sunbirds, white-eyes, Comoro blue pigeons and Madagascar coucals can be seen on Picard.

The great colonies of nesting frigatebirds and red-footed boobies are spectacular. An estimated 10,000 pairs of greater and lesser frigatebirds nest in the canopy of the mangroves lining the shores of the inner lagoon. The acrobatic frigates, with their long, angular wings and deeply forked tails, are true masters of the air and, besides scooping their food from the surface of the water, they will harass any unsuspecting bird, chiefly the boobies. It is mainly the female greater frigatebirds that chase the boobies until, in sheer desperation, they regurgitate their last meals, which the agile frigates catch – classic kleptoparasitism. The frigate nests are squashed, cheek by jowl, among those of the red-footed boobies who tolerate them with dumb acceptance (which probably explains how they got their name). During the breeding season, October to January, the male frigates go courting with their inflated scarlet pouches dangling under their chins.

Dimorphic egrets, grey herons and green-backed herons feed on the exposed reef at low tide. A variety of terns breed on the small islands in the lagoon – common noddies as well as crested, black-naped, Caspian and white fairy terns.

A recently described race of tropical shearwater breeds on the little rocky îlots alongside the tropicbirds.

During the austral summer, many migrant waders visit Aldabra's shores including sandplovers, whimbrels, sandpipers and godwits. It is possible to see flocks of several hundred crab plovers – those enigmatic, elegant, Indian Ocean endemics. Some, particularly the juveniles, will spend a whole season on Aldabra before returning to the sandy shores of Oman to breed.

Plants The vegetation of Aldabra can be broadly divided into six categories: mangroves, pemphis scrub, mixed scrub, tortoise turf, coconuts and casuarinas, and beach pioneer plants. Almost 90% of the lagoon is fringed with a variety of mangrove trees (see box, page 196).

Pemphis acidula, commonly known as pemphis, is a small tree that forms dense impenetrable stands of woody vegetation. In the mixed scrub woodland there is a variety of trees including *Grewia, Sideroxylon, Acalypha, Ficus, Ochna* and *Jasminum elegans* with its fragrantly perfumed, white flowers. The splendid Aldabra lily, a member of the aloe family, which has orange-red flowers, is one of the more spectacular endemic plants found all over the atoll; it flowers at the end of the rainy season. There is also the endemic screw pine, *Pandanus aldabraensis*, which is found only in a few places around the atoll. A subspecies of the tropicbird orchid with sprays of white, waxy flowers, grows on some of the îlots.

Of the 22 species of short grasses identified from the tortoise turf (which constitutes the basic diet of the tortoises), eight are endemic and 12 are genetically dwarfed. There are endemic mosses, lichens, algae and ferns, many of which require further study. Casuarina trees can reach a height of 15m and their wispy, needle-like leaves provide gentle fringing shade along the shoreline. No-one seems sure if they were introduced by man or if they found their own way onto Aldabra by their seeds drifting over the ocean waves. The pioneer plants, *Scaevola, Tournefortia* and *Ipomoea*, line the sandy shoreline.

Mammals The only naturally occurring mammals on Aldabra are bats. The large fruit bats roost in the shady *badamier* trees around the old settlement and can be seen in the early evenings as they fly across the atoll in search of fruits. Differing slightly from the species found on the granitic islands, the Aldabra race is smaller and paler. Three other species of small insectivorous bats are also found on the atoll, though very little is known about them.

From August to October, humpback whales can be seen around Aldabra as they migrate from their feeding grounds in the cold Southern Ocean to calve in warm tropical waters. Huge pods of spinner dolphins regularly frolic in the surging waves just off the reef. It is a spectacular sight as they leap clear out of the water and perform acrobatic aerial twists.

Introduced rats, cats and goats have the potential to cause huge problems. Rats are common all over the atoll but especially around the camps and the settlement. Trapping programmes continue but often coconut crabs get into the traps and have to be extricated (with great care!). Feral cats are found on Grande Terre and their footprints can be found each morning on the sand. There are goats on the eastern and northern parts of Grande Terre where they compete with the tortoises and destroy the trees so desperately needed for shade. Eradication programmes have been carried out from time to time, but with such harsh, jagged terrain and impenetrable vegetation it is a very difficult task. An extensive eradication programme was undertaken in 2007, with good results.

Shore animals The enormous, spectacular robber or coconut crabs are seldom seen by tourists as they spend most of the day hiding in their burrows around tree roots. Adults can grow up to 60cm in overall length, weigh up to 4kg and the colour varies from red to blueish-black. At night, they forage and will eat vegetable matter, baby turtles or even dead tortoises. The mighty crustaceans attack dried coconuts with their massive pincers and use the torn-up fibres to line their burrows. They

MANGROVES

Mangrove is the collective name given to those trees that are capable of surviving in salt water and inundated mud. They generally grow around the shores of quiet estuaries or sheltered lagoons, with the roots of the trees exposed and submerged during the tidal cycle.

Mangrove trees are from several different families of flowering plants and they have thick, leathery leaves to prevent excess water loss. To enable the trees to grow in soft mud, an intricate root system has developed, and some species have strong prop-roots, which do just as the name implies, while others have sturdy buttress roots. Breathing roots or pneumatophores have developed in most species. These may look like pencils or fingers poking up out of the mud, or they may be gnarled, woody bumps. They are generally exposed to the air at low tide, and essentially their job is to supply the trees with oxygen. In non-mangrove plants this takes place in the soil, but as mangrove roots are submerged in waterlogged mud, this special respiration mechanism is required.

Mangrove forests are important ecosystems as, besides providing coastal protection, the tangled root systems slow down currents allowing sediment and decaying plant matter to accumulate, thereby providing a sheltered, nutrient-rich habitat. Many species of fish and crustaceans use mangroves as nursery areas for juveniles. Fiddler and marsh crabs (with their enlarged nippers) and several molluscs also frequent mangroves. Another characteristic species is the mud skipper (*Periopthalmus*), a small fish which is capable of spending considerable time out of the water. The trees provide an evergreen canopy, an ideal nesting site for birds.

On Aldabra there are seven species of mangroves, of which four are common. Fringing the mudflats is the white mangrove (*Avicennia marina*), which can attain 12m. The leaves are grey-green, the bark is smooth and whitish-grey, the seeds are ovoid and can float, and the spreading cable roots have pencil-like pneumatophores (Creole – *mangliye blan*). The black mangrove (*Bruguiera gymnorrhiza*) is a cone-shaped tree reaching 18m (Creole – *mangliye lat*). The aerial roots are knobbly, knee-like bumps, and the bark is rough and reddish-brown. A slender seed up to 25cm long is produced. It germinates on the parent tree before dropping into the mud, whereupon it rapidly develops roots. The Indian mangrove (*Ceriops tagal*) reaches 7m and has a buttressed trunk, prop-roots and elbow-like pneumatophores (Creole – *mangliye zonn*). A 25cm-long seed pod will drop into the mud after germination has started. The bark is smooth and grey. The tallest tree in the mangrove forest is the red mangrove (*Rhizophora mucronata*; Creole – *mangliye rouz*), which reaches 20m. It is characterised by long prop- or stilt roots which form a tangled mass around the tree base. The large, shiny leaves have a spiked tip, fragrant white flowers are present throughout the year, the 30cm-long seed pod is smooth and green, and the fissured bark is dark brown in colour.

have to return to the sea to spawn and, when the larvae metamorphose, the tiny crabs seek out gastropod shells for protection (like hermit crabs). After their first moult they abandon their shell refuges and take up a terrestrial existence. Ghost crabs are very abundant along the sandy shores of the atoll.

Lagoon and reefs The vast lagoon and flat reef platform are rich in marine life. As Aldabra and the surrounding ocean are all part of the World Heritage Site, all the creatures are protected and no shell collecting or fishing is allowed within one nautical mile of the shore.

It is common to see spotted eagle rays and honeycomb stingrays wafting through the lagoon with quiet dignity, though manta rays are more commonly seen offshore. There is a large population of blacktip reef sharks that frequents the shallows. The diverse corals are in good condition and do not appear to have been as badly affected by the 1998 coral bleaching event as those reefs on the shallow Seychelles Bank. Many of the reef fish species are enormous, which is probably due to the protection from fishing afforded these slow-growing species. Diving and snorkelling are spectacular, both in the channels and along the reef drop-off.

Latter-day explorers lucky enough to visit Aldabra treat this amazing natural laboratory with the utmost respect. It can be cruel and harsh but, at the same time, it is extremely fragile. However, for those who never get there, just knowing that this protected, pristine place still exists on the planet should cheer the soul.

GETTING THERE AND AWAY The inaccessibility of Aldabra enhances its desirability. There is no airstrip, helipad or landing jetty. The supply boat from Mahé visits Aldabra every two months and live-aboard dive boats, cruise ships and yachts visit periodically. Aldabra has no tourist facilities. After clearing immigration in Mahé, private yachts and cruise ships wanting to visit the atoll must obtain authorisation from the Seychelles Islands Foundation (📞 4321735; e info@sif.sc; www.sif.sc). Small cruise ships visiting the atoll will anchor on the seaward side of the reef near the settlement. Those passengers lucky enough to go ashore will be accompanied by their expedition leader and transported to the beach adjacent to the station in their ship's inflatable boats.

WHAT TO SEE AND DO Aldabra is awesome in its wild, untamed and natural beauty. The warden and expedition leader will plan any excursions, taking into account the weather and state of the tide. All visitors have to be accompanied by Aldabra personnel at all times; no-one is allowed to wander around on their own and a strict set of guidelines needs to be adhered to regarding the flora and fauna. From the settlement you can walk to La Gigi, a small promontory at Passe Femme on the West Channel where you can see the World Heritage Site plaque resting on a coral cairn. At low tide it is possible to venture a little way up the edge of the lagoon and see four species of mangroves and typical *champignon*, some upright and others collapsed into the shallow water. The breathtaking views across the near-empty channel touch the soul, and the timeless beauty of the vast lagoon merging with the sky will be a lasting memory. Birds feed on the exposed coral reef, and frigates, boobies and white fairy terns wheel overhead as they have done for centuries. The only sounds are the distant thunder of the surf crashing on the reef and the friendly twangs of the white fairy terns as they curiously inspect the visitors.

Another interesting **walk** from the settlement takes one in a northerly direction along the coast to see the remains of the old settlement and the little chapel under the shady *badamier* trees. A little further on, in a coconut grove, there is the old cemetery with the graves of Chinese sea cucumber harvesters. Turtle nesting pits can be seen along the crest of the beach. It is also possible to walk inland along some of the scientific transects but, at all times, it is essential to be aware of the fragility of the ecosystem. The paths are not always easy to follow, and you don't want to get lost on Aldabra. It is very easy to get disorientated as there are no hills or buildings to give an indication of direction and, at first glance, all the vegetation and *champignon* look the same.

Depending on time and tide, it may be possible to visit one of the **frigatebird colonies** inside the lagoon by boat. However, be aware that if the boats approach too close, the noise of the boat engines causes the most incredible disturbance to the courting or nesting birds. While inside the turquoise-green lagoon it might also be possible to stop on Polymnie, Picard or Malabar to look for the white-throated rails. They are curious little birds and will often come to investigate the arrival of strangers.

Diving and snorkelling at Aldabra are fabulous, particularly near the entrances to the channels. However, tidal currents are strong, so take advice from the warden and his staff. There are lots of turtles, big groupers, blacktip reef sharks and stingrays, and the vertical reef drop-off is marvellous. The corals are in good condition and the fish life is prolific.

Appendix 1

LANGUAGE

Creole is the local language in the Seychelles and is a French patois originally used between the French plantation owners and African slaves. Much of the vocabulary is similar to French although the grammar and spelling is simplified and often phonetic. Words and phrases from other languages such as Swahili or Arabic have been incorporated.

USEFUL WORDS AND PHRASES Creole pronunciation is largely phonetic with a tendency towards French, reflecting the origin of many words.

Hello	*Bonzour*	I like it here	*Mon kontan avek*
Goodbye	*Orevwar*		*Sesel*
How are you?	*Konman sava?*	Please stop here	*Aret ici sivouple*
I am well	*Byen*	Good luck	*Bonn sans*
Thank you	*Mersi*	airport	*erport*
Thank you very much	*Mersi bokou*	baggage	*bagaz*
Yes	*Wi*	bank	*labank*
No	*Non*	beach	*lanse*
Please	*Sivouple*	beer	*labyer*
Excuse me	*Ekskiz*	bus terminus	*stayson bis*
I am hungry	*Mon fain*	church	*leglize*
I am thirsty	*Mon swaf*	ferry quay	*terminal bato*
How much?	*Konbyen?*	food	*manz*
I have to get change	*Mon fodre ganny*	hospital	*lopital*
	larzen sanze	hotel	*lotel*
Can you speak Creole?	*Ou kabab koz*	island	*zil*
	Kreol?	market	*bazaar*
Only a little	*Zis en pe*	police	*gard*
I don't understand	*Mon pa konpran*	post office	*lapos*
Where do you come from?	*Kote ou sorti?*	today	*ozordi*
		toilet	*kabinnen*
I come from…	*Mon sorti…*	tomorrow	*demen*

NUMBERS

1	*enn*	6	*sis*	20	*ven*
2	*de*	7	*set*	50	*senkant*
3	*trwa*	8	*wit*	100	*san*
4	*kat*	9	*nef*		
5	*senk*	10	*dis*		

Appendix 2

FURTHER INFORMATION

BOOKS
General

Alexander, D *Holiday in Seychelles* Purnell, Cape Town, 1972. 105pp. Though dated, this anecdotal account includes much information about the history, fauna and flora, and life of the Seychellois people.

Burridge, G *Voices from a Corner of Eden* Savy Publishers, Seychelles, 1998. 313pp. Personal account of life on St Joseph's Atoll in the Amirantes. Full of anecdotes, descriptions and astonishing tales of both real events and fantasies.

Grimshaw, B *Another Grain of Sand* Camerapix Publications International, Nairobi, 2009. Former newspaper editor's colourful account of life on Moyenne Island.

Lionnet, G *The Romance of a Palm – Coco de mer* L'île aux images editions, Mauritius, 1986. 95pp. Small book with every possible detail about the unique coco de mer palm.

Lionnet, G *The Seychelles* David & Charles, Newton Abbot, 1972. 200pp. Factual coverage of geology, geography, flora, fauna and history of the Seychelles.

Mancham, J R *Paradise Raped* Methuen, London, 1983. 256pp. Personal account by the first president of independent Seychelles.

Pavard, C *Seychelles from One Island to Another* GMR Group, Seychelles, 1983. 175pp. Marvellous annotated photographs of human activities and wildlife in the Seychelles. Covers inner islands as well as more distant islands of Amirantes, Farquhar, Coëtivy, Aldabra, Cosmoledo and Assumption.

Thomas, A *Forgotten Eden* Longman Group, London, 1973. 185pp. Anecdotal account of life in the Seychelles in the 1960s.

Vine, P *Seychelles* Immel Publishing, London, 1989. 208pp. Colourful book which focuses on the history, natural history, people and traditions of the Seychelles. Includes a section depicting art of Seychellois artists.

History

Bulpin, T V *Islands in a Forgotten Sea* Howard Timmins, Cape Town, 1958. 435pp. Classic text about the history of human exploits in the western Indian Ocean. Great tales of Arab sailors, pirates, colonial powers and the islands in the Sea of Zanj. Includes detailed list of early historical literature about the western Indian Ocean.

Farmer, H V *Seychelles Postage Stamps and Postal History* Robson Lowe Ltd, London, 1955. 123pp. Detailed descriptions of the stamps and postal history of the Seychelles for serious philatelists.

Lee, C *Political Castaways* Elmtree Books, London, 1976. 169pp. Revealing account of political exiles banished to the remote Seychelles.

Travel guides

Carpin, S and Turcotte, P *Seychelles: Garden of Eden in the Indian Ocean* Odyssey Illustrated Guides, 2010. 268pp. Beautiful photographs and plenty of interesting information on history and culture.

Heady, S *Visitor's Guide – Seychelles* Moorland Publishing, Ashbourne, Derby, 1995. 208pp. Insightful guide to Mahé and some of the other granitic islands. Many colourful photographs augment the text.

Skerrett, A and Skerrett, J *Spectrum Guide to Seychelles* Camerapix Publishers International, Nairobi, 1993. 352pp. A comprehensive guide with many colour photographs of what to see when visiting the Seychelles.

Environment

Bowler, J, *Wildlife of Seychelles* WILDGuides Ltd, Hampshire, UK, 2006. 192pp. Beautifully illustrated book about cetaceans, birds, reptiles, frogs and invertebrates by a former warden of Aride.

Gabriel, M, Marshall, S and Jennings, S 'Seychelles' in *Seas at the Millennium: An Environmental Evaluation*, vol 2. Sheppard, C R C (ed). Elsevier Science, Amsterdam, 2000. pp232–42. Marine environment status report for the Seychelles highlighting the importance of the reefs and the effects of recent coral bleaching and human activities.

Hill, M J (ed) *Biodiversity Surveys and Conservation Potential of Inner Seychelles Islands* Atoll Research Bulletin No 495, Smithsonian Institution, USA, 2002. 272pp. Scientific surveys of plants, invertebrates, reptiles, amphibians and birds of the inner Seychelles. Conservation status of terrestrial fauna and flora of each island is assessed.

Hill, M and Currie, D *Wildlife of Seychelles* HarperCollins, London, 2007. 272pp. This traveller's guide is beautifully laid out with photographs on one side of the page and a short, comprehensive text on the other, identifying just about everything you will find – from birds to geckos, turtles and fish, crabs, moths and spiders, flowering plants and trees. Recommended.

Jennings, S M, Marshall, P and Naim, O 'The Seychelles' in *Coral Reefs of the Western Indian Ocean: Their Ecology and Conservation* McClanahan T R & Sheppard, C R C (eds). Oxford University Press, New York, 2000. pp399–432. A summary of the state of knowledge on Seychelles reefs and associated human impacts including fishing, tourism and pollution. Useful tables documenting the history of scientific research and marine conservation as well as lists of relevant conservation organisations.

Samways, M J, Hitchins, P, Bourquin, O and Henwood, J *Tropical Island Recovery: Cousine Island, Seychelles* John Wiley & Sons, Chichester, UK 2010. 260pp. Interesting account of the restoration of Cousine Island.

Seychelles Fishing Authority *Seychelles Fishing Authority Annual Report* 2012. 75pp. Annual report on the Seychelles fishing industry and associated scientific research.

Stoddart, D R (ed) *Biogeography and Ecology of the Seychelles Islands* W Junk Publishers, The Hague, 1984. 691pp. The definitive scientific work about the Seychelles consisting of a collation of chapters written by various authorities. Includes a history of scientific exploration in the Seychelles as well as accounts of the geology, climate, human population and the impact of man. Most of the chapters cover the fauna of the islands and include coral reefs, echinoderms, crabs, shrimps, fish, terrestrial molluscs, insects, butterflies, ticks, frogs, tortoises, lizards, snakes, turtles, birds and mammals. The vegetation of both the granitic and coralline islands is also covered.

Wells, S (ed) 'Seychelles' in *Coral Reefs of the World. Vol 2: Indian Ocean, Red Sea and Gulf* UNEP & IUCN, Cambridge, 1988. pp291–305. Concise summary of information on Seychelles coral reefs as well as details of the various marine protected areas in the Seychelles.

Appendix 2 FURTHER INFORMATION

A2

Marine-life guides

Branch, G M, Griffiths, C L, Branch, M L and Beckley, L E *Two Oceans – A Guide to Marine Life of Southern Africa* Random House Struik Publishers, Cape Town. 2010. 432pp. This authoritative guidebook to the diversity of marine life in southern Africa is profusely illustrated with colour photographs of over 1,000 species of marine plants and animals, many of which occur in Seychelles waters.

Debelius, H *Indian Ocean Reef Guide* Ikan-Unterwasserarchiv, Frankfurt, 1999. 321pp. Profusely illustrated with underwater photographs, this guidebook covers much of the marine life occurring in Seychelles waters. Excellent fish pictures.

Jarrett, A G *Marine Shells of the Seychelles* Carole Green Publishers, 2000. 149pp. Guide to the wonderful array of marine molluscs found in Seychelles waters.

King, D *Reef Fishes & Corals – East Coast of Southern Africa* Struik Publishers, Cape Town, 1996. 128pp. A small guidebook with underwater photographs of many of the fish and corals encountered in the southwestern Indian Ocean.

Lieske, E and Myers, R *Coral Reef Fishes: Indo-Pacific & Caribbean* HarperCollins, London, 1994. 400pp. Concise illustrated pocket guide that includes many of the fish found on the reefs of the Seychelles.

Richmond, M D (ed) *A Guide to the Seashores of Eastern Africa and the Western Indian Ocean Islands* Sida/SAREC, Stockholm, 1997. 448pp. The most comprehensive guide to marine biodiversity of the western Indian Ocean. Covers everything from seaweeds to whales with concise information and colour illustrations. Also has good introductory section dealing with environment, people, human activities and conservation. Available in the UK through Tylers Books (e *tylers@tylers-books.co.uk*).

Smith, J L B and Smith, M M *The Fishes of Seychelles* Rhodes University, Grahamstown, South Africa, 1963. 215pp. Detailed early account of fishes collected during one of the legendary 'JLB' scientific expeditions. Wonderful colour paintings by Margaret Smith.

Veron, J E N *Corals of Australia and the Indo-Pacific* Angus & Robertson Publishers, London, 1986. 644pp. The definitive illustrated scientific work on corals of the Indo-Pacific region. Distribution maps indicate which species are found in Seychelles waters.

Bird guides

Harrison, P *Seabirds – An Identification Guide* Christopher Helm Publishers, London, 1996. 448pp. The authoritative text on seabirds of the world. All species occurring in Seychelles waters are covered and illustrated in this classic work.

Sinclair, I and Langrand, O *Birds of the Indian Ocean Islands* Struik, Cape Town, 2013. 264pp. Excellent field guide to the identification of the birds, both land and sea, occurring on the Seychelles and other Indian Ocean islands. Well illustrated, concise and a handy size.

Skerrett, A *Beautiful Birds of Seychelles* Camerapix Publishers International, Nairobi, 1994. 128pp. Small book with colour photographs of most of the birds breeding in the Seychelles and a short text on each.

Skerrett, A and Bullock, I *A Birdwatchers' Guide to Seychelles* Prion Ltd, Cambridge, 1992. 71pp. Useful guide for the serious birdwatcher who wants to get the most out of a visit to the Seychelles. Includes information on various birdwatching sites as well as a comprehensive checklist of birds to be seen around the islands.

Skerrett, A, Bullock, I and Disley, T *Field Guide to the Birds of the Seychelles* Christopher Helm and Princeton University Press, 2001. 320pp, 53 colour plates. Contains a wealth of information about all the birds in the Seychelles as well as many that may occur here on migration.

Navigation and diving

Hydrographic Department *South Indian Ocean Pilot* British Navy, Somerset, 1971. 333pp. This pilot book amplifies details on Admiralty charts and is a mine of information about the Seychelles islands. Particularly useful for those voyaging in Seychelles waters, it provides extensive information on reefs, shoals, anchorages, currents and weather.

Rondeau, A *Nautical Pilot of the Seychelles* Praxys Marine, Paris, 1997. 252pp. An excellent guide to cruising in Seychelles waters. Text is bilingual (French and English) and accompanied by numerous small charts of anchorages.

Salm, R *A Guide to Snorkelling and Diving in the Seychelles* Octavian Books, London, 1997. 60pp. Useful information for divers and includes details of the dive sites around the granitic islands and Amirantes.

Venter, A J *Under the Indian Ocean* Purnell, Cape Town, 1973. 219pp. Anecdotal accounts of diving adventures at various Indian Ocean localities. Contains information on shipwrecks on the Seychelles islands as well as dive sites on Mahé.

Wood, L *Diving and Snorkeling Guide to the Seychelles* Pisces Books, Orlando, Florida, 1997. 89pp. A well-illustrated guide with information on most of the well-known dive sites of Mahé, Praslin and La Digue as well as notes on the marine life of the Seychelles.

Aldabra

Amin, M, Willetts, D and Skerrett, A *Aldabra World Heritage Site* Camerapix Publishers International, Nairobi, 1995. 192pp. A wonderful, large-format book filled with the excellent photographs of Mohamed Amin and Duncan Willets. Chapters by various authorities showcase the magnificent biodiversity of the atoll which was proclaimed a World Heritage Site in 1982.

Beamish, T *Aldabra Alone* Allen & Unwin, London, 1970. 222pp. Interesting account of how efforts to establish an Anglo-American air-force base on Aldabra were thwarted, and subsequent conservation of the atoll as a World Heritage Site.

Seaton, A J, Beaver, K and Afif, M (eds) *A Focus on Aldabra* Seychelles Islands Foundation, Victoria, 1991. 178pp. This book synthesises much of the scientific research done on the atoll and presents it in a more user-friendly fashion. It covers studies on the geology, marine and terrestrial environments as well as management of the atoll.

WEBSITES There are several websites which provide useful information for travellers visiting the Seychelles, although not all of them are updated that frequently.

www.seychelles.travel An excellent site run by the Seychelles Tourism Board. Lots of tempting photographs and useful information for planning your visit. Specific pages about activities like sailing, diving and fishing.

www.seychellesconnect.com Fairly general information advertising good special offers for accommodation.

www.virtualseychelles.sc Official website of the Republic of Seychelles. Current affairs and a webcam of various destinations.

Coco de Mer Hotel
Black Parrot Suites

Praslin Island - Seychelles
www.cocodemer.com
Once Discovered ~ Never Forgotten

204

Index

Page numbers in **bold** indicate major entries, those in *italics* indicate maps or diagrams.

INDEX OF ADVERTISERS